*Amelia Elizabeth Perry Pride*

# The Slave Children of Thomas Jefferson

by

Samuel H. Sloan

The Orsden Press
Lynchburg, Berkeley, Tokyo

Published by
The Orsden Press
48 Shattuck Square, Suite 66
Berkeley, CA 94704-1140
U.S.A.

ISBN 1-881373-02-9

In Japan this book may be ordered from:

The Orsden Press
CPO Box 2126
Tokyo, Japan

First Printing April 1992
Printed in Japan

# Table of Contents

# About the Author

Samuel H. Sloan was born in Richmond, Virginia in 1944 and grew up entirely in the State of Virginia. His family moved to Bedford County, Virginia, near Lynchburg in 1955. He attended Boonsboro School there and ultimately graduated from E.C. Glass High School in Lynchburg in 1962.

Sloan thereafter attended the University of California at Berkeley, majoring in mathematics. He became actively involved in the Free Speech Movement there and was the president of an on-campus student organization.

In 1968, he got a job working in the over-the-counter trading department of Hayden-Stone, Inc., a stock brokerage firm in New York City. By 1970, he had established his own firm, Samuel H. Sloan & Co., which, over a period of the next several years, made a market in thousands of over-the-counter stocks and bonds.

The S.E.C.'s curiosity about Sloan clashed with Sloan's natural tendency to rebel against governmental authority acquired through active involvement in the Free Speech Movement, which followed the philosophy expounded by Jeffersonian. This led to a series of lawsuits, with the S.E.C. suing Sloan and Sloan suing the S.E.C. Eventually, the matter reached the United States Supreme Court in 1978. Sloan won 9–0, after arguing his appeal pro se. The name of that case is S.E.C. vs. Samuel H. Sloan, 436 U.S. 103 (1978).

He thereafter went to Kabul, Afghanistan, where he nearly lost his life in the 1978 communist take-over. After spending three months as a political prisoner of the new communist government, he went from there to Chitral, Pakistan, where he became fluent in the local language, which is Khowar. Sloan married in Chitral, and eventually wrote the *Khowar–English Dictionary* of that previously almost completely unrecorded language. He later traveled to 74 countries of the world, lived in Japan and Sri Lanka and finally settled in the United Arab Emirates.

In 1990, while residing in the United Arab Emirates, one of Sloan's daughters, Shamema Honzagool Sloan, then aged eight, was kidnapped from his home by a Mr. Charles Roberts, who is a member of an organization of religious fundamentalists headquartered in the Temple Baptist Church in Madison Heights, Virginia near Lynchburg. This kidnapping was organized by one Lawrence Janow, who also happened to be a corrupt Virginia Juvenile and Domestic Relations judge. As a result of this kidnapping, Sloan was forced to close his computer business in the United Arab Emirates and return to the United States, in an effort to recover his kidnapped eight-year-old daughter.

Due to the continuing on-going criminal activities of Judge Janow, Sloan still has not been able to recover his kidnapped daughter, who is now ten years old. Unfortunately, the mother of Shamema resides in Chitral, Pakistan. The mother, whose name is Honzagool, only speaks the Khowar language and has been unable to provide any assistance in this matter.

During the course of his continuing litigation to recover his kidnapped daughter, Sloan was stranded in Lynchburg, Virginia and therefore decided to renew his studies into the Life of Thomas Jefferson. As a result, he has produced this book.

Sloan is also an active writer in the field of chess. He knows personally almost all of the world's leading chess grandmasters, and is friends with many of the world's leading chess personalities, including Bobby Fischer, the Polgar sisters and Xie Jun, the new World's Woman Chess Champion. He was the chess columnist for the *Gulf News* in the United Arab Emirates.

In addition, Sloan is a three-dan player of Japanese Chess (*shogi*) and holds a third-grade certificate in Chinese chess (*xiangqi*). He is considered one of the leading western players in the world in both of these games. In 1989, he finished second in Singapore in the World Championship for non-Chinese of Chinese chess. He is also considered to be the strongest non-Thai player in the world of Thai chess. Sloan is the author of two other books: *Chinese Chess for Beginners* and *How to Take Over an American Public Company*, in addition to the *Khowar–English Dictionary*.

Sloan has seven children, whose names are Peter, Mary, Shamema, Michael, Jessica, George and Anusha.

# Chapter One

## The Unanswered Questions

There are rumors which are so persistent that it seems impossible to stamp them out, regardless of how hard everyone tries.

One of these rumors is that Thomas Jefferson, a Founding Father of the United States of America, was a founding father in more ways than one and that he actually fathered a large number of children by the black slaves on his plantations.

In fact, there is nothing on the surface so startling about this. Slavery was a legal institution in Virginia where Jefferson lived. Thomas Jefferson had inherited a large number of slaves from his father, from his mother, and finally from his father-in-law. Some of those slaves were female. Slave owners in Virginia had the right of *droit du seigneur* over their female slaves. No doubt, many slave owners did not exercise this right, but there were no doubt some who exploited it to the fullest extent. We have only to look at the Governor of Virginia, Douglas Wilder, to see the results of this practice.

*Droit du seigneur* is a French term. It means that the King has the legal right to have sex with any woman within his realm, regardless of who her father or husband might happen to be. In other words, if King Louis XV saw any beautiful girl walking down the street, he could just have his guards pick her up and bring her to him. This was perfectly legal and nobody would raise any question about it.

History does not tell us exactly how many French kings and noblemen exercised this right, and to what extent, but there were no doubt many; otherwise, there would not be a special term for this in the French language.

Returning to Virginia, there were certainly men, perhaps just a few, but men nevertheless, who found pleasure in the company of their black female slaves. Nobody disputes this. The only dispute concerns whether Thomas Jefferson was one of those men, or whether the inordinate number of white-skinned mulatto slaves found on his plantation just happened to be there and were actually the children of other white men.

Stated differently, the question is this: Is it really possible that Thomas Jefferson, the author of the *Declaration of Independence*, the author of the *Virginia Statute of Religious Freedom*, and one of the great champions in history of individual rights, freedoms and liberties, was in the habit of stealing off to the slave's shack for the night after spending his days expounding on great wisdoms and truths?

First, it must be explained that Thomas Jefferson was not merely one of the Founding Fathers of America. He was indeed one of the great geniuses of all time. His name has been ranked right up there with Socrates and Plato. Among modern men, perhaps he came closest to John Stuart Mill (1806–1873), who was also a champion of individual freedom and who is sometimes mentioned as possibly the greatest genius in modern human history.

However, John Stuart Mill merely wrote books and essays. Thomas Jefferson was a man of action. The ideas of Thomas Jefferson are the ideas upon which the United States of America is founded. The only other person who came close in terms of intellect to Thomas Jefferson was Benjamin Franklin, but most consider Jefferson to be the greater thinker. The only other man among the American Founding Fathers who was even in their intellectual league was Alexander Hamilton. However, Hamilton favored strong executive control, as opposed to Jefferson, who wanted freedom for the people. Eventually, the ideas of Jefferson won out, which is why America is the nation that it is today.

George Washington, the Father of his Country, was the general who won the war. He was a great leader of his people, but he was not what one would call a brilliant man. He was not even a good general. He lost more battles than he won. He could not spell and he could barely write. In terms of intellectual capability, there is no comparison at all between Thomas Jefferson and George Washington.

Today, America is often called a 'Jeffersonian Democracy', because the political system of America is based upon the ideas of Jefferson. The political ideas of George Washington have long since been forgotten.

Thus, the fact is that Thomas Jefferson is regarded as not merely one of the smartest men in American history, but as one of the greatest geniuses in all of human history. The troubling question is: Is it this great man who accounts for some of those white faces on black people running around Virginia?

The Great Abolitionist Frederick Douglass thought so. In 1850, commentating on the fact that Thomas Jefferson was believed to have fathered and then sold children by his black slaves, Frederick Douglass wrote:

> It has long been known that the best blood of Virginia may now be found in the slave markets . . .

It must be remembered that Thomas Jefferson was the actual author of the following words, which every school boy learns:

*We hold these truths to be self-evident, that all men are created equal, that they are endowed by their Creator with certain unalienable rights, that among these are life, liberty and the pursuit of happiness.*

Those who claim that Thomas Jefferson could not possibly have fathered children by his black slaves contend essentially that the man who wrote the famous words, 'All men are created equal,' could not possibly at the same time have been having sex with the black girls in the shack behind the house.

However, does this really follow? Indeed, exactly the opposite conclusion seems more likely. If Thomas Jefferson really thought that a black man was just as good as a white man, then he must have also believed that a black woman was just as good as a white woman. If this was true, then why go down to the local bar and try to pick up white girls, when he already had dozens of black girls at his disposal?

So-called 'serious historians', who claim that they are defending Jefferson by saying that he could not possibly have done such a thing, have simply failed to understand the mentality of Jefferson himself. First, it must be noted that the wife of Thomas Jefferson died in 1782, when Jefferson was only 39 years old. Nevertheless, he never married again in the remaining 44 years of his life. His wife had produced six children during their ten years of marriage, so he was clearly attracted to women. Indeed, even before he got married, Thomas Jefferson had been a notorious womanizer. He was once challenged to a duel after he had made advances towards another man's wife.

Clearly, from everything we know about Thomas Jefferson, he was not a man to remain celibate for 44 years, just because his wife died. Therefore, he must have had a woman around somewhere. Now, the question is: Just exactly who was that woman?

Everybody knows the answer to this question. It is one of the deepest, darkest and most poorly kept secrets in American history. The name of the woman was Sally Hemings. Here is what Joseph Dennie, one of the political poets of the day, had to say about her in the *Boston Gazette* in 1802:

*Of all the damsels on the green*
*On mountain or in valley*
*A lass so luscious never was seen*
*As Monticellian Sally*

*Yankee Doodle, whose the noodle?*
*What wife were half so handy?*
*To breed a flock of slaves to stock*
*A blackamoors the dandy*

After this, the poem goes on for many verses. It was intended to be sung to the tune of *Yankee Doodle*.

It is noteworthy that this verse was written and published in the newspapers of America at a time when Thomas Jefferson was actually the President of the United States. Nevertheless, he never denied the story. To the contrary, Sally Hemings stayed right at his side and apparently in the White House throughout the entire controversy. She never left him and he never sent her away. She continued to be with him right up to his death bed.

If the story that Sally Hemings was actually the concubine of Thomas Jefferson, the sitting President of the United States, was not true, then why did he not deny it? Why did he not send her away? The answer is obvious. The story must have been true.

Arguments used by historians who claim that they are defending Thomas Jefferson from this slander are so weak that they can be exploded even by a layman with a little knowledge of simple arithmetic. The common explanation given, which has been advanced by historians Douglass Adair and Virginius Dabney, is that Thomas Jefferson did not dare to deny that he was the father of the children of Sally Hemings, because to do so would have forced him to reveal who the actual father was, who, according to them, was probably either Peter Jefferson Carr or Samuel Jefferson Carr, his nephews. They claim that President Thomas Jefferson remained tight-lipped only to protect his wayward relatives from damage to their reputations.

This, however, does not make any sense at all. In the first place, Thomas Jefferson could have simply denied that the child or children were his, without naming the actual father. However, a more serious problem is that the first child of Sally Hemings was named Tom. He was born in 1790 and must have been conceived in France. At that time, Peter Carr and Samuel Carr were less than twenty years old. They could not possibly have been the father of that child.

To this, the historians counter that there was no baby named Tom who was born in 1790. They claim that according to the record of the *Farm Book*, which Thomas Jefferson maintained, the first child born to Sally Hemings was named Harriet. She was born in 1795. She died two years later, in 1797, according to a letter dated January 22, 1798 by Martha Jefferson, the oldest daughter of Thomas Jefferson.

However, if that was the case, then what was the fuss all about? There was no child around in 1802 who was being claimed as the child of Thomas Jefferson. Obviously, there must have been at least one living child somewhere who was being attributed to Thomas Jefferson, or else this matter would not have been reported in every newspaper in America.

However, the newspapers of the time did not stop with Sally Hemings. It was being alleged that Thomas Jefferson maintained a whole stable of these girls, of which Sally Hemings was only the one most publicly known. More than that, it was even claimed that Thomas Jefferson was fathering large numbers of children by these slave girls in order to sell them at a good profit on the local slave markets.

Here is what one reputable authority has to say about this: "The American people were told that Jefferson maintained at Monticello a 'Congo Harem' and that he deliberately brought children into the world in order that he might sell them and thereby turn his debaucheries into profit." *Thomas Jefferson, A Reference Biography*, Merrill D. Peterson, Editor, 1986, Charles Scribner & Sons., p. 429.

On this point, the scandal mongering newspapers of the day probably over-reached. There was no proof then that Thomas Jefferson ever sold his children into slavery. Indeed, at that point in his life, it seems that he rarely, if ever, sold his slaves at all, much less his own children. In addition, while there is ample evidence regarding his connection with Sally Hemings, there was no other slave woman who was then known to have been associated with him in this way. Thus, it appears likely or at least possible that Sally Hemings was his one and only concubine.

At the same time, many visitors to the estate of Thomas Jefferson at Monticello during that period, including future president John Quincy Adams, noted the presence of a large number of white-skinned mulatto slave children on the premises. It was further noted that many of these children bore a striking resemblance to Thomas Jefferson himself. However, historians say that most of these were actually the children of John Wayles, the father-in-law of Thomas Jefferson, who is known or believed to have fathered many mulatto children by his black slaves. Thomas Jefferson inherited these children when John Wayles died, or so the story goes. Thus, Thomas Jefferson was a man supporting a large number of at least half-white children on his vast estates, but none of those children were his, or so says the official explanation.

However, the controversy regarding this started not while Jefferson was occupying his vast estate at Monticello near Charlottesville, Virginia. Rather, it started in 1802 when Thomas Jefferson was President and was occupying the White House. The accusation that Thomas Jefferson was having sex with his slaves was first published by a political enemy of Jefferson. The story spread like wildfire, far beyond what a single hack writer could have been expected to produce.

After sifting the best historical evidence available, it seems that there is only one possible reason as to why this accusation could have spread so quickly. The reason was that Thomas Jefferson was not merely having sex with his slaves on his remote estate at Monticello. Rather, the unmarried president must have been keeping a slave girl in his bed inside the White

House itself. In fact, Sally Hemings gave birth to three children during the eight years while Jefferson was president. If Thomas Jefferson really was the father of those children, then they were probably conceived inside the White House.

In short, the question is this: Is it really true that Thomas Jefferson so deeply mourned his beloved wife Martha that he remained completely celibate after her death until his own death 44 years later? This is what respectable Virginia historians would have us believe.

Consider the alternative: Is it just barely possible that within a few years after the death of his beloved wife, Jefferson took up with a woman who happened to be her half-sister and who remained with him right up until his death?

The basic facts are believed to be this: Sally Hemings was a white-skinned mulatto woman who was universally known as the concubine of Thomas Jefferson. He took up with her when she went to Paris as the nanny for one of his children while Jefferson was Ambassador to France. John Adams, who was also in Europe at the time, mentioned this in one of his subsequent letters to his wife, Abigail. At that time, Sally Hemings was only 14 to 16 years old. She became pregnant while in France and gave birth to their first son in 1790 shortly after their return to the United States. Jefferson was elected President of the United States in 1800.

Thomas Jefferson would have been attracted to Sally. All evidence indicates that Thomas Jefferson dearly loved his wife, Martha. After Martha died, he never married again in his lifetime. Sally was the half-sister of Martha, so they probably looked like each other and resembled each other in many ways. Also, everybody who ever saw Sally remarked that she was exceptionally beautiful. She was known as 'Dusky Sally' on the Monticello estate. She and Thomas Jefferson spent more than two years together in France. It was during these two years that their relationship started.

That is the summary of the case. Now, let us consider the evidence.

# Chapter Two

## The Beginnings

The grandmother of Sally Hemings had been a full blooded African woman. She became pregnant on the slave ship by the owner of the ship, who was an Englishman named Hemings. Upon their arrival at the Port of Williamsburg, Virginia, the pregnant woman was sold and eventually became the property of a Mr. John Wayles, who later became the father- in-law of Thomas Jefferson. When the child was born, Captain Hemings realized that the child was his and tried to buy the newborn infant at an exceptionally high price. However, the new owner had his own plans for the newborn baby girl and refused to sell at any price. Hemings then attempted to kidnap the child. According to one version, John Wayles removed the newborn child, whose name was Elizabeth, to Central Virginia, where the seagoing Captain Hemings could not find her. Captain Hemings sailed shortly thereafter from the Port of Williamsburg, never to return.

When Elizabeth, who became known as Betty, matured, she produced six children fathered by John Wayles. One of these children was Sally Hemings. Thus, Sally Hemings was 75% white, in spite of being a slave. Wayles reportedly had other children by Betty as well. All of these mulatto children were subsequently inherited by Thomas Jefferson.

John Wayles was married three times to white women. All of these wives died not long after marriage. Three of his legitimate children also died, but four daughters survived. The first born of these was Martha, who became Martha Jefferson, the wife of Thomas Jefferson. Thus, Sally Hemings was the half sister of Martha Jefferson.

We have proof that Betty Hemings was a special person in the life of John Wayles because she was the only slave mentioned by name in his will, in spite of the large number of slaves which he had. The will of John Wayles is included in the appendix to this book.

Thomas Jefferson was the son of a planter and surveyor named Peter Jefferson. The mother of Thomas Jefferson was Jane Randolph. Peter Jefferson died when Thomas Jefferson was only 14, so Thomas Jefferson inherited his estate, which included 2,750 acres and 50 slaves. This was under the law of primogeniture at that time, under which the eldest son inherited the entire estate of his father. As a wealthy man in his own right, Thomas Jefferson was able to marry a wealthy woman, the daughter of John Wayles.

John Wayles was a lawyer from Lancaster, England, born in 1715. He married three times. He became a wealthy man due to his success as a lawyer and a planter, and because he had received land and slaves as a dowry in consideration of his marriage to his first wife, Martha Eppes. He did not make Betty Hemings his mistress until after his third wife had died in 1761. When John Wayles died in 1773, the bulk of his estate was left to his eldest daughter, Martha, and her husband, Thomas Jefferson. Included in this estate was 11,000 acres of land and 135 slaves. One of these slaves was Sally Hemings, less than one year old.

The reason that Martha got the bulk of the estate that John Wayles left was that he had originally received this estate as a dowry as consideration for his marriage to the mother of Martha. Martha Wayles Jefferson was the only surviving child of Martha Eppes Wayles. Three other legitimate daughters of John Wayles by another unknown wife got much less, but were not cut out entirely.

Martha Wayles Jefferson produced six children during her ten years of marriage to Thomas Jefferson. She died in 1782, perhaps the result of having had so many children in such a short time. Jefferson loved her dearly, so much so that he declined to take his seat in the Virginia General Assembly because of her final illness. After her death, he never remarried. Jefferson had been a notorious womanizer in his youth. However, after the death of Martha Jefferson, there is no public record of his ever having female companionship, except for one brief fling in France lasting at most less than six weeks with Maria Cosway, an Italian woman who had married a prominent Englishman and whom he had met in Paris in 1786, before the arrival of Sally Hemings.

Maria Cosway was quickly thereafter taken by her husband to London. A year later, she returned without her husband, hoping to resume her relationship with Thomas Jefferson. However, he no longer seemed interested in her and she returned to London disappointed. Of course, by that time, Sally Hemings had arrived.

Maria Cosway continued to write letters to Thomas Jefferson from Europe for the remainder of his life, the last such letter arriving just before he died in 1826. She kept expressing an interest in coming to Monticello to visit him. He sometimes responded to her letters, but never offered her any encouragement. She could never possibly have guessed why he had dropped her after such a passionate, if brief, romance and after having written her such passionate love letters after they first met. She never knew that he had Sally Hemings.

One point which might cause confusion concerns the fact that there were three persons named Martha Jefferson. Martha Wayles Jefferson, also known as Martha Skelton Jefferson, was the wife of Thomas Jefferson and the widow of Bathurst Skelton. Martha Jefferson Carr was the sister of Thomas Jefferson who married Dabney Carr (1743-1773). Finally, Martha Jefferson Randolph was the eldest daughter of Thomas Jefferson and married Thomas Mann Randolph, Jr.

When Jane Randolph, the mother of Thomas Jefferson, died on March 31, 1776, Jefferson destroyed all of her papers and personal effects. Then, when Martha Wayles Jefferson, the wife of Thomas Jefferson, died on September 6, 1782, he destroyed all of her papers and personal effects as well.

As a result, not one letter, not one portrait, not one necklace, not one ring and not one dress of either of these two women survived. There is one surviving letter by Martha Wayles Jefferson, but that letter was obviously dictated entirely by Thomas Jefferson. At the same time, Thomas Jefferson was intent on saving his own letters and other documents for posterity.

Nobody has ever been able to come up with a good explanation for this, except for those who have suggested that it was because he loved those two women so dearly that he did not want to share them with anybody else. This explanation is not convincing, however. Many men love their wives and their mothers, without destroying every remembrance of them.

There is something strange and almost even psychopathic about the lengths to which Thomas Jefferson went to destroy all remembrances of his mother and his wife after they died. He destroyed both their letters and their portraits, so that we do not have any idea of what these two women, important in American history, looked like. More than that, he even wrote letters to every person who had ever received a letter from either of these women asking them to return that letter. No doubt, these requests were complied with by those assuming that Thomas Jefferson wanted to preserve and remember the letters of his mother and his wife. They could not possibly have known that he wanted to get these letters back just so that he could destroy them.

Thomas Jefferson was appointed the U.S. Ambassador to France in 1786. He was already in France, having reached there in 1784. By 1787, he had summoned his nine-year-old daughter, Maria, also known as Mary or Polly, to come to Paris to join him because of an epidemic of whooping cough which was sweeping America and which had just killed Lucy, one of his few remaining daughters. Polly was accompanied on the trip by a 14-year-old black slave named Sally Hemings. After their arrival in Paris, Sally Hemings took up with Thomas Jefferson.

The fact that they were believed to have been openly and notoriously sleeping together was noted in a subsequent letter by John Adams to his wife, Abigail. Apparently, the true nature of their relationship may have been known in France, although years passed before this news reached America.

In July, 1787, Maria and Sally arrived together in Paris. According to Fawn Brodie, who wrote a general biography entitled *Thomas Jefferson, An Intimate History*, shortly thereafter, on November 6, 1787, Thomas Jefferson had Sally but not Maria inoculated against smallpox. This gives rise to one of the theories of Fawn Brodie that this proves a special relationship between Sally and Thomas Jefferson at that early date, or else why would Thomas Jefferson spend the money to have Sally inoculated.

Unfortunately, this is one of the many theories of Fawn Brodie which is complete nonsense, for a number of reasons.

Smallpox was the most deadly and dangerous disease among the slaves at Monticello. At least five slaves died of this disease in 1781 alone, during the Revolutionary War. Probably, all of the slaves were exposed to smallpox at one time or another. President George Washington had contracted smallpox in 1751 and his face was scarred with pox marks for that reason.

In his detailed instructions regarding how Maria was to be brought to France, Thomas Jefferson had specified that the woman to accompany her should be mature and should be one who had already had the smallpox. He suggested Isabel as a possibility. This is one of the reasons that it seems strange that Sally was the one who was ultimately sent.

Naturally, as soon as Sally arrived, Thomas Jefferson must have realized that she was not immune to smallpox and decided to do something about it.

However, there was little he could do. The smallpox vaccine did not exist yet. Edward Jenner of England did not perform his first famous vaccination against smallpox until 1796, nine years later.

It is really astounding that all of the great and good and wonderfully distinguished historians have never bothered to open any standard reference work to find out when the smallpox vaccine was first developed. Every historian who has discussed this subject, including not only Fawn Brodie but also Virginius Dabney and James A. Bear, Jr., has mentioned Sally as being inoculated against smallpox with Jenner's vaccine in 1787. Fawn Brodie strongly implies that this proves that Sally Hemings and Thomas Jefferson were already sleeping together at that early date.

It is no doubt true that Sally did receive some sort of inoculation on November 6, 1787. However, this was not a vaccination as we know it today. It was an inoculation with a disease called cowpox, which was a serious disease but much milder than smallpox. The person inoculated would actually catch the disease of cowpox and get sick, sometimes fatally, but, upon recovery, would be immune to smallpox. This was an experimental procedure being developed by someone in France prior to Jenner. Like almost all great discoveries, Jenner was not the only one who had the idea of a vaccine against smallpox, even though he gets the full credit for it today. Sally may have been one of the first persons in human history to be inoculated. This also explains the high cost of the inoculation which Fawn Brodie mentions.

What this proves is exactly the opposite of what Fawn Brodie contends. Even after Jenner had developed and published his theories regarding smallpox vaccination in 1798, there were cases, especially in England, of bad vaccine which killed those vaccinated. Years earlier, Jonathan Edwards (1703–1758), the great theologian and the grandfather of Aaron Burr, had been killed by a smallpox inoculation in 1758.

In short, Thomas Jefferson must have been unhappy about the fact that, against his instructions, a person had been sent to accompany his daughter who was not immune to smallpox. He therefore had that person exposed to cowpox, a mild form of that disease, and put into quarantine. In short, he was prepared to use Sally as a human guinea pig to save his daughters from exposure to smallpox. In 1801, after his return to America, he had all of his other slaves inoculated as well. After that, none of his slaves ever died of smallpox, which became a major killer of troops later on, during the American Civil War.

What this really proves is that in November, 1787, Sally was still expendable, but his daughters, Martha and Maria, who had not been inoculated, were not. Therefore, the sexual relationship between Thomas Jefferson and Sally is likely to have started at a later date.

In 1789, Thomas Jefferson returned to America. Sally Hemings was reluctant to go, knowing that as soon as she set foot on America, she would become a slave again, whereas she was a free woman in France. She had already become fluent in the French language. However, Jefferson induced her to return to America by making an agreement that her child would be set free upon reaching maturity. (This last fact tends to prove that she must have been at least pregnant at the time).

Shortly after she arrived back in the U.S. at the Port of Norfolk, Virginia on November 23, 1789, Sally Hemings gave birth to a son named Tom, who must have been born in either 1789 or 1790.

Here is one place where the historians attack this account. Thomas Jefferson kept a *Farm Book*, and there in no mention in this *Farm Book* of the birth of a son named Tom in 1789 or 1790. They say that this proves that Tom did not exist at all.

However, only slaves are mentioned in the *Farm Book*. No mention is made of his daughters, Martha and Maria, for example. Thomas Jefferson may have felt that his son, Tom, was born free and never a slave.

Fortunately, this document, the *Farm Book*, was published in fascimile form by the University Press of Virginia in 1987. This makes this important document accessible to everyone willing to plunk down thirty dollars, not just to the historians.

It is true that the *Farm Book* does not show the birth of a child named Tom in 1789 or 1790. However, among the six known children of Sally Hemings, the birth of only one is recorded in the *Farm Book*. Others have their birth dates mentioned, but are not listed among the births on the farm. Moreover, the editors of the *Farm Book* admit that the book is incomplete and difficult to read and follow. Many pages and entries are missing. Also, there are several alternative explanations for the fact that Tom is not mentioned in the *Farm Book*. The one most likely is that Tom was not born on the farm and never went there. Jefferson had agreed that Tom would not be a slave, so perhaps Tom grew up in the North, or possibly in Washington, D.C., or in Philadelphia, where Jefferson served as Secretary of State from 1790 to 1793, during the period when Tom was born. At that time, Philadelphia, and not Washington, was the Capital of America. There is now living in Washington, D.C. a woman named Minnie Shumate Woodson, who claims that her husband and her children are descendants of that Tom and of Sally Hemings and Thomas Jefferson.

There are several additional possible explanations for why that Tom is not mentioned in the *Farm Book*. For example, the family members of Thomas Jefferson had access to the *Farm Book* after he died and often thumbed through it. Since Tom was born so shortly after the return of Sally Hemings from France, if his birth had been recorded in the *Farm Book*, it would have been clear that he had been conceived in France. Thomas Jefferson might have wanted to conceal this fact. There were, in fact, a few slaves at Monticello named Tom, this being a common name, but none of these were listed in the *Farm Book* as a child of Sally Hemings.

# Chapter Three

## The Farm Book

Thomas Jefferson has left to posterity a wonderful source document which provides details about his life on the Monticello estate near to Charlottesville, Virginia. To those who have never been there, Monticello is a grand palatial estate situated on a mountain-top. It is the closest thing America has to the Taj Mahal. The building is shown on the 'tails' side of the American five-cent coin. No other president in American history ever owned anything approaching Monticello. Thomas Jefferson was almost certainly the richest man of his day to become President. He got his money the old fashioned way: He inherited it.

The *Farm Book* contains a complete list of all slaves at various times, how many blankets each was given and how much food. It shows to which farm each slave was assigned. It also records the births and deaths of slaves.

The *Farm Book* is also a log containing information about the planting of crops and other items. However, it mostly deals with slaves, including how much food, blankets and clothing each slave was to be given. It also records births and deaths of slaves as well as the loans and leases of slaves. It contains long inventories of the names of slaves for various years. However, it does not record the purchase and sale of slaves.

Unfortunately, there is no complete record of the purchase and sale of slaves. In some cases, documents, such as bills of sale, have survived elsewhere, but they are not in the *Farm Book*.

There are only a few instances where Jefferson actually bought slaves. Instead, he bred his own. On June 20, 1820, in a letter to his son-in- law John Eppes, he wrote: 'I consider a woman who brings a child every two years as more profitable than the best man on the farm. What she produces is an addition to the capital, while his labors disappear in mere consumption.'

Almost all of the purchases of slaves by Thomas Jefferson were of pregnant women with children. One of the purchases of slaves took place while Thomas Jefferson was President. In the account book dated August 21, 1805, there is the entry, 'bought a Negro woman, Lucretia, Jame's wife and her two sons John and Randall and the child of which she is pregnant, when born, for 180 pounds, of which 100 pounds to be paid before departure and the residue twelve months hence.'

Thomas Jefferson had several slaves named Sally. One died in 1781, during the American Revolution. Next to her name on page 29 of the *Farm Book* is the entry, 'Cumberland . . . . fled to the enemy and died.' A total of eight names are included in this category. Below is another entry with five more names of slaves who caught smallpox from the enemy and died and five more who caught camp fever from Negroes who returned and died. Altogether, there seems to have been 30 slaves who died in 1781 during the American Revolution. Thomas Jefferson claimed that British General Cornwallis was personally responsible for their deaths. This was not mainly because the British attacked both Richmond and Monticello during the American Revolution in the hopes of capturing Jefferson, who was then the Governor of Virginia at the time. Rather, most of the deaths involved slaves on another plantation belonging to Jefferson named 'Elk Hill', which Lord Cornwallis occupied, using Jefferson's house as his office.

During the Revolution, the British rounded up many slaves as prisoners, not only the slaves of Thomas Jefferson, and kept them at Yorktown, where many of them died of various diseases due to the unsanitary conditions. This is reported by many sources, including Isaac Jefferson, one of the captured slaves, in *Jefferson at Monticello*, p. 10, edited by James A. Bear, Jr. There, Isaac Jefferson states, 'great many colored people died there'. The Americans have often been accused of treating their slaves badly, but the British treated them far worse. This subject is treated in greater detail in Benjamin Quarles, *The Negro in the American Revolution*, Chapel Hill, North Carolina, 1961.

Although the *Farm Book* lists slaves who 'fled with the enemy and died', the *Memoirs of Isaac Jefferson*, p. 10, makes it clear that actually those slaves were taken as prisoners. Isaac Jefferson, then six years old, after being captured by the British along with his parents, was given the nickname 'Sambo' by the British soldiers and allowed to beat the drum during the forced march to Yorktown. Isaac further states that after the fighting was over, General George Washington helped Isaac, along with his parents, Great George and Ursula, get back with their master, Thomas Jefferson.

Those slaves who died clearly did not include the Sally about whom we are concerned. She is listed as 'Sally 73', with 73 being her year of birth. This is the reason that the historians mention Sally as being 16 when she was with Jefferson in 1789 in France.

There is also a Sally 80, who was too young to be of concern to us. However, as will be seen, this causes a lot of confusion, because both Sallys produced many children. The other Sally apparently was pure black and spent her life as a field hand in Bedford.

The *Farm Book* begins with a listing of all of the slaves of Thomas Jefferson and from where obtained on January 14, 1774. Page 5 of the *Farm Book* has a 'Roll of the proper slaves of Thomas Jefferson', with 29 slaves listed at Monticello, four at Lego and eight at Shadwell. Lego and Shadwell were other farms owned by Thomas Jefferson. On page 6 of the *Farm Book* is a listing of 'Slaves conveyed by my mother to me under the power given her in my father's will upon indemnification for the debts I had paid for her.' Eleven slaves are listed: one at Lego, ten at Shadwell.

After that, on pages 7-9 is, 'A Roll of the slaves of John Wayles which were allotted to T.J. in right of his wife on a division of the estate Jan. 14 1774.' This is a listing showing the whereabouts of all of the slaves in January, 1774, at the time that they were inherited from John Wayles. John Wayles had owned the impressive total of 11 different farms when he died. These were: Poplar Forest, Wingo's, Judith Creek, Crank's, Elk Hill, Indian Camp, Angola, Guinea, Bridge Quarter, Liggon's and Forest. Many of these farms were sold by Thomas Jefferson promptly after he inherited them. There were 135 slaves in all originally belonging to John Wayles, including the slaves on each farm.

This shows the importance of the *Farm Book*. We can see that at the beginning, in January, 1774, Thomas Jefferson owned exactly 187 slaves. Through the pages of the *Farm Book*, we can track the movements and the whereabouts of these slaves. Coincidentally, in the last inventory in the *Farm Book*, taken in 1824, just before he died in 1826, Thomas Jefferson also owned exactly 187 slaves.

This gives us a recorded history over the length of 50 years from 1774 to 1824 of the births and deaths and the comings and goings of these 187 slaves. No other slave owner during this period kept such a detailed record.

The entries in the *Farm Book* regarding Sally 73, to the extent that they are legible, along with some other relevant entries, are as follows:

**Page 9.** Sally 73, Guinea. Below the name of Betty Hemings (Betty being short for Elizabeth) are the names of six children and one grandchild. The children are: Nancy, 1761; Jimmy, 1765; Thenia, 1767; Critta, 1769; Peter, Aug. 1770; and Sally, 1773. The grandson is Daniel, 1772. All are listed under the heading of Guinea. Guinea was not the country but rather the name of the farm in Cumberland County belonging to John Wayles where Sally had presumably been born. (Another farm was named Angola, also the name of a country, adding to the confusion). The name of Betty's mother, who was from Africa, does not seem to have been mentioned by any source. Martin, 1756, and Bob, 1762, two other children of Betty Hemings, are listed separately on page 9 of the *Farm Book* as being at 'Forest', the official residence of John Wayles, which was in Charles City County, near Richmond.

**Page 18.** Under Elk Hill (the farm where they were assigned to work in 1774) is the same list of names, except that Jimmy 1765 is missing. At the bottom is the notation '187 [slaves] in all'. From other sources, we know that

'Jimmy', or James Hemings, the son of Betty Hemings, was taken to France by Thomas Jefferson in 1784, and later returned. James Hemings worked as a chef in the house of Thomas Jefferson at what is now 287 Market Street in Philadelphia, while Thomas Jefferson was Secretary of State. Finally, he was given his freedom on February 5, 1796. He and his brother Robert Hemings were the only slaves ever to be officially freed by Thomas Jefferson in his lifetime.

Page 21. Under Deaths in 1774 is listed 'Betty (Sue's Elk Hill) November 15'. However, this Betty who died on November 15, 1774 was another Betty, not the mother of Sally.

At this point, there is a 20-year gap. During this period, Thomas Jefferson went to France and upon his return became Secretary of State. Sally apparently stayed with him and did not return to the farm until 1794. However, there is no absolute proof of this, but it is reported that Aaron Burr in his diary noted the presence of Sally in Philadelphia in March, 1797, to attend the inauguration of Thomas Jefferson as Vice-President. Because of the distance involved, the daughters of Jefferson did not attend that inauguration.

Page 30. 'Roll of the Negroes Nov. 1794 and where to be settled for the year 1795. Monticello Sally 73.'

Page 31. Squeezed in at the bottom of the page there is an illegible entry under births which says, 'H---, Sally's, October 5, 1795'.

Page 39. Sally along with her sisters, Critta and Nancy, are mentioned as having received a blanket in various years.

Page 41. Sally, Critta and others were given clothing in December 1794.

Page 42. Sally was given 2 yards of linen and other items in 1794.

Page 43. Both 'Betty Hem' and several Sallys are on the bread list for 1795.

Page 46. One Sally is mentioned as a gatherer at Shadwell. Another Sally is on the list of eight women who 'would remain to keep half the ploughs a going'.

Page 49. Sally is on the list as receiving various items of clothing in 1795

Page 50. Bread list for 1796. Perhaps the first important entry. Sally is listed as being at Monticello and below her is the name 'Edy'. They are to receive two loaves of bread per week. It appears that Edy is a child of Sally's. Sally 80 is listed under Shadwell. That must have been the Sally who is listed as a gatherer on page 46 above.

Page 51. Ration list for 1796. Sally and Edy are to receive 8 fish.

Page 52. Col. 2. Cloths list 1796. Sally and Harriet are to receive one bed. Col. 3. Bread list 1797. Sally, Harriet and Aggy are to receive 3 bread.

Page 53. Sally and Harriet get 8 fish.

**Page 55.** 1799 Oct. Sally and Beverly 98 get 1 1/2 of something illegible.

**Page 56.** Sally and Beverly get 8 fish and one bread. Below them are Betty Hem., John Hem. and Peter Hem. They each get 4 fish and 1/2 bread.

**Page 57.** Roll of the Negroes in the Winter of 1798-9. Listed below Sally is Beverly, who was born on April 1, 1798. Sally and Beverly get 8 fish and 1 bread.

**Page 58a.** Sally and Beverly are on the ration list for 1800.

**Page 60.** There is a list of 46 'Negroes leased to J. H. Craven' in 1801. There is another list of 'Negroes retained'. Sally and Beverly are on the list of Negroes retained, along with 'Betty Hemings 35 & 07'. This is the only indication of the possible actual birth and death dates of Betty. This shows that Betty was born in 1735 and died in 1807. This would make Betty 26 when she first gave birth to a child of John Wayles, and would make John Wayles only 20 when he bought her. Both seem unlikely.

However, other sources indicate that the reason for this discrepancy is that Madison Hemings, who, as will be seen, was the source for much of the information about the Hemings family history, was wrong when he said that his grandmother had been purchased directly off the slave ship by John Wayles. According to James A. Bear, Jr., the mother of Betty Hemings had first been owned by Col. Francis Eppes IV, who resided in what was then Henrico County, in a place now near to Hopewell, which is south of Richmond. Even recently, there were people named Hemings in that area, before they all changed their names. In 1746, Betty Hemings was deeded to John Wayles as part of the dowry he received in consideration of his marriage to Martha Eppes.

The reason that Betty Hemings did not become the mistress of John Wayles until age 26, after she had already given birth to six children by a slave husband who had died, was that she did not become the mistress of John Wayles until after his third wife, Elizabeth Lomax, had died in 1761. Betty produced her first child from John Wayles in 1762.

All of this may or may not be true. There is no mention of any of this in the *Farm Book*, other than the birth and death dates of Betty Hemings of 1735 and 1807.

The only persons with the name given as Hemings listed in the *Farm Book* are Betty Hemings, Peter Hemings, sometimes Sally Hemings and John Hemings. John Hemings was a son of Betty Hemings who was born long after the death of John Wayles. His father was a carpenter named John Neilson who had worked for Thomas Jefferson.

We know from other correspondence by Thomas Jefferson that there was a James Hemings and a Robert Hemings. Robert Hemings almost never lived on the farm and traveled freely, almost like a white man. He was able to do so easily, being 75% white. He was eventually freed by Thomas Jefferson and settled in Richmond, Virginia, where he had a wife named Dolly and lived in a house on the corner of 7th and Grace Streets, which is now in downtown Richmond and is occupied by a skyscraper. His descendants live in the area of Richmond to this day. In addition, there are still people in the area of Charlottesville, Bedford and Lynchburg, Virginia named Hemmings (note the 'mm'). All of them are undoubtedly descended from Betty Hemings.

After the 1801 entry, this there is a nine-year gap in the *Farm Book*. This apparently reflects the fact that Thomas Jefferson was President during the years 1801 to 1809.

**Page 128.** Contains an entry of great importance. This is the roll of Negroes 1810 Feb. in Albemarle, the county were Monticello was located. Under Monticello is listed 'house . . . Sally 73' and below her Harriet 01 May, Madison 05 Jan. and Eston 08 May 21. This means that during the eight years when Thomas Jefferson was in the White House, Sally Hemings produced three children. Harriet was born in 1801, Madison in 1805 and Eston on May 21, 1808. Also there is Edy 87 and three children, James, Jan. 7, 1805; Maria, October 27, 1807 and Patsy, May 11, 1810. Under Tradesmen is listed John Hemings 75 and Beverly April 1, 1798.

From this it appears that Sally at age 37 already had possibly six children, of whom one had died. Harriet, who perhaps was also called Edy, who was born in 1795, must have died, but now Sally had a new daughter, also named Harriet. Her child Beverly at age 12 is already an emancipated person with a separate place on this list. However, it is important to note that Beverly was a boy, not a girl. Usually, Beverly is a girl's name, but occasionally it is a boy's, as was the case here.

**Page 130.** Roll of the Negroes according to their ages at Albemarle. Betty (the mother) is not on the list and presumably has died. Peter Hemings 1770, Sally 73 and John Hemings 75 are listed. There is also 1798 Beverly run away 22; 1801 Harriet (Sally's) run 22; Madison (Sally's) 1805; Eston (Sally's) 1808; Peter (Edy's) June 5, 1815; Innet Sally's July 1816; Loranan Sally's 1818; Isabella Edy's Jan. 7, 1819; [blank] Sally's May 1821; William Edy's May 1821; Gilly Aggy's Dec. 1822; Isabella, Sally's Cha wife, May 1823.

The above entry is of great importance, because most agree that the notation 'run 22' next to the names of Beverly and Harriet indicates that they ran away in 1822.

**Page 131.** Roll of the Negroes in Bedford according to their ages. This list shows at least three children born to Sally, but this is apparently Sally 80, who was a field hand, not Sally Hemings.

Page 134. Under bread list Feb. 1810 is listed Sally, followed by Beverly, Harriet, Madison and Eston.

Page 135. Under Monticello House is listed Sally grown-2 children-3. Unlike some of the other women on the list, Sally has no husband. Beverly is apparently considered grown. There are a total of 25 adults and 28 children on the house list.

Page 136. Dec. 1810. Again Sally is listed with her four children.

Page 137. Sally gets a blanket in 1808. Harriet, Madison and Eston each get a blanket in 1809.

Page 139. Again Sally is listed with four children.

Page 142. Distribution of blankets, 1812. Sally and four children get blankets.

Page 145. December 1813 clothing list. Sally has three children. Beverly has his own place on the list.

Page 147. December 14, 1814. No change from above.

Page 148. Bread lists for 1815. Sally has all four children again.

Page 151. Dec. 1815. Sally back to three children. Beverly has his own spot on the list.

Page 155. 1816. Same as above.

Page 156. Bread list. Again all four children listed under Sally.

Page 159. There are now a total of 140 slaves. Sally listed with three children.

Page 160. Negroes leased to Thos. Randolph. 29 adults and 31 children, for a total of 60. Sally and her four children are all on the list of 'Negroes retained', of which there are 80.

Page 162. 1818. Sally and three children plus Beverly are on the ration list.

Page 164. 1819-1820. Same as above.

Page 165. Blanket list. Sally and four children are on the list, but lines are drawn through the names of Beverly and Harriet. There is no explanation for this, but it has been explained that at about this time, Beverly and Harriet were allowed to run away and later took up residence in Washington, D.C.

Page 169. Dec. 1823. Sally Hem. is on the list but no mention of the children.

Page 171. Sally and all four children are on the house list.

Page 172. Sally, Madison and Eston only are on the list for 1821-2.

Page 174. 1822. Again the same. No more mention of Beverly and Harriet.

Page 175. December 1823. No change.

Page 176. December 1824. No change. There are now 23 children, 21 men and 16 women on the Monticello house list.

# The End of the Farm Book

Although the ration list of Thomas Jefferson of 8 fish and one bread per week for each slave does not appear to be particularly sumptuous, it shows that, unlike some other masters, Thomas Jefferson did at least feed his slaves. It is often forgotten that some slave owners did not feed their slaves at all. Instead, after a hard days work in the fields, the slaves were left to forage in the woods for whatever food they could find. Slaves ate dandelions, weeds, wild plants and roots, plus the occasional rabbit if they could catch one. They also ate chitlins and other undesirable animal parts which were left-overs the white people were not willing to eat. From this, we have the 'soul food', which is still eaten in fine restaurants in places such as Harlem. Among the best known soul food is 'collard greens'.

Strangely, at least among the slaves mentioned in this book, it appears that they, more often than not, outlived their masters. It is possible that the unusual diet which the slaves were forced to eat was more healthy in the long run. A television documentary entitled *The Civil War* has talked about the deplorable condition of the slaves, stating that they rarely lived to be more than forty or fifty years old. However, this documentary forgot to men-tion that in those days, the life expectancy of white people was even less than that. Of course, this is not an apology for slavery. It merely means that a person who lives by foraging for weeds in the woods might live a longer life than one who is waited on by servants at the dinner table.

From reading the *Farm Book*, it does not appear that Sally was given spe-cial treatment. Nothing in the book identifies her as the President's personal concubine. When the others got eight fish and one bread, she also got the same.

However, other documents show that Sally was different from the other girls. The other women on the Monticello house list had various duties, such as cleaning and cooking. Only Sally, her mother, Betty, and her sister, Critta, had no other job. They were the personal attendants to Thomas Jefferson. Sally is occasionally listed as a seamstress.

Whenever a child was born, Jefferson noted not only the name of the mother but also the name of the father. All of the children produced by field hands at Poplar Forest in Bedford County had the names of their fathers on the lists in the *Farm Book*. However, no father is given for the children of Sally or for many of the other children born at Monticello. This does not, however, mean to imply that Jefferson might have been the father of all of these many children.

Sally is consistently listed as having four children. However, there may have been as many as six or even seven. Tom, the one who was conceived in France, possibly never lived on the farm. Harriet, born in 1795, died in 1797.

The 1796 entry shows a child named Edy. That name never appears again. It seems possible that Edy is the same child as Harriet, who died in 1797. It has been suggested by Fawn Brodie that these were different children, and that both died at about the same time. However, from a careful examination of the *Farm Book*, the statement by Fawn Brodie that Sally Hemings had a child named Edy who died has now been virtually disproven by Jack McLaughlin in his 1988 book *Jefferson and Monticello*, page 406, note 119.

There is another Edy, the daughter of Isabella and the mother of James, Maria, Patsy, Betsy and Peter. She was born in 1787 and is clearly a different person. McLaughlin points out that when the name 'Edy' appears under the name of Sally on page 50 of the *Farm Book*, it disappears under the name of Isabel, the mother of Edy 87. This means, according to McLaughlin, that this Edy was not the child of Sally at all but rather that she had been assigned to Sally to act as a nursemaid to care for the infant Harriet. Later, on page 52, the name of Aggy appears below the name of Sally. Aggy 89 was another child of Isabel. This means that Aggy is now helping Sally to take care of Harriet.

This explanation is almost convincing. However, there is one small problem. Edy and Harriet are not listed together, as they presumably would have been had Edy been the nursemaid of Harriet. At the same time, on page 52 of the *Farm Book*, right hand columns, the names of Sally, Harriet and Aggy appear together. Edy is back under the name of Isabel, her mother. This would seem to indicate that now Aggy has been assigned as a nursemaid to care for Harriet.

Thus, McLaughlin's basic point appears to be correct. From checking several thousand entries in the *Farm Book*, we can see that Thomas Jefferson never made a mistake. His accuracy was almost super-human. Since we exclude the possibility of a mistake, McLaughlin's explanation is the only one which is plausible.

This provides strong evidence that there was something special about Harriet and that she actually was the daughter of Thomas Jefferson. There is no other instance in which anyone besides the mother was assigned as a nursemaid care for an infant slave child.

It is refreshing to learn that there is one author, Jack McLaughlin, who does bother to check these small but extremely important facts and details in the *Farm Book*. This is in contrast to the sloppy work done by so many other writers on this subject, especially Virginius Dabney. Incidentally, this Edy is the same person who later served as a cook in the White House and who became the wife of Joe Fossett. Also, just to remind the reader, the Harriet in question here is the one who died as an infant in 1797, not the second Harriet who was born in 1801.

Many other women at Monticello produced multiple children. One of the most prolific was Ursula, born in 1787, who had seven. These were Joe, Anna, Dolly, Cornelius, Thomas, Louisa, and Caroline.

Critta only bore one child. However, another woman on the house list with a similar name, Cretia, had seven children. This was apparently the same person as Lucretia, who was purchased while pregnant in 1805.

The allegation that Jefferson had children by at least one of his slaves seems likely. However, the allegation that he actually sold his children into slavery was clearly without foundation when made. Jefferson sold no slaves during that period. However, in just the last few years of his life, when Thomas Jefferson was desperately broke and short of cash, he started selling his slaves. There is one especially pathetic instance regarding this.

On November 30, 1815, when Thomas Jefferson was 72 years old, he entered into a contract to sell a three year old girl, coincidentally named Sally, daughter of Aggy, for the sum of one hundred fifty dollars, to a Mr. Jeremiah Goodman of Bedford County.

After making that contract, an addendum was added stating that the child would remain in the possession of her mother until either Mr. Goodman or Thomas Jefferson desired that she be taken into his possession.

Two years later, on July 20, 1817, Thomas Jefferson must have realized that he had done a terrible thing, because he wrote a letter to Mr. Goodman stating that he wanted the contract to be annulled. He said, however, that he did not have the money to pay back the 150 dollars. He therefore requested that he be given two years credit to repay this sum.

This is truly a pathetic specter. Here is a former President of the United States, in the waning years of his life, who actually does not have $150 which he needs to rescue a by this time five-year-old girl.

One of the last entries of his life, when he was 81 years old, shows that by that time Thomas Jefferson was so desperately broke that he just wanted to sell his slaves for any money he could get for him. This was the first time he had reached that level of desperation.

A letter dated January 5, 1824 to Bernard Payton states: 'Jefferson returned last night from a sale of some Negroes in Bedford. He could make no hand off selling for any portion of ready money. He sold therefore at one and two years credit.'

Jefferson died completely insolvent on July 4, 1826, when he was 83 years old. His debts amounted to $107,000, a huge amount in that time. It is said that it took fifty years before they were completely paid off.

On January 15, 1827, after the death of Thomas Jefferson, there was an auction advertised in the *Richmond Enquirer*. That notice, published in the Richmond Enquirer dated November 7, 1826, said:

# EXECUTOR'S SALE

*On the fifteenth of January, at Monticello, in the county of Albemarle, the whole of the residue of the personal property of Thomas Jefferson, dec., consisting of valuable negroes, stock, crops, etc., household and kitchen furniture. The attention of the public is earnestly invited to this property. The negroes are believed to be the most valuable for their number ever offered in the state of Virginia. . . . .*

As a result of this ad, all of the personal property and effects of Thomas Jefferson at Monticello were sold at this auction in an attempt to pay his debts. Included in the sale were almost all of his slaves at Monticello. A second slave auction took place in January, 1829, regarding the slaves in Bedford County.

However, in his will he had decreed freedom for five of his slaves. All five of them were males who had white fathers. The five were Burwell Colburn, John Hemings, Joe Fossett (the son of Mary, who was the first-born child of Betty Hemings and a slave father), Madison Hemings and Eston Hemings. The name of Sally Hemings was not on the list, but apparently there was a private understanding that she would not be sold. All the rest of the slaves were sold. Nobody knows this for certain, however. There is no absolute proof that the terms of the will of Thomas Jefferson were carried out, but the descendants of these five claim that this was done. Also, there was apparently a special act passed by the Virginia legislature in 1827 which decreed that the five slaves freed in the will of Thomas Jefferson were allowed to remain in the State of Virginia. Otherwise, all freed slaves were required to go north, under the law of Virginia at that time.

Sally Hemings continued to live at Monticello after the death of Jefferson along with her sons, Madison and Eston, but all the other slaves were dispersed to various parts of the South. Sally Hemings died at Monticello in 1835. When she died, she and her two sons were the only former slaves of Thomas Jefferson still living at Monticello. Of course, they did not live in the 'big house', but in a nearby cabin. By that time, the big house at Monticello had a new owner. After Sally Hemings died, her sons, Madison and Eston, moved to the area of Chillicothe, Ohio.

# Chapter Four

## Madison Hemings

The most important piece of evidence concerning this entire question did not surface until 47 years after the death of Thomas Jefferson. That was in an interview of Madison Hemings in 1873, published in the *Pike County Republican* in Waverly, Ohio.

Historians have jumped on that interview with a hatchet and tried to tear it to ribbons. They say that it was impossible for Madison Hemings to have known the things he claimed that he knew, but that even if he knew them, he must have learned them from a library book. According to historian Douglass Adair, all the information provided by Madison Hemings could have been found in 'any well regulated library' with works on the life of Jefferson. Adair concluded that the interview was entirely fake and was composed by a political enemy of Thomas Jefferson.

The vehemence with which this interview was attacked shows that Adair and others like him were not really engaged in a search for the truth. There are so many holes and flaws in Adair's argument that it is clear that he was not even writing in good faith.

For example, there is his statement that everything said by Madison Hemings could have been learned in the library, but since Madison Hemings had taught himself how to read, Adair claims that somebody else must have composed the interview.

However, this entire line of reasoning misses the point. The *Farm Book* contains more than a dozen entries showing that a person named Madison Hemings was born in 1805 and lived on the Monticello estate for more than twenty years up until the death of Thomas Jefferson. If the man who gave the interview in Ohio really was the same man, then he didn't need to check out a book in the library. He would have known more about the personal habits of Jefferson than any author of any book, regardless of whether he happened to be the son of Thomas Jefferson or not.

Thus, the only valid question is: Was this really the same man?

The details about the life of Thomas Jefferson provided by Madison Hemings are not details to be found in library books. Madison Hemings talks about what Thomas Jefferson did in the mornings, and what he did at night. He talks about his attitudes towards and his treatment of slaves. 'He was very undemonstrative', said Madison Hemings. There are hundreds if not thousands of books on the life of Thomas Jefferson. However, almost all of these books deal with the great events of his life, such as the *Declaration of Independence* and the Louisiana Purchase.

For example, Madison Hemings in his interview provided the names of the twelve grandchildren of Thomas Jefferson, in their correct order of birth. Surely, this information is readily available in a book somewhere. But, where is that book?

Recent books have appeared on this subject but, prior to that time, even the fact that Jefferson had six children by his wife Martha, but four of them died as children, was not a fact easily ascertainable, nor was the fact that his other surviving daughter, Maria, had only one surviving child before she also died. Almost nowhere else but in the interview of Madison Hemings is there a complete list of the names of the eleven surviving children of Martha, the eldest daughter of Thomas Jefferson.

At the same time, if this was really the same Madison Hemings who lived in the house of Thomas Jefferson for 20 years, he would have been able effortlessly to reel off the names of all 12 of these children without consulting notes.

The reason that Adair went to the trouble to attack this interview with such vehemence is that Madison Hemings said that his mother, Sally, had told him that he, Madison, was the son of Thomas Jefferson.

Adair claims that Sally must have told her son, Madison, this only to lead her son to believe that his father had been an important person and 'to protect the real father, who was married'. However, does this really sound logical? Sally Hemings was devoted to Thomas Jefferson. She stayed with him right until he died. She continued to live on at Monticello even after his death. Why would she tell a lie to her son about who his father was?

Also, Adair claims that the true father of Madison Hemings was Peter Jefferson Carr, who died in 1815. Why would Sally Hemings slander the reputation of Thomas Jefferson just to protect the reputation of a dead man?

Then, there is the contention by Adair that this entire interview was faked by a political enemy of Thomas Jefferson. This is stupid. Thomas Jefferson had more personal and political enemies than most in the period 1801 to 1809 when he was president, but by 1873 he was a deity. He had no political enemies. He had been dead for nearly fifty years. His face was about to be chiseled into Mount Rushmore. Everybody worshipped Thomas Jefferson. For anyone to criticize or attack him would have been political suicide.

Virginius Dabney agrees with Adair and says that the interview of Madison Hemings expresses ideas and words beyond the intellectual range of a man like Madison Hemings, who says that he taught himself how to read. However, Dabney fails to consider the possibility that a son of Thomas Jefferson might just possibly have been able to use the big words found in this interview. Also, Dabney overlooks the fact that Madison Hemings had to say that he taught himself how to read. It was illegal in Virginia to teach a slave how to read. Madison Hemings was not going to confess that any person close to him had broken the law, so he had to say that he had taught himself how to read.

There were a few mistakes in the interview of Madison Hemings, but all of them are of such a nature as to tend to prove that the interview was real, and not fake. For example, he 'thinks' that the wife of Thomas Jefferson was named Martha, but is not completely sure. This is no great surprise. Martha Wayles Jefferson had died in 1782, twenty- three years before Madison was born. On the other hand, he recites with ease the names of all eleven surviving children of Martha Jefferson Randolph and the correct order of their birth. He was able to do this because they were his contemporaries. He grew up with them.

The most important mistake in the interview of Madison Hemings was his statement that his great-grandmother had been sold while pregnant directly off the slave ship to John Wayles. The official bibliographical information on John Wayles in the *Encyclopedia of Virginia Biography*, Vol. I, p. 354 says that John Wayles was an eminent lawyer, born in 1715 in Lancaster, England. However, according to *Thomas Jefferson's Farm Book*, Betty Hemings was born in 1735. That would make John Wayles only twenty years old when he purchased the mother of Betty Hemings, but at that age he was still studying law in England. This is a point which all other authors on this subject have overlooked.

It is, of course, possible that it is true that John Wayles at age twenty purchased the mother of Betty while pregnant just off the ship with the plan in mind that her soon-to-be-born daughter would become his concubine when she grew up. However, another explanation seems more likely. That was put forth by James A. Bear Jr. in a article in *Virginia Cavalcade*, Autumn 1979, p. 78. There, he states:

> *Although the exact location of her birth is unknown, evidence indicates that her mother belonged to Francis Eppes IV, who resided at Bermuda Hundred, then in Henrico County. Betty Hemings was a chattel of Eppes from about 1735 until 1746. In that year, she was deeded to John Wayles as part of his marriage dower with Martha Eppes.*

The unfortunate part about the above quotation comes with the words 'evidence indicates'. We would like to know what that evidence is and where to find it. This is an important part of the story. Nevertheless, it seems logical and reasonable to conclude that Bear is correct and that some person other than John Wayles was the original owner of Betty Hemings, especially since John Wayles apparently did not arrive in America until the 1740's.

This mistake by Madison Hemings is quite understandable when one considers that it concerns events which took place 138 years before the interview. Madison gave his interview in 1873. Betty Hemings was born in 1735.

An interesting point contained in the interview of Madison Hemings concerns how he was given the unusual name of 'Madison'. He said that Dolly Madison was at Monticello at the time that his mother, Sally, gave birth to him. Dolly promised to give Sally a nice present if she would give Dolly the privilege of naming her son. Sally agreed, and Dolly promptly gave the newborn baby boy the name 'Madison'. After that, Dolly Madison completely forgot all about her promise to give Sally a present.

This anecdote has led some persons to the conclusion that Madison Hemings was actually born in the White House. In January, 1805, when Madison was born, James Madison was serving under Thomas Jefferson as Secretary of State. Both men were in Washington. The personal home of James Madison was not far from Monticello. Therefore, it is entirely possible that Dolly Madison was at Monticello when Madison Hemings was born. However, it seems somewhat more likely that James Madison, Dolly Madison, Thomas Jefferson and Sally Hemings were all in Washington, D.C. when Madison Hemings was born.

Other factors make it clear that the Madison Hemings who gave the interview to the *Pike County Republican* in 1873 really was the same Madison Hemings who is repeatedly listed in the *Farm Book*. For example, he provided information to the *Pike County Republican* about the lives of Harriet Hemings and Beverly Hemings. Both were 87.5% white, married whites and lived their lives as whites in Washington, D.C. Nobody ever guessed that they were part black. He correctly identifies Beverly as a man, not as a woman (a mistake others have made). He says that he cannot reveal the new family name of Harriet, because she does not want it to be known that actually she is part black. He talks about his own children, one of whom died in a Confederate jail while being held as a prisoner-of-war. It is most unlikely that anyone would have composed this interview, and for what reason?

However, there is one tidbit in the interview of Madison Hemings which proves this this really was the same Madison Hemings who was the son of Sally Hemings. This, indeed, is one of the main points attacked by Virginius Dabney. Dabney notes that in his interview, Madison Hemings used the French word *enceinte* instead of the English term *pregnant* to describe the condition of his mother when she arrived in America back from France. Dabney notes that Madison Hemings was not a man of letters. He says that he taught himself how to read and write. Therefore, according to Dabney,

Madison Hemings could not possibly have known how to speak French and therefore the entire interview must have been faked.

However, Dabney forgot one thing: **Sally Hemings was a fluent speaker of the French language.** She had spent more than two years in France at an early age. She was reluctant to leave France because she spoke French so fluently that she had become accustomed to living there. In speaking with her children, it is entirely likely that she would have used the polite French term to explain to her son that she was pregnant, rather than the vulgar English term.

Nobody faking the interview would attribute to Madison Hemings the use of a French word when an English word would better suit the readers. Thus, the fact that Madison Hemings used this French word proves that this was really the same Madison Hemings who was the son of Sally Hemings.

There is, however, a second interview. This is of Israel Jefferson, one of the other slaves of Thomas Jefferson. Israel Jefferson said that he believes Madison Hemings to be the son of Thomas Jefferson as a 'fact which I believe from circumstances but do not positively know'.

The reason that this second interview was published in the *Pike County Republican* was that nobody believed the first interview. Therefore, the editor of was in search of somebody to corroborate the story of Madison Hemings. Madison knew of Israel Jefferson, a former slave of Thomas Jefferson, who was living in the vicinity of Waverly, Ohio. Therefore, the same reporter contacted Israel and took down his interview.

However, Virginius Dabney and others have seized upon one clear error in this second interview. They point out that Israel Jefferson said that he thinks he was born on Christmas Day, in about 1797, and can still remember his family moving into the White House. Dabney says that according to the *Farm Book*, Israel was born in 1800 and was too young to remember the Presidential inauguration which took place only a few months later. (At that time, the president was inaugurated in March, not in January, as at present.)

However, that error is not fatal. Thomas Jefferson was inaugurated president a second time, in 1805, and it is possible that the by then five-year-old Israel Jefferson would have been old enough to remember that event.

The *Farm Book* contains a dozen entries showing that Madison Hemings was born in 1805. It also contains an entry on page 130 showing that 'Israel Ned's' was born in 1800. The only record of any slave having been born on exactly Christmas Day was Brown, the son of Betty Brown, who was born on December 25, 1785. Brown was sold in 1806, according to page 60, col. 2, of the *Farm Book*. In any event, it hardly matters whether Israel Jefferson was born in 1797 or in 1800. Nobody is claiming that he was the son of Thomas Jefferson.

In addition, there is little of vital importance in the interview of Israel

Jefferson. Much of it deals with what happened to Israel after he reached Ohio. This might have been of more interest to the readers of the *Pike County Republican*, because they also lived in Ohio.

The interviews of Madison Hemings and of Israel Jefferson provide a wealth of information not available elsewhere. For example, Israel Jefferson describes his return to Monticello in 1866, just after the American Civil War. There, he met his former master, Thomas Jefferson Randolph, the grandson who had been the administrator of the estate of Thomas Jefferson. At that time, Thomas Jefferson Randolph was living in poverty at Edgehill, near to the decayed ruins of what had once been the grand old estate of Monticello. All the slaves were, of course, gone, having been freed by the Civil War. Thomas Jefferson Randolph was left with nothing more than 'one old blind mule'. Israel Jefferson was then living in Ohio, much better off financially than his former master.

A letter discovered by Judith P. Justus in the archives of the Alderman Library of the University of Virginia in Charlottesville confirms this story. This letter by Thomas Jefferson Randolph was intended to be a rebuttal of the article in the *Pike County Republican* but apparently was never mailed. In it, Thomas Jefferson Randolph discussed the visit he had received in 1866 at Edgehill from his former slave, Israel Jefferson. Thomas Jefferson Randolph wrote that his financial position was even worse than that which Israel Jefferson had described. Of course, the Civil War was just then over. Thomas Jefferson Randolph was lucky to be alive.

In spite of being a short interview, the story of Madison Hemings provides much information not available elsewhere. The story rings true. Madison Hemings made a few mistakes, but these were the normal mistakes of a man speaking from his own recollection about events which had occurred more than 50 years earlier. It is too bad the story did not go on longer. However, apparently, the *Pike County Republican*, the newspaper which published the story, intended this to be the first of a series of articles, but it received so much flack over this interview that it stopped publication about this subject.

In the interview, Madison Hemings states that he and the other children of Sally Hemings were the only children of the slaves of Thomas Jefferson. In other words, this means that Betty, Betsy, Mary, Ursula, Cretia, Edy and the other woman at Monticello who were giving birth to multiple children in that house were producing children from other fathers. We can all breath a sigh of relief at this news.

# Chapter Five

## Contrary Evidence

A number of serious historians in Virginia, including Douglas Adair, Virginius Dabney, Dumas Malone and George Shackleford, have disputed this entire story. They say that Thomas Jefferson was not the father of these children. They say that the author of the *Declaration of Independence* and the *Virginia Statute of Religious Freedom* could not possibly have 'seduced' a 16-year-old black slave. Rather, according to them, the fathers of the children of Sally Hemings probably must have been Peter Carr (1770-1815) and/or Samuel Jefferson Carr (1771-1855), who were the sons of Martha Jefferson Carr, a widowed sister of Thomas Jefferson. Peter Carr and Samuel Carr had lived at Monticello for a time as infants after their father, Dabney Carr (1743-1773), had died.

The reason that the so-called 'defenders' of Thomas Jefferson feel the need to blame the Carr brothers for these children is that they have no other good explanation for the fact that so many slave children at Monticello looked just like Thomas Jefferson. Everyone agrees that if Thomas Jefferson did not father these children, the father must have been his close relative.

However, even if it were true that one or both of the Carr brothers were responsible for these children, that would still make the children of Sally Hemings as blood relations and collateral descendants of Thomas Jefferson. They would still carry similar DNA.

Among those historians who have staked their reputations on 'defending' Thomas Jefferson from the charge that he fathered children by his black slaves, the current leader is Virginius Dabney, a former editor of the *Richmond Times-Dispatch* and the author many books, including the *History of the University of Virginia*, which was founded by Thomas Jefferson himself. Virginius Dabney is the grandson of an even more prominent Virginius Dabney (1835-1894) who is listed in the *Encyclopedia of Virginia Biography*, Vol. 3, p. 190 and who was novelist and a captain in the Confederate Army.

The present Virginius Dabney has written an article in *Virginia Cavalcade* and a book entitled *The Jefferson Scandals, a Rebuttal*, which was published in 1991 by Madison Books in Lanham, Maryland. The copyright notice states that Dabney wrote the book in 1981, when it was published under hard cover.

In his article and in his book, Dabney criticizes all of these critics by saying that their works are 'not the result of a historian's careful sifting and weighing of evidence'. See *Virginia Cavalcade*, Volume XXIX, Autumn 1979, Number 2, page 55. He accuses them of scandal mongering just to sell books and magazines and playing fast and loose with the facts.

However, it is clearly Dabney himself, who has devoted considerable time to the study of Thomas Jefferson, who has not sifted the evidence on this particular point very well. Everything written by Dabney is riddled with factual errors.

First, it must be pointed out that one can hardly blame Virginius Dabney and fellow historian Douglas Adair from fudging the facts on this particular point. Both have eminent positions at universities devoted to the study of the life of Thomas Jefferson. If they were to come out with the conclusion that Thomas Jefferson had sex with his slaves, they would be out of a job on the same day. They must defend their president, right or wrong. They have no choice but to proclaim him completely innocent. Adair was, prior to his death, the Editor of the *William and Mary Quarterly* in Williamsburg, Virginia. Dabney is associated with the Virginia Commonwealth University.

The first and the best point which Virginius Dabney and Douglas Adair make in attacking the story that Thomas Jefferson fathered children by his slaves, is to focus on the writer who first published that story. His name was James Thompson Callender. He was, without exaggeration, one of the most vicious political writers in all of history. His place in hell is secure. Callender did not merely sully the reputation of Thomas Jefferson. Callender also wrote the story which led to the duel years later in which Alexander Hamilton was killed by Aaron Burr. In addition, Callender first published the story of a sexual episode involving Thomas Jefferson and Elizabeth Walker.

However, Callender did not live long enough to see the fruits of his labors. The story which led to the duel between Hamilton and Burr became known as as 'The Reynolds Affair'. By the time of that duel, Callender himself was already dead, presumably murdered by somebody who did not appreciate his writing style.

In any case like this, focusing on the writer, however disreputable, misses the point. Callender may have been a political hack writer, but his story would have fallen flat had there been no truth to it. It is therefore necessary to look beyond the personality of the writer who first published the story to see whether the story was true or not.

All of the evidence of Virginius Dabney and others, which, according to them, proves that there was no relationship between Thomas Jefferson and Sally Hemings, is transparent and weak. For example, there is their statement that the children of Sally Hemings were fathered by either Peter Jefferson

Carr or Samuel Jefferson Carr, the nephews of Thomas Jefferson. However, the source for this is none other than Thomas Jefferson Randolph, the grandson of Thomas Jefferson and the administrator of his estate after he died. Could anyone seriously believe that Thomas Jefferson Randolph would say that his long deceased grandfather had sex with his slaves? Would Thomas Jefferson Randolph have admitted that Madison Hemings was his uncle?

The other 'independent' source is Ellen Randolph Coolidge, a granddaughter of Thomas Jefferson, who wrote a letter in 1858 stating that, according to her brother, Thomas Jefferson Randolph, 'Dusky Sally' had been the mistress of 'a married man'. The full text of this letter was kept secret by the family for years until it was finally published for the first time in the New York Times on May 18, 1974.

Ellen Randolph Coolidge claimed that Thomas Jefferson could not have been the father of the children of Sally Hemings because he had not been near Sally for fifteen months before one of her children was born. (She did not say which child.) However, this has been proven wrong by historian Winthrop Jordan. Thomas Jefferson had been with Sally nine months before the birth of each of her children. For example, on April 17, 1804, Maria, the daughter of Thomas Jefferson, died and both Thomas Jefferson and Sally Hemings attended the funeral at Monticello. On January 19, 1805, exactly nine months and two days later, Madison Hemings was born.

Next, there is the interview of an overseer named Edmund Bacon, who worked at Monticello in the period 1806 to 1822. This interview has been published in *Jefferson at Monticello*, edited by James A. Bear, Jr., University Press of Virginia, 1981. In this interview, Bacon said that he knew that some person other than Thomas Jefferson was the father of Sally Hemings' children, but he would not say who that person was, or else that name was deleted by the reverend who published the interview. Bacon also positively proclaimed that he knew who the father of Harriet was, having often seen that man emerge from the room of Sally Hemings early in the morning. He gave his interview in 1862 in Kentucky, where he had become a wealthy planter and horse- breeder, long after the death of Thomas Jefferson.

However, Harriet (the second Harriet) was born on May 22, 1801, and therefore was conceived in 1800. Bacon did not come to work at Monticello until 1806. Even if one believes his story about wanting to protect the unidentified lover of Sally 62 years later, Bacon could not possibly have known whom she was sleeping with in 1800. Also, it appears possible that Sally was not on the farm in 1800, but rather was with Thomas Jefferson in Washington, D.C. or in Philadelphia where he was Vice-President. (The capital of the United States was moved from Philadelphia to Washington, D.C. in the year of 1800).

In addition, whenever this interview is quoted, an important part of it is left out. In that part, Edmund Bacon said about Harriet, 'People said that he [Thomas Jefferson] freed her because she was his own daughter.' Bacon further said that, acting pursuant to Jefferson's instructions, he had personally handed to Harriet $50 plus the stage fare to pay for her transportation north. This happened in 1822, the last year that Bacon worked at Monticello. This appears to indicate that Harriet really was the daughter of Thomas Jefferson, in spite of Bacon's denial.

For various reasons, it seems unlikely that either Peter Carr or Samuel Jefferson Carr was the father of Sally Hemings' children. At the time that most of her children were born, Peter and Samuel Carr were married and had their own plantations and their own slaves. They did not have much contact with Thomas Jefferson during this period. The fact that descendants of Thomas Jefferson have been quick to slander the Carr brothers suggests that there was not much love lost between them. It seems unlikely that the the Carr brothers would have left their own plantations to go and bother the personal attendants of Thomas Jefferson, namely Sally Hemings and her half-sister, Betty Brown. They had plenty of other women to choose from, if that was what interested them.

In addition, it is interesting to note that a third Carr brother, Dabney Jr. (1773-1837), has never been accused of this. Perhaps, that is because he was an eminent Justice of the Supreme Court of Virginia.

Of significance is the fact that two of the five children of Sally were born after this scandal had been published extensively in the newspapers. The story was first published in 1802, and yet Sally produced children in 1805 and 1808. Would Peter Carr or Samuel Carr or any other prudent white man have dared to lay a hand on Sally Hemings after she had become world famous as the concubine of Thomas Jefferson?

Next, there is the question of utmost importance, which is why did not Thomas Jefferson himself deny the story. In a court of law, this would constitute clear and convincing evidence that Thomas Jefferson really was the father. A paternity case is not like other types of cases. In a paternity case, silence tends to create the presumption that the accused man is the father of the child.

However, according to Virginius Dabney and others, Thomas Jefferson did deny it by implication although not directly in a letter dealing with another episode, this concerning his repeated approaches years earlier towards a married woman named Elizabeth Walker, who happened to be his best friend's wife.

One of the main reasons why Thomas Jefferson is considered to have been a notorious womanizer in his youth concerned his ardent advances towards a number of young women. In 1764, he proposed or intended to propose marriage to Rebecca Burwell, aged 17, but wanted for her to wait for six months until he went on a journey to England and then returned. She did not wait but after four months got married to another man. Thomas Jefferson never went on his journey.

The correspondence Jefferson left behind on this subject does not make it clear whether Rebecca Burwell actually rejected him and spurned his advances or whether, being only 21 years old and presumably inexperienced with women, Thomas Jefferson did not press his case hard enough. However, history does tell us that Rebecca Burwell did just as well if not better with the marriage partner she actually selected. She married Jaquelin Ambler (1742–1798), who became the Treasurer of the State of Virginia. One of their daughters, Polly Ambler, married John Marshall, who was Chief Justice of the United States Supreme Court from 1801 to 1835. Marshall decided the famous case of *Marbury v. Madison*. According to many historians, Marshall was more influential in his 34 years as Chief Justice in shaping the modern United States of America than any president who ever served.

Rebecca Burwell and Jaquelin Ambler had seven daughters. One daughter, Mary Willis Ambler, also known as Polly, who married Chief Justice John Marshall, gave him six surviving children. This was a prolific family. The six surviving children of Chief Justice John Marshall produced a total of 48 grandchildren. See *Descendants of Jaquelin Ambler* by George D. Fisher, Richmond, Virginia (1890). Another daughter of Rebecca Burwell, Betsy Ambler, later wrote a letter criticizing all Virginia politicians, including Thomas Jefferson, for running away when the British attacked Richmond in 1781. This letter came to be published in the *Atlantic Monthly*, vol. 84, p. 538 (1899).

Unfortunately, the only son of Rebecca Burwell died in infancy. For this reason, the Ambler name did not survive.

The woman who actually did eventually marry Thomas Jefferson unfortunately died after ten years of marriage because of complications resulting from having too many children in such a short time.

One wonders: If Thomas Jefferson had married Rebecca Burwell, how would history have been different? Would her sturdier constitution have produced a brood of children for Thomas Jefferson as it did for Jaquelin Ambler, the man whom she actually married. Or, would Thomas Jefferson have killed her off, as he did the woman he actually married?

In any event, it is clear from his letters that his failure to get Rebecca Burwell when he wanted her was truly a painful experience for the young Thomas Jefferson. He danced with her on October 6, 1763. This apparently excited him greatly, but left him tongue-tied and speechless. He did not put the question to her. Years later, at the inaugural ball of James Madison in 1809 at the conclusion of his presidency, Jefferson remarked that he had not attended a ball in over 40 years. Perhaps his dance with Rebecca Burwell was the last time he danced in his entire life.

Thereby frustrated, in 1768 he turned his attentions to a married woman, namely his best friend's and neighbor's wife. Never one to do things in a small time way, Jefferson selected as the object of his desires the granddaughter of Governor Alexander Spotswood (1676–1740), who is credited with having killed Blackbeard the Pirate and who first appointed Benjamin Franklin as the Postmaster of Pennsylvania. Her husband, John Walker, went off to serve in the French and Indian Wars, where he greatly distinguished himself, leading to a later appointment to the United States Senate, after asking the young Thomas Jefferson to look after his wife. Thomas Jefferson took this request to heart and invited himself into the young woman's bed. She claimed to have spurned his advances, but that he continued his hot pursuit of her for more than ten years until 1779, even after he married Martha Wayles Jefferson.

There was an episode in 1770 when Thomas Jefferson was lodged in the same house with Walker and his wife. They were in nearby quarters. Walker left his wife alone in their room. Seizing upon this opportunity, Thomas Jefferson somehow got into the room of Walker's wife while she was either undressing or in bed. Again, in as late as 1779, there was an incident where Thomas Jefferson and his wife, Martha, were lodged in the same house with Walker and his wife. Jefferson learned the habits of Elizabeth Walker and, leaving his own wife asleep in bed, stood in the hallway in the wee hours of the morning in only his shirt waiting to seize Elizabeth Walker as she walked from her bedroom to the toilet.

John Walker remained oblivious to this for years. In the mean time, he rose to the rank of colonel and served as a staff aid to General George Washington during the Revolutionary War. According to the official version, his wife waited until 1786, when Thomas Jefferson was safely in France, before revealing this affair to her husband, and did so then only because John Walker intended to name Thomas Jefferson in his will. When this matter subsequently became public, Walker felt obliged as a man of honor to challenge Thomas Jefferson to a duel, but he later withdrew the offer. Pathetically, years later, in 1809, as Walker lay on his death bed, he sent a message asking Thomas Jefferson to come and visit him. Jefferson refused to come.

The official version is that the wife of Walker maintained her virtue and never ever had sex at all with Thomas Jefferson. But who can really believe that he hotly pursued her for more than ten years and never got any little bit of encouragement? Elizabeth Walker had only one child by her husband, John Walker. Perhaps there was something missing in her married life.

This episode, like the Sally Hemings affair, got in the newspapers while

Thomas Jefferson was president. Responding to these charges, Thomas Jefferson wrote in a note in 1805: 'I plead guilty to one of [the] charges . . . . that when young and single I offered love to a handsome lady.' According to Virginius Dabney, this means that he is denying the charges regarding Sally Hemings but admitting to some of the charges regarding Elizabeth Walker.

However, this does not follow. The key word is 'guilty'. When he says, 'I plead guilty', this means that he admits that he did something wrong. Even here, Thomas Jefferson fudged the question. There was nothing, in itself, wrong with him offering love to a handsome lady. The only thing wrong with it was that this particular handsome lady happened to be his best friend's wife.

It is not even clear that Thomas Jefferson was confessing to having made approaches towards Walker's wife. Perhaps, when he said that he had once offered his love to a handsome lady, he was referring to Rebecca Burwell, 17, who was unmarried at the time.

However, the main point about this 1805 letter is the context in which it was written. After this matter had been splashed all over the newspapers of America, Walker felt humiliated with being publicly known to have been cuckolded. He therefore demanded a public letter from Thomas Jefferson, confessing his own guilt and defending the virtue of Walker's wife. The 1805 letter by Thomas Jefferson was actually a note to his Secretary of the Navy attached to a longer letter which has been lost to history but which was intended to satisfy this demand. Thus, no real credence can be placed in a letter written under these circumstances. In addition, it is strange that among the thousands of letters written by Thomas Jefferson, only this one letter has been lost, in spite of the fact that he kept a copy of all of his letters.

More important to the question here, this letter was not intended to deal in any way with the Sally Hemings affair. It concerned only the matter of John Walker and his wife, Elizabeth. Considering the seriousness of the situation at the time, with John Walker, a military officer and a former United States Senator, threatening to fight a duel with the President of the United States, it would have trivialized the matter for Thomas Jefferson to digress and allude to the unrelated Sally Hemings affair in such a letter.

Also, if Thomas Jefferson had implied, as Virginius Dabney states, that he was 'not guilty' of the Sally Hemings episode, he might merely have been saying that there was nothing wrong with it. At the time that he was presumably sleeping with Sally Hemings, he was not married and neither was she. It is also significant that, at that time, she was not a slave, although the subsequent 1857 *Dred Scott* decision of the U.S. Supreme Court ruled otherwise.

This is a point of utmost importance, and a point which is consistently overlooked. The relationship between Sally Hemings and Thomas Jefferson started in France. In France, slavery was illegal, so Sally Hemings was a free woman. Thomas Jefferson had no power to force her to sleep with him. She must have done it of her own free will. Later, three children were born while Thomas Jefferson was in the White House. Apparently, Sally Hemings was sleeping with Thomas Jefferson in the official President's bed in the White House. As soon as she stepped across the line into the State of Virginia, Sally Hemings became a slave again. However, at least two of her five surviving children may have been conceived in the White House.

All five of the surviving children of Sally Hemings were conceived while Thomas Jefferson was employed as a government servant in places outside of Virginia. The first child, Tom, was conceived in France, where Thomas Jefferson was the United States Ambassador. The next two, Beverly and Harriet, born in 1798 and 1801, were conceived while Thomas Jefferson was Vice-President of the United States in Philadelphia. The last two, Madison and Eston, born in 1805 and 1808, were conceived while Thomas Jefferson was President in Washington, D.C. In other words, assuming that Sally came to him and he did not go to her (we do not have any certain information on this point), all five children were conceived in places where Sally was a free woman.

In 1801, Sally Hemings probably moved into the White House. If not, she stayed at the Jefferson estate at Monticello, near Charlottesville, Virginia, 120 miles away. Historian Winthrop Jordan has proven that, in fact, Thomas Jefferson visited Monticello for two or three weeks just about exactly nine months before the births of each of the four children. This does not count Tom, who was conceived in France. However, it seems more likely that Sally Hemings was in the White House itself when the last two children were conceived.

The statement of his grandson, Thomas Jefferson Randolph, which was intended to prove that Thomas Jefferson was not the father of these children, tends to prove otherwise. He recounted an incident where a guest of Thomas Jefferson was eating at the dinner table. The guest thought that Thomas Jefferson was standing over him. When he raised his eyes from the dinner table, however, he was surprised to realize that it was not Thomas Jefferson at all, but rather one of the mulatto slaves who looked like him.

There are many other anecdotes along the same lines. John Quincy Adams visited Monticello and noted the large number of mulattos who bore a striking resemblance to Thomas Jefferson. No good explanation was given for this.

Comte de Volney, a French republican refugee, visited Monticello in 1796 and later wrote in French that he had seen slave children 'as white as me'. (His words, in original French, were that the children were 'des enfants aussi blanc que moi'.) This quote tends to show that already by 1796 there were many white slave children at Monticello and, therefore, that Thomas Jefferson may have had other slave concubines prior to Sally Hemings, who had only one child at that time.

Occasionally, the possibility has been suggested that Betty Brown, the older half-sister of Sally Hemings, among others, might also have produced children for Thomas Jefferson. However, while Betty Brown was at Monticello at the same time, there is little to indicate that she was so close to Thomas Jefferson.

In an attempt to defend Thomas Jefferson from the charge that Sally Hemings was his concubine, his friend Meriwether Jones wrote in the *Richmond Examiner* on September 25, 1802: 'That this servant woman has a child is true . . . . ' but the child is not the child of Thomas Jefferson. In so doing, Meriwether Jones, in a left-handed way, confirmed the existence of a child of Sally named Tom.

In 1802, the scandal broke, with every newspaper in America carrying the story. Jefferson never denied it. This was made a major issue in his re-election campaign, but Jefferson was re-elected. The electoral count was 162 votes to 14, one of the biggest landslides in American history.

Sally Hemings is known to have produced at least five children after 1790, of which four survived to maturity. She stayed with Jefferson at Monticello until his death at age 83 in 1826. After his death, Sally was given an appraised value of $50 for the purposes of evaluation of the estate. The will of Thomas Jefferson decreed that five of his slaves were to be given their freedom, two upon reaching maturity. These were: Burwell, Joe Fossett, John Hemings, Madison Hemings and Eston Hemings. Sally Hemings was not on the list. However, as a reward for a lifetime of dedicated service, she was not sold. The other slaves, along with their children and grandchildren, were put on the auction block to pay off the enormous debts which Jefferson left when died. A nominal price of $50 dollars was put on Sally Hemings, but she was never sold either because she was too old or else because Jefferson had privately informed his family that she was to be set free upon his death. According to Madison Hemings, she died in 1835.

The other slaves were dispersed to various parts of the South. There is no record of what happened to most of them, but some of them were able to keep in touch, presumably through the mails. The last reported sighting came in 1838, when *The Liberator*, an abolitionist newspaper in Boston, published a letter which claimed that someone had been heard to state that a daughter of Thomas Jefferson had been sold at a slave auction in New Orleans for one thousand dollars. However, this report has been widely disbelieved and is almost certainly not true.

Fifteen years later, in 1853, this claim was repeated in a purely fictional novel entitled *Clotel, or the President's Daughter* by William Wells Brown, who had also written for *The Liberator* in Boston. The novel was published in England, but some copies reached the United States and the controversy re-erupted.

Serious efforts have been made to verify this story by searching all of the records of all slave trades in New Orleans during that period. No record of the sale of any such slave has ever been found. In addition, Sally Hemings only had one daughter who survived: Harriet. She was virtually white and is believed to have been allowed to run away in 1822. There is no proof of this, but her brother, Madison Hemings, claimed to have maintained contact with her in Washington, D.C.

The original quote from *The Liberator* dated September 21, 1838, which started this entire furor, was as follows:

> *In a recent conversation with Mr. Otis Reynolds, a gentleman from St. Louis, Missouri, himself a practical as well as a theoretical supporter of slavery, in our discussion on the subject, Mr. Reynolds endeavored an apology for the 'domestic institutions' of the South, by assuming, as a fact, the alleged inferiority of the colored race.*
>
> *I replied that it was currently reported here that the 'best blood of Virginia flowed in the veins of the slaves' and the argument could, therefore, be of no force in regard to the amalgamated position of the slaves. Said he, with much emphasis,*
> *'That's true; I saw myself the DAUGHTER of THOMAS JEFFERSON sold in New Orleans for ONE THOUSAND DOLLARS.'*
>
> *What a fact for the contemplation of this free republic and what a comment on our professions of love for liberty, and practice of slavery.*
>
> *The daughter of the President of the United States, the boasted land of freedom, sold into interminable bondage. Look at it, citizens of our free republic. Here is no violation of law–you have the natural, legalized working of the system.*

Reading the above quotation carefully, it is being alleged that a Mr. Otis Reynolds, himself a proponent of slavery, told Mr. Gaylord Levi, in the course of a heated conversation, that he had personally seen a daughter of Jefferson sold at a slave auction. Under normal circumstances, such an off-hand remark, without corroboration, would be given little credence. Yet, this single statement has been repeated and realleged in publications throughout the world for the past 150 years.

One rumor which has circulated orally in Virginia but does not seem to have appeared in print is that actually the father of Thomas Jefferson, name-ly, Peter Jefferson, was also to blame for some of these mulatto children. This accusation would be serious, if true. It would mean that Thomas Jefferson kept his own half-brothers as slaves and that then they and their children were sold after his death. However, this is probably a mistake. It may result from confusion between Peter Jefferson, the father of Thomas Jefferson, and Peter Jefferson Carr, his nephew.

One reason why it seems reasonable to suggest that Peter Jefferson, the father of Thomas Jefferson, did not father children by his slaves, whereas just about all of the others did, is that he, unlike John Wayles and Thomas Jefferson, had a living wife, Jane Randolph, who survived him. No doubt she must have been checking the slave house on a regular basis to make sure that she did not catch Peter Jefferson in there.

Also, it must be noted that Peter Jefferson died in 1757. Therefore, if he fathered any children, they would have been quite old or would have died long before Thomas Jefferson did. About the only slave old enough would have been Tom Shackleford, who died in 1801. Tom Shackleford, who never belonged to Peter Jefferson but was inherited from the estate of John Wayles, is often mentioned as a 'white driver'. Many observers apparently thought that he was a free white man, both by his appearance and by his status. However, on Thomas Jefferson's inventory of 'Negroes', the name of Tom Shackleford consistently appears.

Tom Shackleford, the elderly mulatto who worked as a driver, may have been an ancestor of Professor George Shackleford, a Professor of History at Virginia Polytechnic University. However, Professor Shackleford presumably is a descendant of George Scott Shackleford, who in 1884 married Virginia Minor Randolph, a daughter of Thomas Jefferson Randolph, who was the grandson of Thomas Jefferson. This makes Professor Shackleford the great-great-great-grandson of Thomas Jefferson. Professor Shackleford has been one of the most vehement defenders of Thomas Jefferson and insists that he never ever fathered children by his slaves.

Another way in which historians attack this entire story is by focusing upon the person who first publicized it. He was a hack writer named James Thompson Callender. To call him a hack writer is no understatement. He attacked most of the leading political figures of his day at one time or another. For example, he once said in print that then President John Adams was 'a British spy'. Here is what Callender said in the *Richmond Recorder* about James Madison, then Secretary of State under Thomas Jefferson and a future president of the United States:

> *As for Madison, he is a poor consumptive thing; 5 foot 2 or 3 inches high; deeply wrinkled, and nothing but skin and bone. He has not a constitution capable of supporting official fatigue.*

Truly, this is hack writing at its worst. It is hard to understand why the newspapers of this day had such a shortage of talent that they could not publish something better than this. Indeed, Callender had often been in trouble for writing this sort of tripe. Originally from Scotland, he had published attacks against the British Government there and had apparently fled that country to save himself from being arrested on sedition charges. Not long after his arrival in America, he was arrested, tried, convicted and sentenced by Supreme Court Justice Samuel Chase to nine months in prison for writing defamatory material. (In those days, justices of the Supreme Court did not have many cases, so they also sat as 'circuit judges' and tried local cases.) Callender was freed from jail on a pardon issued by Jefferson himself, who had also once given him $50 to help him out financially and to encourage his attacks on Jefferson's political opponents.

However, Callender wanted more from Jefferson. He wanted to be appointed the postmaster of Richmond, an inappropriate post for a man who had just gotten out of jail essentially for sending false and defamatory material through the mails. When Jefferson refused to appoint Callender as the postmaster, Callender demanded blackmail money, stating that he would reveal a secret about Jefferson if he did not give the money he was demanding. James Monroe, then Governor of Virginia, advised Jefferson to give in and pay the money demanded by Callender. However, Jefferson declared that he had nothing to hide and refused. Then, Callender published his story, the story which was to make him famous: The story that Thomas Jefferson had fathered children by his slave, Sally Hemings.

Callender may have eventually gotten what he deserved. On July 16, 1803, his editor Henry Pace was beaten up on the streets of Richmond, Virginia by a gang of thugs, one of whom may have been a friend of Thomas Jefferson named Meriwether Jones. The next day, Callender's dead body was found in the James River. Some said that he had gotten drunk and fallen into the water. Others felt that he had committed suicide. It was also possible that he was murdered.

After the death of Callender, the *Richmond Recorder* quickly folded. The semi-weekly newspaper enjoyed a short life span. It was apparently established on July 11, 1801, just after Callender had gotten out of jail on sedition charges. Henry Pace was the sole publisher at the time, but in early 1802 the name of Callender had been added as co-publisher. With the issue of June 22, 1803, the first issue after the death of Callender, Pace again became the sole publisher. Only two months later, the newspaper folded. The last known issue was dated August 24, 1803. The Frederickstown, Maryland *Republican Advocate* of September 20, 1803 stated that 'The Recorder . . . . is stopped entirely. Callender was drowned, and Pace is now in jail.'

In spite of its short life span, the name of the *Richmond Recorder* will live in infamy. Because of the fact that Callender at one time or another published a vicious and often baseless attack against almost every politician in America, he became a sort of 'Jack Anderson' of his day. Any politician who had some dirty linen he wanted revealed about his opponents would hand the secret damaging documents or whatever it might be over to Callender. In this way, Callender ruined the reputation of Alexander Hamilton, the Secretary of the Treasury, by the publication in 1797 of a charge which was completely false although, like a ricocheting bullet, it coincidentally happened to hit something which was possibly true. This libelous publication about Alexander Hamilton indirectly not only ruined his reputation but also led eventually to the duels in which first his son, Philip Hamilton, and then Alexander Hamilton himself, were killed.

Briefly, the story of the Reynolds affair is as follows: One summer day in 1791, while in office as the Secretary of the Treasury, Alexander Hamilton was called upon by an attractive young woman named Maria Reynolds, who told him a sad tale of poverty and cruelty on the part of her husband. She implored him to visit her at her residence.

That evening, Hamilton came to her address in a rooming house, was shown to her room and, within a few minutes, was in bed with her.

This relationship, thus started, continued for some months. Meanwhile, Alexander Hamilton happened to meet her husband, James Reynolds, when he came to Hamilton's office to apply for a job and to complain about what he considered to be speculation of funds in the Department of the Treasury.

On December 15, 1791, Hamilton received two letters, one from Mrs. Reynolds and the other from her husband. Maria Reynolds informed Alexander Hamilton that her husband wanted money; otherwise he was going to inform the wife of Hamilton about these goings on. Mr. Reynolds complained to Hamilton about the fact that Hamilton had been having sex with his wife. However, in a subsequent follow-up note, he informed Alexander Hamilton that merely upon payment of one thousand dollars, he would forget the entire matter and leave town. According to Mr. Reynolds, Alexander Hamilton could then have Mrs. Reynolds 'to do as you think proper'. However, if the money was not paid, Mr. Reynolds would tell Hamilton's wife.

Hamilton then made a cardinal error in such situations. He paid the one thousand dollars in two installments. Mr. Reynolds did not leave town. Mrs. Reynolds wanted more sex. She kept writing more letters asking Hamilton come and visit her. Mr. Reynolds also wrote letters which said, in summary, 'My wife wants you. Please go and visit her. Also, send me more money.'

This evolved into an arrangement of prostitution. Hamilton had sex with the wife and paid money to the husband.

This relationship was short-lived. In 1793, Mrs. Reynolds got a divorce from her husband. Naturally, she wanted the best legal representation, so she hired the best attorney. The name of that attorney was Aaron Burr.

None of this would have amounted to anything. It certainly would not have changed the course of American history, had not the contents of some of the Reynolds letters been leaked to an unscrupulous reporter named James Thompson Callender five years later. Callender did not work for a newspaper at that time, so he published it in a pamphlet entitled *History of the United States for the Year 1796*.

Callender did not know the entire story. He only knew a small fragment. What he knew was that Hamilton had paid some money to Mr. Reynolds and that Mr. Reynolds had made an accusation of speculation with treasury funds. Being an Anti-Federalist, Callender assumed that this meant that Alexander Hamilton had had his fingers in the till. He did not realize that Alexander Hamilton had had his fingers in Mrs. Reynolds.

The reason this leak occurred was that in the meantime, Mr. Reynolds had been arrested for filing false claims with the Treasury Department on behalf of Revolutionary War soldiers who had never been paid their salaries. (If George Washington had paid his troops, this would never have happened.) One soldier whom Reynolds claimed to be dead turned up alive and Reynolds went to jail.

From his jail cell, Reynolds informed the authorities that, in return for his release, he would prove that Alexander Hamilton was guilty of treasury speculation. Mr. Reynolds got out of jail, but disappeared without providing the proof. An informal congressional committee, which included James Monroe, went to look for Mr. Reynolds, but found Mrs. Reynolds instead. She showed them some of the letters, claiming to have burned the rest. This committee then went to Hamilton, who told them the entire story.

Hamilton gave them copies of the letters. In those days, there were no photocopying machines, so copies were made by hand. Monroe had John Beckley, Clerk of the House of Representatives, make copies of the letters and return the copies and the originals to Monroe. Monroe then had these documents sealed. Monroe had no way of knowing that Beckley had also made an extra copy for himself.

That extra copy for himself was what Beckley leaked to Callender five years later, after Beckley had been fired as Clerk of the House. When Callender published this story, Hamilton was enraged. He naturally assumed that James Monroe had leaked the story to the press. He came to Monroe's residence, accompanied by John B. Church, the husband of Hamilton's sister-in-law, Angelica Church, and promptly challenged Monroe to a duel. Aaron Burr, among others, intervened.

Alexander Hamilton then published, in 1797, an astounding pamphlet, still available in the libraries, with his own portrait on the cover, in which he stated that he had not speculated in treasury funds but rather that he had merely paid some blackmail money so that his wife would not find out that he was having sex with Mrs. Reynolds.

Hamilton clearly felt that the charge of speculation with treasury funds was a serious matter which must be defended as a point of honor, whereas the charge of committing adultery with another man's wife, with the consent of the husband, was not. Unfortunately, the reading public disagreed. Nobody, neither his friends and his supporters nor his enemies, could believe that he had published such a thing. Nobody had believed Callender's story, and no response had been necessary. General David Cobb wrote:

> *Hamilton is fallen for the present, but even if he fornicates with every female in the cities of New York and Philadelphia, he will rise again, for purity of character, after a period of political existence, is not necessary for public patronage.*

Unfortunately, Hamilton did not rise again. He never again in his life held a political office. General Cobb would have been correct and the Reynolds affair would have been forgotten, except that Alexander Hamilton himself considered this to be such a serious point of honor that he was prepared to fight a duel over it. Eventually, in 1804, he fought a duel with Aaron Burr. Hamilton was killed. The widow of Alexander Hamilton never forgave James Monroe.

One strange thing about this concerns the original threat made by Reynolds that, unless he was paid one thousand dollars, he would inform Hamilton's wife. Hamilton had the most devoted wife that any man could hope to have. She was also the richest wife that any man could hope to have. Her father was Gen. Philip Schuyler, one of the richest men in New York. She gave her husband, Alexander Hamilton, nine children.

One of the best sources for the above is *The Notorious Affair of Mrs. Reynolds*, by Robert C. Alberts, *American Heritage*, February, 1973, p. 8.

Meanwhile, James Thompson Callender was arrested, not for this, but for publishing attacks on President John Adams. Even after being arrested and imprisoned for writing defamatory articles, Callender did not become discouraged. During his nine months in jail, he continued to write his virulent attacks in his prison cell, passing them through the bars to be published in the outside world.

Some of the things which Callender published were true and some were false. History will never know whether he actually saw the 'Yellow Tom' whom he so vividly described as the illegitimate son of Thomas Jefferson, whether he had solid information about the existence of this person, or whether this was just a story which he made up. However, it does appear that most of those who knew Thomas Jefferson personally believed this story, including John Adams, who had seen Sally in the flesh. In addition, there is evidence that the tendency of Thomas Jefferson, among many others, to dally with his slaves was well known and privately discussed in Virginia circles years before Callender first published these charges in a newspaper.

Even today, there is scarcely even one person who was born in Virginia who does not believe that Thomas Jefferson fathered children by his slaves. Those such as Dumas Malone who deny the story are almost all rank outsiders who came to Virginia from someplace else.

It no doubt was true that Callender was a hack writer, but he must have been onto something when he started publicizing the claim that Thomas Jefferson had a child by one of his slaves. Callender said that he did not invent the story, but that he got it from gossiping with neighbors in the Monticello area. Even Virginius Dabney admits, in a surprising concession on page 10 of *The Jefferson Scandals*, that Callender did not invent the story but that it had been floating around for some time and had even been hinted at by other Federalist newspapers. What Callender did that was new and different was that he spelled out the accusation in graphic detail, with his description of 'Yellow Tom', whose mother was a 'wench' named Sally. Suddenly, his allegation was being repeated everywhere, and by respectable writers with their own reputations to protect. Had there not been at least some truth to his accusation, this would not have happened.

For example, Thomas Moore, the famous Irish poet, who had visited America during this time, published this poem in 1806:

> *The weary statesman for repose hath fled*
> *From halls of council to his negro's shed*
> *Where blest he woos some black Aspasia's grace,*
> *And dreams of freedom in his slaves embrace!*

To this, Virginius Dabney counters that Thomas Moore did not like America, and for this reason circulated this slander about the American president.

Jefferson correctly concluded that the best response to the charge that he was maintaining a 'Congo Harem' was no response at all. In so doing, he established a great precedent for future presidents faced with the same situation.

Nowadays, whenever a presidential candidate is faced with the situation where he is being publicly accused of adultery, he makes a speech with his wife standing at his side. It is important for the wife to be standing there, although she says nothing. Tradition has it that the wife must stand by her man, and remain silent. After the campaign rally is over, the wife goes home and the candidate goes to the motel room to meet his mistress.

In so doing, they are following in the great tradition of Thomas Jefferson. Jefferson did not have a wife, but he had two daughters. In October, 1802, as soon as this scandal hit the newspapers, he summoned his two daughters, Martha and Maria, to come to Washington to join him. This involved a long journey in those days. Martha was at Edgehill, near Monticello. Maria was at Bermuda Hundred, near Hopewell. Both were about 120 miles away. Yet, within a few days, both of them arrived at the White House, leaving their husbands and most of their children behind. They arrived near the end of November, 1802 and stayed six weeks. This was the only time that they both visited the White House together during the eight years that Thomas Jefferson was president.

Here is a typical example of what they had to endure in the daily newspapers, while staying with their father. It was published in the *Philadelphia Port Folio* on January 22, 1803.

> *Cease, cease old man, for soon you must,*
> *Your faithless cunning, pride, and lust,*
> *Which death shall quickly level:*
> . . . .
> *Thy tricks with Sooty Sal give over;*
> *Indulge thy body, Tom, no more;*
> *But try to save thy soul.*

'Sooty Sal' referred, of course, to the fact Callender in his articles had said that she was known at Monticello as 'Dusky Sally'.

In spite of their short stay in the White House, there are indications that the presence of Martha and Maria Jefferson there at this critical point in time was a considerable factor in turning the sympathies of the public in favor of the beleaguered president. Even now, nearly two hundred years later, Virginius Dabney cites Thomas Jefferson's closeness with his daughters as proof that there was no sexual relationship between Thomas Jefferson and Sally Hemings.

Another verse, which appeared in newspapers in Philadelphia and New York in April, 1803, after Maria and Martha had left the White House and gone back to their families, was entitled *Black and White* and went as follows:

> *A statesman so great, and a damsel so neat,*
> *Conversed about things where they were;*
> *They ogled and chatted, and made it quite late,*
> *Tall Tom was the name of the statesman so great,*
> *And Sally the name of the fair.*

The above quote is, compared with the others, somewhat sympathetic to the President and may reflect a turn in the tide of public opinion in his favor. 'Tall Tom' refers, of course, to Thomas Jefferson, who was six feet two inches tall.

The well known saying 'where there's smoke, there's fire,' does not really apply to this sort of case. However, it seems difficult to believe that so many different writers would have circulated the same story had there not been some truth to it.

Prior to Dabney, a Virginia historian named Douglass Adair claimed that this entire story about Thomas Jefferson having children by his slaves was a pure fabrication by the political enemies of Jefferson. His primary evidence was the fact that there is no record of the birth of a child named Tom in the *Monticello Farm Book*. He says that the first child of Sally Hemings recorded in that book was named Harriet, who was born in 1795 and died two years later. Thus, there was no Tom at all.

There are many theories about this. Madison Hemings stated in his interview that Tom lived only short time and died in infancy. Others have suggested that Tom was born in the North and grew up there. Still others say that Tom might have been one of several persons named Tom living at Monticello. One of them was named Tom Shackleford, a driver. There was also a 'Tom Buck' and a 'Tom Lee', both of whom were listed as hired at the bottom of page 136 of the *Farm Book*, which reflects an inventory taken in December, 1810.

Newspapers attacking Thomas Jefferson in 1802 spoke of Tom as though he was a known person living in the Washington, D.C., or Charlottesville area. Minnie Shumate Woodson claims that her husband and her children are direct descendants of this Tom.

This is a question of critical importance. If Tom existed, we have the virtual proof of a relationship between Thomas Jefferson and Sally Hemings. If some random Frenchman had been the father of Tom, it is unlikely that a pregnant Sally Hemings would have returned from France with Thomas Jefferson, or that Thomas Jefferson would have been willing to bring her along to accompany his daughters in such an advanced state of pregnancy.

Over the past 200 years that this controversy has been raging, there have been a number of best selling books on this subject. The most recent was *Thomas Jefferson, An Intimate History*, New York 1974. The author was the late Fawn M. Brodie, a professor of history at UCLA. However, her contentions have been dismissed by Virginius Dabney as 'absurd'.

Another much less reliable but popular book is a novel entitled: *Sally Hemings*. The author, Barbara Chase-Riboud, appears to have read only one book on this subject. She has lifted all of her basic facts from *Thomas Jefferson, An Intimate History*, and has woven them into a historical novel. However, it seems that either she knows much more than anyone else about this subject, or else she knows much less. Some of her 'facts' are known to be actual facts as published by Brodie. Others appear to have been the result of her liberties taken as a novelist. In her defense, she never claims that what she wrote was true. She always says that it is a novel.

Indeed, it is surprising that her book was even accepted by a publisher. Any publisher with a basic knowledge of history should have been able to observe flaws in her manuscript and should have told her to look up the basic facts about the life of Thomas Jefferson in the *Encyclopedia Britannica* and try to do better.

Of Caribbean origin and a mulatto herself, Barbara Chase-Riboud received her elementary school education outside of the United States. Also, she attended university in England. This shows in her book. She makes errors about the life and times of Thomas Jefferson which would earn a high school student a failing mark. It is, of course, a great tribute to our democracy that a foreigner such as Barbara Chase- Riboud, who does know the difference between the 'House of Burgesses' and the 'Virginia House of Delegates', can come to our shores and, knowing nothing about the subject, get a book published about one of our presidents. However, a problem arises when a large number of people, who should know better, read the book and take it seriously.

All of this provides fuel for the contention by Virginius Dabney that Thomas Jefferson was not the father of the children of Sally Hemings. Dabney finds flaws in the books by Fawn Brodie and Barbara Chase- Riboud, implying that these errors negate the claim that Thomas Jefferson was the father. No doubt, the flaws are there, but Virginius Dabney makes some even bigger factual errors in his book.

Dabney devotes a chapter to attacking with vehemence the 1838 story that a daughter of Thomas Jefferson was sold at a slave auction in New Orleans for one thousand dollars. This is a story which no reasonable person believes.

Dabney cites four items of documentary evidence which he claims come from completely independent sources and which show that Peter Carr and not Thomas Jefferson was the father of the children of Sally Hemings. However, his first item of documentary evidence is a letter reporting a statement made by Thomas Jefferson Randolph who, for obvious reasons, would not want it said that his grandfather, Thomas Jefferson, had sex with his slaves. The second comes from a sister of Thomas Jefferson Randolph, who merely reflected what her brother had told her. The third comes from Edmund Bacon, speaking in Kentucky in 1862, but the critical paragraph had the name of the father deleted or omitted and the text had obviously been tampered with. The fourth is a note by Thomas Jefferson himself which has been lost to history but which only dealt with the Elizabeth Walker affair. It had nothing to do with the allegations involving Sally Hemings.

Dabney spends a long chapter quoting letters written by Thomas Jefferson to his daughters and by his daughters to him. His point to all this is to prove that Jefferson loved his daughters, that his daughters loved him, and that therefore it is not possible that Thomas Jefferson had been having sex with one of his slaves. In summary, Dabney concludes, 'The foregoing letters . . . . demonstrate conclusively the devotion of Jefferson's daughters and their complete confidence in his innocence of the charges which were being published so widely'. *The Jefferson Scandals*, p. 90.

A detailed response to this assertion by Dabney is not necessary. The letters he cites show nothing more or less than that Thomas Jefferson loved and was loved by his daughters. No reference is contained in any of these letters to the Sally Hemings scandal. The assumption that a man who loves his daughters would never have sex with another woman is without basis.

The other arguments advanced by Virginius Dabney are utterly without merit. His attacks on the interviews of Madison Hemings and Israel Jefferson fail to achieve any point. Although those interviews do contain a few small errors, it is nevertheless obvious that those two men were the same men who lived at Monticello 50 years before the interviews were taken down. For example, the 'rebuttal' written by Thomas Jefferson Randolph confirms the truth of the most important statement made by Israel Jefferson. In particular, it confirms that the Israel who gave the interview to the newspaper in Ohio was the same man as the Israel who was formerly his slave.

Having considered all of the pros and cons, the evidence seems convincing that Sally Hemings really was the concubine of Thomas Jefferson and that her children were all his. The evidence in favor of this is overwhelming and the evidence against as presented by Virginius Dabney is almost non-existent.

# Chapter Six

## The Mentality of Thomas Jefferson

The question which might well be asked is: 'What makes this subject so interesting? There is no doubt that many white masters had children by their black slaves. Even George Washington is said to have done it. Everybody was doing it. Why pick on poor Thomas Jefferson?'

However, there is something especially intriguing about the fact this was done by Thomas Jefferson himself, as opposed to others. No doubt, one reason for this is that among all the Founding Fathers, Thomas Jefferson was the most vocal opponent of slavery. When America was still a British colony, Thomas Jefferson wrote a pamphlet entitled *A Summary View of the Rights of British America*, which, among other things, attacked King George III for engaging in the slave trade. It was substantially this pamphlet which made Thomas Jefferson famous and earned him the assignment of writing the *Declaration of Independence*. He put an anti-slavery clause in the *Declaration of Independence*. It was the only clause to be deleted by the Continental Congress. He also authored the provision that prohibited the importation of slaves after the year 1808. He was also the author of the *Virginia Statute of Religious Freedom*. He wrote the famous words: 'All Men are created equal.' He wrote hundreds if not thousands of letters, articles and essays attacking slavery and urging its abolition. Yet, he kept his own slaves and fathered children by them.

One over-all point which must be made is not that Jefferson was a bad man, but rather that Jefferson was a good man who did what every good man does when confronted with a beautiful woman. To summarize, the most significant fact is that Sally Hemings was not just any black slave. She was, in fact, the known half-sister of the legitimate wife of Thomas Jefferson. The allegations about Thomas Jefferson that he was selling his children were untrue. He did mortgage almost all of his slaves to pay his debts at various times, however.

On the surface, he seems to have been a hypocrite. No doubt, to a certain extent, he must have been. However, his public life and his private affairs were perhaps not that inconsistent.

In order to explain this statement, it must be understood how the slavery system worked at that time.

For example, it will often be asked: If Thomas Jefferson was an opponent of slavery, why did he not free his own slaves?

First, it must be understood that under the law of Virginia, a freed slave was required to go north within one year of being given his or her freedom. There were even cases where slaves turned down the opportunity for freedom, because they did not want to go north, where it was reported to be cold and where they had never been before. This was an important if not critical point. One slave named Sally Marks, who worked as a nurse and who was briefly owned by Thomas Jefferson just before he died, apparently may have refused her freedom for this reason later on. Some writers have mistakenly confused Sally Marks with Sally Hemings.

The reason for this Virginia law that a freed slave had to go north was obviously that if a black man was seen walking on the road, the law enforcement authorities had to have some way to determine if the man was free or a slave. If free, he would have to have papers proving his freedom. Obviously, the police could not check everybody. Thus, in order to perpetuate slavery and to keep the entire situation under control, they had to make sure that the freed blacks went north. To be sure, there were exceptions to the rule. For example, Sally Hemings herself was one exception. After the death of Thomas Jefferson, she was given her freedom and was not required to go north. However, these exceptions were rare. Sally and her children got special treatment because she was 75% white and her children were 87.5% white. Not many people realized that they were black at all. In addition, as requested by Thomas Jefferson in his will, there was a special act of the Virginia legislature in 1827 which provided that the five slaves freed by that will would not be required to go north.

In a little noticed letter dated October 28, 1813 to John Adams, we have the 'smoking gun', the proof that Thomas Jefferson considered some men to be superior to others and that in an ideal society only the most superior men would be selected to impregnate all the females. This letter can be found in *The Adams-Jefferson Letters*, edited by Lester J. Cappon, University of North Carolina Press, Vol. 2, p. 387. It is also included in the appendix here.

In this letter, Thomas Jefferson considered the situation of the sheep herder. In breeding a flock of sheep, only the best ram would be selected and that one ram would impregnate all the female sheep. Jefferson felt that humans ideally should follow this same practice. However, he also mentioned that if this ever happened, all the men left without women would combine together and kill 'this privileged Solomon'.

Needless to say, among the men available at Monticello, Thomas Jefferson himself was by far the most superior. It would therefore logically follow that he took it upon himself to improve the quality of the race by impregnating all of his female slaves. The pertinent quote is as follows:

> *The selecting the best male for a Harem of well chosen females . . . . would doubtless improve the human, as it does the brute animal, and produce a race of veritable aristocrats. For experience proves that the moral and physical qualities of a man, whether good or evil, are transmissible in a certain degree from father to son. But I suspect that the equal rights of men will rise up against this privileged Solomon. . . . . For I agree that there is a natural aristocracy of men. The grounds of this are virtue and talents. . . . .*

On this last point, Thomas Jefferson expressed the view that the true aristocrats are those with superior gifts and talents, whereas the pseudo-aristocrats are those who inherit the right to be called members of the aristocracy from their parents. Thomas Jefferson himself was the rare example of one man who was both kinds of aristocrat. He was both a man of superior talents and he was born to aristocracy. His mother was Jane Randolph. The Randolphs were an aristocratic family from England.

It is even possible to read in another letter a justification by Thomas Jefferson for incest. One of the well known developments of Thomas Jefferson was the breeding of his world famous 'Monticello sheep'. This was derived from the Merino sheep which came from Spain. Jefferson spent years trying to get two Merino sheep for breeding purposes. However, being newly developed, they were not available and each one cost one thousand dollars. Finally, he got three sheep, one male and three females, but the females died or failed to reproduce. Therefore, he had only one male sheep. He bred it with a normal female sheep. The female offspring of that union was bred with the same male that had been mated with her mother. If a female sheep was again produced, once again the offspring would be mated with the same male. This process was continuously repeated as long as that one male remained alive. After seven generations of this, the result would be a flock of sheep that was more than 99% the offspring of the one original Merino sheep.

After reading about this, one cannot help but wonder if it is not just possible that Thomas Jefferson was doing this too. It is noteworthy that some say that Mary, the oldest daughter of Betty Hemings, was his original concubine, and that Betsy, the daughter of Mary, was also his concubine. Is this really true? Does this really mean that Thomas Jefferson himself personally believed in and actively practiced incest and had sex with his own slave daughters? Indeed, if he was engaged in the regular practice of producing children from his slaves, why would he draw the line at those slaves who also happened to be his daughters?

The *Farm Book* of Thomas Jefferson records 187 slaves at several points.

Other sources say he had more than 200. In any case, he had a lot of slaves. He is only known to have officially freed two slaves during his lifetime. These were Robert Hemings and James Hemings. In both cases, he was not really given a choice. They were so white that they could pass for white. They made it clear that they were going to run away if not given their freedom by legal means.

These freeings had mixed results. Robert Hemings was freed on December 24, 1794 and settled in Richmond, Virginia. He was already married to a slave named Dolly in Fredericksburg, Virginia and they already had a child. Robert had been able to do this because he had been allowed by Thomas Jefferson to travel freely while a slave.

After getting his freedom papers, Robert Hemings purchased his wife Dolly and their child from their master. They then settled in Richmond, Virginia and lived on the corner of Grace and 7th Streets. He became a successful man and his descendants live there to this day. Even before being given his freedom, he had traveled around Virginia like a white man.

James Hemings was a different case. In connection with receiving his freedom on February 5, 1795, he was given ticket money for a journey to Philadelphia. This apparently was a requirement. If any slave owner wanted to give freedom to a slave, he also had to provide money for passage to the North.

James Hemings unfortunately committed suicide in Philadelphia in 1801, only six years after receiving his freedom. Apparently, after a lifetime of slavery, he could not adjust to having his own freedom.

James Hemings should have been well prepared for freedom. He had been taken by Thomas Jefferson to France in 1784, where he had received training as a chef. He had also received French lessons. He apparently wanted to stay in France. Later on, he wanted to stay in Philadelphia after serving as a cook while Jefferson was Secretary of State from 1790 to 1793. With great difficulty, Thomas Jefferson persuaded him to return on the promise that he would be given his freedom as soon as he taught French cooking to the other household slaves.

Thomas Jefferson was not quick to keep his promise, but finally did so in 1795. He also gave him 30 dollars for his passage to Philadelphia. Then, James Hemings went north to take a position as a chef. However, he had always had a drinking problem. Late in 1801 in Philadelphia, apparently after a bout of drinking, he killed himself.

It would clearly have been unfeasible for Thomas Jefferson to have freed all his slaves. While being land and slave rich, he was cash poor. He simply would not have had the money to pay for tickets for all of his slaves to go north. More than that, he held vast acreage of land. At one point, he had about a dozen farms. He needed slaves to work the land. If he freed his slaves, he would have to sell his land.

Indeed, that would not have been a bad idea. He owned so many farms, with names like 'Elk Hill', 'Bear Creek' and 'Tomahawk', that he could not possibly have managed all of them. In fact, his farms mostly lost money, in spite of having free labor. This is the reason that he was born wealthy, inherited vast amounts of land and slaves, and nevertheless died hopelessly insolvent.

Many reasons have been given as to why his farms lost money. One most commonly mentioned is that he was constantly experimenting with new agricultural methods. He was proud of having invented a new kind of plow, for example. He also tried out new kinds of crops.

However, in this field, he did not have the same level of genius as he had for writing political proclamations. Many of his crops failed. Even he admitted that if he wanted to make money, he should have stuck to a cash crop like tobacco. He did grow tobacco on his farms, but not nearly as much as he should have.

Another factor is that Virginia land is not really that productive. For example, Poplar Forest, his biggest farm, is located less than seven miles from where this book is being written. However, most of the land there is no longer used for farming, even with modern tractors and more efficient farming methods.

In addition, much of the land which Thomas Jefferson owned was not productive at all. He had vast acres of timber, but with little commercial value. He also owned the Natural Bridge, which is now a major tourist attraction. However, except as a tourist trap, it has no economic value, and the Natural Bridge was not commercialized at that time.

Thus, if he freed his slaves, he would have to sell his land. However, if the land was not all that productive, why did he not do that?

One cannot answer this question with exactness. However, at the end of his life, the answer was clear. He was buried under such a sea of debt that even if he sold all his land and all his slaves, he could never pay his debt.

At the same time, he seems to have been out of touch with reality. In the last years of his life, while tottering on the brink of bankruptcy, he was proceeding with work on a grand new palatial estate being constructed at Poplar Forest. John Hemings, one of his slaves, was in charge of that project, but he needed money to buy nails. Construction of the house was substantially delayed when one shipment of nails was mistakenly sent to Monticello when it should have been sent to Poplar Forest instead. Thomas Jefferson does not seem to have come to grips with the fact that this was not a suitable time to be building a new gigantic group of houses when he was flat broke and insolvent. The Poplar Forest estate had to be sold to pay his debts just three years after he died.

In other words, Thomas Jefferson was like a gigantic insolvent corporation which might seek protection under Chapter XI. His only chance was to keep his entire operation going, negotiate with his creditors, and hope that something would turn up. At the time of his death, a special Virginia lottery was being organized to help him pay his debts. His intended benefactors probably did not realize that his own financial mismanagement was the cause of his misfortune.

Actually, there is a long story about this lottery. The Virginia State Legislature was apparently prepared to grant Thomas Jefferson $80,000 to make him solvent again. (As it turned out, even that amount would not have been completely adequate.) However, Thomas Jefferson was too proud to ask for the money. See *Virginia Historical Magazine*, Vol. 10, p. 331 (1903). Instead, he had the strange idea of selling lottery tickets. The money from the tickets would be enough to pay his debts. The winner of the lottery would get his land. However, his land was a 'white elephant'. Not many people at that time would have wanted it. Now, of course, Monticello is worth millions as a tourist attraction. Every tourist pays seven dollars to get in, and a thousand tourists come every day. However, it is not even clear whether Thomas Jefferson intended to include Monticello in the lottery.

During the last years of his life, Thomas Jefferson used his reputation as a former President of the United States to the fullest extent. He borrowed heavily and persuaded his creditors not to foreclose. He had even had to borrow $8,000 when he left Washington at the conclusion of his presidency to liquidate the debts he had accumulated while president.

At the same time, he seems not to have come to grips with reality. He kept all of his lands and almost all of his slaves right up until his death. He never really sold anything. Yet, he was flat broke. It is said that when guests came to dinner, he could not turn them away. Edmund Bacon complained in 1862 that most of these guests did not really want to converse with Thomas Jefferson. They just wanted the free food and the free wine. See *Jefferson at Monticello*, p. 114. Sometimes, Thomas Jefferson entertained fifty guests at the dinner table, while having no money of his own in his pocket. It is also said that in the last years of his life, he stopped eating meat, because it was too expensive for him.

It seems difficult to reconcile this picture with the publicly better known picture of Thomas Jefferson being one of the greatest geniuses in all of human history. Actually, this is not that remote. From the above picture, it does not seem that Thomas Jefferson was a great genius, but he really was. His *Declaration of Independence* was arguably the greatest political manifesto in all of human history. Look at the history of England, France and other countries with democratic institutions. Do they have anything which can compare with the *Declaration of Independence*? Not at all; nothing even close.

Nevertheless, the *Declaration of Independence* was written entirely by Thomas Jefferson himself, with just a few minor editorial revisions made by Benjamin Franklin and others.

The problem with Thomas Jefferson is that like most other geniuses, he was a genius at only one thing: writing political manifestoes. Thomas Jefferson almost never in his life made a public speech, a strange fact for a politician. He apparently thought that he was an all around genius; a genius at everything. He is often described as such. It is said that he was an architect, an inventor, a scientist, an agronomist, etc., etc. All this was true. The problem is that he wasn't really any good at any of those things. He was only good at two things: reading and writing.

How did he get to be good at those things, if he wasn't any good at anything else? The answer is simple. That is what he did. From what he produced, we can see that he must have spent almost all day, every day, reading and writing. It is believed that he may have written and received 50,000 letters in his lifetime. Of these, we have the amazing total of 18,000 private letters, all hand written by Thomas Jefferson, and copied with a laboriously difficult method.

Thomas Jefferson had a copying instrument which enabled him to keep copies of each letter. This machine, which was was said to have been invented by Thomas Jefferson himself, but was actually invented by another man, worked by having two pens. As he wrote with one pen, levers moved the other pen in exactly the same way.

As for reading, he had the largest private library in America. He sold his library on April 15, 1815 to the federal government for $23,950. It became the nucleus of the new Library of Congress, after the first library had been burned by the British during the War of 1812. However, he did not make this sale for the governmental good, as has often been claimed. He sold it because he desperately needed money. As soon as he sold it, he started buying more books again.

This is how one gets to be a 'genius'. One does it by practice and hard work. Talent helps only a little bit.

What does all this have to do with the subject of Sally Hemings and children by slaves?

Of course, it has everything to do with it.

How did Thomas Jefferson have the time to write 18,000 private letters? The answer is obvious. He was able to do it because he had 187 slaves to do his bidding. It seems that he must have let them run almost more or less free. He was not much of a whip cracking slave driver. Perhaps his black slaves working in the fields at Poplar Forest in Bedford County were given discipline, but his slaves at Monticello were not. They pretty much had free run of the house. He usually kept one white overseer, but most of the real authority must have been delegated to his slaves. Thus, the situation probably was that the slaves actually ran Monticello, while he sat alone in his study and wrote letters.

Obviously, his slaves could have run away. Why did they not do so? Nobody can say, but it probably wasn't easy to run away. Charlottesville is about 120 miles from Washington, D.C. That is only a two hour drive today, but the trip took four or five days on foot or horseback at that time. Obviously, with 187 slaves and generally only two or three adult white men on the plantation, nothing could have stopped the slaves of Thomas Jefferson from running away. However, they probably would have been caught by the police on the public road.

Another important factor which is often overlooked is that Maryland was actually a slave state. The Mason-Dixon line separates Maryland from Pennsylvania. South of that line, slavery was legal. Any slave running away would have had to make it by foot not only across Virginia but also across Maryland as well.

Later in history, slavery virtually died out in Maryland for the reason that the types of farm land and crops produced in Maryland were not conducive to slavery. Maryland took the side of the North in the American Civil War, but it was a close question as to which way Maryland would go. Abraham Lincoln ordered the Mayor of Baltimore to be arrested and ignored a writ of habeas corpus issued by the United States Supreme Court directing his release, because the Mayor of Baltimore was among those who wanted Maryland to succeed from the Union.

Almost everyone who has ever passed through Washington, D.C. has no doubt wondered why the population of that city is about 90% black, something which has not been characteristic of any other city in America. However, from this history, the reason is obvious.

Virginia, within its present borders, had two great natural boundaries: the Appalachian Mountains to the West and the wide Potomac River to the north, across which there were no bridges at that time.

Any slave trying to run away or even having his freedom papers had essentially only three ways out. He could cross the Appalachian Mountains through what is now Lewisburg, West Virginia, finally reaching Ohio. This is the route eventually taken by Tom, Madison, and Eston, all sons of Sally Hemings. This is a difficult, miserable and unpleasant journey even today by car. Nobody takes that road if they can possibly avoid it.

The second way would have been up the Shenandoah Valley and through Hagerstown, Maryland. This would have been a long road through dangerous slave territory for a man on foot.

The last way would be Northeast, avoiding the Shenandoah Valley, and straight into Washington, D.C. Turning the map of Virginia upside down, the entire state looks like a funnel, with all roads leading to Washington, D.C. Even today, almost the only northern route out of Virginia is through Washington.

This means that the slaves, not only from Virginia, but also from North Carolina, South Carolina and Georgia, if they wanted to get out, had to pass through Washington, D.C. Technically, it was legal to own slaves in Washington, D.C., but the slave trade there was illegal.

Obviously, having finally taken their first breath of freedom, many of the newly freed slaves or runaways who crossed into Washington, stopped right there and saw no reason to proceed further. They remained in Washington, D.C. and spent the rest of their lives there. This is apparently what may have happened to Beverly and Harriet.

A few who were brave enough went on to the major cities of Philadelphia and New York. However, it would have been dangerous to cross Maryland. Even slaves with their freedom papers were often kidnaped, had their papers taken away from them, and were taken back to the Deep South to be sold again into slavery.

In short, compared to other cities, there has always been a disproportionate black population in Washington, D.C., since at least before the Civil War.

Finally, a question which is often asked is: Why would Thomas Jefferson have wanted to have a black mistress, when he was a famous person who could have had any wife he wanted? It is that he favored black women over white women? Indeed, the statement that 'Jefferson preferred dark meat,' is one which is often heard.

However, the question should be asked in the opposite way. Why would Thomas Jefferson bother with going out and looking for a wife, when he already had all the women he wanted?

Thomas Jefferson best expressed this sentiment when he said in his famous *My Head and My Heart* letter to Maria Cosway dated October 12, 1786: 'Do not bite at the bait of pleasure until you know there is no hook beneath it.'

Every man of wealth faces a big problem when it comes to looking for a wife. Most women are looking for a husband with money. Thomas Jefferson would have been a prime target for many women. With all of the land and slaves he owned, nobody would have guessed that actually he had no cash money at all. He was broke.

Probably, he thought about it and decided that there were substantial risks in getting entangled with any white woman, not knowing what her motives might be. Also, if he got married, there was always the possibility that his new wife might not fully approve of the 'Congo Harem' which everybody said that he kept behind the house.

Probably, he must have thought that his best chance would be to marry a woman who had some money herself, so that he could pay his debts. This indeed is how he had gotten most of his money, through his marriage to Martha Wayles. However, he was probably too proud to reduce himself to marrying for money, knowing that his new wife would probably not realize that he had no money himself.

So, it was perfectly logical for him to stick to the women he had, rather than to go out and find a new one.

Every book ever written about the life of Thomas Jefferson contains an appendix which includes a bunch of his letters. This book also follows that practice. This practice is unavoidable because these letters are, in fact, almost the entire life's work of Thomas Jefferson. Indeed, a number of published books contain almost nothing more than a collection of letters written by Jefferson about one particular subject or another.

One of the easiest things in the world to do is to write a book about Thomas Jefferson. All one needs to do is to collect a bunch of letters on any particular subject, such as gardening, astronomy, architecture, etc., include a short preface, and publish it under a hard cover. The title of the book will be 'Jefferson on Gardening' or whatever. Be sure to include a nice four-color cover. With a total of 18,000 letters written by Thomas Jefferson, there are plenty of subjects to choose from, with enough letters to fill a book.

Jefferson occasionally wrote letters under pseudonyms or letters to be published under the names of real persons which were actually his. Most other political figures of his day did this frequently. Jefferson did it only a few times. He even once claimed that he had never done it at all. There are cases where it has only recently been proven that a letter previously believed to have been written by somebody else was actually written by Thomas Jefferson. However, apparently this did not happen often. There were few writers of his day capable of approaching his brilliance, so generally any letter he tried to write under somebody else's name was promptly identified as his.

Letter writing was not merely something extra which Thomas Jefferson did in his spare time when he was not doing something more important. Almost the only thing for which he is remembered today are the letters and short essays which he wrote, one of which was the *Declaration of Independence.*

Although it is often said that he was an inventor, he only invented two things which are certifiably his. One was a wooden plow which was almost never put to use except by the slaves of Jefferson himself. That became obsolete when better metal plows came on the market. The other was a cipher machine, also never put to practical use.

Jefferson only wrote one published book in his entire life. That was his

*Notes on the State of Virginia*, published in Paris in 1785, while he was the Ambassador (then called the Minister) to France. It was first published in the French language in an edition of only 200 copies, without his name being mentioned anywhere. He later authorized an English language edition to be published in London in a very limited quantity to stop the pirating which would otherwise have taken place. He did his best to stop the wide spread circulation of this book, especially in America, with good reason since the book contained attacks on the institutions of religion and slavery which were later used against him by his political opponents.

This book does contain one quotation which is important in this context regarding miscegenation. There, it states:

> *The improvement of the blacks in body and mind, in the first instance of their mixture with the whites, has been observed by everyone.*

It must be pointed out that the theory of the superiority of genetic diversity was not yet known in the time of Jefferson. The science of genetics had not yet been invented. In his *Notes,* Jefferson expressed the view that this 'improvement of body and mind' showed that blacks were in some, but not all, ways inferior to whites. He said about the Negroes that 'in memory they are equal to the whites . . . . are at least as brave and more adventuresome . . . . are more generally gifted than the whites with accurate ears for time and tune', whereas the whites have greater 'beauty and reason'.

This explains one of the reasons why he did not want *Notes on the State of Virginia* to be published in America, because it gave the blacks too much credit for intelligence to suit most Americans in that time. The other reason was his complaint that, 'Millions of innocent men, women and children . . . . have been burnt, tortured, fined, imprisoned' because of Christianity.

The quotation about how blacks improve upon being mixed with whites, at a time when it was not yet understood that a mixture of diverse races will automatically produce a superior offspring, tends to show what has long been suspected, that Thomas Jefferson felt that he was performing a vital public service by impregnating his female black slaves, thereby mixing in them his own superior genes.

Besides that one book, which did not contribute much to his reputation in his lifetime, and the other things which he was able to do only because of who he already was, such as the Louisiana Purchase and the founding of the University of Virginia, almost everything Jefferson did which is remembered today consists of his letters and short essays. He rarely made a public speech in his entire life and those few which he made were entirely unmemorable. He apparently did not have a good speaking voice.

The one document which first made Thomas Jefferson famous and which earned him the assignment of writing the *Declaration of Independence* was a pamphlet entitled *A Summary View of the Rights of British America*. This really turned out to be the first draft of the *Declaration of Independence*. The basic arguments presented were exactly the same. However, it is often forgotten that this, too, was a private letter. Jefferson did not anticipate that it would be published. The recipients passed it around and made copies. In 1774, it appeared as a pamphlet without the name of the author being revealed and without Thomas Jefferson giving permission for its publication.

Among the charges faced by Thomas Jefferson in his lifetime was one that he was an atheist. To counter this accusation, one of the walls of the Jefferson Memorial is filled with quotes of Thomas Jefferson which makes reference to God. However, these quotes are misleading. Often, he referred to God only when he was attacking the church. In other words, he was fighting fire with fire.

For example, his letter to Benjamin Rush dated September 23, 1800 contains the following famous quote: 'I have sworn upon the alter of God eternal hostility against every form of tyranny over the minds of men.'

This quote was not a profession of the belief in God which it seems to be but was actually an expression of opposition towards the aspirations of the Episcopalian and Congregationalist Churches to be named as the official churches of the United States, which would have entitled them to receive taxpayer's money and support by the state.

It appears that Thomas Jefferson sincerely believed in God, he did not believe in a god who manipulated men like puppets on the end of a string. He definitely did not believe in the Holy Trinity. For this reason, he has been called a 'Unitarian'. His philosophy is perhaps best expressed in a letter dated August 10, 1787 to Peter Carr in which he stated:

> *Question with boldness even the existence of a god; because, if there be one, he must more approve of the homage of reason than the blindfold of fear.*

Of course, there is at least one problem with this philosophy. If this is the sort god which exists, then only the smart people will get into heaven. For any religion to be successful, there must be a more basic appeal to the masses.

Nevertheless, we can state categorically that Thomas Jefferson did believe in God. Late in his life, he became prone towards writing lengthy discourses proving the existence of God, the god who created the universe. He followed in some respects the line of reasoning of the French philosopher, Descartes. However, he did not believe in a manipulative god or in a god who sends to hell all those who do not believe in Christianity.

Regarding the mentality of Jefferson, Dr. Bernard Diamond, the late

Chairman of the Department of Criminology at the University of California at Berkeley, did a study during the 'Free Speech Movement' in the mid-1960's of all of the campus leaders of the Berkeley student revolution. He made the remarkable finding that all of these campus revolutionaries had highly educated mothers. They also had highly educated father's, but, in this respect, they were statistically no different from other students of their rank and category. It was particularly the mothers of these revolutionaries who were outstanding and who were far above the educational level of the mother of the average student.

From this, we can conclude that since Thomas Jefferson was one of the greatest revolutionaries of all time, he must have had a strong and highly educated mother. This is not surprising, because his mother was Jane Randolph, a member of the Randolph family, the most highly educated family in Virginia at that time.

However, this is merely an inference. We have no actual information at all about the mother of Thomas Jefferson. He destroyed all of her letters after her death. It is presumed that he disliked his mother. In the thousands of letters which he wrote, he only mentioned her once. That was in a letter he wrote in June, 1776 to her brother, William Randolph, who was residing in England. The letter rambles on about inane topics and, then, at the very end, says that, by the way, you probably have not heard about this but your sister, Jane, died three months ago.

It is generally believed that Thomas Jefferson lived with his mother until she died in 1776 when Thomas Jefferson was 33 or at least until Shadwell burned down in 1770. In all probability, his mother was a domineering woman whom Thomas Jefferson did not like.

At the same time, Thomas Jefferson was clearly proud of his father. Peter Jefferson was described as a giant of a man, enormously strong. Peter Jefferson was a surveyor and a civil engineer who explored the Appalachian Mountains on horseback. He and a collaborator developed the first good map of Virginia. This map was attached by Thomas Jefferson as a fold-out to his book *Notes on the State of Virginia*. Because of this, one wag commented that the only good thing about the book was the map. When one hears references to 'Jefferson's map of Virginia', this refers to the map of Peter Jefferson, not Thomas Jefferson.

Thomas Jefferson also inherited a number of personality characteristics from his father. He never explored the Appalachian Mountains the way that his father did, but he certainly knew how to get around them on horseback. This ability served him in good stead during the Revolutionary War, when the troops of Cornwallis were chasing and trying to catch him.

While Thomas Jefferson was not an explorer himself, he did acquire the title to the Natural Bridge, which possibly had been discovered by his father.

His interest in exploration and discovery no doubt contributed to his bold decision to make the Louisiana Purchase and definitely led him to authorize the Lewis and Clark Expedition, which established the first land route to the Pacific Ocean. That Lewis was Meriwether Lewis (1774–1809), who served as his personal secretary in the White House until the expedition commenced. Strangely, shortly after returning from this great journey of discovery, Meriwether Lewis committed suicide, although one source states that he was murdered by his French servant in Tennessee while returning to Washington from the Missouri Territory, where he was the governor at the time. See *Genealogy of Virginia Families*, Vol. 3, p. 393.

Perhaps the most noteworthy tendency which Thomas Jefferson inherited from his father was to gather a large family about him. The best friend of Peter Jefferson had been William Randolph, who died prematurely in 1746 at age 33, his wife having died four years before him. Before his death, William Randolph got his friend to promise to take care of his children and raise them up. As a result, Peter Jefferson raised up the three children of William Randolph, essentially as adopted children. One of these was Thomas Mann Randolph, Senior. In addition, Peter Jefferson had ten children of his own, two of whom died in infancy. Thus, the house of Peter Jefferson consisted at a minimum of his wife, eleven children, and numerous slaves. This explains the tendency of Thomas Jefferson also to try to keep his numerous family together under the same roof.

The real reason that Thomas Jefferson was so insistent that his daughter Maria come to join him in France was that he was afraid of losing her. She had already been separated from him for four years and he feared that if the separation continued much longer, she would forget who he was.

His fears were well founded. Maria failed to recognize her father and her sister when she was finally reunited with them in Paris. More than that, it is clear that Maria never developed the close personal bond with her father that her sister, Martha, had. Maria had previously written that she did not want to come to France and that she wanted to stay with her Aunt Eppes at Bermuda Hundred. Later, after their return to America, Maria married John Wayles Eppes, the son of Aunt Eppes, and moved back to Bermuda Hundred, the same place where she has spent her childhood. Tragically, Maria died, possibly of breast cancer, at age 25.

Her sister, Martha Jefferson Randolph, perhaps as the result of producing so many children in such a short time, was in the habit of just dropping her children off at Monticello and abandoning them there, sometimes for years at a time. In a letter dated February 14, 1796, Thomas Jefferson wrote to his daughter, Martha, that poor little Thomas Jefferson Randolph, then less than four years old, was so sad at having been abandoned by his mother, who had promised to return for him, but never did.

Probably the actual reason for this was not that Martha Jefferson Randolph was a bad mother but rather that her erratic husband was incapable of supporting her and her children financially. The fact that she often did not keep the children with her and presumably did not breast feed them, also helps to explain the fact that she came to give birth to twelve children.

On the other hand, it has been noted that in 1827, when his wife temporarily left him and went to Boston, Thomas Mann Randolph, Jr. suddenly recovered his sanity and actually went out and got a job! He did excellent work, mapping the Florida border. However, when his wife returned, he became crazy again. He died shortly thereafter, in 1828.

From reading somewhat deeply into the life of Thomas Jefferson, one can easily understand everything he did and why he did it, something which professional historians have been unable to fathom. As one can imagine, many people would have done exactly what he did. It seems that almost all of the big plantation owners in that area of Virginia had two sets of children. Even his father, Peter Jefferson, has been accused of this. Every history book says that Thomas Jefferson was a great admirer of George Wythe, for whom the town of Wytheville, Virginia, was named. George Wythe, the teacher and mentor of Thomas Jefferson and a famous person in his own right, is said to have fathered a son, Michael Brown, by his slave, Lydia Broadnax. If Thomas Jefferson did not engage in the practice of producing children from his slaves, he was just about the only one.

# Chapter Seven

## Life In France

Thomas Jefferson arrived in France in 1784, bringing with him his oldest daughter, Martha, and his slave, James Hemings, who was brought to be trained as a chef.

In 1796, Thomas Jefferson was appointed Ambassador to France, an important position because France was America's most important ally at the time, since they had a mutual enemy: England. In 1784, an epidemic of whooping cough had swept America and his daughter Lucy had died. Already, three of Jefferson's children had died before Lucy. One of his children, a son, had died before he had even been given a name.

The same epidemic which had killed Lucy had killed at the same time another child also named Lucy, a daughter of Elizabeth Eppes and her husband, Col. Francis Eppes, who had been taking care of the two Lucys plus Maria Jefferson while Thomas Jefferson was in France.

Concerned about the health of his remaining daughter, Maria, also known as Mary or Polly, Thomas Jefferson wrote a letter dated September 20, 1785, telling her to come to join him in France. He also sent instructions that one of her servants, as he called them, should be sent along. He specified that the servant to be sent should be one who had already had the smallpox, which would make her immune from transmitting the disease to his daughters.

For no particular reason, Sally Hemings was selected as the one to accompany Polly, in spite of the fact that Sally was only 14 years old. There is some debate as to the reason for this. The most likely reason is that Sally was the closest friend of Polly. In addition, for various reasons, the other women at Monticello may have been unavailable. Isabel, a woman who had already had the smallpox and whom Thomas Jefferson had suggested to be the one to accompany Polly to France, was just in the process of giving birth to a child. That child became Edy, who was born on April 10, 1787 and who later became a cook in the White House. Possibly, Sally was selected because she was nearly white and would adjust better in France. For whatever reason, Sally was the one selected.

One reason this subject is so often debated is that it is known that Sally was 'decidedly good looking', as one observer put it. Every person who ever saw Sally has in some way described her as beautiful. Abigail Adams, who saw Sally when she first got off the boat, was apparently concerned about this. This may have been one of the reasons why Abigail Adams is believed to have demanded that Sally be put back on the same boat and returned to America.

Nevertheless, it is clear from all the correspondence on this subject that Thomas Jefferson himself played no role in the last minute selection of Sally. That decision was made by the Eppes family. By the time that Thomas Jefferson found out about it, Sally was already on the boat on the way over. If Thomas Jefferson had known that Sally was being considered for this assignment, he probably would have objected, because Sally, unlike Isabel, had not had the smallpox.

It appears that Maria did not want to go to France. Indeed, Maria had written an undated letter to her father on about May 22, 1786 which said: 'I am very sorry that you have sent for me. I don't want to go to France. I had rather stay with Aunt Eppes . . . . Your most happy and dutiful daughter, Polly Jefferson.'

The way that Maria and Sally were finally forced to go was that they were taken on an innocent tour of the boat with other children who ran around and played. Maria fell asleep on the boat, and, when she awoke, she and Sally were already on the high seas. They were the only females on the boat, but they were apparently well taken care of by the captain, whose name was Captain Ramsey.

The boat took them from America to England, where they were met on arrival by John Adams and his wife, Abigail. One theory has it that Abigail Adams, who thought that Sally was 15 or 16, was mortified to learn that she was a slave. The stuffy lady absolutely insisted that Sally be put back on the same boat on which she had come and sent back to America. Fawn Brodie, always quick to suggest a sexual innuendo, implies that Captain Ramsey concurred, because he wanted to take Sally back to America alone with him so as to give him the opportunity to have sex with Sally on the boat. John Adams, however, insisted that they should await word from Thomas Jefferson on what to do about this. There was apparently quite a disturbance between the husband and wife over this issue.

Apparently, John Adams eventually prevailed through the argument that whereas Sally was a slave in America, she would be free in France. To put her back on the boat would be to condemn her to a lifetime of slavery.

Inexplicably, Thomas Jefferson did not send immediately to England for Polly and Sally. They had to be brought to him in France. After they had spent some weeks in England, Jefferson sent a Frenchman named Adrien Petit who spoke no English to pick them up. Abigail Adams was mortified at this incident and for a time refused to send the two girls with this strange man. However, she eventually gave up and let them go.

Adrien Petit is another person who pops in and out of this story from time to time. Later, in 1792, he came from France to Monticello to work for Thomas Jefferson. However, he did not like it there and left after a few weeks. One of the slaves at Monticello had accused him of being a homosexual. This suggests another possible reason why Abigail Adams did not want to send Jefferson's daughters with Petit in 1787.

This entire incident may have contributed to the complete break in relations between Thomas Jefferson and John Adams which subsequently took place. At this time, they were still clearly close friends, but later on they became bitter political enemies. It has been reported that Abigail Adams never forgave Thomas Jefferson for the Sally Hemings episode.

It was in France that the affair between Thomas Jefferson and Sally Hemings must have started. Those 'defending' Thomas Jefferson claim that no such sexual affair could have happened, because Sally was only 14 when she came to France and only 16 when she left. However, knowledge of human nature tells us that 16 is old enough for sex. At this time, 16 was the average age for marriage of women in America. Even Thomas Jefferson's own daughter, Martha, got married when she was 17.

If a relationship between Sally Hemings and Thomas Jefferson existed, it may have started as early as 1788. Unfortunately, the volume of letters written by Thomas Jefferson in the years 1788 and 1789 is missing. Of all the letters written by Thomas Jefferson, this is the only missing volume. Speculation by Fawn Brodie is that it contained love letters to or about Sally Hemings and was destroyed by some unknown person for that reason.

However, we still have the account book written by Thomas Jefferson. This account book contains clear and convincing evidence of some special relationship between Thomas Jefferson and Sally Hemings. The main thing which the account book shows is that Thomas Jefferson suddenly started spending large amounts of money on Sally Hemings in April, 1789, inconsistent with her status as a slave. In particular, Thomas Jefferson suddenly started buying Sally Hemings dresses and fine clothing.

This is rather convincing proof. What is the first thing that a man does after he has had sex with a woman for the first time? Everybody knows the answer to this question. He buys her a dress. (The other possibility is that he dumps her completely and never calls her again, an experience which almost every woman has felt at one time or another. This did not happen with Sally Hemings).

The next thing which happens, if the relationship really gets serious, is that he rents her an apartment. This is exactly what Thomas Jefferson did. Sally Hemings had her own apartment in Paris, in a different section of town from the other family members of Thomas Jefferson. Jefferson lived at the Hotel de Langeac on the Champs–Elysees, where James Hemings was in training as a chef.

Stronger proof would be hard to imagine. There is a saying, 'When in Rome, do as the Romans do.' In Paris at this time, every man of importance kept a mistress on the other side of town.

The account book shows that on April 6, 1789, Thomas Jefferson spent 96 francs on 'clothes for Sally.' Then, on April 16, 1789, he spent 72 francs on more clothes. Then, on April 26, 1789, he spent 23 francs on 'making clothes for servants'. Finally, on May 25, 1789, he 'paid making clothes for Sally 25 francs.' Thus, he spent a grand total of 216 francs on clothing for Sally in just a period of seven weeks.

There is no other record before or after at any time from 1773 to 1826 of Thomas Jefferson ever buying clothing for Sally. Of course, after these initial purchases of clothing for Sally in 1789, there was no pressing need to buy her any more clothing. He already had her 'barefoot and pregnant', as they say.

Similarly, his account book shows that on April 29, 1789, he paid Madame Dupre, the landlady of Sally, 105 francs for rent for her apartment and 41.9 francs for 'washing', for a total of 146.9 francs.

Thus, we can put almost an exact date on the beginning of their sexual involvement. It happened in exactly April, 1789, when he started lavishing dresses on her and rented her own apartment. She was sixteen, hardly too young for this sort of thing. Their baby, Tom, was born not much more than nine months later.

Sally Hemings came to France to be a nanny for Polly. If that relationship had continued, she would have lived in the same quarters and in the same room with Polly, who had, in fact, joined her sister, Martha, in school in a convent. However, the evidence is that starting in April, 1789, Sally Hemings was kept away from not only Polly, but also from her own brother, James Hemings, who was studying cooking in the same hotel where Thomas Jefferson lived.

Incidentally, various alternative explanations have been suggested for the payment of rent by Thomas Jefferson to Madame Dupre. It has been suggested that Madame Dupre was a teacher of some sort. It has been said that she taught Sally French, music or that she even gave Sally lessons in how to be a French chambermaid. However, there is a note stating that Madame Dupre was "Sally Hemings' landlady." Also, the account book shows that Madame Dupre did the washing for Sally, indicating that now Sally had achieved such a high status that she no longer had to wash her own clothes.

Another piece of evidence concerns the plight of Maria Cosway. Maria Cosway was an Italian woman of English descent who happened to be in

France with her English husband when Thomas Jefferson was there. She was born in Florence, Italy in 1759. She was a talented artist and musician. She had been elected to the Academy of Fine Arts in Florence. Her paintings had been exhibited at London's Royal Academy. She played the harp and the pianoforte and was a singer and a composer. Her husband was Richard Cosway, an eminent miniaturist painter, but less than five feet tall and possibly a homosexual. Maria Cosway and Thomas Jefferson had a passionate romance, which involved at least one long walk through the gardens, but which lasted not more than five or six weeks.

History does not provide us with the exact date on which they met, except that it was in August, 1786, but only the date on which they parted, which was October 5, 1786. On that date, the husband of Maria Cosway took her back to England.

This relationship with Maria Cosway permanently changed the life of Thomas Jefferson in one way. On one outing with Maria, he apparently jumped over a fence trying to impress her, and fractured his right wrist. The wrist never mended perfectly and caused him pain for the remainder of his life. He even had to give up practicing the violin from that date forward. He wrote with his left hand for a time. Years later, he sometimes halted his writing of letters, because of the pain in his wrist.

Thomas Jefferson wrote Maria Cosway many love letters, one of which is famous. This is entitled *The Head and the Heart*, with the head telling him to do one thing and the heart telling him to do another. An entire book by that name has been published about that letter. This letter was dated October 12, 1786 and was written with his left hand immediately after Thomas Jefferson had followed Maria Cosway and her husband for several miles down the road from Paris and had finally seen her off on their journey to England.

The result of these love letters was that later Maria Cosway came alone to France in 1787, without her husband, just to see Thomas Jefferson.

After her arrival, she was horrified to discover that she was simply ignored by Thomas Jefferson. When she first arrived, she sent him a discrete note informing him that she just might find time in her busy schedule to see him. There was no response. Then, she came to see him. Still, he did not seem much interested. The indications are that she just sat in her room for four months waiting for him to call. He never called. Ironically, when he finally decided to pay her a courtesy call on December 7, 1787, he discovered that she had gone back to England only a few hours earlier. They never met again.

Her reaction shows that she must have had a blind spot. Here she was, the recipient of a love letter which still stands today as one of the great compositions of this sort in the history of the English language. Yet, when she went to see the man who had written her the love letter, he displayed no interest in her.

Surely, she must have guessed the truth. She must have realized that there had to be another woman there somewhere. But, where was that woman? Perhaps, she had Thomas Jefferson followed. She must have checked, through her own sources, everything about the private life of Thomas Jefferson. If she had found another woman, surely she would have written him off. The fact that she did not write him off shows that she could find no evidence of any other woman.

Of course, how could she possibly have guessed that her competition was a 16-year-old black slave?

Probably, the evidence was right under her nose. She may have seen Sally Hemings in the flesh. However, she dismissed her as just another servant. She never guessed the true relationship. Sally had arrived between the date of the love letters from Thomas Jefferson to Maria Cosway and the return of Maria Cosway to France. However, Maria Cosway could never have realized the significance of this.

This is proven by the fact that Maria Cosway continued to write love letters to Thomas Jefferson for the remainder of his life. Throughout most of this time, she remained outwardly faithful to her husband, who died in 1821. However, it was obvious from her letters that she was ready to drop her husband at any moment if only she received the slightest bit of encouragement from Thomas Jefferson.

Her letters to him often chided him for not answering her previous letters. She wrote often of how much she would like to see Washington, D.C. (This proves that it must have been true love). She said that she dreamed of seeing Monticello. All Thomas Jefferson had to do was write one single word of encouragement, and she would have been on the boat on the way over. However, that one word of encouragement never came. The last letter she wrote him was in 1825, just before he died.

Although the parents of Maria Cosway were English, she was born in Italy and was not completely fluent in the English language. Her letters often alternated between broken English and her native Italian. However, this caused no problem, because Thomas Jefferson was able to read Italian, along with French, Spanish, Greek and Latin. After her husband died, Maria Cosway went back to Lodi, Italy, where she spent the remainder of her life.

There are several sources among the slaves at Monticello for the story that when Martha Wayles Jefferson, the wife of Thomas Jefferson, was on her death bed, Thomas Jefferson and a number of his slaves were present in the room, including Sally Hemings and her mother Betty. Just before Martha died, according to this tradition, Thomas Jefferson promised his wife that after her death he would never marry again. In fact, he never did.

This story is almost undoubtedly true, because it comes from a number of independent sources. However, Thomas Jefferson never said that he would never have sex again. Indeed, the fact that he solemnly swore to his dying beloved wife that he would never marry again could just possibly be the result of the fact that he was already having sex with his slaves.

Here is what Edmund Bacon had to say about this, as quoted in *Jefferson at Monticello*, p. 99-100:

> The house servants were Betty Brown, Sally, Critta, and Betty Hemings, Nance and Ursula. They were old family servants and great favorites. They were in the room when Mrs. Jefferson died. She died before I went to live with him, and left four little children. He never married again. They have often told my wife that when Mrs. Jefferson died they stood around the bed. Mr. Jefferson sat by her, and she gave them directions about a good many things that she wanted done. When she came to the children, she wept and could not speak for some time. Finally she held up her hand, and spreading out her four fingers, she told them that she could not die happy if she thought her four children were ever to have a step mother brought in over them. And he never did. He was then quite a young man and very handsome, and I suppose that he could have married well; but he always kept his promise.

A number of authors have been determined to prove that Thomas Jefferson remained pristine pure and that he never had sex at all in the remaining 44 years of his life. They therefore find it important to prove that his relationship with Maria Cosway was non-sexual in nature.

Of course, history will never know exactly what Thomas Jefferson and Maria Cosway were doing during the many hours in which they were alone in the private quarters of Thomas Jefferson in Paris together. Nevertheless, author Thomas Fleming has written that, 'The lady was married and too religious to commit adultery.' Similarly, Fawn Brodie says on page 294 of her book that Maria Cosway was 'guilt ridden and ill equipped for adultery.'

The remark that Maria Cosway was 'too religious to commit adultery' is laughable when one considers a fact which Thomas Jefferson almost certainly never knew, which is that Maria Cosway carried on affairs with a number of different men during her lifetime. Indeed, one of the possible lovers of Maria Cosway was none other than the Prince of Wales, who later on became King George IV. In addition, when Maria gave birth to her only child, she promptly abandoned it to her husband and ran off to Europe with another man. The child eventually died at age six. This happened years after her presumed affair with Thomas Jefferson.

In view of the variety of sexual partners which Maria Cosway is known to have had, one wonders whether Richard Cosway was really the father of that child.

Maria Cosway remained loyal and faithful to her husband for the same reason that so many women remain faithful to their husbands: He sent her money. In addition, he got her paintings exhibited in art galleries. Later on, Maria found that without her husband's backing, no art gallery would exhibit her paintings. This is the reason that she became upset when she received letters from her husband expressing disapproval at her gallivanting around Europe with other men. She was afraid that he would stop sending her money.

Richard Cosway, the husband of Maria, was referred to as a 'fop' by none other an authority than King George III himself. Years later, in a letter to her husband dated March 22, 1815, Maria indicated that she had not objected too much to her husband having an affair with another woman, a certain 'Miss P'. However, when he took up with a certain Mr. Hammersmith, followed by several other men, this was more than she could bear.

Notwithstanding the claim that Maria Cosway was 'too religious to commit adultery', her letters to Thomas Jefferson contain unmistakable innuendoes that their relationship had been sexual in nature. For example, in her letter to Thomas Jefferson from England dated December 25, 1787, Maria stated: 'Have you seen the lovely Mrs. Church. . . . . I give you free permission to love her with all your heart, and I shall feel happy if I think you keep me in a little corner of it.'

At the time of this letter, Angelica Church, the wife, famed for her beauty, of John Church, a member of the British Parliament, had just arrived in Paris from England. For some reason, Maria Cosway knew or believed that Angelica Church would be looking up Thomas Jefferson. Maria presumably wanted to hide her jealousy. In other words, Maria Cosway seems to be saying in her letter that since Maria will be occupied and will not be coming to France for some time, she therefore gives full permission for Thomas Jefferson to have sex with Mrs. Church, provided only that Thomas Jefferson thinks about Maria Cosway while doing it.

This Mrs. Church, as it turns out, was a somewhat important person in history. She happened to be the sister-in-law of Alexander Hamilton. After undoubtedly meeting up with Thomas Jefferson in Paris, she later on showed up in society circles in Philadelphia, where she was noted for her great beauty. She was also noted for the great number of her boyfriends. By then, the competition was too stiff and Thomas Jefferson had no longer any chance to get her, if indeed that idea had crossed his mind earlier due to Maria Cosway's letter.

Another interesting fact about Angelica Church is that her husband, John B. Church, later on fought a duel with Aaron Burr. However, both shots missed their mark and later on they became friends again.

It seems that sometimes these duels were a facade. A duel would be fought, with both parties intending not to shoot the other. This duel between John Church and Aaron Burr took place at the Weehawken Dueling ground, the same place where Aaron Burr later on killed Alexander Hamilton.

For the backdrop, it most be noted that another thing which has not changed in the last 200 years is that Europe is far more permissive sexually than is America. In France at that time, a man would openly keep another man's wife as his mistress, often with her husband's permission. In America, then as now, such behavior would be outrageous and unheard of. Maria Cosway and possibly Angelica Church were just two of the many women who openly slept with men other than their husbands, without any notice being taken of it.

Such behavior was not acceptable in America. One example of this was when Lafayette toured America in 1824, he was uncertain as to whether to bring along his 29-year-old mistress, Frances Wright. It was finally agreed that she would be accompanied by her sister, that they would call him 'father' and that he would call them 'my daughters', all this to hide the true nature of their relationship. Later, Frances Wright became famous in her own right because of her books and her other writings and because she attempted to establish a commune in Tennessee with the considerable money she had inherited. This commune was intended to consist of freed blacks mixed with whites, but it failed immediately.

An excellent article in the August, 1971 issue of *American Heritage* magazine entitled *Thomas Jefferson and Maria Cosway* by Charles B. Van Pelt, concerns their love affair in 1786. It shows that while the the question of whether it was requited love or unrequited love will never be answered, they clearly spent plenty of time alone together. Even the husband of Maria Cosway would politely excuse himself when Thomas Jefferson came calling and leave them alone together. Maria Cosway also came to the residence of Thomas Jefferson unannounced frequently.

Regarding her return to France without her husband in 1787, this article suggests that perhaps there was active sex between them at that time as well. Most commentators believe that Thomas Jefferson ignored Maria during that second period. However, Charles Van Pelt implies that the lack of surviving correspondence between them during this period was not because of a lack of interest on the part of Thomas Jefferson, but rather because that was the time when the hard core sex really got started. However, if that was true, why would Maria Cosway give up and leave after just four months? Why did she not come again during the next two years while Thomas Jefferson still remained in France?

Further evidence of a connection between Thomas Jefferson and Sally Hemings in France is of a negative nature. France was and still is a country noted for its fine ladies. Surely, in that environment, Thomas Jefferson, being a fluent speaker of French, would have acquired a lady companion, if not two or three. Benjamin Franklin, who had come to France on a similar mission a few years earlier and who went back to America shortly after the arrival of Thomas Jefferson, did not have trouble meeting French ladies. Franklin is believed to have fathered several illegitimate children there. Indeed, Franklin, who was an open advocate of sexual freedom, introduced Thomas Jefferson to a number of his lady friends prior to his departure. Why did Thomas Jefferson, who tried to seize Elizabeth Walker, his best friend's wife, in the hallway in the early hours of the morning when her husband was around some years earlier, not bother with any of those women? The answer must have been that he did not bother with any of the available French ladies because he had imported a woman of his own.

It must also be mentioned that Benjamin Franklin apparently contracted venereal disease in France. Franklin died shortly thereafter in 1790, at the age of 84. Perhaps Jefferson knew about this. This could easily explain the fact that Thomas Jefferson apparently never touched any of the fine French women, in spite of spending five years in France. He might have preferred a woman whom he knew for certain had not been tainted with venereal disease.

This might also explain why Jefferson did not have much to do with Maria Cosway when she came back to France a second time in 1787. He might have learned that she was not a pure woman, that she had other lovers and that therefore she might have venereal disease. It is perhaps Thomas Jefferson's fastidious avoidance of disease during an era when most diseases could not be cured which enabled Thomas Jefferson to remain strong and healthy until age 83, when the average life expectancy at that time was less than half of that.

One reason why we do not have complete information about the life of Thomas Jefferson in France is that all but one of the family letters written by him during the years 1788 and 1789 have disappeared. This was the period when his affair with Sally Hemings started.

Fawn Brodie has a theory that the letters are missing because they contained love letters to or about Sally. Here, Fawn Brodie made one critical mistake. She said that only the letters for 1788 are missing and that the letters for every other year are available. Actually, the gap is bigger and, with the exception of one letter, covers a period of nearly three years. We have frequent letters coming and going on a regular basis up until July 6, 1787. After that, there is a gap of nearly one year. Then, there is a letter dated June 16, 1788. After that, there is a bigger gap. The next document is not a letter but rather a marriage contract dated February 21, 1790. In this contract, Thomas Jefferson granted in marriage his daughter Martha to Thomas Mann Randolph, Jr. In consideration of this marriage, the senior Thomas Mann Randolph contributed 950 acres of land at Varina and 40 slaves. Thomas Jefferson contributed a dowry of 1000 acres at Poplar Forest in Bedford County plus 27 slaves who are listed in the contract by name as Jack, Patty, Betty, Judy, Tom, Lucy, Polly, Davy, Jeffery, Joan, Scilla, Nancy, Lundy, Betty, Jupiter, Phyllis the Elder, Phyllis the Younger, Sandy, John, Sam, Betty, Sarah, Peg, Louis, Abby, Patty, and Harry, plus various unnamed horses, cattle, hogs and sheep.

After that, the letters start coming again, with great frequency.

It has been suggested by Fawn Brodie that some unknown person destroyed the letters for the years 1788 and 1789, because they included love letters to Sally Hemings. All of the other women in the life of Thomas Jefferson, with the exception of Elizabeth Walker, who was married, received love letters from him.

Actually, there are several possible reasons why the letters are missing, most of which have nothing to do with Sally. To begin with, it is just possible that his letter copying machine broke down, although, considering the lengths Thomas Jefferson went to keep copies of all his letters, this seems unlikely.

Secondly, it is more likely that the missing volume contained love letters to and from Maria Cosway. In fact, a large collection of these letters were kept secret and have only been revealed in recent years. This, indeed, is possibly the best explanation for the missing volumes.

Another possible reason concerns the fact that Jefferson had fractured his wrist in 1786. He did write several letters with his left hand, but his volume of letters greatly diminished during this period. Possibly, his wrist was not strong enough to write with comfort letters to his family until 1790.

It is unlikely that the missing volumes contained love letters to Sally Hemings. There is no proof that Sally even knew how to read. Thomas Jefferson never mentioned her name in any of his letters, nor did he often mention the name of any of his other slaves, for that matter. At the same time, there is almost no doubt that if love letters to Sally Hemings ever existed, they would have been destroyed or at least removed, as were the letters to Maria Cosway.

The final and perhaps the most conclusive evidence proving a relationship between Sally Hemings and Thomas Jefferson in France concerns the fact that at first she refused to return to America. She was happy in France and was becoming fluent in the French language. Finally, Thomas Jefferson convinced her to return with him, by promising her that her children would receive their freedom upon reaching maturity.

This agreement, in itself, proves that she must have been pregnant at the time. If she already had a baby, the baby would already be free borne in France. There would have been no need for an agreement. On the other hand, if Sally Hemings was still a virgin, it is inconceivable that such an agreement would have been made. She would have stayed in France. With no husband and no attachment to any male, who would make an agreement concerning the totally speculative possibility of children at some distant future date?

Thus, the nature of the agreement itself shows that Sally Hemings had a baby inside when the agreement was made. It also shows that the father of that unborn baby must have been Thomas Jefferson. Otherwise, why would he suffer the embarrassment of bringing a pregnant girl back to America? Why not just leave her with her French lover, if one existed? There were plenty of slave girls available in America, just for the price of purchase.

It must be mentioned, however, that there is one problem with this last point. We don't have the agreement. If a hard copy of the agreement could be produced, this would be proof positive. However, it appears that the agreement was verbal or, if reduced to writing, the writing has been lost. We only know that there was such an agreement from the oral tradition among the slaves at Monticello. However, this latter fact shows that all of the slaves knew that he had made such an agreement. Therefore, he was honor-bound to carry out the terms of the agreement when the children of Sally reached maturity years later.

What we do have is proof that all five members of Jefferson's extended family traveled together on the same boat back to America. There are several documents proving this. One is a passport issued by King Louis XVI allowing them all to leave the country.

This was one of the last things which King Louis XVI did. He was overthrown and finally beheaded in 1793. The French Revolution had already started when Thomas Jefferson and his family left the country. They were in Paris on July 14, 1789, on the occasion of the storming of the Bastille. James Hemings may have participated in that storming. In fact, Thomas Jefferson himself contributed money towards the revolutionary cause, hardly appropriate behavior for an official diplomat to the King. Their decision to leave may have been influenced by the unstable political situation in that country. At the same time, Thomas Jefferson wanted to watch the revolution unfold and was interested in returning to France quickly. He never came back.

On their way back to America, they stopped in England at the Isle of Wight. John Adams was no longer in England. He was already in America, as Vice-President under George Washington. Maria Cosway had written a letter to Thomas Jefferson saying that if he stopped in England on his way to America, he should to let her know. However, he did not do so.

Another point which 'defenders' of Thomas Jefferson, including Virginius Dabney, use to attack this account concerns the fact that they all five traveled on the same boat together in nearby or adjoining quarters. It is claimed by Virginius Dabney and Douglas Adair that it is 'impossible' that Thomas Jefferson would have allowed his two minor daughters to associate with an obviously pregnant Sally Hemings.

However, what else was he going to do? Was he going to abandon his faithful slave and their unborn child in France, just to keep her out of the sight of his two daughters?

Today, in a nation of single parents, we often have this situation. A divorced mother brings her latest boyfriend home where he has the occasion to meet her children. It is just not practical always to rent a hotel room and to hire a baby sitter for these occasions. It happens every day. Life goes on. Thomas Jefferson faced the same problem and he resolved it in the same way.

In fact, there is also some slight evidence which may indicate that the relationship was upsetting to his oldest daughter Martha (the youngest daughter being possibly too young to know what was going on). It might be a coincidence, but on April 18, 1789, Martha wrote a note to her father stating that she had decided to become a nun. This was exactly the week when Thomas Jefferson was buying dresses for Sally. Thomas Jefferson is known for his views opposing organized religion, and his reaction was swift and appropriate. Two days later, he showed up at the door of the convent where Martha had been living and going to school for the past five years. He had a brief conversation with the headmaster and then walked out of the front door with Martha, never to return.

Indeed, this was the last day in her life when Martha ever attended school. The account book shows that on May 7, 1789, Thomas Jefferson paid 12 france to buy a whip for Martha. On February 23, 1790, within three months after their arrival back in America, Martha married Thomas Mann Randolph, Jr. Martha was only 17 years old. Thomas Mann Randolph, Jr. was given a substantial dowry by Thomas Jefferson, including land and 27 slaves. Then, Martha and her new husband moved to their new property.

This sudden change in the life of Martha, where she was quietly attending school in a convent in France and then suddenly became a whip-cracking slave owner in Virginia a few months later, has been attributed by historian Fawn Brodie to be possibly the result of the fact that Martha was upset at the discovery that her father was sleeping with a black slave. However, this is just a theory. There is no proof of this.

This marriage was successful in some ways and a failure in others. It was successful in that it produced twelve children, of which eleven survived, thereby ensuring the survival of the known blood lines of Thomas Jefferson.

On the other hand, Thomas Mann Randolph, Jr. turned out to be a worthless person. Within a few years, he had squandered the entire dowry and was virtually bankrupt. All the land and the 27 slaves had to be sold to pay his debts. This must have been especially upsetting to Thomas Jefferson, after all the work he had done to cultivate these slaves.

For the remainder of his life, Thomas Jefferson had to be concerned with keeping his daughter, Martha, and her many children, out of poverty and destitution, while, at the same time, keeping any money from falling into the hands of Thomas Mann Randolph, Jr., who immediately squandered any funds he received. One result of all this was that Martha and her husband had no permanent place to live, so they moved into and out of Monticello. They moved back to Monticello in 1809, after the Presidency of Thomas Jefferson had concluded. Martha continued to mass produce children for her husband throughout this period, however.

History tells us that Thomas Mann Randolph, Jr. was later elected the Governor of Virginia. However, that was only because of his family name and his connection with Thomas Jefferson. It had nothing to do with his abilities. Even today, Randolph is a big historical name in Virginia.

Going back to their time in France, Martha always referred to Sally as her maid-in-waiting or as her personal servant. She never let on to the fact that Sally was actually providing a very important service to her father. It is clear that Martha did not really like having Sally around and many times pressed her father to get rid of her, but her father refused.

# Chapter Eight

## Life in the White House

It must have come as a great shock to Sally Hemings, after having been showered with fine clothing and given her own apartment and her own washer woman in Paris, to find herself back in Monticello and back on the ration list, where she was allowed only one blanket every three years and 8 fish and one bread per week. No doubt there were many times she wished that she had stayed in France.

However, the evidence is that she did not stay all the time at Monticello. It seems more than likely that where Thomas Jefferson went, he took Sally Hemings with him. In those days, a white man could not walk openly on the streets in the company of a black woman, as the French Minister, Tallyrand, discovered when he once escorted a black woman in Philadelphia. However, Sally would have been accompanied by her brother, James, who always followed Thomas Jefferson as his personal chef. She would have been known as the personal servant and the chambermaid of Thomas Jefferson, and no attention would have been paid to this arrangement.

After Thomas Jefferson returned from France, he became the first Secretary of State under President George Washington. In fact, it took him several months to get around to traveling to Philadelphia to assume his duties, perhaps because he did not like the idea of serving on the same cabinet with Alexander Hamilton. This is the reason why Thomas Jefferson did not assume office as the Secretary of State until 1790, although George Washington had become president and had appointed him the previous year.

It is not clear exactly where Sally Hemings was during this period. Although Thomas Jefferson did pay brief visits to Monticello, there are no entries at all in the *Farm Book* from 1777 to 1792. However, the exact whereabouts of Sally Hemings during this period is not a matter of importance because, with the exception of Tom, she produced no children.

A letter has surfaced from Adrien Petit dated July 28, 1792 which appears to demonstrate that Sally was in Philadelphia with Thomas Jefferson at this time. This letter is included the appendix. It has never been published before in English. The original French version can be found in volume 24 of *The Papers of Thomas Jefferson*, by Princeton University Press, which was just published in 1991.

If Sally was in Philadelphia in 1792, this would be further evidence that she was the concubine of Thomas Jefferson. Moreover, even if she was not with him at all times, the fact that Sally Hemings had only six children shows that she did not conceive any child during the long periods when Thomas Jefferson was away. This, therefore, shows that she remained sexually faithful and loyal to him during her entire child bearing years.

Three of the surviving children of Sally were born while Thomas Jefferson was president. Therefore, the exact whereabouts of Sally Hemings during this period is a matter of critical importance.

Historians claiming that Thomas Jefferson was not the father of these children say that Thomas Jefferson was in Washington during this period whereas Sally Hemings was at Monticello. On the map, these two places are a distance of only 120 miles away. However, travel in those days was by horse and buggy. Roads were not well developed. The commute from Monticello to Washington was a five day journey each way.

This is an important point, as it comes up repeatedly in our calculations of the time it took to do things. It seems that the rate of travel was consistently about 25 miles for one day, regardless of the mode of transportation, whether it be by horseback, the usual mode of transportation for Thomas Jefferson, or by wagon or horse and buggy, or even by walking, as the slaves had to do. For example, when Thomas Jefferson married Martha Wayles, it took them three or four days by horseback to reach the 90 miles from what is now Hopewell to what is now Charlottesville on their honeymoon. Similarly, a his letter to his daughter, Martha, dated January 14, 1793, Thomas Jefferson stated that it normally took ten days for him to reach from Philadelphia to Monticello on horseback. This trip is now a distance of 250 miles on modern roads. The rate of 25 miles per day seems to us to be uncommonly slow, as a man can even walk at that rate, but it must be remembered that there were no modern roads nor were their bridges at that time.

One careful historian has discovered that Thomas Jefferson did visit Monticello almost exactly nine months before the birth of each one of Sally Hemings' three children. Therefore, Thomas Jefferson could have been the father.

However, this misses the point. It seems more likely that Sally Hemings was actually living in the White House at the time. At the same time, it is an intriguing fact that Maria, the daughter of Thomas Jefferson, died on April 17, 1804 and Thomas Jefferson went to Monticello to attend her funeral. Then, on January 19, 1805, almost exactly nine months later, Madison Hemings was born. Madison himself gives his birth date as January 19, 1805. The *Farm Book* only gives the date as January, 1805.

To this, Virginius Dabney asserts that it is impossible that Thomas Jefferson could possibly have defiled the memory of his just deceased daughter by having sex with Sally Hemings on the occasion of his daughter's funeral.

On the other hand, it is often a natural reaction by a parent whose child has died to want to make another one right away.

In his 1873 interview, Madison Hemings clearly stated that he had been born in Monticello in January, 1805, that Dolly Madison had been present at the time of his birth, and that she had given him the name of 'Madison'. However, there is no evidence that Dolly Madison was at Monticello at this particular time, although she easily might have been, as the Madison family home was not far from Monticello.

It is known that Dolly Madison was in Washington, D.C. in January, 1805, where her husband was serving as Jefferson's Secretary of State at an important time in American history. This raises the possibility that Madison Hemings was correct about the circumstances of his birth and merely wrong about the place, and that he actually was born in the White House.

The White House, which was then known as the President's House or the President's Palace, was first occupied by John Adams during the last few months of his presidency. The name 'The White House' was not officially adopted until the presidency of Theodore Roosevelt in this century. John Adams, being from Massachusetts, did not own any slaves, so it is recorded in history that Abigail Adams first hung up her own wash to dry in the uncompleted East Room of the White House in November, 1800.

Thomas Jefferson was inaugurated president in March, 1801. Thus, he became the first president to fully occupy what is now called The White House.

In fact, the President's House of that time is not the present structure. The original President's House was burned by the British during the War of 1812. The present White House was thereafter rebuilt on the same original design.

No doubt, the White House at that time did not have the present system of several hundred full time mostly black servants, gardeners, and chambermaids. Anyone visiting there can see that it would take a large staff to maintain such a place. That permanent staff did not exist in 1801.

Therefore, the conclusion is obvious. Thomas Jefferson probably brought his own slaves. Edmund Bacon says that he brought eleven servants with him to Washington from Monticello. See *Jefferson at Monticello*, p. 104. However, Bacon did not list the names, so we do not know if Sally was among them.

Anything else would have been inconsistent with his life style. When Thomas Jefferson went to France, he took James Hemings with him and later on called for another slave to join him over there too. Surely, for the much shorter trip to Washington, he must have taken many if not all of his personal servants from Monticello.

The interview of Israel Jefferson published in 1873 says that his 'earliest recollections are the exciting events attending the preparations of Mr. Jefferson and other members of his family on their removal to Washington.' Although this interview has been attacked on the grounds that Israel Jefferson was just a baby and too young to remember this, still, it seems likely, knowing Thomas Jefferson's life style, that the entire family did in fact move to Washington.

Now, the question is: What exactly is the 'entire family'?

The actual acknowledged family of Thomas Jefferson at that point was just himself and his two daughters, Martha and Maria. However, Martha, also known as Patsy, had married in 1790 and Maria, also known as Polly, had married in 1797. Thus, Thomas Jefferson was alone, except for his slaves. While Martha was living near Monticello with her husband, the evidence is that she stayed there and did not go to Washington while Thomas Jefferson was president, except for brief visits, or to accompany her husband, when he was elected to Congress. In the latter capacity, she gave birth to a child in the White House in 1806.

Therefore, either Thomas Jefferson went alone to Washington, or else he took along at least some of his slaves. Throughout his life, Thomas Jefferson was a man who was always surrounded by an entourage of his people. His slaves were his family. It seems inconceivable that he would have left his slaves alone at Monticello with nothing to do and condemned himself to eight years of solitary confinement in the spacious but empty White House.

There is ample proof that at least one of his female slaves, Edy, was with him in the White House. This comes, in part, in the form of a letter dated July 31, 1806, from Thomas Jefferson to Joe Daugherty, apparently a police constable of some sort. At that time, Thomas Jefferson was at Monticello on a temporary visit. He wrote a letter to Daugherty to report that a young mulatto man named Joe had run away from Monticello and was on his way to the President's House to see his wife, Edy. 'He may possibly trump up some story to be taken care of at the President's house . . . . or perhaps he may make himself known to Edy only as he was formerly connected with her,' wrote Jefferson. Daugherty was instructed to search all of Washington and Georgetown for this man and, if he was apprehended, to take him into custody. Daugherty was also warned by Jefferson, 'If you can find him, have aid with you to take him, as he is strong and resolute . . . .'

On August 3, 1806, Daugherty reported back that indeed the man had been apprehended in the White House yard on his way out of the White House and 'being informed of his very marks and clothing . . . . I knew it must be him. I immediately took him and brought him to Mr. Perry and has him now in jail. Mr. Perry will start him home tomorrow for Monticello.'

From this, we know that Edy was in the White House. In all likelihood, Sally and many of the other household slaves from Monticello were there as well.

This Joe who was in the White House was the same as 'Joe 80', later known as Joe Fossett, who is listed in many places in the *Farm Book* as the husband of Edy. In spite of being arrested in 1806, Joe may have nevertheless already accomplished his purpose. Their next daughter, Maria, was born the following year. Thus, we have the first confirmed proof of: SEX IN THE WHITE HOUSE. Perhaps, this should go in the official White House records.

On the other hand, one person has suggested that Thomas Jefferson may have been the father of the children born to Edy while she was in the White House. It is said that he bought a coffin in Washington for the funeral of James, a son of Edy, who died while Jefferson was president.

Incidentally, Joe and Edy had a total of seven children, most of whom were born after the incident in question. These were James, born in 1805 (who apparently died), Maria 1807, Patsy 1810, Betsy 1812, Peter 1815, Isabella 1819, and William 1821. Surprisingly, Joe was one of the five slaves later on ordered to be freed by Thomas Jefferson in his will. Even more surprisingly, several descendants of Joe later on became famous.

Joe was the son of Mary, the oldest daughter of Betty Hemings, and, according to a number of sources, of William Fossett, a white apprentice who worked at Monticello for a time. This is the reason that he came to be known as 'Joe Fossett'. However, as will be seen, it can be virtually proven that William Fossett was not the father of Joe Fossett, because Joe was conceived while his mother, Mary, was in Richmond with Thomas Jefferson, who was the governor of Virginia from 1779 to 1781. Mary apparently never went to Monticello during this period. Joe Fossett was the great-grandfather of William Monroe Trotter, who co-founded the NAACP.

In the *Farm Book* for 1801, there is a list of 60 'Negroes leased to J.H. Craven.' These were all field hands. There is also a list of 'Negroes Retained', which included Sally and all of the other mulattos at Monticello. Apparently, Thomas Jefferson leased his land and his field slaves while he was president, which is understandable.

There is almost no doubt that Sally was at Monticello for at least some of the time when Thomas Jefferson was president. There is an undated memorandum from the period of 1806 from Thomas Jefferson to his overseer Edmund Bacon which states in part, 'Mrs. [Martha Jefferson] Randolph always chooses the clothing for the house servants; that is to say, for Peter Hemings, Burwell, Edwin, Critta, and Sally. Colored plains are provided for Betty Brown, Betty Hemings, Nance, Ursula, and indeed all the others. The nailers, laborers and hirelings may have it, if they prefer it to cotton. . . . .'

Bacon started working at Monticello in 1806, so these appear to have been instructions issued when he commenced work. From this, it appears that Sally was probably at Monticello at that time, but this was understandable. She had just given birth to Madison Hemings in 1805. Thomas Jefferson may have flagrantly kept a concubine in the White House, but he would not keep her there with a newborn child of which he was obviously the father. Thus, he would have sent her back to Monticello.

In fact, Thomas Jefferson wrote a thousand letters from the White House to Monticello while he was President, but this memorandum, which was not actually a letter, seems to be the only one which gives any instructions regarding Sally Hemings. Again, this seems to indicate that she was mostly with him during this period.

Another point concerns the fact that when the story broke in the newspapers, it spread like wildfire. Thomas Jefferson kept many women of child-bearing age at Monticello. There was Betty Brown, Ursula, Edy, Mary, Critta, Lucretia and even Betty Hemings, the mother of Sally and of Betty Brown. Why did the newspapers always talk about Sally Hemings? Why not the others?

Unlike today, most newspapers were not going to send a team of investigative reporters to invade the privacy of Monticello to dig up some dirt about the president currently in office. Only the Lynchburg *Virginia Gazette* sent somebody, who interviewed the neighbors and reported back 'nothing but proofs of their authenticity'. For the other newspapers to publish this story, the evidence must have been right there in front of their eyes. Sally Hemings must have been in the White House at that time, plainly for everybody to see. It has been reported that for a time Sally Hemings was the most famous woman of color in the entire United States of America.

In addition, there are many indications that Martha Jefferson Randolph did not like having Sally Hemings around and often pressed her father to sell her or get rid of her in some way. Thus, the forces where strongly pushing Thomas Jefferson to divest himself of Sally Hemings. The press and the general public were accusing her of being his concubine. In addition, his own daughter was pressing him to have her gotten rid of. However, Thomas Jefferson refused to budge. He was not going to get rid of Sally Hemings, no matter what. Indeed, he kept her with him for the remainder of his life.

There is only one reason why a man acts in that way regarding a woman. The reason is obvious.

# Chapter Nine

## Descendants of Betty Hemings and John Wayles

Thomas Jefferson kept many women with him at Monticello, not only Sally. This is the reason that he was accused in the press of maintaining a 'Congo Harem'. It seems that many if not all of them were mulattos. The slaves who were purely black worked in the fields. Those who were partly white served in the house.

Thomas Jefferson was fascinated with the term 'mulatto'. After the arrival of Sally Hemings in France, he often used the word 'mulatto' to describe the color of the fields or other items in nature.

He also did some mathematical equations involving the term: mulatto. On January 1, 1787, a law came into effect in Virginia which provided that a mulatto was any person who was partly white but at least 25% black. Anybody less than 25% black was white. Thus, Sally Hemings was a mulatto, but any children she had from a white father were white.

From this, Thomas Jefferson posed several mathematical problems. What if a person who is half white marries a person who is seven-eighths white and one-eighth black? What will the children be?

The answer is that the children will be five-sixteenths black, which will make them a mulatto. The reader should try to solve this problem.

Another question is: What if one parent is one-quarter black and the other is one-eighth black, what will the children be? The answer is that the children will be three-sixteenths black or, in other words, white.

Thomas Jefferson had a complicated method for solving this problem. However, there is a much simpler way. Just count the great- grandparents.

The person who is one-eighth black had eight great-grandparents. One was black. Seven were white.

The person who is one quarter black had eight great-grandparents. Six were white. Two were black.

Therefore, the resulting child has 16 great-great-grandparents. Of these, three were black and 13 were white. Therefore, the resulting child is 3/16 th black, which is white. Black is white.

Thomas Jefferson was quite interested in this problem. It is hoped that the reader will find it equally amusing.

Getting back to Betty Hemings: She was the matriarch in all this. However, not all the children in the house were hers. There was, for example, Lucretia who was purchased from the outside. No photographs have survived of any of these slaves, except for a photograph of Isaac Jefferson, so there is no way to know if Lucretia was or was not a mulatto. However, it is mentioned in her purchase agreement that she was the wife of Jame, so Lucretia was already some sort of relative and was purchased to reunite a family.

From what we know of Thomas Jefferson, it is probably true that each and every one of his household servants was a mulatto. In other words, none were pure black. To prove this, we should try to establish who these people were.

Almost all of them were the descendants and relatives of Betty Hemings. Working backward, we can try to figure out the line of descent.

According to the statement of Madison Hemings, Betty Hemings had a total of 14 children from four different fathers. Of these, 11 survived. Two of the children who died were of the original slave husband. The third was her last born child, Lucy.

It is possibly incorrect to say that two of the children by the original slave husband of Betty Hemings died. Perhaps, they did not exist at all. James A. Bear, who has researched this subject, can find no trace of those two children. However, another source says that those two children were inherited by Tabitha Wayles, a daughter by the second wife of John Wayles. Tabitha Wayles married Henry Skipwith.

In either event, those two children of Betty Hemings were never heard from again. Whether they died at an early age or not becomes immaterial.

One of the grandsons of Tabitha Wayles Skipwith was a man named William Henry Harrison, who was a cousin of the President of the United States by that name. This means that Presidents William Henry Harrison and Benjamin Harrison are both distant in-laws and relatives of Sally Hemings and the rest of the Hemings family.

Again, the husband of Tabitha Wayles was Henry Skipwith. This brings up another problem. Several sources give the name of second wife of John Wayles as being Tabitha Cocke. However, there were many persons named Tabitha Cocke, but none of them were married to John Wayles. The Cocke family, which is hardly remembered today, was one of the first families of Virginia. It was established in Virginia by the early date of 1620. This family married into many prominent families of Virginia, including the families of Lee and Randolph.

The Cocke family is perhaps the biggest and the best documented family in the early history of Virginia. There are dozens of books and articles about them. If any member of the Cocke family had married an important person like John Wayles, that fact would surely be mentioned in one of the Cocke family histories. Thus, we conclude that it is incorrect to say that John Wayles ever married a person named Tabitha Cocke.

There was another family in Virginia called the Cooke family, which was entirely different. (Look carefully). That was a family of some importance, but of much less importance than the Cocke family. The Cooke family was founded by Mordecai Cooke and was possibly Jewish. That is more likely to have been the family which provided the second wife of John Wayles.

Confusion between these two families no longer exists because many members of the Cocke family changed their name to 'Cox' whereas many members of the Cooke family changed their name to 'Cook'.

Nobody will ever know who the second wife of John Wayles really was, or even if he actually had an additional wife beyond the two we know about. This is a safe statement to make, because genealogists have been searching diligently for the name of that additional wife for the past one hundred years. Not only has her name never been found, but most of those searching are long since dead.

Fawn Brodie claims that Tabitha Wayles, the daughter of this mysterious middle wife, married Robert Skipwith, not Henry Skipwith. Brodie bases this statement solely upon a letter from Thomas Jefferson to Robert Skipwith dated September 20, 1771 in which he referred to 'dear Tibby . . . . the first in your affection, the second in mine.' However, this does not prove that they were married. The will of John Wayles, which is included in the appendix, does leave 250 pounds to Robert Skipwith, but does not say that he was a son-in-law. Henry Skipwith was a witness to that will.

Here is the latest, most up-to-date word on this important subject, published in 1925. It comes from *Tyler's Quarterly Historical and Genealogical Magazine*, Richmond, Virginia, Vol. 6, p. 266:

> *Mr. Wayles was born in Lancashire, England, in 1715, and, after studying law, came to Virginia, where he lived in Charles City County and had an extensive practice in the colonial courts. He called his residence 'The Forest' and was King's attorney in 1756. Mr. Randall, in his Life of Jefferson, says that he was married three times, but we have proof of only two wives. One of these was Martha Eppes, widow, daughter of Col. Francis Eppes of Bermuda Hundred. Mr. Randall says that she was a widow of Llewellen Eppes, Clerk of Charles City County, but this cannot be, as Llewellen Eppes did not die until 1759 and Martha Wayles, the daughter, was born in 1748. She might have been the widow of Col. Littlebury Eppes, father of Llewellen, for he died in 1743, according to the records in Charles City County.*

The other wife of John Wayles was Elizabeth Lomax, widow of Reuben Skelton, brother of Bathurst Skelton. John Wayles married her in 1760, but his will made shortly thereafter during the same year names four children: Martha, Elizabeth, Tabitha and Anne; and the 'Lomax family genealogy' states that Elizabeth Lomax Wayles died without issue.

It is accepted that Elizabeth, Tabitha, and Anne were half sisters of Martha, and who then was their mother? It is a fair guess, but they have names that suggest descent from Col. Ebenezar Adams, of New Kent County. Perhaps she was omitted from the registrar of his children. It is known that the second wife of Richard Eppes, brother of Martha Eppes–Wayles, was Tabitha Adams, one of the daughters of Col. Adams. The will of John Wayles was dated 15 April 1760 and had two codicils, one made March 5, 1772 and the other of February 2, 1773.

His daughter Elizabeth married Francis Eppes (brother of his wife Martha Eppes) of 'Eppington', Chesterfield County, born 1747 died July 4, 1808 and had issue (1) John Wayles and (2) Richard (3) Lucy (4) Mary (5) Martha.

His daughter Anne married Col. Henry Skipwith of Cumberland County and had Elizabeth, who married Edmund Harrison."

One reason for providing the full quotation above is that it illustrates the problems in tracing any family history during this period. At that time, it was customary for cousins to marry. In the quotation above, we see an even closer marriage. Elizabeth Wayles, daughter of John Wayles and Martha Eppes, married her uncle, Col. Francis Eppes. This Elizabeth Wayles was same person as the 'Aunt Eppes' mentioned by Maria Jefferson in her letter to her father in 1786. The first born son, John Wayles Eppes, mentioned above, became the husband of Maria Jefferson.

One commentator has referred to this as 'vaguely incestuous'. However, this is not 'vaguely incestuous'; this is actual incest, prohibited by modern law. Yet, it was commonly practiced at that time.

However, looking carefully, the marriage between Elizabeth Wayles and Francis Eppes was barely legal, because that wife of John Wayles was apparently not the same wife who was the mother of Elizabeth Eppes.

The need to work out the exact details of such relationships is what drove this author to purchase a computer program designed for genealogy for the purpose of preparing this book. These relations are so complex and confusing, that it would be virtually impossible for anyone to keep them in their head.

Another point to note from the quotation above is that when searching for a possible spouse to somebody, researchers immediately start checking all of the cousins and other close relatives. This makes it somewhat easier to find the spouse, because few persons in those days married into the general population. Almost all of them married relatives of some kind.

It has been noted that Henry Skipwith married Tabitha Wayles. It seems that he also married Anne Wayles, her sister. This was not unusual. One sister died, so he married the next one, a common practice in those days.

In this case, it is not completely certain that Henry Skipwith married both Tabitha Wayles and Anne Wayles. Unfortunately, the record of the marriage of Tabitha Wayles has been lost. The reason for this is that 'The Forest', the estate of John Wayles, was burned by the Union Army during the Civil War because the owner of The Forest at that time, Mr. Talman, was a Confederate spy. (At least his place in heaven is secure.) The Forest was near to the present Westover Church in Charles City County, which was attended by John Wayles. The same Union army destroyed the records of the Charles City Courthouse, including the marriage records, although some scattered records have survived, including documents showing the marriage between Henry Skipwith and Anne Wayles on July 7, 1773.

The Mr. Talman who was a Confederate spy was probably a member of the Taliaferro family, as some members of that family changed their name to Talman.

In any event, there is no way to determine who the second wife of John Wayles was. Ebenezar Adams had a wife named Tabitha Cocke. She was born in 1718, making her about the right age, but she did not marry John Wayles. She was busy producing eight children for Ebenezar Adams.

In fact, we just assume that because John Wayles had three daughters unaccounted for that he therefore must have had a wife we don't know about. Illegitimate births did not often happen in those days and, if they did happen, the father was not likely to acknowledge the child, much less three of them. Another possibility suggests itself. Perhaps John Wayles was already married when he came from England, and these daughters are from that marriage. Unfortunately, this cannot be correct. It is clear from the will of John Wayles that Martha Wayles was the oldest of his four surviving daughters.

What difference does it make? The difference is that these two daughters of John Wayles, Tabitha and Anne, married into famous family lines which led to cousins of President William Henry Harrison and President Benjamin Harrison and, going in another direction, into the Robertson family, which provided us with recent long-term United States Senator Willis Robertson of Virginia, and his son, a famous evangelical preacher.

John Wayles was one of the most active lawyers in Virginia at that time. His name appears as attorney of record on many court documents. He was admitted to the practice of law in Virginia in September, 1746, see *Virginia Historical Magazine*, Vol. 22, p. 435 (1914), although his name appears in a court document dated as early as 1744. He represented three infant children named Ward in a suit against their step-mother for their rightful share of the inheritance. He also represented John Chiswell, who had murdered John Routledge in 1766, but who got off because the grand jury failed to return a true bill of indictment. Chiswell committed suicide three months later. John Wayles was a also signer of the Williamsburg Declaration of June 22, 1770, which protested commercial actions of the British. He was also active in the slave trade.

Disaster struck in 1771 when a flood wiped out the holdings of both John Wayles and Thomas Mann Randolph Senior on their islands in the James River. The original colonists preferred to settle on islands, such as Turkey Island. Later colonists settled in the forest, which is the reason that John Wayles called his original estate 'The Forest'. On May 30, 1771, the Lynchburg *Virginia Gazette* reported that everything on Farrar's Island belonging to Thomas Mann Randolph and everything but the people and five horses on Elk Island belonging to John Wayles had been carried away by the river. The loss to John Wayles alone was estimated at four thousand pounds.

John Wayles was, of course, the father of Sally Hemings. Previously, Betty Hemings had had a black slave husband, who died. Betty had six children from him, two of whom may have died. She then had six children by John Wayles, her owner. All survived. The last one was Sally Hemings, who was born at just about the time that John Wayles died, which was on May 23, 1773.

After Thomas Jefferson became the new owner of Betty, she had two more children. One was the child of a white carpenter named Neilson, who worked briefly for Thomas Jefferson. The child was named John, who also became a carpenter. John Hemings became an important person at Monticello and is believed to have made much of the furniture there.

The last child, Lucy, was the child of an unidentified slave. She was born in 1777 and died nine years later, while Thomas Jefferson was in France.

Betty Hemings died at Monticello in 1807 at the age of 72 and was buried in an unmarked grave. An arrow pointing in the direction of the 'Betty Hemings house' was noted on a map of Monticello.

Going back, the original surviving four children of Betty Hemings and the years of their birth were Mary 1753, Martin 1755 or 1756, Bett 1759 and Nancy 1761. Of these, Bett and Nancy were still alive and living at Monticello when Thomas Jefferson died in 1826. Nancy is recorded in the final inventory of Thomas Jefferson's estate in 1827 as 'an old woman with no value'. Martin died in 1807.

Next, there were six children born from John Wayles. These were: Robert (1762–1819), James (1765–1801), Thenia (1767–1795+), Critta (1769–1827+), Peter (1770–1827+), and Sally (1773–1835). Lastly, there were John (1775–

1827+) and Lucy (1777–1786).

Thus, among the 11 surviving children, seven had white fathers and four had black fathers. Those with black fathers were 25% white; those with white fathers were 75% white.

Among the four with black fathers, two were sold. Mary was sold at her own request to Colonel Thomas Bell, Jefferson's friend, in 1792. Martin had a disagreement with Thomas Jefferson and was also sold at his own request. However, it appears that Martin traveled about freely, as did Robert, to such an extent that Thomas Jefferson often did not know where they were. In 1783, Jefferson wrote a letter to a friend in Richmond which stated: 'If you should know anything of my servants Martin and Bob could you give them notice to be at Monticello by the 20th. I should be obliged.'

Among the children of John Wayles, Thenia was much later sold and became the property of future president James Monroe. Critta was also apparently sold. On this point, James A. Bear, a researcher in this field, appears to have possibly made a mistake. Critta was the mother of Jamy, born in 1787. She was not the mother of James Hubbard, also known as Jamy, a trouble maker, who was born in 1783. The confusion arises because both of these slaves named Jamy ran away within one year of each other. Nevertheless, there can be no doubt that these were two different people. This understandable error by a careful researcher shows how difficult research into this subject with so many people having similar names can be. Adding to the confusion, there is another Jame Hubbard, born in 1743, who is on the list of slaves received from the estate of John Wayles in 1774, and who lived at Bedford until at least 1810. It is generally assumed that this James Hubbard was the father of the other James Hubbard, but there is nothing in the *Farm Book* indicating this. At one point, there were at least five slaves named James, and possibly as many as seven or eight. Everybody who has tried to sort them out has made errors.

Since every other authority has repeated this error, this point must be emphasized. There are perhaps ten different entries in the *Farm Book* showing that Critta was not the mother of James Hubbard. The confusion between these two is probably due to the fact that James, the son of Critta, ran away in April, 1804, whereas James Hubbard ran away for the first of two times in September, 1805.

Moving on to the next generation: Betty Brown (1759–1827+) was the most important producer of children. Her children were Billy (1777–1778), Wormley (b. 1780), Burwell (b. Dec. 24, 1783), Brown (b. Dec 25, 1785), Edwin (b. Nov. 2, 1793), Robert (b. Dec. 22, 1799) and Mary (1801).

There is no record of Betty Brown ever having a husband. Perhaps this has led to the speculation that Thomas Jefferson might also be the father of some of these children. This is probably not true but certainly not impossible.

Nancy or Nance apparently had one child.

Critta gave birth to Jamy on April 23, 1787. Jamy ran away in 1804.

Mary gave birth to Joe in 1780 and to Betsy in 1783. Betsy died in 1857 in Buckingham County, Virginia.

Wormley was another important person at Monticello. His wife was Ursula, who was born in 1787. Their children were Joe (1805), Anna (1807), Dolly (1809), Cornelius (1811), Thomas (1813), Louisa (1816), Caroline (1818), Critta (1819) and George (1823).

Other major producers on the farm were Mary, the wife of Moses, born in 1780. (Her name is also listed in several places as Mary Moses'). She produced Billy or William (1801) who died, Davy (1803), Caelia (1806), Tucker (1810), Zacharia (1812), Patsy (1815), Fossett (1817) and Fontaine (1819).

Lucretia was the wife of James, a foreman. The list of her seven children is provided elsewhere.

Joe, son of Mary, and Edy produced seven children. There are several persons named Edy, but this is the one born in 1787. She became a member of the White House staff by the time she was 18.

Davey and Fanny had four children: Ellen (1809), Jenny (1811), Melinda (1817) and Indridge (1819).

Jerry and Isabel gave birth to Jupiter on 1804.

In 1816, Thomas Jefferson gave Edwin, Maria and James to his son-in-law, Thomas Mann Randolph, Jr. He further gave Moses and Johnny to him in 1819. Because of the possibility of other people by these names, it is not certain exactly who these people were. However, Edwin was certainly the son of Betty Brown, as there was no other person named Edwin on the farm.

This is only a partial listing. One of the last inventories before Thomas Jefferson died showed a total of 187 slaves, mostly at Monticello in Albemarle County and at Poplar Forest in Bedford County. There is a clear trend showing that all those at Poplar Forest were pure black and were used as field hands, whereas those at Monticello were at least partly white and had various other tasks, but did not work in the fields. However, there is no firm proof of this.

The last list which clearly separates the slaves at Monticello from the other slaves on the farm is dated 1817 and is found on page 156 of the *Farm Book*. It lists 47 slaves at Monticello. Most of these have already been mentioned above.

Families involving slave husband, wife and children are bracketed together. For example, there is the following listing: [Wormley Ursula & Louisa Joe Anne Dolly Cornelius Thomas]. At first glance, it looks like Wormley has now acquired a second wife named Louisa. However, more careful examination shows that this is just a mistake. Louisa was only born in 1816 and Thomas Jefferson must have forgotten to include her when he wrote out the list and squeezed her name in later. This sort of thing often happens in the *Farm Book*. A list of names is made as of a certain date, and then sometimes years later there are additions, deletions and corrections made. For example, if a person's name is crossed off a list, this means that either the person died, was sold or ran away. If the person died, the year of death is given.

Here is a complete list of the 47 names on the 1817 Monticello house list (families are included in brackets): [Betty Brown, Mary], Billy B., Burwell, Caesar, Critta, [Davy jun?, Fanney, Ellen, Jenny, Ned, Gill, Israel], Dolly, [Joe, Edy, James, Maria, Patsy, Betsy, and Peter], John Hemings, John gardener, Lewis, [Moses, Mary, William, Davy, Caelia, Tucker, Zacharia, Pasty], Nancy, Peter Hemings, [Sally, Beverly, Harriet, Madison, Eston], [Wormley, Ursula & Louisa, Joe, Anne, Dolly, Cornelius, Thomas].

Note that the listing is in exact alphabetical order, except that, in the case of families, the first name in brackets is the husband, next the wife and finally the children in the order of birth.

It is important to note that among these families, there are only two without a husband. These are the families of Betty Brown and of Sally.

On this subject, there are several hints that Betty Brown might also have been a concubine of Thomas Jefferson. Indeed, when this story is being told by old people around Lynchburg, they often give 'Betsy' as the name of the concubine of Thomas Jefferson, not Sally.

In addition, there is a quote from a letter by Henry Stephens Randall, Jefferson's most important 19th-century biographer, which stated that Thomas Jefferson was not the father of the children in question and that Sally was Peter's mistress and her sister, Betsy, was Samuel's mistress. The letter further stated that their 'connection with the Carrs was perfectly notorious at Monticello.'

From this letter, it can be inferred that it was being alleged that Thomas Jefferson had two concubines: Sally and Betsy. Betsy was probably Betty Brown, the older half sister of Sally. There were two people named Betsy on the farm, one born in 1783 and the other born in 1812. Neither was the sister of Sally. Also, the name of the Betsy who was born in 1783 disappears from the farm list after 1796, so it is not likely that she was a concubine of Thomas Jefferson. She was given in dowry to his daughter, Maria, in 1797 and went to live far from Monticello.

By 1817, most of the children of Betty Brown were grown up and had gone away or been sent elsewhere, as in the case of Edwin, or had their own places on the list, as in the case of Burwell and Wormley.

Billy B. is apparently not Billy Brown, who died in 1778, but a Billy Bed. born in 1799. His mother was Hannah, a devoted black slave at Poplar Forest and at nearby Tomahawk, which is now inside the current boundaries of the

City of Lynchburg. It is not clear how Billy Bed. (probably for Bedford County where Poplar Forest and Tomahawk were located) made it to Monticello, but he was there as early as 1813.

On the subject of Hannah, she wrote a remarkable letter to Thomas Jefferson dated November 15, 1818. Slaves were not even supposed to know how to read and write at that time. This is just about the only letter any slave ever wrote to Thomas Jefferson, with the exception of the many letters written by John Hemings. The letter from Hannah said, in part:

> *Master I write you a few lines to let you know that your house and furniture are all safes I expect you will be glad to know I heard that you did not expect to come up that fall I was sorry to hear that you are so unwell you could not come it grieve me many time but I hope as you have been so blessed in this that you considered it was God that done it and no other one we all ought to be thankful for what he has done for us we ought to serve and obey his commandments that you may set to win the prize and after glory run. . . . . adieu, I am your humble servant Hannah.*

Incidentally, there is no record of Hannah ever having a husband either for most of her child-bearing years. In view of the fact that her son Billy was later transferred to Monticello, there is the distinct likelihood that he had a white father. Just who that white father may have been is anybody's guess.

Hannah was born in 1770. Her mother was Cate, who was born in 1747. Hannah had a total of nine children, but, with the exception of Billy B., all of them remained with her at Tomahawk. These were: Lucinda (1791), Reuben (1793), Solomon (1794), Sally (1798), Billy B. (1799), Jany (1805), Phil (1808), Edmund (1809), and George Deli' (1812). Deli' appears to be the father of George. The others do not have fathers listed.

There was another Sally named Sally Marks, who was a maid and a valued nurse. Many writers have confused Sally Marks with Sally Hemings. Sally Marks was much younger. Many letters were written about her. Although legally a slave, she was treated more like an employee. She worked in the homes of wealthy families. It seems that in about 1827, one of her employers, a university professor named Thomas Key, was moving back to England and wanted to take Sally Marks along as a nurse. However, Sally Marks may have preferred to remain as a slave in North Carolina, instead of going to England, where she knew that she would be free. Because she is frequently confused with Sally Hemings, this has added considerable confusion to the different versions of the entire story. The story of Sally Marks can be found in detail in *Monticello, A Family Story*, by Elizabeth Langhorne.

No birth date is given in the *Farm Book* for Sally Marks, apparently because she was not born as the slave of Thomas Jefferson, and therefore he did not know her age. In seems that she was a late arrival at Monticello. Judith P. Justus, in her 1991 book, *Down From the Mountain*, p.127-8, suggests the theory that Sally Marks was originally owned by Hastings Marks, whose wife was Ann Scott Jefferson, one of the many sisters of Thomas Jefferson. After Hastings Marks died, Anna Scott Jefferson came to live at Monticello, bringing Sally Marks with her. Anna Scott Jefferson died in 1828. With the exception of Anna Scott Jefferson, Thomas Jefferson far outlived all of his brothers and sisters. The theory that Sally Marks was actually the slave of Anna Scott Jefferson might best explain the fact that the name of Sally Marks first appears on page 171 of the *Farm Book*, which is for the year 1821.

A fact little known prior to 1980 was that in addition to his estate at Monticello, Thomas Jefferson had a second estate at Poplar Forest. He had inherited the land from John Wayles, but it had no buildings of consequence at that time. Poplar Forest was used as farm land, where the slaves toiled in the fields.

However, Thomas Jefferson planned a palatial estate on that property, just as big or perhaps bigger and better than Monticello. Only starting in 1980 has serious excavation and restoration work been done on Poplar Forest.

Actual construction of Poplar Forest started in 1806. The literature about Poplar Forest mentions that the original floor plans were done by John Neilson and much of the work was directed by John Hemings, a slave. Nowhere is it mentioned that these were actually father and son.

It appears from the correspondence that John Hemings, a slave, was actually the boss man in charge of the construction at Poplar Forest. He clearly was something more than a mere slave. The last exchange of correspondence between John Hemings and Thomas Jefferson took place in August, 1825. John Hemings wrote his last letter to Thomas Jefferson reporting the progress of the work on August 15, 1825. Thomas Jefferson died on July 4, 1826, less than one year later.

Poplar Forest was substantially complete by 1820, or at least sufficiently so to enable Thomas Jefferson to invite a bunch of guests to dinner there in that year. However, construction work continued until the death of Thomas Jefferson.

The fact that Thomas Jefferson was in the process of trying to complete a grand new estate with slave labor when he was over 80 years old at a point when he was on the verge of being forced into bankruptcy shows his lack of realism. It is clear that he never would have sold his land or his slaves until forced by the courts to do so. On October 18, 1820, he wrote a letter to Henry Clark which stated: 'Your favor of Oct. 4 is received. You have been quite misinformed as to my having any intention to lease my possessions in Bedford. Nothing could induce me to put my negroes out of my protection.'

The Poplar Forest property in Bedford was occupied by his grandson,

Francis Eppes, in 1823. However, it was sold in 1829, shortly after the death of Thomas Jefferson, presumably to pay his debts. Francis Eppes moved to Florida. Poplar Forest would have been demolished in 1980 had it not been rescued by a historical society.

John Hemings was an important person, perhaps the most important of all of the slaves, not counting the special contribution made by Sally Hemings. This is clearly the reason why he was on the list of five to be freed upon the death of Thomas Jefferson.

In a 1961 article in the *Journal of Negro History*, XLIV, p. 89- 103, there is an article by Pearl N. Graham entitled *Thomas Jefferson and Sally Hemings*. This article contains the interviews of four elderly women who were still members of the black community (i.e., they had not turned white), who were all born in Charlottesville but who were then living in New Jersey.

These women all claimed to be descendants of Sally Hemings and Thomas Jefferson. However, careful study of the documents they possessed indicated that actually they were all descendants of John Hemings, Sally's younger half-brother. The fact that they were born in Charlottesville also indicates this. The children of Sally Hemings all moved out of Virginia, settling in Washington, D.C., Ohio and Wisconsin.

Regarding the overall question of what happened to all of the descendants of Betty Hemings and her children including Betty Brown, Sally Hemings, John Hemings and the others, this requires major research. The *Farm Book* provides a wealth of hand written information, but that is only the beginning.

Fortunately, there are people willing to do the work and who are actively working on this subject. These are the black descendants of Tom Hemings (Woodson), Madison Hemings and possibly Eston Hemings.

It is known that Eston Hemings married a nice Jewish mulatto girl named Julia and eventually moved to Madison, Wisconsin. He thereafter started using the name of Jefferson, a more suitable name considering the fact that he was probably Thomas Jefferson's son. His descendants still live there and consider themselves white.

Unfortunately, the other white descendants of Sally Hemings are not working on this subject. Presumably, they are cowering in fear of being discovered to be part black. These would be the descendants of Beverly Hemings and Harriet Hemings, who, according to Madison Hemings, married white people in Washington, D.C. By now, there should be almost no trace of any black blood left in them. Beverly and Harriet were already 7/8 ths white. Assuming that there have since been five additional pure white generations, by now they would be only one-two hundred fifty-sixth black (1/256). They would also be one- sixty fourth (1/64) descended from Thomas Jefferson.

In today's still racist society, they are probably not willing to declare themselves descended from Thomas Jefferson if that would also require them to admit that they are just a little bit black.

Consequently, there are those whose souls are wrenched with fear that the horrible secret of their ancestry, the fact that they are descendants of Thomas Jefferson, will be discovered.

Now it has been found out that Edward Graham Jefferson, the retired Chairman of the Board of the DuPont Chemical Corporation and former Director of Research and Development there, is secretly one of those descendants. He is still a member of the Board of Directors of DuPont and was re-elected in 1991. His father was named Edward Hemmings Jefferson of England.

A quote of Thomas Jefferson which is not often published is his statement that comparing a black man to a white man is like comparing a mule to a horse. This unflattering statement has something particularly noteworthy about it in the context of the Sally Hemings story.

A mule is to some remote extent the animal equivalent to a mulatto. A mule is half horse and half donkey. A mule is not as fast as a horse, but it is stronger and sturdier.

The example of the mule is often given as proof for the theory of the superiority of genetic diversity. A mule will be stronger and better than either of his parents, the horse and the donkey. According to the same theory, a mulatto should be better than either of his white or black parents.

Jefferson was obviously fascinated by this well known concept, for good reason.

The white family of Thomas Jefferson was intermarried to an unacceptable degree. His mother was Jane Randolph. His daughter, Martha, married Thomas Mann Randolph, Jr. His mother-in-law, the wife of John Wayles, was Martha Eppes. His daughter, Maria, married John Wayles Eppes, whose mother had been married to her cousin.

One reason for this was the dowry system. At a time when large dowries were passed back and forth at the time of marriage, there was a tendency to marry within the family to keep the money from leaving the family. Even in countries today where the dowry system is still going on, such as India, for example, there is a tendency to marry within the family.

Now, look at the results of this invidious practice. Thomas Jefferson had six children from his wife Martha. Four died in childhood. Of the two surviving daughters, Maria had three children. Two died in childhood. Maria herself died at age 26. Only his daughter, Martha, lived a normal life span. The wife of Thomas Jefferson also died young.

Look at John Wayles. He had three wives. All died. He had seven children from his wives. Three died. Four survived.

These are not unusual examples. Look at the histories of the Kings of England. Almost all of them died as teen-agers or in their early twenties. Remember, these were the ones who lived long enough to become the king. Many of the members of the British Royal family died young, often as children.

Now, just look at Betty Hemings. She had seven children from white fathers. All lived, grew up strong and healthy, and all but possibly one produced children of their own, who produced more children, all strong and healthy.

Of six known children of Sally Hemings, only one is really known to have died. The rest all grew up and produced their own children. One of these alone has a thousand persons who claim him as their ancestor.

The conclusion is clear. The strong survived. The weak died out. The descendants of Betty Hemings are all around us under various assumed names; many of them became successful. We probably see them every day without realizing who they are. On the other hand, the Randolph and Eppes families, with all the money, land and power they controlled two hundred years ago, have almost completely died out now. There are still a few around, but only a vague remnant of the past.

As for Thomas Jefferson himself, he deserves full credit for everything he did. His human weaknesses, which all of us, or almost all of us, share, should be overlooked. Among all the prominent people of his time, he was the only one to campaign prominently against slavery. His reasons for doing that are irrelevant. It is the bottom line that counts.

As for his apparent tendency to father children by his own slaves, we go back to the original quote from Frederick Douglass, who apparently copied it from a statement by Dr. Levi Gaylord in 1838, when he said, 'The best blood of Virginia flows in the veins of the slaves'.

# Chapter Ten

## What Happened to Tom?

The most critical item of importance in this entire question concerns the existence of Tom Hemings, the first born son of Sally Hemings.

The existence of Tom was first revealed in a newspaper article by James Callender dated September 1, 1802 in the *Richmond Recorder*. Callender called him 'President Tom' and claimed that he had an exact 'sable' likeness to Thomas Jefferson. Immediately, defenders of Thomas Jefferson attacked this story. They said that there was no Tom, nor was there even a Sally. At a later date, a mob attacked and beat up the editor who published the story, and the next day the body of Callender himself was found dead in the waters of the James River.

One point which is constantly made is that there is no mention of a child named Tom in the *Farm Book*. His birth is not recorded there, nor is his name included on any list of slaves.

There are many possible explanations for this. Madison Hemings, born 15 years after Tom, said that he died in infancy. Others suggest that he was never a slave and therefore was not on the list. The names of Martha and Maria Jefferson, the legitimate daughters of Thomas and Martha Wayles Jefferson, are nowhere mentioned in the *Farm Book*, and possibly for the same reason Tom was not mentioned.

Nevertheless, there have been enough confirmed sightings of this Tom that it seems hardly likely that he was a figment of the imagination.

The entire story turns on this. Tom was the child who was conceived in France and with whom Sally was pregnant when she arrived in America. If there was a Tom, then Thomas Jefferson almost certainly must have been the father. On the other hand, if there was never any Tom, then the entire story is still possible, but somewhat dubious.

Fortunately, we have in Washington, D.C. a woman named Minnie Shumate Woodson, who claims that her husband is a direct descendant of Tom. She has researched this subject extensively and has provided answers in such detail that it seems most unlikely that Tom never existed. She maintains a roster which contains the names of 1000 descendants of Tom. They hold reunions at which an average of 200 people attend. The next reunion is scheduled to be held in Richmond, Virginia, and in connection with that reunion they intend to visit Monticello.

The name of her book, *The Sable Curtain*, is obviously derived from the statement in the original newspaper article by James Thompson Callender that Tom 'bears an exact sable likeness to Thomas Jefferson.'

*The Sable Curtain* is, however, a novel, and therein lies its weakness. It was apparently not written for commercial publication. It was intended just for circulation among the family members. Probably, it has been far more successful than the author originally intended.

There are a number of errors in the book. However, the errors concern the causes, not the events themselves. Moreover, the author admits that she has no proof for some of her claims. She bases her novel on the oral family history which has been passed down from generation to generation in the style of *Roots*. She tried to write a novel based around the facts as she understands them.

What is clearly her biggest error comes in her statement that Tom had a disagreement with his father [Thomas Jefferson] and for that reason was sent away from the farm in 1802 or 1803. From everything we know about Thomas Jefferson, this is impossible. He never sent anybody away, much less his own son. To the contrary, he constantly collected more people and hung on to everything he had. Indeed, that was his big problem. He never knew when to let go.

At the same time, there is absolutely no doubt that Tom would have been sent away from the farm in 1802 or 1803, but for a different reason. October of 1802 was exactly when the scandal about Sally Hemings was breaking in every newspaper in America. Worse yet, according to reports, Tom Hemings looked exactly like his father, Thomas Jefferson. Sally Hemings could not be sent away because her presence was necessary, due to the vital services she was performing. However, Tom was clearly expendable. He had to be sent away or put out of sight.

Here is the story of Tom, as told by Minnie Shumate Woodson:

Tom was born in 1790, not at Monticello but rather at Shadwell, another farm owned by Thomas Jefferson, close to Monticello. Shadwell, in fact, was the farm where Thomas Jefferson himself was born.

Tom was sent away from Monticello when he was a young boy, about 12 or 13 years old.

Tom married Jemima, who was born in 1783 and was the slave daughter of a master named Drury Woodson of Cumberland County, Virginia. From that point on, Tom called himself Woodson rather than Hemings.

After the master-father of Jemima had died in 1788, she had been bequeathed to his legitimate daughter, Martha Woodson, who married Payton Riddle.

The first son of Tom and Jemima was born in Greenbrier County, Virginia in 1806. This is now in West Virginia. They lived for a time in what is now Lewisburg, West Virginia, which is in the mountains just across the border from Virginia. It must be remembered that West Virginia did not become an independent state until 1863, at the time of the Civil War. Prior to that time, the town was called Lewisburg, Virginia. This is in Greenbrier County. The mother of Jemima also lived there.

Thomas Woodson appears for the first time on the personal property tax records of the area of Lewisburg in 1820 as a lone 'white' male paying no tax. His wife is listed above him, paying tax on three horses. She and her children are listed in the 'Free persons of Color' section at the back of the personal property tax record of 1820. Probably they were listed separately because she was black and he was white and it was illegal for whites and blacks to be married at that time.

In 1829, they moved to Jackson County, Ohio. They settled in Chillicothe, Ohio. By coincidence, it happened that Madison and Eston Hemings settled in neighboring Pike County, Ohio after the death of their mother, Sally Hemings, in 1835. Eston also lived in Chillicothe at some point. There is no convincing evidence that Tom and Eston ever met or were aware of the presence of each other, however.

On the other hand, perhaps this was not a coincidence at all. Judith P. Justus, on page 41 of her book, presents evidence tending to show that Thomas Jefferson owned or at least had an interest in land in Chillicothe, Ohio. At that time, Ohio was not a state but was part of the NorthWest territories and was known as the 'Western Reserve'. Thomas Jefferson, while he never traveled there, was interested in developing this area and apparently paid tax on the ownership of land there. One of the acts of Thomas Jefferson while president was to admit Ohio as a state.

For this reason, it seems possible that it was not a coincidence that Tom Woodson, Madison and Eston all went to Chillicothe, Ohio. Perhaps Thomas Jefferson told them about the place and they all went there for that reason. Chillicothe, Ohio was also a major transit point for slaves on the run. A look at the map reveals the reason for this.

Thomas Woodson died in 1880 at the age of 90. The executor of his estate was his grandson, Rev. Thomas Wesley Woodson. His will and the name of his ancestor (Thomas Jefferson) were published by Richard B. Wright, Jr. in 1916 in the *Centennial Encyclopedia of the African Methodist Episcopal Church*, 631 Pine St., Philadelphia, Pa., pp. 255-256.

The basic details of this story ring true.

Tom was born in the early months of 1790. Callender describes him in September, 1802, as 'a boy of 10 or 12 years old'. In fact, he was 12 years old at the time. When he was 12 or 13 years old, he was sent away from Monticello. This is also logical. The scandal over Tom had broken at just that time. Thomas Jefferson was not going to send Sally Hemings away, because he needed her for a very personal reason. However, Tom clearly had to be gotten out of the way, or at least out of sight, so he was banished from Monticello. Perhaps he was given some money, because he was married at the age of only 16 to a woman seven years older. (This, of course, was a slave marriage, not likely to have been recorded in the county clerk's office.) It appears that he lied about his age, pretending to be older than he was. He did not reveal his true age until just before he died in 1880.

There is only one reference to a Tom, other than hired Toms, being at Monticello, and that is not to be found in the *Farm Book*. That comes in a letter from Martha Jefferson to her father dated January 22, 1798. In this important letter, she describes how, within a few days after Thomas Jefferson had left for Washington on December 4, 1797, two-year-old Harriet had died, but Tom and Goliah had eventually recovered from the illness from which they were all suffering. This is the only news we have about the death of the first Harriet.

The full text of that letter has been published in *The Family Letters of Thomas Jefferson*, Edited by Edwin Morris Betts and James A. Bear, pp. 153-154. However, their footnote contains an error. They say that Harriet died on October 5, 1797, whereas the actual date of the death of Harriet must have been a few days after December 4, 1797.

As for Tom and Goliah, there was an old man at Monticello named Tom Shackleford who worked as a driver. Some sources say that he was white, but he is listed on page 60 of the *Farm Book* and elsewhere as a 'Negro' slave. According to page 60 of the *Farm Book*, someone named Tom died in 1801. This was Tom Shackleford. There was also an old man named Goliah, born in 1831, and also a child aged six named Goliah.

This raises the question of whether the Tom and the Goliah who were sick were young or old.

It appears from the context that all three of these people who were sick in 1797 had the same disease, which was pleurisy, a childhood disease. If that is true, then Tom and Goliah must have been children. Thus, we have the Tom, the son of Sally, we have been looking for.

Other proof of the existence of Tom is speculative. One visitor to Monticello in around 1824 was told that only four slaves had ever been allowed to run away. Three we know about, two of which were Beverly and Harriet. There must have been one we don't know about. Perhaps that one was Tom.

However, this leads us nowhere, because there were several other slaves who ran away. According to page 60 of the *Farm Book*, a slave named James, the son of Critta, ran away in April, 1804. He apparently never came back. Then a different slave named James, this one being James Hubbard, ran away in September, 1805. He was caught, put in jail in Fairfax and returned. Later on, James Hubbard was caught stealing nails, which were being made at a factory on the premises of Monticello in an effort by Jefferson to use his slave labor to engage in a profitable business. After that, James Hubbard ran away again in 1812. His title was thereafter sold to Reuben Perry for $500, of which $300 was paid immediately and the balance of $200 was due upon his re-capture. He was eventually caught and flogged. Edmund Bacon, in his memoirs, p. 102, also describes a slave who ran away by pretending to follow the wagon of James Madison, but does not give the name or the date. However, he indicates that this occurred while James Madison was president, which was from 1809 to 1817.

A slave named Sandy ran away from Thomas Jefferson in 1769, before he started the *Farm Book*. This may have been the former slave of Thomas Jefferson who was the subject of a newspaper advertisement offering a reward for his capture.

In the account book of Thomas Jefferson for August 23, 1800, following a visit from the census taker, there is an inventory of family members. In addition to 93 slaves, it lists among whites, two males and two females under 10, one male between 10 and 16, three males and one female from 16 to 26, one male 26 to 45 and one male 45 and up.

Thomas Jefferson was clearly the one male 45 and up. At that point, Thomas Mann Randolph, Jr. had squandered all the land and slaves given to him as dowry by Thomas Jefferson, so he and his wife were possibly back living at Monticello. In that case, Martha Jefferson was the female from 16 to 26, her husband was the male from 26 to 45. Their son, Thomas Jefferson Randolph, then aged 7, was one male less than ten. Their daughters, Anne, 8, and Ellen, 4, were the females under ten.

This leaves one male under ten, one male from 10 to 16 and three males from 16 to 26. It has been suggested that Tom, aged 11, was the one male between 10 and 16 and his brother Beverly, aged 2, was the male under 10. After all, Tom was so white that Thomas Jefferson considered him white.

The three males from 16 to 26 were most likely any of a number of white workmen who were employed at Monticello from time to time.

Fawn Brodie states that there is a Tom on the clothing lists in the *Farm Book* for 1810 and 1811. If true, this might indicate that after Thomas Jefferson was no longer president, Tom was allowed to return to the farm, collect some clothing and leave again. Brodie is apparently referring to the fact that at the bottom of page 136 of the *Farm Book*, there are three Toms listed as hired. These are 'Tom', 'Tom Buck', and 'Tom Lee'. There also is an entry on page 140 of the *Farm Book* stating that Tom [hired] was to receive 7 linen and 5 1/2 of something else in 1812. However, it seems unlikely that Thomas Jefferson would list his own son as being 'hired'.

There are still some holes and gaps in this story and some details which need to be filled in.

The biggest question is: Why did Madison Hemings in 1873 state that Tom had died when he was only a few years old? There are several possible and completely reasonable explanations for this.

The first is that since Tom left Monticello in 1803 and Madison Hemings was not born until 1805, he may not actually have known the fate of his older brother.

The second is that since Tom was sent away because of the scandal his presence had created, perhaps the other family members were simply told that Tom was dead, as a way to guarantee that some family member might not leak the truth at a later date.

The third is that Madison Hemings actually knew the truth about Tom and might even have met him personally in Ohio, but Tom did not want the truth about who his father was revealed, so Madison Hemings maintained this secret.

It must be mentioned here that Tom Woodson became a famous person in his own right. He became a leader of the black community in Ohio, even though the members of that community were not completely sure whether he was black or white.

This brings us to the next question: Why did Tom use the name Woodson rather than the name Hemings? Why did he not want anybody to know until late in his life his true age and the fact that his father had been the president?

It seems strange from the perspective of nearly 200 years later that anyone would deny being the son of Thomas Jefferson if he actually was. However, one must bear in mind that this story has always met with considerable hostility directed toward anyone who repeated it. The entire story about Sally Hemings has long been taboo. Look what happened to the original editor and to the author of the story. The editor who first published the story was beaten up by a gang of thugs. The author who originally wrote it was found dead in the water ten months after the original publication. In addition, look what happened to George Wythe, the teacher of Thomas Jefferson, who was murdered by arsenic poisoning by a nephew angry that George Wythe had named his mulatto son in his will. Thomas Jefferson had been named as the trustee to that will.

Madison Hemings apparently had been telling his story for years and trying to get it published, before he found someone willing to print it. Even then, it was only published in the *Pike County Republican*, an obscure publication. It was only because some years later that this article was brought to the attention of a historian, that we even know about it today.

No doubt, any time Tom Woodson ever tried to tell anybody the truth about the fact that his father had been Thomas Jefferson, he was met with calumny, ridicule and disbelief. Better to keep his mouth shut about this.

Even the obituary of his grandson does not quite hit the nail directly on the head. It calls him 'a grandson of Thomas Woodson, of Shadwell, Virginia, a direct descendant of Thomas Jefferson, author of the Declaration of Independence'.

Note that it says 'a direct descendant of Thomas Jefferson'. It does not say the son of Thomas Jefferson, as it should have said.

Even the author of *The Sable Curtain*, with all the research she has done, still does not have the courage to come out directly in the main text of the book and say that her husband is actually the direct descendant of Thomas Jefferson. She only gets to it in a very round about way in the appendix to her book and in private correspondence with this author.

There is another book entitled *Down from the Mountain* by Judith P. Justus, which also does not quite grab the issue by the nub. Its subtitle is *The oral history of the Hemings family. Are they the black descendants of Thomas Jefferson?* It was published in 1991 by Jeskurtara, Inc., Perrysville, Ohio. It should say, 'They are the descendants' rather than, 'Are they the descendants?'

If, after the passage of two hundred years, no black person is willing to assert himself publicly as being the descendant of Thomas Jefferson, in spite of the mountain of evidence that this is true, how could Thomas Woodson have been expected to do so more than 150 years ago?

There are many white members of the Woodson family in Virginia. The Woodson family was among the first to be established in America. John Woodson and his wife, Sarah, both from Devonshire, arrived in America on the ship *George*, which left England on January 29, 1619. Only a relative handful of colonists had arrived prior to that date, and most of them had died. Later the same year of 1619 was when a Dutch ship brought the first twenty slaves to America. One uncle by marriage of Thomas Jefferson was Col. John Woodson, who owned a nearby farm. Drury Woodson was his first cousin. It seems logical that Tom, the son of Sally, would have been hidden away on the farm of a distant relative by Thomas Jefferson. Minnie Shumate Woodson found the name of Drury Woodson after an exhaustive search of many Woodson family documents. She finally found a Woodson family with a slave about the right age named 'Mima', with an older half sister named Fanny, this being Fanny Leach, known to be the half sister of Jemima. The gravestone of Jemima Woodson says that she died on March 18, 1868, aged 85 years 10 months 6 days.

However, Minnie Shumate Woodson and the other members of her extensive Woodson family organization may have overlooked the solution to the puzzle of how Tom happened to have acquired the name 'Woodson'. This solution does not become readily apparent until one has created a genealogical database, as this author has done for the purposes of this book.

Thomas Jefferson had the interesting habit of naming the males whom we now believe were his children, after the family names of his ancestors, in-laws and others closely associated with him. In addition to Tom, the male children of Sally Hemings were Beverly, Madison and Eston.

Elizabeth Beverley (spelled with an additional 'e') was the wife of William Randolph the Second of Turkey Island. She was therefore the great-aunt of Thomas Jefferson. Their first born son was named Beverley Randolph. At least six other males in the Randolph family were also named Beverley. One Beverley Randolph (1744-1797) was the Governor of Virginia from 1788 to 1791. Another Beverley Randolph was married to Sarah Wormeley. Invariably, within the Randolph family, Beverley was a boy's name, not a girl's name.

The next son of Sally Hemings was Madison. He was obviously named after James Madison, who was serving as Jefferson's Secretary of State when Madison Hemings was born. James Madison was Thomas Jefferson's hand picked successor as President.

The next and last son of Sally was Eston Hemings. Eston was originally a place name, Eston being the ancestral home of the Randolph family. Eston is also the name of a town in Northern England. That Eston, however, is apparently not the same place as the Randolph ancestral home. According to Randolph family biographers, it has now been proven that the Randolphs originated in Warwickshire, England, not in Yorkshire, as was previously believed. Eston therefore might be the name of the house or the estate where the Randolph family once lived.

Some male members of the Randolph family took the name 'Eston'. One of these was Thomas Eston Randolph, who was the cousin of Thomas Jefferson. He was born in England and was the son of William Randolph, who was the brother of Jane Randolph, the mother of Thomas Jefferson.

As an example of the tendency of the Randolph family towards incest, not only was Thomas Eston Randolph the cousin of Thomas Jefferson, but he also married his second cousin, Jane Cary Randolph (1776-1832), who was the sister of Thomas Mann Randolph Junior.

This brings us to the name 'Woodson'.

The Woodson family intermarried with the Randolphs. Col. John Woodson was an uncle by marriage of Thomas Jefferson. His wife was Dorothy Randolph, who was the sister of Jane Randolph, the mother of Thomas Jefferson. The Woodsons were also neighbors of Thomas Jefferson.

Following the same pattern of Beverley, Madison and Eston, it seems likely that Thomas Jefferson might easily have named his first born slave son 'Woodson'. In all likelihood, 'Tom' was a nickname. He was always referred to as 'Tom', never as 'Thomas'.

Therefore, Minnie Shumate Woodson might be mistaken in her belief that

Tom changed his name to Woodson in order to hide the fact that he was the famous Tom who was the son of Thomas Jefferson. It seems more likely that 'Woodson' was actually the name given to him by Thomas Jefferson at birth. If that is the case, then it is not necessary to go searching old records from the neighboring Woodson families to find evidence of this Tom.

That is not the end, however. Wormley, another slave of Thomas Jefferson, was apparently named after Judith Wormeley, the grandmother of Thomas Mann Randolph Senior. A number of male members of the Randolph family were named Wormeley. Does this mean that Wormley (one 'e'), the slave, was also the son of Thomas Jefferson?

Incidentally, the number of occurrences of the letter 'e' in a persons name back then did not matter. There was no uniform spelling of names at that time. Thus, there was no difference between the names Eppes, Epes and Epps, between Beverley and Beverly and between Wormeley, Wormley and Wormly. All of these variations were used, even by Thomas Jefferson himself.

Wormley (1781-1851+) was the son of Betty Brown. He must have been conceived in Richmond, because both Betty Brown and Thomas Jefferson were there while Thomas Jefferson was the Governor of Virginia from 1779 to 1781. The infant Wormley was among the slaves of Thomas Jefferson captured and held prisoner by the British for several months in 1781 at Yorktown. See *Jefferson at Monticello*, p. 10. It has often been rumored that Betty Brown was the original concubine of Thomas Jefferson. It was clearly possible for Thomas Jefferson to have been the father of Wormley. It was Wormley who dug the grave of Thomas Jefferson in 1826.

If that was the case, why did not Thomas Jefferson free Wormley in his will, as he did all of the other males who were possibly his sons? This question has not been asked before and an answer is not readily available. Perhaps, Wormley got his freedom in some other way. Wormley is on the inventory list of slaves taken at the time of the death of Thomas Jefferson, as are Madison, Eston, John Hemings and Joe Fossett, all of whom were freed by the will. Also, like those others, Wormley does not appear to have been among those sold at either of the two slave auctions. However, his wife, Ursula, and four small children, the oldest being age 7, were sold for $745 to one George Blaettersman, at the auction in January, 1827.

Burwell was another slave of Thomas Jefferson. He was undoubtedly named after the family of Rebecca Burwell who, at age 17, was the first great love in the life of Thomas Jefferson. The Burwell family were neighbors of Thomas Jefferson. Lewis Burwell, the father of Rebecca Burwell, had been in 1750 the acting governor of the Colony of Virginia. William Armistead Burwell (1780–1821), the private secretary of Thomas Jefferson while he was president, was the second cousin one generation removed from Rebecca Burwell. The slave named Burwell (1783-1827+) was a younger brother of the slave named Wormley. He was also a son of Betty Brown and, therefore, was a possible son of Thomas Jefferson. He was among the five freed in the will of Thomas Jefferson.

A significant point must be remembered about Betty Brown. Among all these, she was the only one who was not inherited from John Wayles. Due to circumstances which are unknown, she originally belonged to Thomas Jefferson and was his before the death of John Wayles. We know this because, on page 5 of the *Farm Book*, she is on the list of 'A Roll of the proper slaves of Thomas Jefferson. Jan. 14, 1774.' There are different lists there of the slaves inherited from John Wayles and from Jane Randolph, the mother of Thomas Jefferson.

It is not clear how Thomas Jefferson got Betty Brown or how she came to be separated from her siblings or how she acquired the name 'Brown.' The best guess is that Thomas Jefferson acquired Betty Brown as part of a dowry when he married Martha Wayles, although no dowry is mentioned in any source document we have. Possibly, Betty Brown was simply originally the property of Martha Wayles Jefferson, as a gift from her father. She may have been called 'Brown' to distinguish her from her mother, Betty Hemings.

Jane Lilburne was the great-grandmother of Thomas Jefferson. She was the mother of Jane Rogers, who was the mother of Jane Randolph, who was the mother of Thomas Jefferson. Thomas Jefferson had a slave named Lilburne. He was the son of Cretia and was born in 1809.

The Fontaine family was neighbors and relatives by marriage with the family of Thomas Jefferson. Incidentally, John Fontaine had married a daughter of Patrick Henry. There was also a slave of Thomas Jefferson named Fontaine (b. 1819).

Finally, there were slaves named 'Lewis' and 'Tucker'. While it is true that people often have those as first names, it is also a fact that the Lewis family and the Tucker family had married into the family of Thomas Jefferson. Meriwether Lewis was a member of that Lewis family.

Therefore, we have five slaves with the unusual first names of Beverly, Madison, Eston, Wormley and Burwell, plus slaves named Lilburne and Fontaine, not to mention slaves named Lewis and Tucker. All these are the family names of persons, in-laws or families closely associated with Thomas Jefferson. Woodson was the name of another family closely associated with Thomas Jefferson. Therefore, Thomas Jefferson probably gave Tom Woodson his name.

However, the most conclusive proof of the existence of Tom, the son of Thomas Jefferson, is the roster of more than 1000 people, all of whom say that they are descendants of that Tom. Included on that roster are a number of important people, including a federal district court judge. If Tom never existed, he sure has got a lot of people fooled.

# Chapter Eleven

## The Orgy Room

Perhaps the most startling and convincing bit of evidence regarding this entire matter concerns the discovery that Thomas Jefferson built and maintained a secret trysting place within the walls of Monticello itself.

Like many a 'discovery', this discovery is not new. Anybody taking the standard seven-dollar tour of Monticello can make the same discovery.

This secret sex spot can be found directly over Thomas Jefferson's bed. Naturally, the tour guides do not describe it as such. They say that it is some sort of storage bin where Thomas Jefferson kept things such as 'old clothes'. However, the reader is welcome to take a tour of Monticello to see if this explanation sounds credible.

The secret orgy room of Thomas Jefferson is actually a cubicle approximately eight feet long, ten feet high and four feet wide. It is completely enclosed, with no windows for ventilation, except for three portholes near the top, which let in just a faint amount of light.

This particular room must be contrasted with the architectural design of the remainder of the house.

A depiction of Monticello is one of the most commonly available items and can be found on the American five-cent piece. On the 'heads' side of the nickel is the head of Thomas Jefferson. On the 'tails' side is a view of Monticello. Actually, what is shown there is the rear view of Monticello.

Monticello has an elegant design featuring twenty-foot high ceilings. Everything about the interior conveys a sense of spaciousness. Tour guides are constantly emphasizing the efficiency and utility of every feature of the house. Yet, in the midst of this, there is an unexplained closed space directly above the master's bed.

The tourist pamphlet handed out regarding Monticello states: 'The bedroom with its alcove bed open on both sides served as his dressing room. Above the bed is a long, narrow closet with porthole windows for light and ventilation.'

The claim that the secret room above his bed was merely a closet is based almost entirely on a single letter from Thomas Jefferson to his daughter Martha dated November 4, 1815, in which he stated, "In the closet over my bed you will find a bag tied up, and labeled 'Wolf-skin pelisse', and another labeled 'fur-boots' wherein those articles will be found."

This letter is published in *The Family Letters of Thomas Jefferson*, edited by Betts and Bear. A footnote on page 412 states that this letter is the only reference that Thomas Jefferson ever made to the small room above his bed. It also states, 'The three oval openings, which tradition says were used as look-outs for his body guards, were there only for letting light into the closet.'

This explanation apparently satisfies most tourists. However, anybody looking at this strange structure and contemplating its possible use will find it difficult to consider this to be a likely spot for a 'closet'. Among other things, the ceiling is ten feet high, much too high for any sort of closet.

Another thing which the tour guides go to pains to mention is that the spiral staircase which at one time led up to this room was installed subsequent to the death of Thomas Jefferson by another owner named Jefferson M. Levy. They say that as long as Thomas Jefferson was alive, there was only a rough wooden ladder leading up to this room.

In so stating, they manifest a need to disprove a theory which has been postulated by various others that this cubicle was actually the private bedroom of Sally Hemings and that she would descend the spiral staircase in the night and get into bed with Thomas Jefferson.

It has also been suggested that there might have been another secret entrance to this room, possibly a trap-door from the second floor above or perhaps a door from the side or the end. From that secret entrance, Sally Hemings or some other fair damsel could have lowered herself through the trap door, entered the 'closet', put down the ladder, descended into the bed chamber, and gotten into bed with the great man himself, all without anyone outside having any awareness of this connection.

One person who felt that this 'closet' might well have been the private bed chamber of Sally Hemings was Fawn Brodie. However, here Fawn Brodie demonstrates that in spite of her familiarity with far flung psychoanalytic theories along Freudian lines, she knows little about how sex is actually done between men and women.

It is extremely unlikely that Sally Hemings or any other woman ever slept in the cubicle above the bed of Thomas Jefferson on a regular basis. Indeed, it is readily apparent that this room was not designed for sleeping at all. Thomas Jefferson would not have wanted for any woman to sleep there. There would be no purpose to having a 'secret' room, if the same woman would be sleeping there all the time. Rather, it was clearly an orgy room, especially built and designed for sex itself.

The modus operandi was obvious and simple. The master of the house would simply invite a woman into his room and direct her to climb the rough wooden ladder. After she reached the top and entered the room, he would climb up the ladder himself, pull the ladder up if necessary, shut the hatch, put the woman on to the bed and do his duty.

Presumably, the master of the house preferred his sex almost completely in the dark. Even in the daylight, little light would enter the room through the high portholes. It would have been almost completely black in there.

The question arises: Why bother with such an elaborate scheme? Why not just do it in his own bed?

There are any number of good reasons for this. The bedroom of Thomas Jefferson was never dark, nor would it have been completely secure. There was a skylight in the roof. There were wooden shutters on the windows, but, even when closed, probing eyes could peer between the cracks. There was always the danger that another chambermaid would come into the bedroom for cleaning proposes while the other chambermaid was in the bed with the master himself. Having a secret closed room above the bed solved all of these problems.

However, the main reason for the orgy room was no doubt to give the woman herself a sense of security. The main difficulty in having sex with any woman is just to get her into a place where she feels secure that the other women will not find out what she has been doing. Having achieved that, the battle is 90% won.

Any woman would have felt a bit apprehensive about having sex in the master's bedroom. Perhaps, somebody might have seen her enter the room, or might see her leave when she finished. No woman wants to risk being caught in the act. The cubicle above the bed was the perfect place for secrecy. She could climb up and wait for him to come when the coast was clear, or he could climb and wait for her. He could safely enter the bedroom, making it appear to any outside viewer who might happen to see the door when it was opened that the bedroom was empty, when in actuality there was a woman hiding in the secret room above. Once safely inside the orgy room, nobody would have any way of knowing what was going on up there. The security of the situation was increased by the fact that nobody, not even the daughters of Thomas Jefferson, were ever allowed to enter his bedroom.

The perfection of this design shows that Thomas Jefferson must have planned this for a long time. Again, the standard tourist guide demonstrates this point most clearly. It states:

> 'Few houses in America more accurately reflect the personality of its owner than does Jefferson's Monticello. Its design, construction and remodeling, for which he determined every detail, spanned over forty years, beginning in 1768.'

What we have here is a long range planner at work. The master genius must have realized at an early age that what he really needed was an orgy room above his bed. Every detail about Monticello was planned carefully. Not one inch of space was wasted. The explanation that this room was a clothes closet or, for that matter, that it was a secret bedroom for Sally, is simply not credible.

*Monticello, A Guide Book,* edited by Frederick D. Nichols and James A. Bear, Jr., p. 29, also asserts that, 'Over the bed [of Thomas Jefferson] is a clothes closet, reached by a ladder installed in another closet at the head of the bed.'

Although tourists and other visitors are not allowed to look inside this room, it is still possible to estimate its dimensions and what it must look like inside from an exterior viewing. The main feature of this room is that the only ventilation comes from three portholes which are too high for human reach. It therefore must be dark in there, even in the daytime. It must be remembered that during the years when Thomas Jefferson was living at Monticello, the electric light bulb had not yet been invented. Therefore, anyone entering that room who wanted to see inside would have had to have carried a lamp. Such a lamp would have had a bad smell in such a closed place and the fumes might even have been deadly if kept for a long time in such an unventilated space.

Also, it would have also been impossible for anybody to sleep inside there during the hot summers at Monticello, even without a lamp. In addition, there would be no purpose to building such a large closet where nobody could see inside.

Thus, this space could not reasonably function either as a closet or as a bedroom. However, it was a prefect room for secret sex.

Presumably, Thomas Jefferson must have preferred his sex in the dark, as some men and women do. In that case, there would have been no need to bring a lamp in, as darkness was preferred. The lack of ventilation would not matter much, as the sex act might not take very long, depending on the speed with which Thomas Jefferson acted.

Incidentally, the bedroom, and not the sex room above, was the room in which Thomas Jefferson died on July 4, 1826. It is reported that the obviously dying Thomas Jefferson struggled to keep alive for the last few days of his life so that he could reach the fiftieth anniversary of the signing of the *Declaration of Independence,* which he wrote. Thus, his death on exactly that day was not entirely a coincidence.

It is clear that the orgy room just above the bed of Thomas Jefferson must have been constructed in 1796 or thereafter. During that period, the entire house at Monticello was demolished and then rebuilt. The original house was less than half the size of the present structure. In 1794, Thomas Jefferson established a nail factory and a brick factory at Monticello. Although some of the nails were sold commercially, it is clear that the main purpose of the nail factory was to provide nails for the rebuilding of Monticello. At that time, the process was started of tearing down and reconstructing the house in various stages. Thomas Jefferson tried at all times to keep at least part of the house covered with a roof, so that he would have a place to sleep. As a result, part of the house was always being torn down, while another part was being built up.

One of the first stages of this reconstruction was that what is now considered the front of the house was torn down and the network of tunnels and secret rooms and passageways were dug underneath the house. After these were built over again, the back part of the house, the part which is seen on the American nickel, was torn down. This process continued until after Thomas Jefferson had finished his two terms of office as President.

The engine which drove this 40 year process of construction, tearing down and rebuilding the house at Monticello, was the fact that Thomas Jefferson had a virtually unlimited supply of slave labor. It must be remembered that Monticello was nothing more than a barren mountain top when Thomas Jefferson named it Monticello in 1767 and started construction work on the house in 1768. The finely manicured version of Monticello which forms a tourist trap today was achieved only in the last few years of the life of Thomas Jefferson.

Without free slave labor, his own nail factory and his own brick kiln, the construction of Monticello by a man such as Thomas Jefferson without a nickel to his name would have been impossible. Still, Thomas Jefferson needed money to complete this project. In 1794, he mortgaged 150 of his slaves to provide the money needed for the reconstruction of Monticello. This mortgage was not paid off until more than 20 years later. It was indeed fortunate that Thomas Jefferson lived long enough to see Monticello completely reconstructed and the mortgage paid off. Had he died sooner, he would have left nothing more than the worthless hulk of a partially completed house. Even his slave children would have been sold at auction.

There are many sources for the above information concerning the demolition and reconstruction of Monticello, but by far the best is *Jefferson and Monticello, The Biography of a Builder* by Jack McLaughlin, New York, 1988, especially pp. 259-272.

Getting back to the orgy room, one notable feature of this room is that the three strange portholes which serve as ventilation holes are said to be identical to those found in the painting by Adriaen Van der Werff of Abraham in bed with his wife, Sarah, and his concubine, Hagar, the Egyptian. This seems to be hardly a coincidence. It shows that the orgy room was constructed after 1788, when Thomas Jefferson saw that painting in Europe, and that he had that painting in mind when he constructed the orgy room.

That painting, which is not regarded as especially important in the world of art, created a profound impression on Thomas Jefferson. He frequently mentioned it in his letters. He appears to have been intrigued, some might say obsessed, with the idea of being in bed with two women at the same time, as Abraham is depicted as being in that painting. The painting shows a half-naked Abraham and a nearly-naked Hagar, who appear just to have completed the sex act. A fully dressed Sarah has a worried look on her face, and her concerns are being dismissed by Abraham with a wave of his hand. The fact that, according to one source who found the actual painting still hanging in an art gallery in Europe, the three portholes in his own bedroom were designed based upon the portholes in the painting of Abraham, shows that Thomas Jefferson had group sex on his mind when he designed his own bedroom. Indeed, Thomas Jefferson wrote a letter dated April 24, 1788 to Maria Cosway, in which he described the painting of Van der Werff showing Abraham, his wife Sarah and his concubine Hagar in bed together. In this letter, Thomas Jefferson stated, 'I would have agreed to have been Abraham, although the consequence would have been that I should have been dead five or six thousand years.' It has been suggested that this quotation proves Thomas Jefferson's interest in maintaining a harem and in his preference for being in bed with two women at the same time.

The conclusion that this was some sort of orgy room is by no means new. As early as 1858, Ellen Randolph Coolidge, a granddaughter of Thomas Jefferson, obviously felt a need to deal with this contention when she stated in a letter to her husband the following:

> My brother, then a young man certain to know all that was going on behind the scenes, positively declares his indignant disbelief in the imputations and solemnly affirms that he never saw or heard the smallest thing which could lead him to suspect that his grandfather's life was other than perfectly pure. His apartments had no private entrance not perfectly accessible and visible to all the household. No female domestic ever entered his chambers except at hours when he was known not to be there and none could have entered without being exposed to the public gaze. But again I would put it to any fair mind to decide if a man so admirable in his domestic character as Mr. Jefferson . . . . would be likely to rear a race of half-breeds under their eyes and carry on his low amours in the circle of his family.

More recently, Virginius Dabney has also tried to put aside the contention that this enclosed space was actually an orgy room. He states:

> The closet exists no longer . . . . James Bear states. Bear has consulted various architects who are familiar with the floor plans and other details and who agree that no 'secret' bedroom existed. The Jefferson Scandals, Dabney, p. 71.

However, in spite of these protestations, the secret bedroom is there. Everybody can see it. Just pay seven dollars for a ticket and take a look. More than that, the entire design and layout of the Monticello grounds seems carefully planned and designed for privacy and sex.

One strange feature of Monticello is the lack of normal staircases. The clear purpose of this was also privacy. There were tunnels and secret passageways around and underneath the house. However, a guest entering the house from the front would not have been able to see them. Indeed, it was entirely possible that a guest would not have seen any of the 187 slaves at Monticello. The cooking and other household tasks were done in the subterranean rooms below the house. The food was lifted up to serve the guests by dumb-waiter. The slaves, with the exception of a privileged few, would never have had occasion to enter the house itself.

The semi-underground passageways almost reached from the house to the slave quarters. The slaves were housed behind a wall of trees known as 'Mulberry Row'. A guest looking from the windows of Monticello probably would not have been able to see them, nor would they have been able to see the guest. While the vast majority of the slaves at Monticello lived and worked either on Mulberry Row or in the rooms and passageways underneath the house, just a few such as Sally Hemings, Betty Brown and their mother, Betty Hemings, were allowed to enter through the main doors on the ground floor. Thus, this house was arranged to ensure a maximum of privacy and secrecy.

More than that, Monticello itself was a secretive place. The word 'Monticello' means 'little mountain' in Italian. The mountain was only 867 feet high. However, a steep climb was required to reach the top.

If one wants to build a secret house where nobody can find it, where does one do it? The best place is on an island. However, islands are inherently dangerous. The safest and most secure place would be on the top of a little mountain. That is exactly what Thomas Jefferson selected.

One interesting question is: Where did Sally Hemings actually sleep? We have only one clue about this. This comes in the 1868 letter from Henry S. Randall which stated: 'Walking around moldering Monticello one day with Col. T. J. Randolph (Mr. Jefferson's oldest grandson) he showed me a smoke blackened and sooty room in one of the colonnades, and informed me it was Sally Hemings' room.'

There is a room in Monticello which fits this description perfectly. It is connected to the secret passageway underneath the house. There is now a sign which labels it as the 'smoke room.' While it seems unlikely that anyone ever lived in this room, it was undoubtedly this room to which Col. Thomas Jefferson Randolph referred. This would tend to show that Sally Hemings did not live in the houses and shacks with the slaves on Mulberry Row.

# Chapter Twelve

## Important New Evidence

This author has found something which seems to be completely new, or at least it has not been published anywhere before and is supposed to be secret.

There is a prominent family who lived in Lynchburg, Virginia for many years, which has kept it as a family secret that they are descended from Thomas Jefferson. This author was allowed to see documents pertaining to this by accident, because it was forgotten that this matter is supposed to be a secret. This is what happens when, by mistake, a secret is let out. It gets published.

According to this family secret, Amelia Elizabeth Perry Pride was the great-grand daughter of Thomas Jefferson.

Amelia Elizabeth Perry Pride was born on March 27, 1857. She had unusual hazel eyes and light brown hair. She was a graduate of Hampton Institute, now Hampton University. She was one of the first Negro women to be allowed to teach in the Lynchburg public schools and spent 33 years as a school teacher, spending twenty of those years as the principal of the Polk Street School. She also founded a school of home economics for Negro girls. In short, she rose just about as far as a woman in her age and condition could possibly have risen. She lived in Lynchburg in the Amelia Pride house on 901 Madison Street until her death on June 4, 1932.

This author has spoken to residents of that neighborhood who remember the Pride family well. They were all light-skinned with high cheek bones. There are two old photographs of Amelia Perry Pride which are dated 1881. She looks almost exactly like Thomas Jefferson. Even her grandchildren have the same nose of Thomas Jefferson. There is also an extremely rough photograph of her father, William Perry, which nevertheless shows a likeness to Thomas Jefferson.

Apparently, the persons who gave this author access to the documents realized that they had made a mistake and that nobody was supposed to be allowed to see this. It was a close question as to whether they were going to snatch the documents right of the hands of this author before he had a chance to memorize them.

A note attached to the documents said: "I just don't want to be quizzed about it. Only the family has known this until last summer . . . . . We were always admonished 'This must be kept secret'."

Cases like this pop up from time to time. It has already been mentioned that the descendants of John Hemings and Joe Fossett claim to be descendants of Thomas Jefferson. Still, the case of Amelia Perry Pride is apparently not known.

The most interesting part is that, according to Amelia Perry Pride, her grandmother was the daughter of Thomas Jefferson. However, she does not give the name of her grandmother or of her great-grandmother. She will only say that her grandmother married a white man named John Perry. Their son was William Perry who married a mulatto woman named Ellen Bailey who had been freed by her father-master. Their daughter was Amelia Perry who married Claiborne Pride.

If this claim is true (and that is a big 'if'), what we have here may be an unknown daughter of Thomas Jefferson. The only surviving daughter of Sally was Harriet who, according to Madison Hemings, went to live in Washington, D.C. This seems to make it unlikely that the grandmother of Amelia Perry Pride was Harriet.

What this means is that Thomas Jefferson must have had a second mistress. This should not come as a great surprise. It was always alleged that he maintained a 'Congo Harem'. The question is: Who was that second mistress? The name of Betty Brown has often been mentioned in this capacity. Also, Betty Brown had only one daughter. Her name was Mary and she was born in 1801. This was the same year that Harriet was born. Clearly, it is possible that Mary was the grandmother of Amelia Perry Pride.

In addition, perhaps there really was someone else around named Betsy. The Betsy who was born in 1783 was given in 1797 as part of the dowry at the time of the marriage of Maria, the daughter of Thomas Jefferson, to John Wayles Eppes. Unlike Martha, Maria, after marriage, lived a considerable distance from Monticello. Still, that Betsy remained to some extent in the family and might have returned to Monticello. However, Judith P. Justus has located what appears to be the grave of Betsy Hemings. This is located at Millbrook in Buckingham County. The gravestone says that she died in 1857 at the age of 75. Since the Betsy Hemings of Monticello is known to have been born in 1783, this is undoubtedly the same person.

Millbrook is the place where John Wayles Eppes lived with his second wife, Mary Elizabeth Cleland Randolph, whom he quickly married after his first wife, Maria Jefferson, had died in 1804. This indicates that Betsy Hemings remained the property of John Wayles Eppes and therefore probably did not go back to Monticello and did not become the concubine of Thomas Jefferson.

One potentially significant fact about Betty Brown must again be mentioned. Although all sources say that she was the half-sister of Sally, Robert, and James Hemings, she was apparently separated from them. On page 5 of the *Farm Book*, she is listed in the 'roll of proper slaves of Thomas Jefferson' as of January 14, 1774. On the other hand, Jimmy, Sally, Martin and Bob are listed on page 9 of the *Farm Book* as the former slaves of John Wayles. Still, it appears that they were brothers and sister, because they are bracketed together again on page 15 of the *Farm Book*.

There are two Bettys listed on page 5 of the *Farm Book*. One has an asterisk '*' next to her name which indicates that she was a laborer in the ground. The other is 'Bett 1759', who is clearly Betty Brown. Her name has a plus '+' next to it which indicates that she was a 'person following some other occupation.' Betty Brown was a seamstress.

Probably, the fact that Betty Brown got separated from her brothers and sisters and then was reunited with them has to do with the way in which the families who owned them intermarried, as a result of which the slaves were passed back and forth between family members by way of dowry without ever really leaving the family. The most likely possibility would be that Thomas Jefferson got her when he married Martha Wayles, the daughter of John Wayles, who owned Betty Hemings.

In any event, it is certainly possible that Betty Brown was a mistress of Thomas Jefferson, before Sally got big.

Amelia Perry Pride was buried in at the Old City Cemetery in Lynchburg. Since the grandmother of Amelia Perry Pride may have been buried there as well, it is possible that this information could be dug up. In view of the increasing tendency by Americans to dig up the dead bodies of their past presidents, such as Zachary Taylor, this is a possibility to be considered.

Here is what we know about Amelia Elizabeth Perry Pride: Although she could easily pass for white, she lived in the black community of which she was one of the most prominent members. One wonders the reason for this. It is clear that all of the children of Sally Hemings were white enough to pass for white, yet two of those five chose to remain black. Probably, the simple reason for this was that they felt more comfortable living among blacks, as they had from the beginning of their lives.

According to the family tradition of Amelia Perry Pride, her great-grandmother had been a mulatto slave woman and her great-grandfather was Thomas Jefferson. The daughter of Thomas Jefferson and the mulatto slave married John Perry, who was white. The son of that marriage was William Perry who married Ellen Bailey. The daughter of that marriage was Amelia Perry who married Claiborne Pride, the grandson of Armistead Pride. Their son was Claiborne Pride, Jr., who married Florence Lavender in 1903. They had two daughters. One daughter was Marian Pride who married

George Kyle. Their son is Gregory Pride who is alive today. The other daughter was Mable Pride who married Joseph Jordan. Their children are Amelia Carolin and Josita Claiborne.

Apparently, at one point, Amelia Elizabeth Perry Pride went public with her statement that she was the great-granddaughter of Thomas Jefferson. The following is the text of part of a letter from Amelia Elizabeth Perry Pride to Mr. Francis Gregory of 54 Pleasant St., Cambridge, Massachusetts, dated February 23, 1932:

> *I don't like to write family history. . . . . I gave a talk at Hampton and this was in a Northern paper. 'The paper by Amelia Perry Pride was well rendered and it is well to note here that Amelia Perry Pride is a lineal descendant of Jefferson the author of the Declaration of Independence'. This seemed to stir up some parts of the North and I had many letters from Northern papers asking me for a biography of my life. We on my mother's side were all free. My father's mother was Jefferson's daughter. My father was not treated I am told like a slave but was educated and taught the carpenter's trade and was one of Lynchburg's best carpenters.*

It appears that aside from this one public interview and the letter quoted above, Amelia Elizabeth Perry Pride never publicly mentioned the fact that she was a descendant of Thomas Jefferson. There is nothing to indicate which northern newspaper published the above quote.

Here is what Marian Pride Kyle stated in a letter about this dated May 28, 1980:

> *I feel that these items re Amelia P. Pride belong in the library. However, as far as I am concerned it can rest in peace there. I can understand the importance of the President's daughter being presented as 'unknown' for many reasons at that point in time.*
>
> *I don't think it makes any difference at this late date. I just don't want to be quizzed about it. Only the family has known this until last summer.*
>
> *Mary Page Pride*
>
> *P. S. We were always admonished 'this must be kept secret'.*

Naturally, this author has been sensitive to the wishes of that woman. Her secret will be safe here.

The entire Pride family has now left Lynchburg. They reside in Norfolk, Virginia and in Durham, North Carolina. Mariam Page Pride Kyle, the author of the above letter, resides in Durham and is associated with the North

Carolina State College.

The above letter is a typical example of the clear tendency of the putative descendants of Thomas Jefferson to deny or attempt to hide their ancestry. The above letter keeps saying things like 'I don't want to be quizzed about it' and 'I don't think it makes any difference'.

The basic details of the story ring true. John Perry was a carpenter who worked at Monticello. In addition, according to the memoirs of Isaac Jefferson, John M. Perry was the man who sold the land on which the University of Virginia now stands. There is also a memorandum in which Thomas Jefferson directs Edmund Bacon to order some nails from John Perry. It is not clear whether these were all the same man, or different men who happened to have the same name. In any event, it is clear that there was at least one man named John Perry at Monticello and he could easily have married or had children by Jefferson's slave daughter.

An obituary in the Lynchburg Virginian for September 25, 1837, states:

> Departed this life . . . . in St. Louis (Missouri) on the 4th ult. Mrs. Francis T. Perry, aged 57 years, consort of Capt. John M. Perry, originally of the immediate vicinity of the University of Virginia, but more recently of Louisiana.

What this possibly means is that the grandfather of Amelia Perry Pride was not legally married to the daughter of Thomas Jefferson but rather that he also had a white woman who was his legal 'consort'. However, this might also mean that the grandmother of Amelia Perry Pride was not Harriet but rather was an unknown daughter of Thomas Jefferson. Harriet was white enough to pass for white, so she could have legally married a white man. Another not-so-white daughter could not have legally married a white man under the laws of Virginia prior to 1967, and so would have been forced to remain as a mere concubine.

This author was shown a photograph of a fine old cabinet. At that time, this author was not at all interested in the old cabinet and told the lady to take the photograph back. Only later, it became apparent that this fine old cabinet may have been made by William Perry, the son of John Perry, a carpenter who worked at Monticello.

Court and county records in the City of Lynchburg confirm almost all of the statements made by Amelia Elizabeth Perry Pride and her descendants. For example, she was often actively involved in the purchase of real estate, which was quite unusual for any woman of her times. Her husband, a barber, remained by the sidelines.

For instance, court records show that on June 16, 1892, Amelia Perry Pride purchased at public auction a house at Eighth and Madison Streets for $1520. She later bought another house at Ninth and Madison. In 1903, she sold one house to the City of Lynchburg, presumably at a good profit. One of these houses later became the city school of which she was the principal. It is clear that she was an active person.

Her marriage certificate dated December 27, 1881 shows that her father was William Perry and her mother was Ellen Perry. Her and her husband's ages were both 23. The minister was P. F. Morris. Mr. R. J. Perry swore as to the age of the wife, as was required by the law at that time. One wants to find out exactly who this R. J. Perry was. Was this Reuben Perry or was it perhaps Royal Perry?

Her name first appears in the census of 1860. However, here one encounters a brick wall. Her family is listed as consisting of Ellin Perry, Head of Household, age 30, mulatto female, followed by Amelia E. Perry, age 3, mulatto female, Royal M. Perry, age 8 months, mulatto male, William George Perry, age 14, mulatto male, and Emma Perry, age 11, mulatto female.

No father is listed.

Of course, it is possible that the father had already died. However, there is a more likely explanation. William Perry was considered white. If he really was the grandson of Thomas Jefferson, then he had four generations of white fathers. Nobody would have known that he was part black. At the same time, it was illegal for a white man to marry a mulatto. Therefore, he had to declare himself to be outside of the family.

William Perry does not show up in Lynchburg in the 1860 census but there is a William Perry in Lynchburg in the 1850 census. He is listed as white, age 15 and occupation: carpenter. It would seem that 15 is an early age to have an occupation and one would imagine that he would have been older than that. Still, it is probable that this is the right person. The family photograph of William Perry says that he was a 'master craftsman and carpenter'.

Regarding his father, John Perry, it must be said that there were many persons in Virginia by that name. Looking through these old microfilm records causes terrible eye strain. Some energetic reader is welcome to try to find the right John Perry. Was this the same as John M. Perry, who had a brother named Reuben Perry and who was a close associate of Thomas Jefferson?

One court document from the other side of the family of Amelia Elizabeth Perry Pride is interesting. The husband of Amelia Elizabeth Perry Pride was Claiborne Gladman Pride, Sr., and his grandfather was Armistead Pride, who had been freed by his wife.

This bears repeating. There were apparently many cases in the Old South where a man bought a woman as a slave, lived with her in the town as a wife, produced children by her and eventually gave her freedom to her. Indeed, one such case was the mother of Ellen Bailey (spelled in the 1860 census as Ellin). Ellen Bailey had been brought to Lynchburg and freed by her master-father. Ellen Bailey was the mother of Amelia Elizabeth Perry Pride.

However, the case of Armistead Pride was the opposite. The father of his wife was Stephen Bowles who was born in 1749 and married a woman named Mary Ann. (Perhaps coincidentally, there were slaves by the name of Bowles associated with Thomas Jefferson, including Davy Bowles, his wife, Fanny Bowles, and Suzy Bowles.) The daughter of Stephen Bowles was Patsy Bowles, who apparently was white. Her slave was Armistead Pride and she married him. Then, on February 6, 1821, she gave her husband his freedom. This freedom document is recorded in Book F, page 246 of the deeds book of the City of Lynchburg.

The law against interracial marriage was apparently overcome by his claiming to be of part Indian ancestry.

Armistead Pride was brought to Lynchburg in about 1815 and came to be regarded as an important man there in spite of his modest profession as a barber. He was the first man in Lynchburg with a license to pull teeth, which some barbers did at that time.

The entire Pride family, including Amelia Elizabeth Perry Pride, is buried in section 14, lot 4 of the Old City Cemetery at Fourth and Taylor Streets in Lynchburg. The Pride Family marker is probably the largest marker in the entire cemetery. The initials AEPP are on the individual gravestone of Amelia Elizabeth Perry Pride. Other gravestones in this group have the initials CGP Sr., CGP Jr., HMP, TGP and MPP. The family marker says that the dates of birth and death of Amelia Elizabeth Perry Pride were March 27, 1857 and June 4, 1932. Probably 1857 is correct, since the 1860 census states that she was three years old. However, one family member wrote that she was born in 1858.

This huge graveyard has a fascinating history. It was established in 1805. The previous graveyard could not be expanded because by then it was in downtown Lynchburg. Relatively recently, that former graveyard was deemed to be a suitable spot for the new city police station, jail, district courthouse and parking lot, so all the old bones were dug up and moved elsewhere.

The 1805 City Cemetery appears to be mostly empty at first glance. However, walking around it is treacherous, because one's foot constantly sinks into surprising holes and depressions in the ground. Finally, one realizes that this graveyard is full of graves, most of which are not marked at all.

The majority of Thomas Jefferson's 187 slaves lived not at Monticello but at Poplar Forest, where most of the serious farming was done. No graveyard has ever been found in the immediate vicinity of Poplar Forest, in spite of an extensive search by archaeologists, nor is any other graveyard in the region big enough to accommodate the graves of the one hundred or more slaves from Poplar Forest who had to be buried somewhere. Unless those slave graves are under the new housing developments which have been put up in the neighborhood, the only other likely place where those slaves might be buried would be in the Old City Cemetery in Lynchburg. Although that is seven miles away, which was a considerable distance in an era when most travel was by foot, that is probably the graveyard for most of Jefferson's slaves.

In 1965, the Lynchburg City Council closed this graveyard to further burials, because every time they tried to bury somebody there, they dug up somebody else's grave. No record of burials in this graveyard was ever maintained. There is a 1968 book entitled *Behind the Old Brick Wall, A Cemetery Story*, by Lucy Miller which recounts the heroic efforts by several groups to reconstruct from family and funeral home records who was buried there. Anyone proposing to undertake a visit to this cemetery would be advised first to obtain a copy of that book.

It is clear that among others, slaves and paupers were buried there. This explains the fact that most of the graves were not marked. Also, most of the markers which do exist are completely blank. Finally, most of those markers which ever had words on them are illegible. There is, however, a prominent marker for the infant daughter who died in 1909 of somebody named Emmet Jefferson.

There is a special section of this graveyard with markers for Confederate soldiers who died in the Civil War. There is also a special memorial to those soldiers who died of smallpox. This reminds one of the extraordinary efforts of Thomas Jefferson to inoculate his family members and his slaves against smallpox. However, there is no resting place for the Union soldiers who died in the Civil War. Presumably, their bodies were dumped unceremoniously in a mass grave somewhere.

The main section of the graveyard contains only a few markers compared with the large number of people who were obviously buried there. This huge expanse must have served as the graveyard for the surrounding counties and not only for Lynchburg itself. The slaves and possible descendants of Thomas Jefferson were probably buried there.

One major problem with all of this is that according to people old enough to remember, almost every half-white black person at that time in Lynchburg claimed to be a descendant of Thomas Jefferson. Census records show that there were many people in the Lynchburg area in the period 1850–1930 who were named Thomas Jefferson. All of those people were black. According to those who remember, all of them claimed to be actual descendants of Thomas Jefferson. It was generally accepted among the good white people of Lynchburg that a mulatto family named Shelton was descended from Thomas Jefferson. No such family name ever appears in connection with Monticello, although Sarah Shelton was the first wife of Patrick Henry.

An article appeared in 1929 in the *William and Mary Quarterly*, Vol. 9, Series 2, p. 204, which claimed that research had determined that Shelton and Skelton were actually the same names. However, this theory has been debunked and nobody believes this. The problem arises from the fact that, in the handwriting of Thomas Jefferson, it is impossible to distinguish between the names 'Shelton' and 'Skelton'. If Shelton and Skelton are the same names, then the Sarah Shelton who married Patrick Henry is a likely relative of Bathurst Skelton, the first husband of Martha Wayles. However, more detailed handwriting analysis plus family records have proven this to be incorrect. The person making this claim was a member of the Shelton family, which is a family of much lower prestige than the Skelton family.

Most people in Lynchburg believe that Thomas Jefferson was extremely prolific when it came to producing children from his slaves. The Sally Hemings story is not believed to the extent that they do not believe that she was the only one who produced children for Thomas Jefferson.

It must be recalled that Poplar Forest, just beyond the city limits of Lynchburg, was the second home of Thomas Jefferson. The majority of his slaves lived there, not at Monticello, because the best farm land was there. Sometimes, it is referred to as his 'Summer Home'. This would explain the prevalent stories that his descendants continue to live in that area.

Probably, the actual truth is that those people who openly claimed that they were descended from Thomas Jefferson were not descended from Thomas Jefferson, whereas those who tried to hide their family secret actually were descended from Thomas Jefferson

Regarding Amelia Elizabeth Perry Pride, all of the records she left behind show that she was an extremely serious and capable person. She was a college graduate, rare for 'persons of color' and for women in those days. She was one of the first Negro teachers in the public schools. She became the principal of the Negro public school, a position she held for twenty years. In short, she rose just about as high as any woman in her condition could possibly have risen in a place like Lynchburg. When such a person makes a claim in a private family letter that she is the great-granddaughter of Thomas Jefferson, this claim must be taken seriously.

In addition, the two pictures of her which survive today show a strong resemblance towards Thomas Jefferson. They also show that she was white.

Incidentally, it is noteworthy that the descendants of Thomas Jefferson seemed to like the name 'Madison'. Eston Hemings lived the last years of his life, died and was buried in Madison, Wisconsin. Amelia Perry Pride lived at 901 Madison Street in Lynchburg. Both of these place names existed long before those people moved there.

Finally, on the subject of names, it is noteworthy to consider the names of the above mentioned family members of Amelia Elizabeth Perry Pride. These are: Armistead Pride, Claiborne Pride, William Perry, Ellen Bailey, Royal Pride and Stephen Bowles.

Almost all of these names are also the family names of white people associated with Thomas Jefferson. The Armistead family was one of the big families of Virginia. William Armistead Burwell was the private secretary to Thomas Jefferson while he was president, after his first private secretary, Meriwether Lewis, had been sent on the Lewis and Clark Expedition. The mother of William Armistead Burwell was Mary Armistead. The mother of President John Tyler was a different but related Mary Armistead. In fact, William Armistead Burwell was exactly the fourth cousin of President John Tyler. Another important white family in Virginia was the Claiborne family. In addition, Mary Royall, a white person, was the mother of Col. John Woodson, who was the husband of Dorothy Randolph, the sister of the mother of Thomas Jefferson. Perry, Bailey and Bowles were also all family names of families living in the area and associated with Thomas Jefferson.

Of course, one explanation for this would be simply that these were all originally slaves owned by those families. However, since all of these individuals related to Amelia Elizabeth Perry Pride were mulattos, there is also the possibility that these all were actually fathered by the male members of the above families.

Unfortunately, the birth and death records for Bedford County, where Poplar Forest is located, prior to 1871, are available only on microfilm and are completely illegible. The same is true of the birth and death records for Campbell County, which included Lynchburg at that time. However, from 1871 to 1896, there were many people who died in Bedford County with the name of Jefferson. It must be remembered that Thomas Jefferson himself left no white descendants with that name, so all of these Jeffersons who died were probably the children of his slaves.

Most of the names of those who died are clearly recognizable as names used by the slaves of Thomas Jefferson. The complete list of first names of those persons named Jefferson who died in Bedford County from 1871 to 1896 is as follows: William, Thomas, Eddie, Sally, Jenny, Maria, John, Fanny, Unnamed, Nelson, Sallie, Beverly, Harritt, Duggie, John, Dug, John, Harrett and Minnie.

Almost all of these names are familiar. However, 'Harritt' died in 1894 and 'Harrett' died in 1895. Neither one was likely to have been the Harriet Hemings who was born in 1801.

Social Security records show that two persons named Harriet Hemmings have died within recent years. One Harriet Hemmings, who was born on May 6, 1888, died in Troy, New York in November, 1973. Another Harriet

Hemmings, was born on September 23, 1880, died in Auburn, Washington in November, 1974. These would not, however, be descendants of the original Harriet Hemings, who would have married and taken her husband's name. Most likely, these are descendants of Madison Hemings or, possibly, of a son of Betty Hemings. In addition, social security records show a person named Peyton Hemmings, born in 1883, died in 1980. Peyton Randolph was a relative and a close associate of Thomas Jefferson.

Nobody named Hemings is ever recorded to have died in Bedford County. Indeed, the name 'Hemings' (one 'm') itself appears to have died out everywhere. Anybody who ever had that name changed it to something else because of the Sally Hemings story. There are, however, still a few people named 'Hemmings'. This is just a different way of spelling the same name. There are people named Hemmings who still live in Albemarle County. There are also two people named Hemmings in Lynchburg, Virginia.

One of these is Mrs. Willis Hemmings, who lives at the corner of 9th and Wise Streets in Lynchburg. She says that her husband, Gordon Hemmings (1909–1986), was the youngest of four brothers named Hemmings, all of whom died without male issue. Therefore, she is almost the last of the Hemmings.

She says that the family of her husband came from places named Bent Creek and Five Forks. Both are small dots, not shown on many maps. Bent Creek is in Buckingham County, Virginia, about 25 miles down the James River from Lynchburg. It looks like a place where one might have stopped while walking from Charlottesville to Lynchburg. Five Forks is much further away. It is next to Williamsburg and exactly one mile from Jamestown, where the first Virginia colony was established.

In all probability, the husband of Willis Hemmings was a descendant of Betsy Hemings, the one who died at Millbrook in Buckingham County in 1857. If not, it is possible that he was a descendent of John, Peter, Robert or some other Hemings. Willis Hemmings doesn't have any idea herself. She says that there is a cousin named Steven Hemmings in Lynchburg, but he was raised by people other than his parents, so he knows absolutely zero about his heritage. 'Willis', by the way, is another historical family name in Virginia, associated more closely with Henry Willis and the family of George Washington.

Willis Hemmings knew the Pride family well, because they lived only a few blocks away. However, she never knew that they were possibly descendants of Thomas Jefferson and that her husband might therefore have been distantly related to them.

Some of the best new research in this field has been done by Judith P. Justus. She has made many discoveries, some of which she has not even published in her own book, *Down From the Mountain*, for fear that she will be proven wrong. In addition, her book really concerns a different subject, because it never expresses any opinion as to whether these are the descendants of Thomas Jefferson. Here are a few of the possibilities which she suggests, but only in private correspondence:

She says that while Thomas Jefferson was in Washington as President, a child of Edy died and Thomas Jefferson bought a coffin for the funeral. Since it seems unlikely that the chronically broke Thomas Jefferson would spend the money to buy a coffin for a mere servant, this may mean that this was his own child.

Here it must be mentioned that Edy stayed with Thomas Jefferson in the White House for a number of years, while her husband Joe Fossett was required to remain at Monticello. In 1807, Edy gave birth to a child named Maria. Perhaps Thomas Jefferson was the father of that child. It should be recalled that in early 1806, Thomas Jefferson had ordered Joe to be arrested on the White House yard where he had come to visit Edy.

After being arrested, Joe had been taken back to Monticello by Reuben Perry, a white carpenter who worked for Thomas Jefferson. Later on, Reuben Perry worked on the construction of the Poplar Forest Estate in what is now Lynchburg, Virginia. The brother of Reuben Perry was John Perry, also a carpenter. John Perry worked on Monticello.

Almost undoubtedly, that John Perry was the same John Perry who was the grandfather of Amelia Elizabeth Perry Pride. Further confirmation of this lies in the fact that according to the letters of Amelia Elizabeth Perry Pride, the son of John Perry was William Perry who was one of the best carpenters in Lynchburg. There is still a photograph of a fine old cabinet said to have been made by this William Perry.

The next part of the story is very important: According to sources in the black community in the Charlottesville area, Harriet Hemings never actually went to Washington, D.C., and Madison Hemings was wrong about that. Instead, according to Judith P. Justus, the tradition is that Harriet got married to a man named Reuben in Charlottesville and eventually, some years later, went to Canada. If so, that could actually be the Reuben Perry who was the carpenter mentioned in the letters of Thomas Jefferson.

Further evidence that Harriet did not go to Washington, at least not right away, comes from Israel Jefferson who stated in 1873 that seven slaves were given their freedom in the will of Thomas Jefferson. These were, according to him, Burwell, Joe, John, Madison, Eston, Sally and Harriet. Of course, he was mistaken. Sally and Harriet were not actually named in the will. Nevertheless, the fact that Israel believed that Harriet had been freed by the will indicates that she was probably still at Monticello in 1826, when Thomas Jefferson died. She would not have been able to travel so freely alone as a single woman as her brother Beverly had done before her.

This means that Harriet could very possibly be the grandmother of Amelia Elizabeth Perry Pride. Of course, the astute reader will have noticed one problem with this. The family of Amelia Elizabeth Perry Pride says that her grandmother got married to John Perry, not to his brother, Reuben Perry.

Moving to another subject, Judith P. Justus has been searching for the grave of Sally Hemings. She has found an old square tombstone in a black cemetery in Charlottesville that has the initials of 'S H' on it plus a small heart, but no names or dates. Somebody tried to scratch out the 'S' and change it to a 'B'. The cemetery is on the road to Monticello.

Another interesting question concerns that fact that according to James A. Bear, Jr., Mary Hemings, the daughter of Betty Hemings and the mother of Joe Fossett and of Betsy Hemings, was sold at her own request to Col. Tom Bell in 1792. Judith P. Justus questions whether this may have been the result of female jealousy. Perhaps, Mary was upset when a pregnant Sally Hemings returned from France with Thomas Jefferson in November, 1789.

Here, however, we reach the twilight zone of pure speculation, which should be avoided. The possibility we are here being asked to consider is that Thomas Jefferson also had a sexual relationship with Mary, who was born in 1753, and who therefore was upset when Thomas Jefferson took up with Sally Hemings. If true, the next question which would arise would be whether Thomas Jefferson might possibly be the father of Joe Fossett, who, incidentally, was one of the five slaves ordered to be freed.

This would also mean that Thomas Jefferson might just possibly be the father of the children of Mary or the father of the children of her daughter Betsy or even both. Therefore, we have the possibility of Thomas Jefferson going even so far as to have committed incest.

These purely speculative possibilities must be rejected or at least avoided. The evidence connecting Thomas Jefferson to Sally Hemings is concrete. The evidence connecting him to other women is virtually non- existent.

Still, it must be mentioned that it is quite possible that at one time or another both William Fossett and Thomas Jefferson had relations with Mary Hemings. In that case, they might not have known exactly who the father was. Joe might have been given the name Fossett simply because that possible father was no longer on the farm. If that practice was followed, this would make the paternity of John Hemings and also of Burwell Colburn similarly unknown. In other words, Thomas Jefferson could possibly have been the father of all of them, even though they were being attributed to other white men.

Another type of 'new evidence' concerns old letters not yet published. Here it must be mentioned that there is really no such thing as new evidence regarding this entire matter. Anything new would simply be old evidence which has been hidden or kept secret for a long time. Also, an old gravestone previously unnoticed would qualify as 'new evidence'.

According to David C. Dickey, a lawyer practicing in the Charlottesville area, there once was a framed letter hanging on a wall at Monticello which was written by George Washington to Thomas Jefferson which implied that they both shared a common interest in having sex with their slaves. This letter caused considerable comment. It was taken down some time after 1957. It is not clear what happened to it. Judith P. Justus has heard that there is a letter at Mt. Vernon from George Washington to Thomas Jefferson in which the Father of His Country invited the author of the Declaration of Independence to visit him and said that if he comes, 'The same high yellow will entertain you as before.' 'High yellow' was a term repeatedly used to describe the mulatto slaves at Monticello. These appear to be two different sightings of the same letter.

No such letter has ever been published. This seems to make it apparent that only the clean and wholesome letters to Thomas Jefferson get published, not the dirty ones. Almost none of the published letters of Thomas Jefferson contain any reference to slaves at all. Is this because Thomas Jefferson never wrote about his slaves, or is it because all of those letters were taken out?

There have already been published a heavy volume of letters between George Washington and Thomas Jefferson. However, the letter between George Washington and Thomas Jefferson referred to above must have been written after 1792, at which time George Washington was still president. Everything up to and including 1792 has already been published in *The Papers of Thomas Jefferson* by Princeton University Press. George Washington died in 1799.

None of the letters which have been published thus far which were written by Thomas Jefferson contain any mention of Sally. However, there were four letters written by others to Thomas Jefferson which mention Sally. The fact that Sally was mentioned so rarely in spite of being a constant companion of Thomas Jefferson shows that she was a taboo subject.

Thomas Jefferson wrote 18,000 letters, of which several thousand have been published in various collections by James A. Bear, Jr., and by Edwin Morris Betts. This means that most of them have not yet been published. There are still letters for which permission to publish has apparently been denied. Also, the descendants of Thomas Jefferson in Boston are apparently holding large numbers of letters which were sold by other descendants of Thomas Jefferson to his relatives to raise cash. These have not been published or cannot be published except upon payment of a fee.

It is hoped that all the letters of Thomas Jefferson will eventually be published. This work is going on at the Princeton University Press. *The Papers of Thomas Jefferson* is currently being edited by John Catanzariti, the most recent of several editors, after the original editor, Julian P. Boyd, retired years ago. It has now reached Volume 24, since publication began in 1950, and is up to the year 1792. It is hoped that the publication of the projected 100 volumes of this great work will be completed within the lifetimes of our children, so that they will have complete access to the writings of Thomas Jefferson.

This glacially slow process of publication can be explained by the fact that the papers of Thomas Jefferson have been scattered in a variety places. Some are in private hands. Some descendants of Thomas Jefferson who are holding letters are not cooperative and some of those letters may contain secrets which the family does not want to be revealed. Some sources may be demanding payment for the publication of these letters. In short, the papers of Thomas Jefferson have been scattered asunder, whereas Gerald Ford, one of the weakest presidents in American history, has a federally funded library devoted exclusively to his works.

To illustrate the problems associated with re-collecting the personal papers of Thomas Jefferson, there is an inventory item in the estate of David Isaacs showing that certain correspondence of Thomas Jefferson was sold to one Jesse Scott in 1837 for the grand amount of $2.25. See *Down from the Mountain*, by Judith P. Justus, p. 122. David Isaacs was a shopkeeper on Main Street in downtown Charlottesville, who often sold nails and other supplies to Thomas Jefferson. See *Early Charlottesville, Recollections of James Alexander, 1828-1874*, p. 83.

Occasionally, Thomas Jefferson corresponded in the French language. He received a letter in French dated July 28, 1792 from Adrien Petit, who had been previously employed by him in Paris, which mentions Sally. This letter can be found in the original French in volume 24, page 262 of *The Papers of Thomas Jefferson*, which was published in 1991 and is the most recent volume to be published. It has been translated and is published for the first time in English in the appendix here.

From this interesting letter, it appears that Petit had by then been brought to America by Jefferson to work for him at Monticello. However, this was essentially a letter of resignation. Petit was frustrated and angry that the slaves were walking freely in and out of the doors and not respecting his authority. In addition, one of them had accused him of being a homosexual. It must be mentioned here that Europeans often, from the point of view of Americans, appear to be homosexual, even when they are not. Petit was angry about this. He was packing his bags and was going back to France, even though he had not even been there for long enough to say hello to Martha Jefferson Randolph, whom he had known in Paris.

In 1792, at the time of this letter, Thomas Jefferson was in Philadelphia as the Secretary of State. Jimmy Hemings is known to have been there with him too, working as a chef. If this letter has been interpreted correctly, it indicates that Sally Hemings was also at that time in Philadelphia with Thomas Jefferson. The letter concludes, 'Give my regards to Jimmy and Sally.'

It must be mentioned here, with caution, that this is the first time that this important letter has ever appeared in print in English and there might be other explanations. We are able to confirm the presence of Adrien Petit in America at this time because of a letter dated July 3, 1792 from Thomas Jefferson in Philadelphia to his daughter Martha at Monticello. That letter stated that on the previous day, Petit had left Philadelphia and was on his way to Virginia by boat. The route he was to take was to come down to the Chesapeake Bay and then up the James River to Richmond. This was apparently a quicker route than the ten days by horseback normally used by Thomas Jefferson.

From that plus the subsequent letter of Petit dated July 28, 1792, we conclude that he quit his job at Monticello and left there after staying for less than three weeks. He must have come to America and then turned around and gone back to France almost immediately. He did not stay long enough at Monticello to find out about and taste the tender pleasures available there. Or, perhaps, who knows, maybe he really was a homosexual and was not interested in that sort of thing.

This letter, however, does tend to confirm what we know to the effect that the slaves were given the free run of the house, were totally undisciplined and could do whatever they wanted at Monticello. More importantly, this letter constitutes proof that Sally was in Philadelphia with Thomas Jefferson at this time. This is further evidence that Sally was the concubine of Thomas Jefferson. The letter concludes with the words 'Give my regards to Jimmy and Sally'. It is known that James Hemings was at that time in Philadelphia working for Thomas Jefferson as a chef. Therefore, from this context, we know that Sally must have been in Philadelphia then as well.

The fact that this important letter has only surfaced in 1991 shows that the information available now is not complete. One cannot say whether there is unpublished but conclusive proof regarding the Sally Hemings affair. However, one can say conclusively that if such evidence existed, it would not have been published even until now.

# Chapter Thirteen

## Other Documentary Evidence

There are only eight basic documents which provide real evidence regarding the Sally Hemings story. Everybody who argues the pros and cons of what Sally did or didn't do invariably just debates the significance of these eight documents. Stated differently, anyone who has read these eight documents and has studied them in detail knows just about everything which is presently knowable about this story.

The first document is, of course, the *Farm Book*. The original is a bound notebook of 178 pages, some of which are blank. It contains entries starting from 1774 and continuing until 1824, just before the death of Thomas Jefferson in 1826. One problem with the *Farm Book* is that many of the pages are missing. Thomas Jefferson Randolph kept it with him for years after his grandfather died. Many pages were removed. Fortunately, the pages were all numbered and several of the removed pages have been located and restored to their proper place. However, some pages are still missing. It is also suspected that Thomas Jefferson Randolph may have altered some of the pages to hide the secrets of his grandfather.

The original *Farm Book* is now in the possession of the Massachusetts Historical Society. A facsimile copy has been published by the University Press of Virginia.

The other seven documents are written statements and letters. It was originally intended that five among these would be included in the appendix to this book. However, a decision has since been made that the appendix should concentrate on those documents which the reader will have difficulty in obtaining elsewhere. Also, the most important parts of the seven basic documents are already quoted in various places in this book. Two documents were too long for inclusion anyway but are readily available in *Jefferson at Monticello*, edited by James A. Bear, Jr., and published by the University Press of Virginia. In addition, only about two paragraphs from those two documents bear directly on the Sally Hemings story. As a result, among this list of seven documents, only the will of Thomas Jefferson is included in the appendix to this book.

The complete seven documents in question are:

1. The will of Thomas Jefferson, dated 1826.
2. The Statement of Madison Hemings published in 1873.
3. The Statement of Israel Jefferson published in 1873.
4. The letter by Ellen Randolph Coolidge dated October 24, 1858.
5. The letter by Henry S. Randall dated June 1, 1868.
6. The Memoirs of Isaac Jefferson dated 1847.
7. The recollections of Edmund Bacon dated 1862.

Among these seven documents, the first, sixth and seventh can be found in *Jefferson at Monticello*, published by University Press of Virginia in 1981. The second, third, fourth and fifth are to be found in the appendix to *Thomas Jefferson, An Intimate History*, by Fawn M. Brodie, published in 1974, and have been published in numerous other places as well

The first thing one notices about the above list is that, with the exception of the will, all of the documents are dated long after the events in question. The last child of Sally Hemings was born in 1808. One is asked to believe that documents dated 1858 and even later can tell us who the father of the children of Sally Hemings was.

Here is a brief description of what the above documents do and do not tell us:

1. **The Will of Thomas Jefferson.** This will was written in March, 1826, just four months before he died. It tells us that his son-in-law, Thomas Mann Randolph, Jr., was hopelessly insolvent. For this reason, the will goes to lengths to make sure that none of the property of Thomas Jefferson will go directly to his daughter, Martha, for so long as Thomas Mann Randolph is still alive. It sets up a committee to manage the money. There were two reasons for this. One was to prevent Thomas Mann Randolph from grabbing the money and spending it, which would have left Martha and her children completely destitute. The other was that since all of the property of a woman in that era belonged to her husband, the creditors of Thomas Mann Randolph might try to take any money Thomas Jefferson left to Martha.

However, regarding the Sally Hemings story, the main item of interest is contained in the codicil to the will, which provides freedom for five slaves, namely, Burwell, John Hemings, Joe Fossett, Madison Hemings and Eston Hemings. It also implies that the wives and children of these five will get their freedom in some unspecified way. It directs that a comfortable log cabin be built for each of his three 'servants', Burwell, John Hemings and Joe Fossett and their respective wives. It leaves to Burwell three hundred dollars to buy necessities to commence his trade as a painter. It also gives freedom to 'two apprentices' of John Hemings, namely Madison and Eston Hemings, upon reaching maturity. It is perhaps significant that while it refers to Burwell, John and Joe his 'servants', it does not use that term to describe Madison and Eston.

We would like to know the end of this story. Were the three log cabins built? Was the rented house where Sally Hemings lived with her two sons, Madison and Eston, until 1835, one of those cabins? Did Joe ever get to live with his wife, Edy, in one of those cabins. We know that Edy was sold along with her children at the 1827 slave auction. We do not know whether Joe ever got her back. Joe went to Cincinnati in the 1840s. Edy apparently never made it to Cincinnati, but several of her children did, and one became famous there.

2. **The Statement of Madison Hemings.** This is by far the most important document. It is the main and, in some cases, the only written source for much of the crucial information. The story of how the great- grandmother of Madison became pregnant on the slave ship by the owner of the ship and of how his mother became pregnant in France are all contained in this interview.

Although this interview has been attacked vehemently, almost everybody now accepts its validity. The details which are provided could not have been provided by anyone other than someone with a detailed knowledge of life at Monticello. There are a few mistakes in the interview, but all concern matters which occurred before Madison Hemings was born.

3. **The Interview of Israel Jefferson.** Here, we initially reach a different conclusion. This interview at first seems questionable. Fortunately, this does not constitute a serious problem. The interview contains nothing of importance. Indeed, that in itself is part of the reason that this interview seems questionable.

A problem which arises in connection with this interview is that Israel Jefferson says that he was born in about 1797 and that his mother's name was Jane and his father's name was Edwin Gillett. He says that his mother had 13 children with the same father and that they were named Barnaby, Edward, Priscilla, Agnes, Richard, James, Fanny, Lucy, Gilly, Israel, Moses, Susan, and Jane. He also says that his mother, Jane, was born at Monticello, lived all her life there and died there.

However, it seems at first that there was no woman named Jane at Monticello, and no man named Edward Gillett at Monticello. There was a man named Barnaby on the farm born in 1783. Agnes, Fanny, Gill, Israel and Moses were all names of people on the farm, but there is nothing connecting these people as all being members of one family. Such a family would have been the biggest family at Monticello, bigger even that the family of Betty Hemings, who had 14 children, but three of them died. It seems impossible that such a big family could have existed on the farm without it being mentioned in the *Farm Book*.

Fortunately, Minnie Shumate Woodson, in private correspondence with this author, has salvaged this interview which otherwise appears to be doubtful. She points out the extensive use of nicknames at Monticello. For example, Martha was also called Patsy and Maria was also called Polly.

Therefore, according to Minnie Shumate Woodson, Ned, the father of the Israel whose birth is mentioned in the *Farm Book*, might have been a nickname. His real name might not have been Ned, but might have been Edwin instead. Similarly, Jane might have been Jenny, another person living on the farm. In this manner, most of the people on the list of the brothers and sisters of Israel Jefferson can be associated with names listed in the *Farm Book* as people on the farm.

Therefore, the truth seems to be that there was a person named Israel Jefferson and he did live at Pee Pee Creek in Ohio and many if not all the events described in the interview actually occurred. Moreover, those people listed as his brothers and sisters were also on the farm. However, it is almost definitely not true that the mother of Israel was born at Monticello, had 13 children there and remained there until six years after the death of Thomas Jefferson. There was simply no such person like that. The mountain on which Monticello sits was just a barren mountain top prior to 1768 when construction of Monticello began. Nobody lived there. Most of the slaves arrived there in 1774, after the death of John Wayles. The mother of Israel was born in 1764 and therefore was not born at Monticello.

What we find consulting the initial pages of the *Farm Book* is that Ned 60 is on the list of slaves originally owned by Thomas Jefferson. On the other hand, Jenny 64, daughter of Aggy, was inherited from John Wayles. Jenny 64 came from Guinea, the same farm from which Sally Hemings and her mother Betty had come after the death of John Wayles. This Jenny 64 was the mother of Israel Jefferson.

Assuming the use of nicknames, there are several places in the *Farm Book* where a family such as the one described by Israel Jefferson is identified. The first is on page 30, on the 'Roll of Negroes in November 1794 and where to be settled for the year 1795'. Listed at a farm called 'Tufton', which was several miles from Monticello, are the following: [Ned 60, Jenny (Aggy's) 64, Ned 86 Feb. 15, Fanny 88 Mar 31, Dick 90 Mar. 19, Gill 92 Mar. 18, Scilla 94 April 14].

According to the system used by Thomas Jefferson, this means that Ned was born in 1760, his wife, Jenny, the daughter of Aggy, was born in 1764, and they had five children: Ned, born on February 15, 1786, Fanny born on March 31, 1788, Dick born on March 19, 1790, Gill born on March 18, 1792 and Scilla, born on April 14, 1794.

According to the interview of Israel Jefferson, the children of his mother were: Barnaby, Edward, Priscilla, Agnes, Richard, James, Fanny, Lucy, Gilly, Israel, Moses, Susan and Jane. Thus, the similarity of the names is there, even though the order of birth is wrong. We only need to assume that of the five children on the *Farm Book* list, Ned is short for Edward, Scilla is short for Priscilla and Dick is short for Richard. The remaining eight children listed by Israel Jefferson had not been born yet.

Incidentally, there were two Jennys at the farm. One was the wife of Ned, born in 1764. The other was the wife of Lewis, born in 1768. Both are listed on page 50 of the *Farm Book* as laboring hands at Tufton. The Jenny who was the wife of Lewis was on the list of the original slaves of Thomas Jefferson whom he did not get from either his mother or from John Wayles.

On page 55 of the *Farm Book*, on a list for 1799, we have the same list of five children, plus two new children: James born in 1796 and Aggy born in 1798. Another child named Barnaby is listed as having been born in 1783, but his name is crossed off the list for an unknown reason. (He did not die, as he is again mentioned starting on page 128 of the *Farm Book* as being a tradesman in 1810.)

The names of Ned and Jenny plus these children consistently appear on every *Farm Book* list up until 1801. Then, on page 60, there is a list of Negroes leased to J. H. Craven. Ned, Jenny and the seven children, including Israel, are on that list. From then on, their names as a family disappear from the *Farm Book*.

When Thomas Jefferson was elected president, he was obviously not going to be in a position to manage the farms which he owned. Therefore, he leased his land and most of his slaves to J. H. Craven. Israel Jefferson and his parents, brothers and sisters were field hands who did not work in the house. They were among those leased to J. H. Craven. This is the reason that we were not previously aware of this existence of such a large family. Thomas Jefferson had 187 slaves, but we do not know much about many of them except for what we know about those who worked in the house.

We first find the name of Israel on page 130 of the *Farm Book* under 'Roll of Negroes according to their ages at Albemarle'. This gives '1800 Israel Ned's'. Apparently, the father's and not the mother's name is given here in order to avoid confusion between the two Jennys. This shows that Israel was born in 1800, not in 1797 as he believed.

On page 136 of the *Farm Book*, under a list for 1810, there is listed Jenny and below her four children, Aggy 1798, Israel 1800, Moses 1803 and Sucky 1806. Apparently, 'Sucky' is the Susan on the list of brothers and sisters as given by Israel Jefferson.

On page 172 of the *Farm Book*, for the years 1821-1822, the names of Ned, Jenny, Moses and Sucky are listed together. Finally, on page 176, the last page of the *Farm Book*, the names of Ned and Jenny are still listed together.

Thus, assuming that Ned is the nickname of Edwin Gillett and that Jenny was the nickname for Jane, it seems that there was such a family which worked as field hands and laborers at or near to Monticello. Therefore, we arrive at the truth, which is that there was such a family, but mostly they were field hands. They were not kept together. Some were at Monticello; others worked the fields on the nearby farms such as Tufton and Lego. Some were leased. These farms were only four miles away, so they rightfully considered themselves to be 'at Monticello'. We do not know their living arrangements. Perhaps, they spent their nights in the slave quarters at Monticello, and then walked to the fields where they worked by day. They were not kept together as a family unit the way that the Hemings family was and, for that reason, were less noticeable to us.

In any event, the interview of Israel Jefferson does not tell us much of importance about Monticello. Mostly, it tells us what happened to Israel Jefferson after he reached Ohio. He became the slave of Governor Gilmer of Ohio, who gave him his freedom and then later on was killed by an explosion on the ship 'Princeton'. This was a famous incident in which two members of the cabinet of President John Tyler were killed in 1844.

However, one tidbit of information about Monticello might be significant. Israel Jefferson lists seven slaves who were freed in the will of Thomas Jefferson. This clearly was erroneous. Only five were actually freed. The other two mentioned by Israel, Sally and Harriet, were not freed by the will itself. However, even though this is a mistake, it still constitutes further evidence that Sally did get her freedom after the death of Thomas Jefferson and that also Harriet had not yet gone to Washington and was still in the vicinity of Monticello in 1826.

The interview of Israel Jefferson described a meeting between Thomas Jefferson and Lafayette. He says that his 'ears were eagerly taking in every sound' while he was driving their coach. He reports certain remarks having been made about the condition of slavery. However, the meetings between Thomas Jefferson and Lafayette were famous. Any 'well regulated library' has dozens of books which report what was said between Thomas Jefferson and Lafayette.

When comparing the two interviews, we can see that the richness of detail in the interview of Madison Hemings is completely missing in the interview of Israel Jefferson, even though both interviews were about the same length and were apparently taken down by the same newspaper reporter. However, the best explanation for this is that Madison Hemings was simply a more intelligent man than was Israel Jefferson.

There is only one paragraph in the interview of Israel Jefferson which tells us anything about the Sally Hemings episode. That comes at the end, where he says that Sally Hemings was the concubine of Thomas Jefferson and that Madison Hemings was their son 'as any other fact which I believe from circumstances but do not positively know.'

Judith P. Justus has discovered in the archives of the University of Virginia an old hand-written letter from Thomas Jefferson Randolph to the *Pike County Republican* in which he claimed to have refuted the statements made in the interview of Israel Jefferson. However, this letter was never published in the *Pike County Republican* and probably never reached there. Judith P. Justus has published this letter for the first time in her book, *Down From the Mountain*.

In fact, the refutation turns out to be a confirmation. In his letter, Thomas Jefferson Randolph stated that the same Israel Jefferson who had been the subject of the interview had visited him at his residence at Edgehill near to Monticello in 1866. This, indeed, was one of the most important and most difficult to believe points in the interview of Israel Jefferson. It was surprising to read that just one year after the conclusion of the Civil War, Israel Jefferson had made the long journey from Ohio back to see Monticello. Of course, that was his first opportunity to do so without running the risk of being detained and made into a slave again.

The actual objections to this interview by Thomas Jefferson Randolph amount to little more than minor quibbling. He refers to the fact that Israel Jefferson and his family had been leased to J. H. Craven in 1801 and therefore were not always at Monticello. However, that is immaterial to the main issue. They were clearly living in the vicinity, even if they were not always at Monticello.

One noteworthy point is that Thomas Jefferson Randolph only disputed the interview of Israel Jefferson. He did not dispute the interview of Madison Hemings, except to the extent that he said that Madison Hemings was not the son of Thomas Jefferson. Otherwise, he would have been forced to admit that Madison Hemings was his own uncle.

4. The Letter by Ellen Randolph Coolidge Dated October 24, 1858. This letter is always cited by those wishing to claim that Thomas Jefferson never had anything to do with Sally Hemings. The full text of the letter was kept secret by the family, until it was published by the New York Times on May 18, 1974. This letter, along with a subsequent letter by Henry S. Randall, is given as proof that the actual fathers of the children of Sally Hemings were Peter Jefferson Carr and Samuel Jefferson Carr.

It must be mentioned that the Carr brothers were prominent people in their own right. There were actually three Carr brothers. Peter Carr was born on January 21, 1770. Samuel Carr was born on October 9, 1771 and Dabney Carr, Jr., was born on April 25, 1773. Their father, Dabney Carr, Sr., died on

May 16, 1773, just three weeks after the birth of Dabney Carr, Jr.

Peter Carr acquired the title of colonel and was one of the co-founders, along with Jefferson, of the University of Virginia. He died in 1815. Dabney Carr, Jr., was by far the most famous of the three brothers. He became a Justice of the Supreme Court of Virginia. He sat on the Supreme Court bench until his death on January 8, 1837. Samuel Carr, who was also known as colonel, lived the longest, dying in 1855, but was the least distinguished. He had little if anything to do with Thomas Jefferson after his childhood.

In those days, titles such as 'colonel' did not mean much. Almost everybody of any prominence at all had some sort of title. Even Thomas Jefferson Randolph is sometimes referred to as 'Col. Randolph', although there is no indication that he had actual military experience.

Nobody dared to accuse Peter Carr and Samuel Carr of fathering children by Sally Hemings while they were still alive. Yet, in 1874, nearly twenty years after the death of the longest living of the three of them, a biographer, Henry Randall, for the first time quoted Thomas Jefferson Randolph, who by then was also deceased, as stating that they were the ones who did it. This biographer also reported that he had been prohibited from publishing this information earlier by Thomas Jefferson Randolph, who said that: 'If I should allow you to take Peter Carr's corpse into court and plead guilty over it to shelter Mr. Jefferson, I should not dare again to walk by his grave: He would rise and spurn me.' Peter Carr was buried at Monticello.

However, this statement implies that the claim that Peter Carr fathered the children of Sally Hemings is not true. Corpses, if they rise at all, do not rise when true statements are made about them.

Strangely, the allegation that Peter Carr fathered the children of Sally Hemings is accepted without hesitation by those such as Virginius Dabney who are anxious to pin the blame on anyone other than Thomas Jefferson himself.

**5. The Letter by Henry S. Randall Dated June 1, 1868.** This letter is the second primary element in the proof offered that the actual fathers of the children of Sally Hemings were either Peter Jefferson Carr or Samuel Jefferson Carr or both. However, by admitting that there were a large number of mulatto slaves at Monticello who so strongly resembled Thomas Jefferson that the guests were constantly getting them mixed up, Thomas Jefferson Randolph seems to have strengthened the argument that these all were the children of Thomas Jefferson.

**6. The Memoirs of Isaac Jefferson Dated 1847.** This can be found in *Jefferson at Monticello* edited by James A. Bear, Jr. It is interesting to contrast the interview of Isaac Jefferson with the interview of Israel Jefferson.

It is clear from his interview that Isaac Jefferson was completely illiterate, and that Charles Campbell, the person who wrote down his interview, was hardly better. Campbell tried to capture the speaking style of Isaac Jefferson.

The interview is filled with childish errors and mistakes. According to the editors, the original text, prior to having been edited by James A. Bear, was far worse. For example, Isaac Jefferson states that in 1790, at age 15, he accompanied Thomas Jefferson to Philadelphia where he was the President of the United States. Actually, Thomas Jefferson was only the Secretary of State at that time. He did not become President until 1801.

An even bigger blunder comes when Isaac Jefferson lists the children of John Wayles. Actually, the children on his list were the children of Peter Jefferson, the father of Thomas Jefferson.

At the same time, in spite of his illiteracy, the interview of Isaac Jefferson provides us with a tremendous quantity of useful information. This should be contrasted with the interview of Israel Jefferson, which was written in flowing English, but provides us with almost no useful information at all.

For example, everyone has heard of the *Midnight Ride of Paul Revere*, 'one if by land and two if by sea', and the glorious American victory at the battle of Lexington in Massachusetts.

However, what about the glorious Battle of Richmond? What about that? By some oversight, they forget to mention that in the American history books.

However, Isaac Jefferson knows all about that. Although still a child, aged 6, he was there.

> *As soon as the British formed a line, three cannon was wheeled 'round all at once and fired three rounds. . . . . That moment they fired everybody knew it was the British. . . . . In ten minutes, not a white man was to be seen in Richmond. They all ran as hard as they could . . .*
>
> *There was a monstrous hollering and screaming of women and children. Isaac was out in the yard; his mother ran out and cotch him up by the hand and carried him into the kitchen hollering. Mary Hemings, she jerked her daughter the same way. . . . The British was dressed in red. Isaac saw them marching. . . . . They formed a line and marched up to the palace with drums beating; it was a awful sight – seemed like the Day of Judgment was come. When they fired the cannon, Old Master called out to John to fetch his horse Caractacus from the stable and rode off.*
>
> *Isaac never see his Old Master arter dat for six months.*

Thus, when the British attacked Richmond on January 5, 1781 under General Benedict Arnold, all of the white men fled. Only the Negro slaves remained to face the advancing British army.

Thereafter, all of the slaves of Thomas Jefferson at Richmond were taken prisoner by the British and marched to Yorktown. These included Isaac, plus Jupiter, Sukey, Ursula, Big George, Mary, Molly, Daniel, Joe and Wormley. (No mention of Sally). Although many other slaves died at Yorktown, the slaves of Thomas Jefferson were given special treatment and fortunately all of them survived.

The editors of *Jefferson at Monticello* in footnote 32, p. 125 state that Isaac and the other slaves remained at Yorktown and were not liberated until the British surrendered on October 19, 1781. After taking Richmond, the main force of the British withdrew from Virginia, only to return several months later. Isaac vividly describes the *Battle of Yorktown*, with cannons firing and wounded soldiers screaming in agony.

> *There was tremendous firing and smoke – seemed like heaven and earth was come together. Every time the great guns fire Isaac jump up off of the ground. Heard the wounded men hollering. When the smoke blow off, you see the dead men laying on the ground.*

There can be little doubt that Isaac Jefferson was there at Yorktown. He also said that General George Washington personally came and liberated them after the surrender of Cornwallis, whom Isaac Jefferson referred to as 'Wallis'. General George Washington did not even arrive in Virginia and show up at Yorktown until must of the serious fighting was over. He came just in time to take full credit for the glorious American victory.

This entire incident led to articles of impeachment being drawn up against Thomas Jefferson for insufficient military preparation while Governor of Virginia. It was said that Jefferson should not have run away from Richmond but should have directed the battle against the British. Jefferson resigned in June, 1781 rather than face impeachment. This remained as a blot on his career until he was forgiven and exonerated by the Virginia legislature before he became President.

It is clear that Isaac Jefferson knew his 'Old Master' well. Whereas Israel Jefferson kept referring to Thomas Jefferson as 'a good and great man', as though a slave would be able to perceive these qualities in his master, Isaac Jefferson had a more realistic view. 'He want rich himself – only his larnin,' he said of Thomas Jefferson.

This short quote proves that Isaac Jefferson knew what he was talking about. Most people believed that Thomas Jefferson, who lived like a king, was a rich man. Only somebody close to him like Isaac Jefferson would have known that in spite of being well educated, he had no money at all.

There is only one paragraph in the interview of Isaac Jefferson which tells us much about Sally Hemings and the others, but this paragraph is of great importance.

*Mr. Jefferson came down to Williamsburg in a phaeton made by Davy Watson. . . . . His family with him in a coach of four. Bob Hemings drove the phaeton; Jim Hemings was a body servant; Martin Hemings the butler. These three were brothers; Mary Hemings and Sally, their sisters. Jim and Bob bright mulattos; Martin darker. Jim and Martin rode on horseback. Bob went afterwards to live with old Dr. Strauss in Richmond and unfortunately had his hand shot off with a blunderbuss. Mary Hemings rode in the wagon. Sally Hemings' mother Betty was a bright mulatto woman, and Sally mighty near white; she was the youngest child. Folks said that these Hemings was Mr. Wayles children. Sally was very handsome, long straight hair down her back. She was about eleven years old when Mr. Jefferson took her to France to wait on Miss Polly. She and Sally went to France a year after Mr. Jefferson went. Patsy went with him first, but she carried no maid with her. Harriet, one of Sally's daughters, was very handsome. Sally had a son named Madison, who learned to be a great fiddler. He has been in Petersburg twice; was here when the balloon went up, the balloon that Beverly sent off.*

It must be pointed out that the Beverly who sent the balloon off was the 'scientifically minded' son who is the probable ancestor of a man who has a Ph. D. in chemistry and is the now retired former Chairman of the Board of DuPont Chemical Corporation.

It is noteworthy that in one short paragraph, the reader is provided with a vast amount of information which is unquestionably accurate and is mostly not available from any other source. Indeed, the entire interview of Isaac Jefferson is like that. The facts are occasionally mixed up. For example, he states that Sally was 11 years old when she was taken to France, whereas she was actually 14. However, these are relatively minor points. Every page in the interview of Isaac Jefferson provides us with insights into the life and times of Thomas Jefferson. This is a valuable source document, providing a wealth of information not available elsewhere.

Late in his life, Thomas Jefferson told his daughter's son-in-law, Nicholas Trist, that during a dozen years he had practiced the violin three hours a day. (He had been forced to give up the violin when he had fractured his right wrist while on an outing with Maria Cosway in France in 1786). The memoirs of Isaac Jefferson notes that Madison Hemings was an 'excellent fiddler'. Since a violin is an expensive instrument and is far beyond the purchasing power of the average slave, it seems reasonable to conclude that Thomas Jefferson might have taught Madison Hemings how to play and may have loaned him the use of his violin. This also tends to show that

Madison may have been the son of Thomas Jefferson.

7. **The Recollections of Edmund Bacon Dated 1862.** This is a lengthy interview taken town over a period of several weeks of the most important overseer who ever worked for Thomas Jefferson. He was born in 1785 and came to work for Thomas Jefferson in 1806.

The accuracy of this interview was hotly disputed by Thomas Jefferson Randolph, and for good reason. Edmund Bacon portrays Thomas Jefferson Randolph as a little bit stupid. Bacon says that Thomas Jefferson Randolph inherited his grandfather's looks but none of his talent. Bacon characterizes Thomas Jefferson Randolph as being incapable of writing anything himself and unable to do anything without help.

Edmund Bacon also had a dim view of the talents of President James Monroe, who lived less than three miles from Monticello. Bacon said, 'You could write better with your toes than Mr. Monroe wrote.'

These disparaging remarks about others have led to his interview being questioned. For example, Edmund Bacon describes himself as having ready access to Thomas Jefferson at all times. He says that in all the years, whenever he entered the private study of Thomas Jefferson at Monticello, there were only two times when he did not find Jefferson actively occupied at something such as writing, reading, or developing a mechanical device.

Thomas Jefferson Randolph countered that it was impossible for an employee such as Bacon to have had the authority to walk into the door of his private study at any time to see Thomas Jefferson without even knocking. Thomas Jefferson Randolph said that even the daughters of Thomas Jefferson were not allowed to do that.

However, being a daughter is different from being an overseer. Edmund Bacon was the supervisor in charge of everything which went on at Monticello and the surrounding four farms. If he came to see Thomas Jefferson, it would have been on important business. Naturally, such a person would have been allowed instant access to his boss, especially since it appears that Thomas Jefferson spent most of his waking hours in his study and rarely left there.

The daughters were another matter. What about the orgy room which Thomas Jefferson maintained directly over his bed? What would have happened if the daughters had walked in unannounced, knowing their father to be inside, and yet could not find him in the study? Would they have tried to climb the rough wooden ladder and knock on the entrance to the orgy room? Clearly, the daughters were not going to be allowed to enter the private study and bedroom of Thomas Jefferson.

The interview of Edmund Bacon provides a pathetic example of the incompetency of Governor Thomas Mann Randolph, Jr., the husband of Martha Jefferson and the father of Thomas Jefferson Randolph. It must be mentioned here that Thomas Mann Randolph, Jr., has been variously described by others as 'strange', 'eccentric' and even 'mentally ill'.

> While he was Governor, his debts troubled him a great deal. I often loaned him money, and he often applied to me to help him raise it from others. When he must have it and could get it in no other way, he would be obliged to sell some of his Negroes. Here is one of his letters to me. . . .

> Dear Sir: It is so absolutely necessary to me to have as much as $150 by tomorrow evening . . . . that I am forced, against my will, to importune you farther with the offer of the little girl at Edgehill . . . .

> Your Friend, Th. M. Randolph
> May 9, 1819'

> I raised the money and the next day paid him two hundred dollars for Edy. She was a little girl four years old. He gave me this receipt. . . . .
> He was finally unable to meet his obligations, failed completely and lost everything. Mr. Jefferson, in making his will, had to take special care to prevent Mr. Randolph's creditors from getting what property he left for Mrs. Randolph.
> Before he died his mind became shattered, and he pretty much lost his reason.

It is easy to see why Thomas Jefferson Randolph, the son of Thomas Mann Randolph, Jr., did not like this interview. However, this assessment of Thomas Mann Randolph, Jr., was shared by everybody from his slaves up to his peers.

Ironically, after disputing every other significant part of the interview of Edmund Bacon, Thomas Jefferson Randolph wholeheartedly agreed with what he said about Sally. Here is the full text of the relevant part of that interview.

> Joe Fossett made the iron-work. He was a very fine workman; could do anything it was necessary with steel or iron. He learned his trade of Stewart. Mr. Jefferson kept Stewart several years longer than he otherwise would have done in order that his own servants might learn his trade thoroughly. Stewart was a very superior workman, but he would drink. And Burwell was a fine painter. He painted the carriage and always kept the house painted. He painted a good deal at the University.
> Mr. Jefferson freed a number of servants in his will. I think he would have freed all of them if his affairs had not been so much involved that he could not

*do it. He freed one girl some years before he died, and there was a great deal of talk about it. She was nearly as white as anybody and very beautiful. People said he freed her because she was his own daughter. She was not his daughter; she was _____ _____'s daughter. I know that. I have seen him come out of her mother's room many a morning when I went up to Monticello very early. When she was nearly grown, by Mr. Jefferson's direction I paid her stage fare to Philadelphia and gave her fifty dollars. I have never seen her since and don't know what became of her. From the time she was large enough, she always worked in the cotton factory. She never did any hard work.*

*When Mr. Madison was President, one of our slaves ran away, and we never got him again. As soon as I learned he was gone, I was satisfied he had gone with Mr. Madison's cart to Washington and had passed himself off as Mr. Madison's servant. But Jeff Randolph did not believe it. He said he had hid himself somewhere around the plantation, and he hunted everywhere for him. . . . . We afterwards learned that he went off as Mr. Madison's servant, as I had supposed. No servants ever had a kinder master that Mr. Jefferson's. He did not like slavery. I have heard him talk a great deal about it. He thought it a bad system. I have heard him prophesy that we should have just such trouble as we are having now.*

'Just such trouble as we are having now' referred to the Civil War. It must be recalled that this interview was taken down in 1862, while the Civil War was going on.

The statement by Edmund Bacon that he knew that the girl in question was _____ _____'s daughter has repeatedly been cited as proof that Harriet was not the daughter of Thomas Jefferson. However, there are serious questions about this. Harriet was born in 1801 and therefore was conceived in 1800. Edmund Bacon did not come to work at Monticello until 1806. It is true that he grew up in the neighborhood of Monticello, but he was born in 1785 and at age 15 was probably too young to have paid much attention to a man coming out of the room of Sally Hemings in the morning, even if he had happened to be at Monticello even before he worked there.

Another factor is that the name of the putative father of the children of Sally was deleted. It appears that the editor of this interview, The Reverend Hamilton Wilcox Pierson, made this deletion. There are any number of possible reasons for this. It could be that the entire sentence was inserted by Pierson, along with the two sentences following that. Perhaps the blank spaces were to be filled in later. Unfortunately, the original handwritten text has been lost to history, in spite of monumental efforts to find it.

In addition, there is something suspicious about Edmund Bacon's statement that after giving Harriet $50 plus her stage fare to Philadelphia, he had never seen her since. The fact is that Harriet left Monticello in 1822 and Edmund Bacon left Monticello and went to St. Louis on horseback, also in 1822. Therefore, Harriet might easily have remained in Charlottesville, as the local tradition says that she did, without Edmund Bacon ever knowing that she was still there.

In fact, in his interview, Bacon never mentions the name 'Harriet' or the name 'Sally'. It is only assumed from the context that he is referring to Harriet, the only daughter of Sally. There is always the chance that he was referring to some other daughter by some other possible concubine of Thomas Jefferson. This circumstance indicates that there is considerable doubt about Edmund Bacon's entire statement regarding Harriet.

Thus, what we really have is a document which has a clear mistake in the date and which has also been tampered with and the original text has been lost. In a court of law, this document would clearly be inadmissible. We cannot say that this document proves anything at all about who the father of Harriet may have been. It is strange that this paragraph was tampered with when the remainder of the lengthy document appears to be highly accurate. However, this is not so strange when one considers that this single paragraph had received considerable attention, whereas the rest of the lengthy interview had been largely ignored.

One theory which must be considered is that the Reverend Pierson may have had his own reasons for wanting to exonerate the 'good and great' name of Thomas Jefferson. It must be considered that with the exception of a few fiery abolitionists, no white person has until relatively recently been willing to acknowledge in print the possibility of Thomas Jefferson fathering children by his slaves. Thus, it is entirely plausible and indeed likely that the good reverend himself inserted the three sentences which seem to put the blame for fathering these children on some other person. In addition, it is entirely probable that the document might never have seen the light of publication had it not been for those three sentences clearing the name of Thomas Jefferson. It almost certainly would otherwise not have been reprinted by the University Press of Virginia now.

There is much of interest in the remainder of the statement of Edmund Bacon. For example, on page 104 of *Jefferson at Monticello*, he states that Thomas Jefferson had eleven servants from Monticello with him at the White House. However, he only mentions the names of three of them: Edy, Fanny and Davy. One wants to know whether Sally was ever in the White House. Edmund Bacon does not answer this question.

Edmund Bacon also mentions that Thomas Jefferson had a French cook in Washington named Julien. Edy and Fanny were in the White House to learn French cookery. Edy and Fanny were afterwards cooks in Monticello.

Bacon also describes an incident involving Davy and Fanny:

*The second time I went [to the White House] he had got very much dis-
pleased with two of his servants, Davy and Fanny, and he wished me to take
them to Alexandria and sell them. They were married and had got into a
terrible quarrel. Davy was jealous of his wife and, I reckon, with good reason.
When I got there, they learned what I had come for, and they were in great
trouble. They wept and begged and made good promises and made such an
ado that they begged the old gentleman out of it. But it was a good lesson for
them. I never heard any more complaint of them; and when I left Mr. Jefferson, I left them both at Monticello.*

It is noteworthy that Bacon intended to take Davy and Fanny to
Alexandria to sell them. This confirms the fact that at that time, it was legal to
own slaves in Washington, D.C., but illegal to buy or sell them there. This is
the reason that he had to take them to Alexandria, Virginia if he wanted to
sell them.

What happened is that two members of the official White House staff,
upon giving displeasure to the President, were almost taken out and sold on
the local slave market.

Edmund Bacon also has valuable insights about Thomas Mann Randolph, Jr., confirming what we know from other sources. He states:

*Governor Randolph, Mr. Jefferson's son-in-law, was a very eccentric man. . .
. . He was generally dressed in the most indifferent manner and was very
queer anyway. The Randolphs were all strange people. John Randolph, you
know, was one of the most eccentric men that ever lived, and I think Governor Randolph was full out as strange a man as he. They were as much alike
as any two steers you ever saw.*

The above mentioned 'John Randolph' was John Randolph of Roanoke, a
brilliant United States Senator and one of the great men of that era. He was
also known to be eccentric. He never married and was known to hate
women. He was the brother of the Richard Randolph, who was charged in
an infanticide case in 1793.

Edmund Bacon left Monticello with a considerable amount of money in
his pocket. He went on horseback all the way to St. Louis, where he twice
turned down an opportunity to buy a large piece of land which later on
became the better part of downtown St. Louis. Instead, he bought farm land
in Kentucky, where he became a successful horse breeder and one of the
wealthiest men in that area.

On the whole, the interview of Edmund Bacon provides a great
storehouse of information, in spite of the doubts concerning the single paragraph regarding who the father of Harriet might have been.

# Chapter Fourteen

## Jefferson as a Statesman

The reader might think that the author of this book has a dim view of the overall abilities of Thomas Jefferson and is skeptical as to whether he really was one of the great men in all of human history.

Nothing could be further from the truth.

Not only was Thomas Jefferson a great man who, perhaps more than any other man of his time, made America the great nation it is today, but he was, more than any other person of his era, responsible for the eventual abolition of slavery.

As to his relationship with Sally Hemings, there was nothing in that relationship to indicate that he was not a good man. Rather he was a good man who does what every good man does when confronted with a beautiful woman.

The reason that so many black people have taken the name of Jefferson is not, as one might imagine from reading this book, that Thomas Jefferson personally fathered all of them, but rather that among all the founding fathers, he was the one who was the most vocal opponent of slavery and did the most to contribute to its abolition.

A detailed discussion of this subject is beyond the scope of this book, especially because there are a hundred books on this subject which can be found in any well regulated library. However, here are a few of the highlights of Jefferson's lifelong opposition to slavery.

Thomas Jefferson filled a desperate need which existed in pre-Revolutionary War America. In the *Diary and Autobiography of John Adams* for June 25, 1774, p. 97, the future president John Adams wrote:

> We have not men, fit for the times. We are deficient in genius, in education, in gravel, in fortune, in everything. I feel unutterable anxiety. God grant us wisdom and fortitude.

John Adams wrote these words before he had ever met or heard of Thomas Jefferson, who did not come to prominence until his *Summary View of the Rights of British America* was published later the same year, in August,

1774. Before that, nobody knew about the young man who spent all his time reading books in Monticello. Jefferson had read everything ever published that he could get his hands on in Greek, Latin, French, Italian and Spanish. He had absorbed all of the knowledge which had been published and which existed in the world at that time. There was nobody in America approaching him in general knowledge and education. He far exceeded everybody else. Yet, nobody knew about him. He grew up in the countryside and had never in his life visited a town with a population of more than 2000, until after his *Summary View* had been published in August, 1774.

Because of his *Summary View*, he was sent as a junior substitute delegate to attend the Continental Congress in Philadelphia in 1775. As soon as they discovered that they had finally found a man who knew how to write, the delegates put him to work drafting documents in various committees. He rarely, if ever, joined in the public debates. Instead, he served on 34 committees and probably drafted substantially all of the documents which these committees produced.

No doubt, much of what he did consisted merely of putting the ideas of others onto the written page. Nevertheless, it was Jefferson who was doing the actual writing, and he had the opportunity to try and slip in what he wanted.

Nobody outside of these committees knew at the time that it was Jefferson who was producing all of these documents. It was even not revealed until years later that he was the author of the *Declaration of Independence*. However, the convoluted writing style was clearly his, as anyone who has read a few thousand of his letters can readily testify.

Later, Jefferson began to write his own documents. Although he was merely a member of the committee assigned to draft a declaration of independence, it is clear that he personally wrote the *Declaration of Independence* himself. He included a clause opposing slavery. The other signers insisted that this clause be taken out. Otherwise, the entire document was adopted almost exactly as Jefferson wrote it.

In the Continental Congress of 1783, Jefferson became the author of the *Northwest Ordinance*, which set up the system under which the newly emerging territories, which include such present states as Ohio, Indiana and Illinois, were developed. He included in the *Northwest Ordinance* a clause prohibiting the introduction of slavery in these territories after 1800. Otherwise, if Ohio, for example, had become a slave state, the balance of political power would have shifted and slavery might never have been abolished.

While president, Thomas Jefferson pushed through Congress a bill prohibiting the importation of slaves. This bill authorized the navy to seize ships on the high seas, to confiscate property, and to impose fines to stop the slave trade. This law came into effect in 1808, while Jefferson was president.

In negotiating the Louisiana Purchase, which more than doubled the territory of the United States, Thomas Jefferson included a provision which prohibited the introduction of slavery into these new areas.

These are just the highlights. In hundreds of political documents, private letters and elsewhere, Thomas Jefferson reiterated his opposition to slavery. This was not mere political posturing. His views were unpopular and cost him considerable support. He became president in spite of, not because of, these views.

Much of what he did or tried to do to eliminate slavery had little effect, due to circumstances beyond his control. In spite of his law prohibiting the importation of slaves, the slaves still came in through smuggling. Even now in America, a similar problem exists. Boatloads of Haitians are always entering through international waters. The United States Coast Guard keeps trying to stop them and send them back, with mixed results. If today, with radar and modern technology, it is impossible to stop ships on the high seas from coming in, imagine how much more difficult it must have been in Jefferson's time.

However, that is not the point. The point is that Jefferson did as much as any one man could possibly have done to bring to an end the practice of slavery. Nobody did more than he did. Even John Adams, who came from Massachusetts, still by far the most liberal state of the United States on these matters, did not have the solid record of Jefferson of opposing slavery. The fact that Jefferson was not successful in bringing about the abolition of slavery reflected the fact that his ideas were way ahead of his time.

Thomas Jefferson, among all the founding fathers, was responsible for the establishment of democratic institutions in America. After the American Revolution, it was by no means certain what type of government was going to be established. Several experiments were tried, most notably the Continental Congress of which Jefferson was a member. There were no doubt others besides Jefferson who favored a democratic form of government, but none were more vocal or persuasive than he. He was the one, more than any other, who favored rule by the people, as opposed to a strong central government.

At that time, democracy was just a theoretical idea which had never really been tried in practice. The idea of a government freely elected by the people had been talked about but never really tested. In fact, it was Jefferson himself who later brought about the constitutional amendment which provided for a direct election of the President and the Vice-President by the people. The Twelfth Amendment of the Constitution of the United States was passed by Congress under Jefferson in 1803 and ratified and signed into law in 1804, all during his first term of office. This radical concept, of allowing the people to elect their own president directly, might well never have become the law, had not Jefferson, using the full powers of his presidency, pushed for it.

Jefferson became president at a critical turning point in the history of America. He was not the first president, but he was perhaps the one whose actions had the most lasting impact. His predecessors, Washington and Adams, were actually his political opponents. They were members of the Federalist Party. Jefferson was a Democratic-Republican. He was the first of an uninterrupted string of Democratic-Republican presidents, which included Madison, who was hand picked by Jefferson, followed by Monroe and John Quincy Adams. Through this line of presidents, most of the democratic institutions in America today were established. Had Thomas Jefferson never lived, America would undoubtedly be a different place.

Even more than that, the ideas of Thomas Jefferson thereafter swept across Europe. His writings were the inspiration, especially in the early stages, for the French Revolution. Some of the early documents in that revolution were virtually translations of documents written by Jefferson to inspire the American Revolution.

After that, a wave of democratic reform swept Europe, all inspired by Thomas Jefferson and the example set by the American Revolution. It will surprise most readers to learn that Karl Marx was a great admirer of Thomas Jefferson and the American Revolution. The American Revolution was always revered by the top Communist Party officials in the Soviet Union, an amazing and seldom mentioned fact, in view of the vastly different forms of government which were ultimately established in those two countries.

In short, it was truly the ideals of Thomas Jefferson which formed the shape of the world political horizon which continues up until this day. In that case, why not give the poor fellow the right to a brief repast in the slave shack behind the house?

There is another question as to what exactly his reasons were for opposing slavery. Of course, there was the moral high ground, that slavery is an immoral and invidious practice. This may have been one of his reasons, but he did not often mention it.

Often his arguments turned on the point that slavery was bad for the economy. It was mentioned that Quakers had experimented with the idea of freeing their slaves and then hiring them back at regular salaries. The idea was that a free man paid a salary will produce more than the same man while a slave.

Thomas Jefferson took a tour of Germany while he was living in France. He discussed the idea of hiring Germans, importing them to America, and putting them on his farms in competition with his own unpaid slaves. He felt that even after the payment of salaries, the freed men would bring him more of a profit than the slaves.

It must be mentioned here that these sort of arguments were more likely to persuade his fellow Virginians that slavery should be abolished, than to try to say that black men were just as good as white men. Even today, if someone tries to say in Virginia that the blacks are just as good as the whites, one will encounter a stiff argument, to say the least.

Jefferson took the right approach when he tried to tell Virginians that they could make more money if they abolished slavery. This sort of contention would make people listen.

However, we know from his treatment of his own slaves that he did not sincerely believe that blacks were completely equal to whites. In particular, it seems that he kept all of his purely black slaves working in the fields at Poplar Forest in Bedford County, whereas the partly white slaves were employed as carpenters, mechanics and household servants at Monticello.

This indeed was part of a larger pattern. An example of this is a famous quote which is enshrined in the Jefferson Memorial in Washington, D.C., which states the following:

> *Nothing is more clearly written in the book of fate, than that these people are to be free . . . .*

This indeed is a wonderful quote, but look at the '. . . .' at the end. What is this? They forgot to finish the sentence!

The rest of the original sentence goes on to state that the blacks and the whites will never be able to live together under one government.

It is easy to see why they left that part of the sentence off of the Jefferson Memorial. This view also seems to explain why Jefferson put the purely blacks on one farm and the part-whites on another.

In short, Jefferson wanted not only freedom for the slaves, but he also wanted to establish a separate homeland for them. He apparently favored establishing a colony in the Caribbean or else in Africa, perhaps in the area which subsequently became Liberia, a country which President James Monroe helped establish and which has a capital named Monrovia. Thomas Jefferson may have believed in the flawed doctrine of 'separate but equal'.

The actual anti-slavery quote on that section of the wall of the Jefferson Memorial in Washington is really a patch work of various quotes which were put together and made to look like one. In other words, Thomas Jefferson wrote all of the things quoted there, but did not write them all at the same time.

Here are the actual words inscribed on that part of the wall at the Jefferson Memorial. One can readily see that these are disjointed words, not part of a single unified quote.

> *God who gave us life gave us liberty. Can the liberties of a nation be secure*

*when we have removed the conviction that these liberties are a gift from God. Indeed, I tremble for my country when I reflect that God is just, that his justice cannot sleep forever. Commerce between master and slave is despotism. Nothing is more certainly written in the book of fate than that these people are to be free. Establish the law for educating the common people. This is the business of the state to effect on a general plan.*

These semi-literate ramblings were clearly never written in that form by one of the world's great writers like Thomas Jefferson. However, the architects of the Jefferson Memorial put a quote like that together on the wall because they were faced with a problem. Although Jefferson often wrote about freeing the slaves, he would then always in the same sentence write about sending them back to Africa or separating them from the white people in some way. These views are unacceptable today.

Perhaps one reason that Thomas Jefferson felt so strongly about this was that while he was President, a slave revolution occurred in what is now the country of Haiti, concluding in 1804. Haiti was a slave colony of France, and the vast majority of the population there were slaves. As a result, the slaves rose up and overthrew the French. More than that, in one of the greatest bloodlettings in human history up until that time, the Haitians under their new King Christopher killed not only every French man, woman and child, but also killed every person there who was tainted by even the slightest bit of white blood. As a result, any tourist who goes to Haiti today will observe that the entire population there is pure black of the deepest dark variety.

While the slave revolution was going on in Haiti, Napoleon in 1802 sent a detachment of 10,000 of his finest French forces to subdue the population. However, after landing on that island, they disappeared. Not one French soldier was ever seen alive again.

Reinforcements met a similar fate. More than 24,000 French troops died in Haiti before Napoleon finally realized that the situation there was hopeless. The armies of the Czar of Russia hardly did better against the troops of Napoleon than the Haitians did.

President Thomas Jefferson knew about this debacle because, in 1802, the French asked him for American assistance, which he wisely declined. Jefferson was happy that the French army was bogged down in Haiti, because otherwise they would have occupied New Orleans. The slave revolution in Haiti helped make possible the Louisiana Purchase.

Thomas Jefferson was concerned about this sort of revolution spreading to America. In hundreds of his letters, he kept referring to the bloody revolution of St. Domingo, the island upon which Haiti is located. The following is an excerpt from a letter which is his most authoritative statement of his views on slavery. This was a letter dated August 25, 1814 to Edward Coles. Edward

Coles was a neighbor who became famous because he inherited a large number of slaves, took them to Illinois, bought land for them, gave them all their freedom, and eventually was elected as the Governor of Illinois in 1822 for these noble deeds:

> *Yet the hour of emancipation is advancing in the march of time. It will come; and whether brought on by the generous energy of our minds, or by the bloody process of St. Domingo, excited and conducted by the power of our present enemy, if one stationed permanently within our country, & offering asylum & arms to the oppressed, is a leaf of our history not yet turned over.*
> *As to the method by which this difficult work is to be effected, if permitted to be done by ourselves, I have seen no proposition so expedient on the whole, as that of emancipation of those born after a given day, and of their education and expatriation at a proper age. . . . . The idea of emancipating the whole at once, the old as well as the young, and retaining them here, is of those who have not the guide of either knowledge or experience of the subject. . . .*
> *My opinion has ever been that, until more can be done for them, we should endeavor, with those whom fortune has thrown on our hands, to feed & cloth them well, protect them from ill usage, require such reasonable labor only as performed voluntarily by freemen, and be led by no repugnancies to abdicate them, and our duties to them. The laws do not permit us to turn them loose, if that were for their good; and to commute them for other property is to commit them to those whose usage of them we cannot control. I hope then, my dear Sir, you will reconcile yourself to your country and its unfortunate condition. . . . .*

These are the actual views on slavery of Thomas Jefferson. He favored freeing the slaves, but only gradually, with those under a certain age freed first. The reason for this belief was the view, expressed in other parts of this lengthy letter, that the older slaves who had spent their entire lives in slavery would not be able to adjust to sudden freedom and would behave like children.

It must be mentioned here that of the only two slaves officially freed by Thomas Jefferson in his lifetime, one of them, James Hemings, committed suicide only a few years after gaining his freedom. The other, Robert Hemings, 'unfortunately got his hand shot off with a blunderbuss', according to the statement of Isaac Jefferson. See *Jefferson at Monticello*, p. 4. Robert Hemings died in 1819 at the early age of 57.

There were a few minor slave revolutions which took place in Virginia. The one which came closest to succeeding was the Gabriel conspiracy, organized by Gabriel Prosser, a freed black. According to Gabriel's carefully worked out plan, word was passed among all the plantations in the Richmond area that on exactly the night of August 30, 1800, more than one thousand crudely armed slaves would assemble at a certain designated point, from which they would march on Richmond, easily outnumbering and over-powering the small militia there, and would attack the penitentiary, where they would gain control of the muskets and other arms and ammunition contained therein.

There is a saying about the best laid plans of mice and men. On exactly the night of August 30, 1800, a tremendously violent thunder storm occurred. Most of the would-be black army did not attempt to slough through the rain and the deep mud of the back trails necessary to reach the rendezvous point, which was by a brook. Therefore, they did not keep their appointment to show up and fight. Most of those who did show up, got stuck in the mud and never reached their military objective. After the sun came up the next morning, two slaves told their master about this plan, and the authorities were alerted. Gabriel and the remnants of his army were easily rounded up and captured. Twenty-five blacks, including Gabriel, were publicly hung in Richmond, to the great approval of the white population.

Prior to being executed, Gabriel Prosser was personally interviewed by James Monroe, who was then the Governor of Virginia. Monroe reported that Gabriel displayed a high level of intelligence, a complete lack of fear and a full understanding of his human rights. Better to kill a man like that.

By coincidence, the fellow conspirators of Gabriel were imprisoned in the Richmond City Jail just at the time that James Thompson Callender was also there. Callender complained that he could not sleep in the night because Gabriel's men were always singing.

The Gabriel affair was never far from the mind of Thomas Jefferson, who always feared that something like that could happen again. He disapproved of the mass hangings, but, as they took place before he assumed the office of president, he could do nothing to stop them. Later, as President, Jefferson wrote a letter dated July 13, 1802 to Rufus King asking that the lives of such persons be spared and that they be deported to Sierra Leone in Africa. He said that these men were not common criminals and that they merely wanted to gain their human rights to freedom.

There are parts of the above quoted letter to Edward Coles which are wrongly used by Fawn Brodie and Virginius Dabney, among many others, to prove that Thomas Jefferson did or did not have sex with Sally Hemings. For example, at some point in this letter, Thomas Jefferson said that he opposed the political amalgamation of the races. This is taken by those to mean that he opposes miscegenation between persons of different race. However, this letter does not deal with that issue at all. It advocates a political separation between white and blacks, with both groups heaving their own countries and their own governments. Interracial sex was not a subject addressed in that letter. Since this letter is of such great importance regarding his views on slavery, it is included in full in the appendix.

His view was that the slaves, once freed, should be first educated and then expatriated; in other words, sent back to Africa. His famous quote about this is that the keeping of slaves is like 'holding a wolf by the ears', you do not want to keep it, but are afraid to let go. Everything Jefferson wrote on the subject of slavery contained the constant theme that sooner or later the slaves were bound to be freed. The longer that this inevitable event was put off, the greater the social upheaval when it finally occurred.

He studied the great slave revolutions of history, going back to Spartacus. This was at a time when almost nobody else in America was even thinking about this subject. Everybody else thought that the status quo could go on forever. They thought that more and more slaves could be imported to open up the vast new lands of the American West. Thomas Jefferson was almost alone in realizing that a tremendous explosion was bound to occur eventually. He felt that the only way out of this that he could see was the education and the extirpation of the slaves either back to Africa or to some other place where they could establish their own government.

Only with the perfect hindsight of history do we know that these views, however noble, would never have worked in practice. There were simply too many slaves in America for any significant part of them to be sent to Africa. The sudden freeing of all the slaves, even if it meant bringing on the bloody process of St. Domingo, was really the only practical solution.

However, the actual process which eventually took place was far more bloody than even the murderous revolution of St. Domingo. The slave revolution which Thomas Jefferson feared in America never materialized, except for a few minor revolts such as the Gabriel conspiracy of 1800, which was quickly put down. However, the American Civil War was by far the bloodiest war in all of human history up until that time, with nearly one million deaths, including battle casualties, deaths by poorly treated prisoners, and the countless men, women and children who died as a consequence of the war. Also, the Old South, once the richest part of America, was ruined economically. It took one hundred years for the South to recover from the poverty brought on by the Civil War.

History will always debate whether it was really necessary for so many people to die just for the sake of achieving the goal of freeing the slaves. There were many unlucky factors which led to the war and to the large number of battle deaths. There was the unfortunate 1857 *Dred Scott* decision of the United States Supreme Court, which declared that even slaves living in the non-slave states were still slaves and could be reclaimed by their masters. That decision thereby in effect extended slavery to the entire United States. That decision is regarded by most to have directly led to the American

Civil War, four years later. There was also the election of Abraham Lincoln as a minority president who only received 39.9% of the popular vote, thereby convincing the South of the unfairness of the electoral process and of their moral and legal right to break away from the Union.

Traditionally, both the North and the South have agreed that slavery was not the real issue which caused the Civil War. The North has always said that the reason for the war was 'to preserve the Union', not to free the slaves. The South has always said that they had the legal right to succeed from the Union, at any time and for any reason.

This was undeniably true, just as the Republics of the Soviet Union always had the legal right to succeed from that union. However, when they tried to exercise that right under Stalin, the results were not beneficial.

The Civil War caused such a deep wound in the psyche of America that only within the last twenty or thirty years has it become possible to face the reality that slavery was the underlying cause of the war. For example, the South elected Jefferson Davis as its president, and Jefferson Davis was the most rabid proponent of slavery which the South had. However, even that point is still being debated. In reality, slavery both was and was not the issue. Abraham Lincoln, in his campaign for president, never said that he intended to free the slaves and probably had no intention of doing so. He merely opposed the extension of slavery into the newly emerging territories of the American West. Lincoln did not free the slaves until 1863, after the war had already been under way for three years, and probably freed them then only to gain a battlefield advantage. Significantly, he did not free all the slaves in 1863. He only freed those slaves residing in states in open rebellion against the United States. Thus, the slaves residing in slave states such as Maryland and Missouri, which were not in open rebellion, were not freed.

The truth about Abraham Lincoln is that he was not the holy man sitting on the right hand of God as he is depicted as being nowadays. The Emancipation Proclamation, which freed the slaves, was, if anything, issued just to cause turmoil in the South and gain an advantage in the war. During the American Revolutionary War, the British had done the same thing, offering freedom to every slave who ran away, even though it was the British slave ships that were bringing the slaves to America, both before and after the war.

Even while the Civil War was going on, the Union Army enforced slavery and returned runaway slaves to their Southern masters. In one famous incident, while General Sherman, of 'War is Hell' fame, was in the process of burning his way across Georgia, a group of several hundred runaway slaves, including women and children, tried to cross a temporary bridge which would have taken them to freedom. They were chased off the bridge by the Union Army several times. Finally, the pontoon bridge itself was disconnected and demolished while the slaves were still trying to cross, with the result that women with babies in their arms fell into the river and drowned. The surviving slaves were then rounded up by the Union Army and returned to their Southern masters. General Sherman, under whose command this happened, was angry about this because of the time wasted by his officers on this matter. They could have better spent their valuable time setting fire to neighboring houses and barns. A few months later, General Robert E. Lee surrendered at Appomattox and the war was over.

Atrocities like these tend not to be mentioned in history books dealing with the Civil War. They show that, with the exception of a few extreme abolitionists, almost no white person, either in the North or in the South, including Abraham Lincoln, was prepared to contemplate a time when a black man would be just as free as a white man. Those in favor of freeing the slaves still had the idea of sending them all back to Africa.

This is the reason that former President Jimmy Carter of Georgia always refers to this war as 'The War between The States'. He never calls it the Civil War because, according to the Southern view, it was not a civil war. The South had the legal right to secede and they properly exercised that right. The northern invasion of the South was completely illegal, according to them.

It was indeed this attitude that caused the South to lose the war. The South won the the first major battle of the war, which was the Battle of Bull Run, which took place on July 21, 1861, at Manassas, Virginia, just across the river from Washington, D.C. After that battle, the Northern Army disintegrated. The Army of Virginia could easily have crossed the Potomac, marched into Washington, D.C. unopposed, arrested Abraham Lincoln, had him transferred to a Richmond jail, and the war would have been over. Lincoln could not have escaped. He could not have ridden his horse off into the mountains the way that Thomas Jefferson did during the Revolutionary War. Lincoln was not that popular and had nowhere to hide. Maryland was leaning towards the South. The Mayor of Baltimore, who was arrested by Lincoln, was in favor of succession.

However, the South was determined at that time to proceed in a proper and legal manner. It did not want to arrest Abraham Lincoln. It did not want to invade the North, although it finally did so two years later. During that intervening two years, General McClellan was able to rebuild the Union Army from scratch and to import troops plus superior arms and ammunition from Europe, including repeater rifles rather than muzzle loaded rifles, which finally enabled the North to win the Civil War.

No doubt it is true that there must have been some way for the slaves to have eventually been freed without a million people having to die in the process. However, it must also be stated that the direst predictions of Thomas Jefferson of a repeat of 'the bloody process of St. Domingo' proved ultimately to be true.

In the waning years of his life, when Thomas Jefferson was getting old, he seemed to accommodate himself more and more to the necessity of keeping the slaves in bondage. According to Israel Jefferson, when a law was passed in Virginia making it illegal to teach a slave how to read and write, Thomas Jefferson remarked that slaves should be taught how to read, but not how to write. If taught how to write, they would learn how to forge their own freedom papers and the police would not be able to tell which black man was free and which was a slave. It seemed that Thomas Jefferson felt that this would be a bad thing.

For all his imperfections, Thomas Jefferson was clearly a man of action who produced results. We can only respect him for it. Although the name of Jefferson is included on every list of Great Presidents, his actual contribution is, if anything, underestimated. There is a tendency to assume that the Louisiana Purchase just fell into his lap, that his presidency was otherwise uneventful, and that his best achievements had occurred before he was president.

Actually, a strong case can be made that Jefferson was by far the greatest president of all, for the reason that, had he not won the election in 1800, there might shortly thereafter have been no longer any United States of America.

The presidency of John Adams from 1797 to 1801 had been disastrous. The problem was that not only was John Adams an inept administrator, but his policy of attempting to establish a strong central government was wrong. By the end of his term as President, New England was on the verge of succeeding from the Union, as were the states of the Deep South of Georgia and South Carolina. In addition, under Adams, the hated Alien and Sedition Acts had been passed. Foreigners, especially refugees from France, were in danger of being rounded up and sent back to their country, where they faced the guillotine. Newspaper editors and reporters were imprisoned for writing articles critical of the President. James Thompson Callender, who later on published the Sally Hemings story, was just one of the many political writers put in jail during this period. For example, Journalist Thomas Cooper was sentenced to prison in 1800 because 'he intended to mislead the ignorant . . . . against the President, and . . . . influence their votes in the next election.'

In addition, Adams had sounded the alarm that France was about to invade America! As improbable as this may seem, General George Washington was recalled to active service, supposedly to repel the impending French invasion. At Washington's insistence, Hamilton was named as the second in command.

At this time, the two great superpowers in the world were England and France. In every dispute, Jefferson took the side of France whereas Adams and Hamilton took the side of England. Jefferson, of course, knew the French language and had spent five years in France. He also felt that France was more inclined towards democracy and would never pose the threat to America that England did. He remembered that it was due to the assistance of France that America had won the Revolutionary War.

The State of the Union was in such disarray by the conclusion of the Adams' Presidency that it seemed that the Articles of Confederation, which had lasted only 10 years from 1777 until 1787, were going to survive only slightly less longer than the Constitution of the United States.

As soon as he became President, Jefferson brought all this to an end. One of the first things he did was to let the newspaper editors out of jail. He also stopped the deportations of the foreigners. Indeed, he appointed as his Secretary of the Treasury a Frenchman who had been on the list of those scheduled to be deported. He acknowledged the legal right of the States to succeed from the Union, or to 'nullify' their decision to join the Union, as it was called at the time. In so doing, he convinced the states not to carry out their threat to succeed, postponing the act of succession for 60 years.

Thus, the peaceful presidency of Jefferson was not due to any lackluster character on his part but rather was due to his success in soothing the passions of the rival groups.

The single great event of the presidency of Thomas Jefferson was the Louisiana Purchase. This huge tract of land, five times the size of France, was purchased by the United States from Napoleon for 27 million dollars in 1803. Napoleon was ready to sell, apparently being discouraged by the revolution and the massacre just then taking place in the island of St. Domingo, in the part now known as Haiti, in which the entire French population was eventually killed. However, is it often forgotten that the Louisiana Purchase was made illegally. There was nothing in the Constitution of the United States which gave the President the power to undertake such a massive purchase of land or to borrow such a huge amount of money for this purpose. The Congress never approved of this purchase. Jefferson just did it on his own, negotiating directly with his friends in France, through his Secretary of State, James Madison, and his 'envoy extraordinary' to Paris, James Monroe.

James Monroe signed the treaty with France on behalf of the United States in total absence of all legal authority to do so. Since the President controlled the purse strings, Congress found itself powerless to do anything to stop this transaction from taking place. By this one transaction, Jefferson changed the course of world history, doubling the size of the United States of America and also nearly doubling its national debt.

Another result of the Presidency of Jefferson was that the Supreme Court was greatly strengthened. Previously, under Chief Justice John Jay, the Supreme Court had been essentially a weak arm of the executive branch, as it is in most other countries of the world. Under Jefferson, the Supreme Court became much stronger. However, this was for the opposite reason from that which one might imagine. The Chief Justice was John Marshall, a political opponent of Thomas Jefferson. Marshall had been appointed by President Adams in the final days of his presidency. Jefferson got along with John Marshall about as well as Hamilton got along with Burr. All of the famous decisions of John Marshall as Chief Justice, including the most famous decision of all, *Marbury v. Madison*, established the power of the Supreme Court to over-rule the decisions of the legislative and executive branches. The Madison who lost that case was James Madison, the Secretary of State under Jefferson. This infuriated Jefferson, who kept seeing his legislative acts being declared unconstitutional by his political enemy, John Marshall.

Jefferson never forgave Adams for the fact that Adams stayed up late at night in the final evening of his presidency and appointed all of Jefferson's political opponents as federal judges. These became known in American history as the 'Midnight Judges'. Adams then left town and did not attend the inauguration of Jefferson a few hours later.

In spite of his re-election by an overwhelming landslide, Thomas Jefferson was not a universally popular president. His popularity was hurt by his economic embargo imposed against Europe. This caused great hardship in America, particularly in the South, because the plantation owners were forced to the verge of bankruptcy because they could not sell their cotton to the textile mills in England.

However, with the hindsight of history, it can be seen that the embargo had a valid justification and was the lesser of two evils, because the only viable alternatives to the embargo were a declaration of war against England or the permanent humiliation of America.

The embargo was the result of the 'Chesapeake Affair' of 1807. The American Battleship 'Chesapeake' was taken by surprise and captured by the British ship 'Leopard', just off the Virginia coastline. When the British boarded the ship, they found one British deserter. This man was strung up from the galleys and hanged on the spot. This was clearly an act of war. More than that, in 1806, England had passed 'Orders of Council' which gave English ships the right to seize American ships and cargoes on the high seas, and indeed they often did so.

These outrageous acts caused the American public to clamor for war. However, Jefferson did not want a war. Therefore, he declared an embargo. This made him even more unpopular.

However, we know now that his decision was the right one. At that time, the entire Europe was embroiled in war. The Chesapeake Affair was merely a manifestation of that war, plus the fact that England still considered America to be a colony.

Public pressure forced Thomas Jefferson to rescind the embargo near the end of his presidency. The result of this was that his successor, James Madison, got involved in the same war which Thomas Jefferson had succeeded in avoiding. Every tenth grade American history book tells us that the War of 1812 was a great American victory. However, during this 'victory', Washington, D.C. was overrun by the British and the White House and the Library of Congress was burned to the ground. Along with it, all of the books contained therein were burned. As a result of this, Jefferson sold his personal library to start a new Library of Congress later on. Baltimore was also attacked and nearly fell to the British.

Of course, the War of 1812 was an American victory, of sorts. However, in reality, like so many wars, it was a war that nobody won. It is true that after this war, England stopped seizing American ships on the high seas. Still, rather than fight this war, Jefferson's approach of an embargo against England was probably better.

The other event which marred the Presidency of Thomas Jefferson was the trial for treason of Aaron Burr. In the light of history, the entire matter seems ridiculous. At various times, it was alleged that Aaron Burr intended to lead the Army of New England in a War of Succession against America, that he had assembled a group of men for the purpose of attacking New Orleans, and that he intended to set himself up as the Emperor of Mexico.

There can be no doubt that Thomas Jefferson was perfectly capable of carrying out a personal vendetta against his own former Vice-President and that at least some of these charges could have been trumped up. Aaron Burr is one man about whom the full truth will never be known. He is often depicted as a short, balding, dark-skinned man with two little horns growing out of the back of his head. However, to say that Aaron Burr was the epitome of the devil is an exaggeration. Nevertheless, the question will always remain: Was this man who missed becoming the President of the United States by a single vote, really a demented genius?

The answer probably is that the charges against Aaron Burr were basically true. It was just bad luck that such a strange case arose while Thomas Jefferson happened to be president. Another different sort of question can be raised as to whether there was anything illegal under American law for an American citizen to hatch a plot to become the Emperor of Mexico, as unlikely as this prospect might have seemed.

Burr was tried and ultimately acquitted by Chief Justice John Marshall, who, in the practice of those days, also served as a trial judge in addition to his duties as Chief Justice of the United States Supreme Court. During the trial, Burr and Marshall had tried to serve a subpoena upon President Jefferson to compel him to testify as a witness. Jefferson had refused to attend court, citing sovereign immunity, even though he was clearly involved in the case, having personally ordered the arrest and extradition of Burr. This provided the precedent for President Richard Nixon 170 years later to attempt to refuse to provide the Watergate tapes to the court.

There can be little doubt that next to Thomas Jefferson, the two most gifted and brilliant men in America at that time were Alexander Hamilton and Aaron Burr. They were still young men in 1804 and either or both of them might easily have eventually become president of the United States had not one of them killed the other.

Both had remarkably similar backgrounds. Both were about the same age. (Hamilton was born in 1755, Burr in 1756). Unlike Thomas Jefferson, both were decidedly not born with a silver spoon in their mouths. They both suffered extreme poverty and destitution during their early youths. Both had essentially no father. Both had many children. Both rose quickly to the top, by dent of sheer brilliance. Both got involved with women other than their wives and got into political trouble because of it. Both came to prominence as military commanders at an early age. Both fought duels against other persons before they fought against each other.

It is often said that Alexander Hamilton was illegitimate. This is technically true, because, prior to the birth of Alexander Hamilton, his mother, who died when he was 13, had been divorced by her husband on the grounds of adultery. As part of this divorce decree, the judge had ordered that she could never remarry for the remainder of her natural life. This was the standard ruling made in cases in those days involving divorce by reason of adultery.

The specific allegation against the mother of Alexander Hamilton was that she had been a prostitute working in a whorehouse in Barbados, where Alexander himself was subsequently born.

One of the strange rumors which went around was that George Washington, who visited Barbados in 1751, might have been a customer of the mother of Alexander Hamilton and therefore might have been his father. However, the IQ of Alexander Hamilton was much too high for George Washington to have been his father.

The parental background of Aaron Burr was hardly better. He had distinguished parents. His father had been the president of what became Princeton University. His maternal grandfather was Jonathan Edwards, who is still considered by historians today to be possibly the greatest philosopher and theologian that America has ever produced. Edwards was the author of the famous doctrine of *Original Sin*, which was published in 1758. He died of a smallpox inoculation the same year.

Unfortunately, both of the parents of Aaron Burr died before Aaron was two years old. He was bounced around from place to place and was eventually raised by a bachelor uncle, Timothy Edwards, who was a strict disciplinarian in accordance with the Puritan tradition of his famous father.

Aaron Burr tried to run away from home many times, starting from the age of four, once boarding a ship destined for the high seas. These traumatic experiences during his early childhood no doubt contributed to the demented nature of his character observed later on. Nevertheless, he was gifted with high intelligence and gained admission to what became Princeton University at the age of 13! He graduated at age 16.

The daring exploits of Aaron Burr during the early stages of the Revolutionary War earned him a high military rank at the age of 21. However, he did not like George Washington, nor did George Washington like him. He sat out the end of the war.

Aaron Burr was an avid chess player. His diary shows that while in Europe, he often stayed up until one o'clock in the morning playing. He must have been somewhat accomplished at the game. He generally gave his favorite opponent the handicap of a rook to equalize their chances. Thomas Jefferson was also a chess player. He said that he played even against Benjamin Franklin. However, the implication was that Franklin, who had spent more time in Europe where chess was popular, was the better player.

Burr has certainly received a raw deal from American history. He was a hard working and active person. Without the backing of Burr, Thomas Jefferson might never have become President. It was Burr's idea to make Jefferson the presidential candidate in 1796. That was the first election contested by two parties. Jefferson refused to campaign at all. In 1795, Jefferson had retired to Monticello. Burr came there to visit him. At that time, Jefferson had partially demolished Monticello and was struggling to get his walls up before the winter set in. He seemed to have little interest in campaigning for president. If Jefferson had made some effort, he might easily have become the president four years earlier than he did. As it was, he lost that election by only three electoral votes.

Hamilton and Burr had both become aids to General George Washington during the Revolutionary War. They were useful to Washington because they both knew how to read and write at a competent level, which few other officers could do, plus Hamilton and Burr had both distinguished themselves in the line of battle. The details of the relationship between Hamilton and Burr are recorded in many other history books, but suffice it to say that they were rivals almost from the start. The tragic result of this was that one of them killed the other some 28 years later, while Jefferson was president.

Although Alexander Hamilton is remembered today as a brilliant writer and thinker, he was also an irascible person. His ongoing feuds with Thomas Jefferson, a person not easily drawn into personal disputes, were legendary. He also once agreed to a duel with James Monroe, but it was called off, surprisingly through the intervention of Aaron Burr. Perhaps the most tragic consequence of his personality was that the son of Alexander Hamilton,

Philip Hamilton, age 20, was killed in a duel in November, 1801, on the same Weehawken Dueling Ground in the same spot and in the same way that his father was to be killed three years later. Philip Hamilton fought that duel against a man who had insulted the personal reputation of his father.

With all of the personal disputes that Alexander Hamilton got into, it seems likely that eventually somebody would have killed him, had not Aaron Burr been the one to do it. Still, it seems unbelievable even after the passage of almost two hundred years that the Vice-President of the United States, in office at that time, engaged in a shoot-out and killed the former Secretary of the Treasury of the United States.

As to Alexander Hamilton's constant feuding with Thomas Jefferson, it appears that he sincerely believed that Thomas Jefferson would make a weak president, in view of his libertarian ideas and his radical concept of giving freedom to the people. Alexander Hamilton opposed this, because he favored a strong central government, somewhat more similar to the government which we have today. As to his assessment that Thomas Jefferson would make a weak president and that the nation would lapse into anarchy, Alexander Hamilton was eventually to be proven wrong, but he cannot be faulted for having that belief.

It is often said that Thomas Jefferson was an architect, an inventor, a scientist, and agronomist and so on. However, it has never yet been alleged that he was a master of military strategy. In defending the charge that, while Governor, Thomas Jefferson had been so inept that he had not posted a lookout to see if the British were coming, thereby allowing the British under General Benedict Arnold to march into Richmond virtually unopposed, Thomas Jefferson stated that he had not thought to post a lookout because none of his predecessors had done so either. Unfortunately, he did not have the opportunity to read about the *Midnight Ride of Paul Revere* ('One if by land and two if by sea' and the 'Old North Church tower as a signal light'), because that yarn by Longfellow was not composed until 1863, long after Thomas Jefferson had died.

The one thing which Thomas Jefferson did for which he was most severely criticized during his lifetime and which almost ended his political career was his act of running away into the Appalachian Mountains when the British attacked first Richmond, then Jefferson's estate at Elk Hill and finally Monticello in an effort to capture and arrest him. His detractors stated that, as he was the Governor of Virginia at the time, he should have stayed behind and directed the battle against the British, instead of running away. Because of this criticism, he resigned as Governor of Virginia in June, 1781.

However, it has been pointed out that the British Army exhausted itself by chasing around Virginia in an effort to catch Jefferson. In addition, the entire population of Virginia turned against the British because of the acts of

Lord Cornwallis in burning fences, barns and crops in a single minded effort to capture Jefferson. Both factors contributed to the British surrender at Yorktown, only four months after Thomas Jefferson resigned as governor.

The British raid on Monticello under Gen. Banastre Tarleton took place on June 3-4, 1781. The local legend in Charlottesville has it that it was John Jouette who saw Gen. Tarleton and his troop of cavalry coming, got on a fleet horse, took a route shorter than the main, and arrived at Monticello in time to warn Jefferson and members of the legislature who were also there, giving them time to escape. See *Early Charlottesville, Recollections of James Alexander 1828-1874*, p. 16. Jefferson got onto his trusty horse, Caractacus, and rode off into the mountains. Only a few weeks later, he submitted his resignation as Governor of Virginia. We now know from the *Memoirs of Isaac Jefferson* that his hide-out from then until the end of the war was at Poplar Forest, near Lynchburg.

It is surprising that the British thought that an army on foot could catch a single man on horseback, as familiar with the mountains and the terrain of Virginia as Thomas Jefferson was. General Light-Horse Henry Lee (not to be confused, of course, with his son, Black-Horse Henry Lee), referred derisively in his 1812 book *Memoirs of the War*, Vol. II, p. 234, to the troops of Cornwallis 'chasing our governor from hill to hill'. This was a snipe at both Cornwallis and at Thomas Jefferson himself.

Apparently, General Light-Horse Henry Lee, the father of General Robert E. Lee, felt that Thomas Jefferson should have fought off the entire British Army himself when they attacked Monticello or should have allowed himself to be captured, in which case he might easily have been hanged for treason on the spot. This was a real possibility. The Americans hanged as a spy Major Andre, who was caught passing secret messages from Gen. Benedict Arnold to British Governor Clinton. This execution was personally supervised by Alexander Hamilton, who said that he had executed a better man than he. The British also hung spies and deserters during the Revolutionary War. Clearly, writing the *Declaration of Independence* was itself a treasonable act from the point of view of the British, punishable by death.

General Cornwallis later went to India, where he played a large role in subduing the population there with the same slash and burn tactics which were unsuccessful in Virginia.

In case the reader ever appears on a quiz program and the MC asks the question: What was the name of the horse of Thomas Jefferson? Remember the answer: Caractacus. Thomas Jefferson used about five primary horses during his lifetime, but Caractacus was by far the most famous. One legend has it that Caractacus did not agree with Thomas Jefferson's plan of retreat in the face of the advancing British army, so threw him off, breaking his arm.

One often hears attempts to compare George Washington to Thomas Jefferson. In fact, there is no comparison and no similarity at all between these two men. Jefferson was a great thinker, but certainly not a military man. In contrast, George Washington was not a great thinker, but he was even more certainly not a great military man. His great ability was in surrounding himself with sycophants, who would protect his position as commander-in-chief, while letting others do the actual fighting. There was not one battle-field victory for which General George Washington really deserves credit. His best known battle, the great 'Battle of Monmouth Court House', was actually an attempt by George Washington to chase the British who had decided on their own to make a strategic withdrawal from Philadelphia to New York.

Even that battle was by no stretch of the imagination a victory. It might have become a victory, except for the fact that General Charles Lee, who had disagreed with Washington's plan of attack in the first place, disobeyed Washington's order to attack and retreated instead. With this momentum lost, the British were allowed to continue on their way to New York relatively unmolested. That great battle took place on June 28, 1778. It was the last battlefield engagement by General George Washington during the entire Revolutionary War, which ended with the surrender of Cornwallis in October, 1781.

Washington does, however, deserve full credit for his ability to keep people working together towards a common cause. He was a 'unifier'. In this respect, perhaps he does deserve the the the title he received from history as the 'Father of his Country'. Later, as president, he headed what would now be called a 'unity' or coalition government. He brought into his cabinet both Thomas Jefferson and Alexander Hamilton, two of the most bitter rivals imaginable. Jefferson was reluctant to join. He preferred to be reappointed as the Ambassador to France. Washington had to write him two personal letters before he agreed to become Secretary of State. Jefferson did not arrive in Philadelphia to assume his duties until early 1790, nearly one year after Washington had become president.

One great thing which George Washington did was that he appointed the best two men for their respective jobs. Alexander Hamilton was unquestionably the best man to become the first Secretary of the Treasury. Thomas Jefferson was unquestionably the best man to become the first Secretary of State. However, Washington could never stop the constant feuding between Jefferson and Hamilton. Both quit the cabinet while Washington was still in his first term of office. Jefferson resigned on December 31, 1793.

The French military officers sent by King Louis XVI to assist America in the Revolutionary War appear to have done more than just help out George Washington. Of course, there can be no doubt that George Washington made a great contribution to the American victory, because he showed up at the surrender ceremonies just in time to accept the sword of Cornwallis.

George Washington spent most of the war in various stages of retreat in New York and Pennsylvania. By the end of the war, he had few troops left, most of them having gone home because of not being paid their salaries. The majority of the army was at that point French. George Washington did not campaign in Virginia and fought no battles there, where the victory was ultimately won.

This is not to say that George Washington was completely passive during the war. He did maneuver around and is famous for crossing the Delaware River by rowboat several times. The famous painting of *Washington Crossing the Delaware* has a romantic version of him standing in the bow of the rowboat. If he had done this in real life, he would probably have fallen into the river. Anybody who has studied the actual history of that war, as opposed to the official elementary school version, has quickly realized that General George Washington contributed little to the ultimate American victory.

For example, when the British landed 35,000 troops on Staten Island, New York, Washington did not attack them as they were getting off the ship, as he obviously should have done. Instead, he waited in the luxury of Brooklyn Heights. When the British came there looking for him, he retreated to Manhattan. When the British crossed the East River, Washington decided that Harlem was the place for him and camped out on what is now approximately the campus of Columbia University. This high ground, now known as 'Morningside Heights' but then known as 'Harlem Heights', was a good place for an army which was not anxious to fight. When the British came there, Washington decided that New Jersey was a good place to be. As a result, the British captured all of New York City, without ever being engaged in a serious battle.

After that, George Washington maneuvered even more backward, giving up New Jersey, and finally camping for one famous winter of 1777 at Valley Forge, Pennsylvania, where his un-paid troops suffered from frost-bitten feet, while General George Washington lounged by the fireside in the luxury of a private home.

It was the French officers, of whom Lafayette was one, who had studied the scientific art of war and who knew how to formulate a proper strategic plan of attack. Lafayette, with an army of 3,000 men in Virginia, attacked the army of Cornwallis, who had 7,000 under his command, on July 6, 1781. Cornwallis was never actually defeated in battle. He eventually surrendered on October 19, 1781 because he was surrounded and had nowhere to go. The French generals, including Rochambeau and Lafayette, had cut off all escape routs by land, whereas French Admiral Francios de Grasse had blockaded Yorktown by sea. This led Cornwallis to give up.

Technically, the war was not yet over. The British still occupied New York. However, they were simply ignored. Two years later, in 1783, realizing that the population was against them, and lacking the ability and the will simply to envelop the colonies and burn all the major cities to the ground, as the North did to the South in the subsequent American Civil War, the British finally withdrew.

In spite of what we all have learned in our high school history books, the American Revolution was won more at sea than by land. This was partly due to the exploits of John Paul Jones (a collateral ancestor of this author) who sailed all the way around the island of Britain, entering the British harbors and sinking British ships while moored at anchor. The main problem which the British faced during the war was the need to supply their army across 3,000 miles of ocean, while being engaged at sea by the French and Dutch navies who had come to the assistance of the Americans plus, of course, Captain John Paul Jones, who was operating from the safety of French harbors. If one counts the battles actually fought on land, the British won the overwhelming majority, and the few victories of the Americans included mostly those won by General Benedict Arnold, who later on changed sides, after being wrongfully subjected to a politically motivated court martial.

The general who truly was a great commander during the war was none other than Benedict Arnold. He was a pure 'red-blooded' American, whose ancestors had been among the earliest colonists. His grandfather had been the governor of Rhode Island. He was perhaps the only American general with a winning record during the Revolutionary War. Without the victories which he won, America might easily have lost the Revolutionary War. Had Benedict Arnold not changed sides near the end of the war, he probably would have emerged as the greatest hero of that war, greater even than General George Washington, rather than as the worst villain.

General Benedict Arnold was arguably the ablest military officer in the entire Revolutionary War. He won battles for both sides. For the Americans, he won the battle of Saratoga and successfully occupied Montreal. He retreated only when overwhelmed by a vastly superior force. For the British, he won the Battle of Richmond and nearly captured Jefferson.

Benedict Arnold won an impressive series of victories at a time when all of the other American military officers were losing. However, he was too thin skinned for the political in-fighting which is also part of every war. After one of his greatest victories, he was enraged at being passed over for promotion in favor of junior officers. However, a few kind words from General George Washington caused him to fight and win again. He even fought successfully as a common foot-soldier on occasions when his political opponents in the military denied him an official rank.

Eventually, the Continental Congress did award Benedict Arnold the rank of major general, but later on he repeatedly felt slighted again. He eventually changed sides and won some victories for the British. The British also awarded him the rank of general but never respected him in view of the fact that he was a turn-coat. They sent him to London before the war was over and refused to give him further military assignments. He died there in 1801, scorned in his adopted country, a broken and bitter man, despised on both sides of the Atlantic. However, next only to General George Washington, among all the Revolutionary War generals, his name will ring forever in the annals of history. Just about the worst thing that you can say about a person is to call him 'a Benedict Arnold'.

Jefferson had nothing to do with either the *Constitution of the United States* or the *Bill of Rights*, because he was in France from 1784 until nearly the end of 1789. Had he been in America during this period, the Constitution might have been a very different document. Surprisingly, none of his letters appear to express any strong opinion as to whether the new Constitution was a good or a bad thing. He was completely out of the picture because of his long stay in France during the period of adoption and ratification.

Unlike the *Declaration of Independence*, no one person can be considered the architect of the *Constitution of the United States*. Alexander Hamilton, the sole signing delegate from New York (the remainder of the New York delegation having walked out in protest), was high on the list of framers, as was Gouverneur Morris, who represented Pennsylvania at the time, and George Wythe of Virginia. However, George Wythe was among the many delegates to the Constitutional Convention who did not sign the final document for one reason or another. The Constitution was signed on September 17, 1787, exactly when Thomas Jefferson was carousing about with Maria Cosway over in France and more than two years before he returned to America.

Only six persons signed both the *Declaration of Independence* and the *Constitution of the United States*. These were Benjamin Franklin, George Clymer, Robert Morris, James Wilson (all of Pennsylvania), George Read (Delaware) and Roger Sherman (Conn.).

The minutes of the Constitutional Convention were deliberately destroyed so that the acrimonious debates which resulted in the compromises and the adoption of the Constitution would never be made public. However, to Hamilton goes the credit for securing ratification by the key State of New York. Hamilton probably did not play a major role in the drafting of the Constitution itself, but he became the primary author of the brilliantly written *Federalist Papers*, which convinced the public of the benefits of ratifying the Constitution.

This was no small achievement. Almost everybody seemed to object to the Constitution for one reason or another. The battle against the ratification of the constitution was led by Patrick Henry, who, by choice, spent most of his career as a perpetual outsider. The biggest state, New York, and the smallest state, Rhode Island, both thought that the Constitution was unfair to them. The South reluctantly joined the Union with the understanding, later reneged upon, that they could withdraw at any time. Near the end, both North Carolina and Rhode Island refused to join. Because of this, they were threatened with an embargo. They were told that if they did not join the Union, their goods would be taxed the same as imports from foreign countries. As a result, they finally both joined.

The *Bill of Rights* was passed by Congress on September 25, 1789, just two months before Thomas Jefferson returned from France. The chief architect of the Bill of Rights is considered to have been George Mason of Virginia, who refused to sign the Constitution on the grounds that it did not contain a bill of rights. However, Thomas Jefferson was clearly in sympathy with the *Bill of Rights* and was in America as the Secretary of State during its period of ratification, which lasted from 1789 until 1791.

Earlier, while a member of the Virginia Assembly from 1776 until 1779, Thomas Jefferson tried to amend the *Virginia Constitution* with articles similar to those contained in the *Bill of Rights*. However, his radical ideas went much further and included free public education and gradual emancipation of the slaves. Almost all of his amendments were rejected. The one about freeing the slaves did not even come up for a vote in the Virginia House of Delegates. He did, however, get passed a law abolishing the automatic right of primogeniture, which had been designed to preserve the British aristocracy and which had meant that the oldest son inherited everything from his father and that the younger sons and the daughters got nothing. Jefferson had been the beneficiary of this law, as he had inherited all of the assets of his father, Peter Jefferson, whereas his lackluster younger brother, Randolph Jefferson, and his many sisters had received nothing.

Some of the other proposals of Thomas Jefferson were accepted later on, however. His proposal for the separation of the church and state was accepted in 1786.

While in France, Thomas Jefferson, in 1786, had the audacity to go to England and present his credentials to King George III. It was reported that Thomas Jefferson was deeply offended when King George III turned his back on him. However, considering what Thomas Jefferson had said about King George III in the *Declaration of Independence*, it is amazing that King George III received him at all and/or that he did not have him strung up and hanged on the spot.

Tradition has it that the decision to move the capital of the United States from Philadelphia to what is now Washington, D.C. came as the result of a deal between Hamilton and Jefferson. Hamilton wanted the United States to assume the debts incurred by individual states during the Revolutionary War and thereafter. Jefferson and other Virginians would not agree. They opposed the strong central government which the assumption of these debts would entail. Jefferson believed that under the Constitution, the central government did not have the authority to go into debt. He also believed that once the central government went into debt, it would never be paid off and this debt would continue to burden future generations. (This prediction proved to be entirely correct). In addition, Virginia itself had no debt and therefore had no reason to want the central government to assume it.

Another thing which has not changed in the last two hundred years was that New York was heavily in debt and had no means to pay. The money issued under the *Articles of Confederation* had become worthless. Also, for reasons of political philosophy, Hamilton wanted to establish the Bank of the United States (a predecessor of the Federal Reserve Bank), which Jefferson opposed. However, Jefferson did not want to have to travel all the way to Philadelphia to serve in the government.

This dispute led to a historic deal. Jefferson agreed that the United States would assume the debts of New York and the other states. Hamilton agreed to move the capital to the boarder between Maryland and Virginia. This deal was approved by Congress in 1790. Congress passed a resolution that the capital would be situated on the banks of the Potomac River on an area 'not exceeding ten miles square'.

This explains the odd fact that, if one looks at a map of Washington, D.C. plus Arlington County on the Virginia side, one finds a perfect square exactly ten miles long on each side. This probably makes Washington, D.C. the only perfectly square city in the entire world. However, the Virginia side was returned to that state by an improvident act of Congress in 1846.

In summary, Thomas Jefferson, more than any other man of his time, played a decisive role in making America the country that it is today. He and his direct political successors governed America for 28 years, from 1801 to 1829. His most important and remembered contribution was the idea of a democratically elected government by the people. None of the other leading politicians of his time, including George Washington, John Adams and Alexander Hamilton, favored that idea. Washington and Hamilton were actually admirers of King George III. They might even have favored establishing a monarchy were it not for the fact that George Washington never had a legitimate child. John Adams favored establishing something similar to the British House of Lords, where the rich and the powerful would have an extra voice in the government. Only Jefferson argued in favor of a government by majority rule, where all the votes counted equally. That is the reason that Jefferson gets the full credit for our present system of government. The term 'Jeffersonian Democracy' today means 'one man, one vote'.

# Chapter Fifteen

## And What Was Wrong with It Anyway?

In the endless debate over these historical events, the underlying presumption always seems to be that if this really happened, there was really something terribly wrong with it.

For example, Fawn Brodie keeps talking about the 'deep sense of guilt and shame' felt by Thomas Jefferson, whereas Virginius Dabney says that Thomas Jefferson did not feel any sense of guilt and shame at all.

Both operate under the presumption that if Thomas Jefferson fathered children by Sally Hemings, he would have felt guilt and shame. Therefore, they claim that they can prove whether he fathered the children or not by proving whether he felt shame or not.

Everybody seems to have overlooked the fact that it is at least barely possible for a man to have sex with a woman without feeling guilty about it.

Slavery was an immoral institution. There is no doubt about this, even though one will still find people in Virginia prepared to argue this point.

However, once slavery is accepted, why is having sex with slaves and fathering children by them more immoral than owning slaves itself?

Stated differently, which is worse: To force a man to toil in the fields at backbreaking labor for all his life at no pay at all.

Or is it worse for a man to have sex with a woman who has essentially no real choice in the matter?

Feminists are always arguing that women never have any choice in the matter of sex, anyway. They are all victims of economic exploitation and, therefore, they are all slaves.

Thomas Jefferson spent his life surrounded by slave women. Perhaps he only did it with Sally, but all of them were presumably available to him.

It is likely that any of the women available to him would have welcomed his advances. Their prospects for advancement otherwise were not merely bleak; they were zero. A woman basically goes with a man to improve her life. Even a ration of nine fish per week instead of the normal eight would have been an improvement for these women. If they didn't do it, the only possible reason would have been fear of Sally. A woman in their position would never refuse Thomas Jefferson himself.

One only wonders how Sally managed to keep her man under tow, with all the other slave girls around.

The living situation of Thomas Jefferson was not unique. It seems that everybody was doing it and that this practice was accepted. In fact, Thomas Jefferson took the moral high ground as compared to the others. He never had a wife while this was going on. Other plantation owners did it behind the backs of or perhaps even with the full knowledge of their wives.

Mary Boykin Chesnut (1823–1886) of Camden, South Carolina, near Columbia, wrote the best diary ever written of the Civil War. She was the daughter of the pro-slavery Governor of South Carolina, Stephen Miller, who founded the 'States Rights Movement' and favored 'nullification', which was a predecessor to the movement for succession from the Union, as early as 1828. She was educated in French in a school in South Carolina run by a refugee from Santo Domingo, thereby becoming fluent in Haitian Creole. She studied the history of the slave revolution which had taken place in Haiti, in which every white or part white person had been killed, with the exception of those few who, like her teacher, had escaped. However, she found it difficult to use her knowledge of Creole to communicate with the speakers of another kind of Creole she met in Louisiana. She married her husband, James Chesnut, a future Senator from South Carolina, and lived on a plantation with more than five hundred slaves.

Mary Boykin Chesnut said that her husband never bought slaves, but that their numbers just kept increasing by rapid reproduction, and were never sold. The exact number of slaves was never counted except that it was known to be more than 500 as early as 1849. Her husband resigned from the United States Senate on November 10, 1860, immediately upon receiving the news that Lincoln had been elected president. He went to South Carolina to help draft the Ordinance of Succession, making South Carolina the first state to secede from the Union. He then went to Montgomery, Alabama with his wife to attend the first Confederate Congress. Mary Boykin Chesnut personally witnessed the Battle of Fort Sumter, which started the Civil War. She was a close friend of Varina Davis, the wife of Jefferson Davis, who was the President of the Confederacy.

The husband of Mary Boykin Chesnut declined appointment as a high military officer and, for that reason, survived the Civil War. After the war, Mary and her husband were absolutely penniless, their only income being derived from the eggs and butter which her maid, a former slave, sold on the street. She later estimated that her income from this activity was twelve dollars a month.

When she and her husband returned to their plantation after the war, they found that all of their slaves were still there. "Not a soul was absent from his or her post. I said, 'Good Colored folks, when are you going to kick off the traces and be free?' In their furious emotional way, they swore devotion to us to their dying day." (See p. 821 of her diary).

Their slaves did not leave the plantation, having themselves nowhere else to go. They continued to work the fields and farm the land, which at least provided them with enough food to eat during a time of great poverty in the South. More than that, the population of her plantation, located at Camden, South Carolina, actually increased, as relatives displaced by the war, whose husbands or fathers had been killed, continued to move in. In the 1870s, Mary Chesnut and her husband sold a portrait of George Washington by Gilbert Stuart which had been hanging in their living room. That famous portrait now hangs in the Library of Congress.

Commentators on her works have expressed surprise at the fact that Mary Boykin Chesnut consistently expressed abhorrence at the institution of slavery, in spite of the fact that she herself was thoroughly imbued in that system, living her life in the Deep South, with her father and her husband both being political leaders who defended slavery. However, her abhorrence at slavery was at least in part derived from the corruption caused by the tendency of Southern men to use their female slaves as concubines. She wrote that women and slaves were in the same predicament and that all Southern women shared her objection to slavery, and for the same reason. Mary Chesnut apparently believed that her father-in-law had produced a brood of children by one of his slaves named Rachel. She never accused her husband of this practice, however.

Mary Chesnut proved unable to bear children. For that reason, she devoted her life to voracious reading and voluminous writing. Among all of her volumes of writing, she is best remembered for the following quote, the original handwritten version of which is reproduced in facsimile form, on pages 29-31, of *Mary Chesnut's Civil War*, edited by C. Vann Woodward, Yale University Press, 1981. This was originally published as *A Diary from Dixie*, a title coined after her death by an editor of *The Saturday Evening Post*, although Mary Chesnut personally hated both the term 'Dixie' and the song by that name:

> *I wonder if it be a sin to think slavery a curse to any land. . . . . God forgive us, but ours is a monstrous system, a wrong and iniquity! Perhaps the rest of the world is as bad – this only I see. Like the patriarchs of old, our men all live in one house with their wives and their concubines; and the mulattos one sees in every family partly resemble the white children. Any lady is ready to tell you who is the father of all the mulatto children in everybody's household but her own. Those, she seems to think, drop from the clouds, or pretends so to think. Good women we have, but they talk of all nastiness – though they never do wrong, they talk all day and night. . . . . My disgust is sometimes*

*boiling over – but they are, I believe in conduct the purest women God ever made. Thank God for my countrywomen – alas for the men! No worse than men everywhere, but the lower their mistresses, the more degraded they must be.*

. . . .

*It was so patriarchal. So it is – flocks and herds and slaves — and wife Leah does not suffice. Rachel must be added. And all the time they seem to think themselves patterns — models of husbands and fathers.*

This last phrase, 'Rachel must be added', refers to the well known story found in *Genesis 29–30* of the *Bible* that Jacob, dissatisfied with his wife Leah, took a second wife Rachel, and then her handmaid, Bilhah, and finally Leah's handmaid, Zilpah, eventually producing sons by all four of his wives and concubines. The total of twelve sons from these four women became the Twelve Tribes of Israel. Not only is this story found in the Bible, but it is also found in the Holy Koran and forms the basis for the Islamic rule that a man may have up to four wives, but not more.

Thus, by 'the patriarchs of old', Mary Chesnut was referring to the Biblical personalities such as Jacob and Abraham who maintained both wives and concubines. Indeed, Thomas Jefferson himself wrote a letter dated April 24, 1788, to Maria Cosway in which he described a painting of Van der Werff showing Abraham, his wife Sarah and his concubine Hagar in bed together. In this letter, Thomas Jefferson stated, 'I would have agreed to be Abraham.' It has been suggested that this quote proves Thomas Jefferson's interest in maintaining a concubine and his preference for being in bed with two women at the same time.

In a 1991 book entitled *Brain Sex: The Real Difference Between Men and Women,* by Anne Moir, the theory is advanced that the brains of men and women are structured differently. The British author of this work has a doctorate in genetics from Oxford University. This book represents the latest, most up to date findings in genetics research. That research is still going on.

Dr. Anne Moir claims that the brain is 'wired' differently in men and women, as the result of the differences between male and female hormones. This difference, she says, explains why it is that women are superior in verbal and language skills but men are better in spatial relations games like chess.

Indeed, it is a fact that the best writers are women and that women learn foreign languages more readily than men, but that the best chess players are men.

This 'hard-wiring' of the brain takes place at an early age. It explains the fact that children can learn a foreign language more thoroughly than an adult. It explains the fact that Judith Polgar can play chess at the grandmaster level, because her brain was hard-wired to play chess from the age of five, by an average of eight hours per day of play and practice from that age.

Dr. Anne Moir says that the sex-related differences in the structure of the brain explain the fact that men have a genetic drive to seek sexual variety and to produce children by more than one women, whereas women have a counter-balancing and equally strong drive to have all of their children by the same man. The drive by men to seek sexual variety is, of course, what leads to conflicts between men, producing wars, murders and so on.

The theories of Dr. Anne Moir, however well researched and documented, will never be accepted in America because of the potential political consequences, leading to sex discrimination. Nevertheless, women, of whom Anne Moir is one, have always said that they are different from men in this respect. Even Mary Boykin Chesnut, in her quote found in *Mary Chesnut's Civil War*, said that 'Good women we have . . . . they never do wrong . . . . they are, I believe in conduct the purest women God ever made. Thank God for my countrywomen — alas for the men! No worse than men everywhere, but the lower their mistresses, the more degraded they must be.'

In other words, she wrote that all Southern women were faithful to their husbands and did not sleep with men other than their husbands, but that all Southern men maintained slaves as their concubines and mistresses.

The above quotation by Mary Boykin Chesnut has often been dismissed as an exaggeration, but was it really?

This practice must have been more widespread that anyone today can imagine. The first Virginia census in which slaves were counted as people was the 1850 census. Slaves were then listed as black or as mulatto. A high percentage of slaves were listed as mulatto, perhaps more than 15%, although exact statistics are not available.

Every woman in the world faces essentially the same problem: How to keep her man from wandering. A woman who doesn't worry about this runs the risk of someday finding herself out of the street with another woman taking her place in the house.

The wife of the plantation owner was really in an enviable position as compared to other women. She did not have to worry about being replaced. If her man had an inclination to dally, he would do it with the slaves in the back of the house. He would not bother to go into the town and look for women there.

The wife of the plantation owner did not have any reason to feel insecure about her husband's slaves. He was not going to divorce her to marry a slave. In the first place, that would have been illegal.

Even if he produced children from his slaves, that would not threaten her own children. The children of a slave could not get any inheritance.

Thus, the plantation owner's wife could feel completely secure, both about her own position and about the position of her children. Many probably felt it was far preferable to see her husband steal into the slave shack, than to have him make a play for thy neighbor's wife, the neighbor's daughter, or some floozy in a bar in the town. No doubt many wives encouraged their husbands to go with the slaves as the lesser of two evils.

If Thomas Jefferson didn't do it, he was just about the only one who didn't. Certainly, everyone says that his father-in-law and his nephews did it.

Just to give an idea of how widely this story is known, this author happened to ask Judge Preston Sawyer, a prominent lawyer who is a former circuit court judge in Lynchburg, if he believed that Thomas Jefferson had produced children from his slaves. 'Sure,' was the reply, shrugging his shoulders, 'everybody accepts that.' He then mentioned that the family of his own brother-in-law had once owned Poplar Forest for nearly forty years.

In short, this author has not yet met anybody in Lynchburg whose family has been here for any length of time, who has not both heard the story that Thomas Jefferson fathered children by his slaves and who doesn't believe it. This sort of widespread acceptance in the very place where many of these events actually occurred would not be possible if the story wasn't true.

The next question is: What is it precisely that is so objectionable about this practice?

Almost everybody will agree that if an unmarried man spends time with an unmarried woman, there is nothing really wrong with that. The church might be opposed to this but no law has ever been passed against it.

Benjamin Franklin is known or believed to have had possibly fathered as many as eighteen illegitimate children. This is nothing more than a curious fact in American history. Nobody expresses moral outrage about this. There is an anecdote that when he heard that one of his illegitimate children had been appointed the Royal Governor of New Jersey, he commented: 'Serves the bastard right!'

If the fact that Thomas Jefferson had a relationship with Sally Hemings is itself not so shocking, perhaps it is the age factor. It has often been claimed that it was 'impossible' for a morally upright man like Thomas Jefferson to have 'seduced' a sixteen-year-old girl.

This was hardly a seduction. The two of them lived together in close quarters for almost two years before anything started. If any man and any woman are put close together for two years, something like this is going to happen. It is only human nature.

At the time when we believe that this relationship started, which was April, 1789, Sally was 16 and Thomas Jefferson was 46. That would be illegal in many states today. However, 16 or 17 was the average age for marriage back then. Indeed, it was necessary for the survival of the human race, with the high infant mortality rate which existed at that time.

Next, there is the fact that Sally was part black. That is a hot subject, especially in Virginia. In fact, until 1967, the law of Virginia did not allow marriage between races. That was changed in the 1967 United States Supreme Court decision of *Loving vs. Virginia*. It seems hard to believe that it was only so recently that a white man became legally allowed to marry a black woman in Virginia.

Before that, there were differing laws regarding whether either the white or the black race could marry Indians. There are in Virginia today and other parts of the South so-called 'Indian tribes' which are actually black people with a small amount of Indian blood. The exact legal reason for this is unclear, but it had to do with the need to get around the prohibition on interracial marriage. Indeed, Thomas Jefferson was thinking about this when he encouraged blacks to get married to Indians.

Apparently, if a black person married an Indian, the children would be free. This is the reason that so many black persons claim some Indian ancestry, even though there are few real Indians left in Virginia. However, there is another side to this. Originally, there were many Indians in Virginia. The main tribe was the Cherokee. The Cherokee tribe is often thought of as being from Oklahoma. That is entirely false. The Cherokee is a tribe of the Allegheny Mountains of North Carolina and Virginia which was deported to Oklahoma. Some of the Cherokee went to Oklahoma voluntarily. In 1838, the remaining 17,000 Cherokee in Virginia were rounded up by troops and forced to move to Oklahoma. An estimated 4,000 of them died on the journey.

However, some Indians managed to evade these round-ups and lived as fugitives in the mountains. Most likely to be successful were those who spoke English and agreed to convert to Christianity. See Horace R. Rice, *The Buffalo Ridge Cherokee: The Colors and Culture of a Virginian Indian Community*, Madison Heights, Virginia, 1991, p. 9. The Indians called themselves 'colored' to hide their ancestry and to avoid deportation. They also freely mixed and intermarried with blacks for the same reason. Thus, we have blacks claiming that they were Indians to gain their freedom, and Indians claiming that they were black to avoid deportation. Both were classified as 'mulatto' by Virginia census takers in 1850 and 1860.

Indian children went to the 'colored schools' along with the blacks in the segregated school system of Virginia which existed until 1962. However, the number of actual Indians still in Virginia at that time was statistically insignificant.

A person named Charles Lewis, a first cousin of Charles Lilburne Lewis, the brother-in-law of Thomas Jefferson, married into one of these part-white, part-black, part-Indian tribes. That tribe is called the 'Issues' of Amherst County. The wife of Charles Lewis was Garthrey Johns, a name which only the Issues have. The Lewis family biographers seem to be unaware of this connection, which would be known only to a person familiar with this region.

In fact, Sally was not really black. She was 75% white. However, according to the law of Virginia, she was black. Among her five children, Beverly, Harriet and Eston married whites and became white. Tom and Madison married blacks or half-blacks and became black.

Finally, there is the fact that Sally was a slave. This is really the point. If she had been a free black woman, not many people would have complained about it. However, she was not free. She was a slave.

Actually, at the beginning of their relationship, she was not a slave. They got together in France. At that time, she was free, because slavery itself did not exist in France. She knew her rights. At first, she refused to return to America, but finally Thomas Jefferson convinced her. She was pregnant with his child at the time. In all likelihood, if she had not been pregnant, she would have stayed in France, rather than re-enslave herself by going back to Virginia.

Finally, there is the allegation which is still heard that Thomas Jefferson sold his own children into slavery. In fact, it appears that this allegation is not true in the case of Thomas Jefferson, but this very allegation puts the finger on the main inherent evil in this entire system.

Consider the case of the plantation owner who has two sets of children, one by his wife and the other by his slaves. Everything might go fine as long as the plantation owner is alive and can secretly look after the welfare of his slave children. However, as soon as he dies, as eventually he must, the fate of his half-black children will be at the mercy of his white children. The half-black children might easily wind up being sold at public auction and sent down the river.

The slave children of Thomas Jefferson were lucky. Although he stated in his will that Madison and Eston Hemings were to be freed, his heirs were not legally obliged to honor this. Thomas Jefferson died completely insolvent. Both his heirs and his creditors had the legal right to insist that Madison and Eston be sold at auction to pay his debts. It was indeed quite fortunate that this was not done. We actually have no written proof that they were set free. All we have is the statements by them and their descendants that they were set free and went to live in Ohio. Otherwise, there is no proof.

The story of Thomas Jefferson and Sally Hemings was originally spread by Federalists, political opponents of Thomas Jefferson. By the time Jefferson had died, the Federalist Party had died out, Jefferson having thoroughly defeated them in the battle of political ideals. The election of 1824, the last election before Thomas Jefferson died, was fought between differing factions of the Democratic Republican Party, the party of Jefferson. Both John Quincy Adams and Andrew Jackson called themselves Democratic Republicans. Jackson got more popular votes, but Adams was elected anyway, so the party split in two. Both the current Democratic and the Republican parties of today claim their heritage from Jefferson.

The political ideas of George Washington and his Federalist Party have long since disappeared and been forgotten. This is the reason that America today is often called a 'Jeffersonian Democracy'.

During this period after 1809, the story of Sally Hemings and the slave children of Thomas Jefferson appears to have been largely forgotten. However, when abolitionist fever started to sweep America, the story was revamped. In 1838, Dr. Levi Gaylord made his claim that he had heard that a daughter of Thomas Jefferson had been sold at a slave action in New Orleans for one thousand dollars. That story was subsequently embellished further. It has even been written that Thomas Jefferson personally took his daughter Harriet down to New Orleans and sold her to a house of prostitution there to raise cash. As recently as 1959, a book appeared entitled the *Image of America* by Father R. L. Bruckburger, which stated that two daughters of Jefferson's were taken to New Orleans for that purpose. According to this book, one daughter was sold; the other 'committed suicide by drowning herself to escape the horrors of her position.' The source for this information was said to be none other than Abraham Lincoln.

In fact, Abraham Lincoln was once quoted in the newspapers as citing the fact Thomas Jefferson had produced children from his slaves. However, Lincoln immediately repudiated that quote, stating that he had always had the utmost respect for Jefferson.

There seems to be no way to kill off this story about Jefferson selling his own daughter for one thousand dollars (a goodly sum on the slave market of those days, incidentally). This story will undoubtedly be repeated, retold and republished forever.

The question is: Why is it exactly that abolitionists and other people opposing slavery keep repeating this particular story? What difference does it make if the slave that was sold was Jefferson's daughter or was a poor hungry woman just off the boat from Africa. Slavery was a great evil, regardless of who the slave happened to be.

Thomas Jefferson discussed this very topic in his private letters. He pointed out that the ancient Romans kept white people as their slaves. There was no racial difference between master and slave in ancient Rome. He realized that slavery was not inherently dependent on racism, even though in Virginia it seemed to be that way.

According to some authorities, the story that Harriet was sold for $1,000, got started as the story about another plantation owner who actually lived in

Louisiana. This story was later modified by another editor who put in the famous name of Thomas Jefferson to sell more copies. Harriet got her name included to further embellish the story because she was known to be the only daughter of Sally Hemings. This all came to be published in a novel by William Wells Brown entitled, *Clotel, or the President's Daughter, A Narrative of Slave Life in the United States*, (London, 1853). This book became popular in America. The subsequent U.S.A. edition, published in 1864, and entitled, *Clotelle, A Tale of the Southern States*, deleted the name of Thomas Jefferson and substituted in the name of a mythical United States Senator who, according to this novel, sold his slave daughter into prostitution. Nevertheless, the story continues to be told, in spite of the fact that it was fiction all along.

In summary, the evidence shows beyond a reasonable doubt that many Virginia plantation owners produced children from their slaves. Obviously, this happened in other parts of the South as well. One question is: Was this more prevalent in Virginia than elsewhere?

Nobody can answer this question. However, in terms of percentage, it is possible that this was more frequent in Virginia, for the following reason:

The success or failure of slavery was dependent on what type of crops were grown. Slavery was legal in Maryland but died out naturally, because the crops there were not conducive to it. Corn and wheat are not good crops for slavery. Tobacco, which was grown in Virginia, is a crop somewhat suitable for slavery. A tobacco grower was called a planter, which is where the word 'plantation' comes from. A person who grew corn or wheat was called a 'farmer'.

The ideal crop for slavery was cotton, which had to be hand picked. Cotton was King in South Carolina, Georgia, Alabama, Mississippi, and Louisiana. This is where the preponderance of the slaves lived.

Even today, a form of slavery still exists in those areas, except that instead of being called slaves, they are called migrant farm workers. Efforts are constantly being made to eliminate the poverty and illiteracy of these people, but that will never really happen because that type of worker is necessary for the production of crops like cotton and vegetables in those states. Thus, we can say that slavery would never have died out of its own accord in those areas.

Thomas Jefferson was apparently one of the biggest owners of slaves in the entire state of Virginia at the time of his death. However, by the standards of the cotton producing states, he was strictly small time. For example, one plantation owner in South Carolina alone, General Wade Hampton, owned 5,000 slaves. He was made a general in the Civil War. Even after the war was over, he was not wiped out. He served as a Senator from South Carolina.

Thus, it appears that in the Deep South, fewer people owned slaves, but those who did owned larger numbers. At the beginning of the Civil War, there were more than three million slaves in the South. These were owned by less than five percent of the white population. In Virginia, there may have been more slave owners, but each owned on the average fewer slaves.

This might tend to indicate that the practice of fathering children by one's slaves was more prevalent in Virginia on a percentage basis. For example, Wade Hampton may have had 5,000 slaves out in the fields picking cotton, but it probably was a bit beyond his range personally to go out and impregnate all of them. If he kept a few in the house for his own proposes, it was probably at the most two or three, from the total of 5,000.

On the other hand, Thomas Jefferson had the capability, if he really wanted to do so, of virtually monopolizing all of the women in his house. He could have had, not only Sally, but Betty, Betsy, Edy, Ursula, Cretia, Critta, Thenia, Mary and even the mother, Betty Hemings. Nobody would have refused him, if that was what he wanted.

There is no reason to believe that Thomas Jefferson did that on such a grand scale, but there were no doubt at least a few plantation owners who did. That accounts for the heavy mulatto population in the State of Virginia today. The Damn Yankees who come down here to Virginia and think that we Southerners don't know what to do with our women, find it shocking and unbelievable to hear stories about white fathers producing children from their black slaves. However, this is something which all native Virginians naturally assume to have been a common occurrence.

One school teacher from New York City who came to Lynchburg to teach fourth grade has related to this author that two of the little black children in his fourth grade class say that they are descendants of Thomas Jefferson. He assumed that they did not know what they were talking about or even who Thomas Jefferson was. Finally, he asked one of the other school teachers about this and was informed that, in fact, they probably were descendants of Thomas Jefferson.

It is a mistake to assume that all racial mixing in early Virginia history was the result of a combination of white-master-father and black-slave-mother. According to James Dishman, a local historian in Lynchburg, old court order books and church parish records dating back to the early seventeenth century show many cases of English servant girls imported to serve the wealthy families of Virginia and coming down with cases of pregnancy from the black slaves. A typical court record shows 'Susan, English servant girl', fined 15 pounds by the court for giving birth to a bastard child by 'Slave Jack'.

There was, however, a darker side to this. If the mother of the half- black child was not a servant girl but rather was a proper married lady from a prominent family, she would claim that she had been 'raped' by the slave.

Court records show more than 60 cases where the offending slave was hung until dead. It did not matter how many hundred witnesses could be assembled to testify that the slave was regularly invited by the woman to join her in bed. The testimony of one white woman far outweighed the testimony of one hundred slaves.

The children of such unions were born free. The church took custody of these bastard children and hired what we would today call foster care parents. Typical church parish records show a person being paid 100 pounds of tobacco per year for taking care of a bastard child. Abstracts of these old parish records for various counties of Virginia dating back to the sixteen hundreds have been published in book form in limited editions and are available in the libraries. They show how many pounds of tobacco were paid by each farmer into the church and how many pounds of tobacco were paid out by the church for social welfare purposes such as taking care of all of these bastard children produced by these ubiquitous English servant girls.

This was a major problem in those days. As early as 1618, a law had to be passed making illegal the practice of 'Kidnapping maidens, to be sold in Virginia'. This official law prohibited 'Kidnapping persons to be sold as servants in the colonies, or inducing them, under false pretenses to emigrate.' See *Virginia Historical Magazine*, Vol. 6, p. 228 (1899). It must be pointed out that these kidnapped persons were not black slaves from Africa; these were white girls from England.

Even that 1618 law did not put an end to this practice. Eventually, the wrong person was kidnaped. James Annesly, the son of British Lord Altham, was kidnaped in 1728, through the connivance of an uncle who wanted to get his inheritance. It took him 15 years for him to do so, but in 1743, he made it back to Ireland and successfully prosecuted a suit to regain his birthright.

At that time, the Church of England was an arm of the state. All farmers were required to pay ten percent of their tobacco crop to the church, whether they believed in that church or not. This was one of the abuses which Patrick Henry and Thomas Jefferson railed against.

After the American Revolution, the Church of England changed its name in America to the Episcopal Church. Many of the churches were burned to the ground by a population bent on revenge. The Right Reverend William Meade, Bishop of Virginia, whose mother was an in-law of the Randolphs, wrote a book on the history of the Episcopal church entitled *Old Churches, Ministers, Families of Virginia*, Philadelphia, 1857, as a way of preserving this historical record at a time when the fortunes of the church had reached its nadir and the church itself was in danger of going out of existence.

Slavery has existed throughout recorded human history. The ancient Greeks and Romans kept slaves. However, the colonization of the Americas is considered to mark perhaps one of the first times in human history when slaves were imported to do hard physical labor. It occurred at a unique period of world history, the time of the discovery of a 'New World'. A vast under-populated wilderness had been opened and there was an unprecedented need for the large scale importation of labor.

In contrast, the Arabs kept slaves until recently. However, that was for a different purpose altogether. Slave women were brought from Africa to Arabia to populate the harems of the sheikhs. This practice continued until at least the 1950's and was officially abolished in Saudi Arabia only in 1968. Today, an Arab man is required by decisions of the courts to pay his additional wives a regular salary of at least the equivalent of about $135 per month for being employed as a wife. Nowadays, only a few of the additional wives still come from African counties such as Ethiopia and Kenya. Mostly, they come from places such as India and the Philippines, where women can easily be found who are overjoyed to receive the high salary of $135 per month for the easy job of working as an extra wife.

Many people have been seeing a lot of the Emir of Kuwait on television recently, as well as of his son, the Prime Minister and Heir Apparent of Kuwait. However, how many have noticed that the Emir of Kuwait, who speaks no English, is white but his son, the Prime Minister of Kuwait, who speaks fluent English, is black? How many realize that this is because the Prime Minister of Kuwait is the son of the Emir and of a black slave woman from Africa? English is the predominant language of black Africa. No doubt, the Prime Minister of Kuwait can speak English fluently because he was taught that language by his slave mother.

An amusing incident related to this happened in the barren desert sands of Arabia in Dubai in 1990. A woman arrived on a flight from India. Two men showed up at the airport to collect her. One man said, 'This is my wife'. The other man said, 'No. This is my wife.' Both men had complete documentation on the same woman. Both men had a photocopy of the same passport of the same woman. Both men had an official government approved employment contract to employ this same woman as a wife. The police intervened and took all three of them to the police station. The end result was that the two marriage contracts were legally dissolved. The woman was put in jail and deported back to India.

This is one of those sources which does not need a footnote. The author was there at the airport when this happened.

# Chapter Sixteen

## The Randolph Family

The Randolph Family, of which Thomas Jefferson was a member, was by far the leading family of Virginia if not of all America. The Randolphs were of noble origin. The *Doomsday Book* of Medieval England mentioned a Thomas Randolph in the year 1294. Robert the Bruce and the Kings of Scotland were relatives of the Randolphs.

The first permanent English settlement in America was established at Jamestown, Virginia, in 1607. The first plantations were established at Henrico and Bermuda Hundred in 1611. The first Randolph in America was Henry Randolph (1623–1673), who arrived in 1650. However, the branch of the Randolph family which became the ancestors of Thomas Jefferson was established in America with the arrival in 1672 of William (1650–1711), who became known as William Randolph of Turkey Island. He became the Clerk of Henrico County in 1673, succeeding his uncle, Henry Randolph. He was the great-grandfather of Thomas Jefferson.

There were so many important branches of the Randolph family who provided so many of the governors and other high public officials of Virginia, both before and after independence from England, that it would be pointless to attempt to name all of the famous people who were Randolphs. Chief Justice John Marshall was a Randolph as was General Robert E. Lee, who was a direct sixth generation descendant of the second daughter of William Randolph of Turkey Island.

There is no doubt that the Randolphs were a family of great intellect. They married into the other leading families of Scotland and England. Sir Richard Lane (1584–1650), the brother of the grandmother of William Randolph of Turkey Island, is still regarded today as perhaps the greatest legal mind in all of British history. He was knighted in Oxford in 1643 and later became both the Chief Lord Baron and the Lord Keeper of England.

From the great number of their prominent descendants, William Randolph of Turkey Island and his wife, Mary Isham, became known as 'the Adam and Eve of Virginia'. They had seven sons and two daughters. The third of these sons was Isham Randolph of Dungeness, 'Dungeness' being the name of the home that he built. Isham Randolph was born in January,

1685, and died in November, 1742. During his life, he spent many years as the colonial agent for Virginia in England, starting in 1708. He married Jane Rogers in London in 1717. He later returned to Virginia, where he became the Lieutenant General of the Colony. He left six daughters and three sons. The oldest of these was Jane Randolph, the mother of Thomas Jefferson. She was born in London in 1720.

Turkey Island was an island located in the James River where William Randolph built his estate. Some original source documents refer to him as being from 'Appomattox'. This should not be confused with the town of Appomattox, now famous as the place where General Robert E. Lee surrendered to General Grant at the conclusion of the American Civil War. The river which flows through Appomattox town is called the Appomattox River. It continues for another 80 miles downstream until it joins the James River at Bermuda Hundred across from what is now Hopewell. That confluence of these two rivers is where William Randolph of Turkey Island and his sons lived. Turkey Island is the largest Island in the James River. It is now a national wildlife reserve.

The history of the Randolph family can be found, among other places, in 32 dense pages in the *Genealogies of Virginia Families*, Vol. V, Genealogical Publishing Co., Baltimore, 1981. There are many Randolph family biographers and many other books about the Randolph family, including those by Wessel Randolph, who has traced 3000 direct descendants of the first Henry Randolph alone. Wessel Randolph has noted on page 36 of his genealogy of the *Family of Henry Randolph I* that in the case of the family of William Randolph of Turkey Island 'the opportunity for multiplication in the first generation and thereafter was pregnant and this opportunity was not neglected.'

All but one of the nine children of William Randolph of Turkey Island produced many children, who in turn produced more children. The Randolphs were careful to keep their wives pregnant at all times. Thomas Jefferson followed in this great tradition, as did his son-in- law, Thomas Mann Randolph Junior, who had twelve children, and his grandson, Thomas Jefferson Randolph, who had thirteen.

Suffice it to say that the list of distinguished persons who were members of the Randolph family is so long that there can be little doubt that Thomas Jefferson got much of his great genius and high intellect from them. Less is known about the family of his father, Peter Jefferson, a civil engineer. However, to Peter Jefferson goes the full credit for teaching his son that all men are created equal and the benefits of a pluralistic democracy, a concept with which the aristocratic Randolphs could not have been comfortable.

An interesting fact is that Thomas Jefferson was a direct descendant of Lady Godiva, who had many children and whose husband died in 1057.

Biographers of the Randolph family believe that one of their ancestors may have accompanied William the Conqueror across the English Channel and fought under him in the Battle of Hastings in 1066. They are seriously worried about this, because this might mean that they are Normans and not pure Saxons or Celts. However, they are relieved to discover that there were two Randolph families, one English and one Scotch, and these two families were probably not related to each other. The Randolphs of Virginia are of Scotch ancestry.

Although the genealogy of the mother of Thomas Jefferson is well known, no biographer has ever attempted to trace the family history of Peter Jefferson, the father of Thomas Jefferson. Typical of all biographers is the statement by Fawn Brodie that Peter Jefferson knew nothing about his ancestry, except that his grandfather was from Wales.

There is one fact about Peter Jefferson which tells us that he was probably a member of the upper class. This is that he was easily able to register land titles. He could claim any land he wanted in Virginia, within reasonable limits. This procedure was known as 'patenting' land. This is how he got the land which became Monticello. Only the members of the gentry class were allowed to do this.

Actually, there is a story about this. After registering the title of this land, Peter Jefferson discovered that his best friend, William Randolph, had registered the same title a few hours earlier. As a result, they exchanged land titles, which is how Peter Jefferson came to acquire title to the land which became Monticello.

On the other hand, some sources believe that Peter Jefferson was merely a member of the 'respectable' middle class.

Through the use of a computer program developed by the world's largest genealogical database at the headquarters of the Mormon Church in Salt Lake City, Utah, this author has now been able to trace back the ancestry of Peter Jefferson. For the purposes of preparing this book, this author has created a computer database with more than 3000 names of members of the Randolph family and their in-laws, including, of course, Sally Hemings and her descendants. This is only a fraction of the total names of the family members.

Among these 3000 plus names are in-laws and in-laws of in-laws and their families. As a result, the families of almost every leading personality of early Virginia history are included in this database, including the families of President George Washington, President James Madison, President John Tyler, President Zachary Taylor and President Benjamin Harrison. All of these people were distantly related to each other, through in-laws. Only President James Monroe, the son of a joiner, does not have any clear connection with these families.

The creation of this database had led to discoveries of relationships which nobody previously believed existed. For example, there was an obscure woman born in England named Lucy Higginson. (Some say her name was 'Hickerson'.) She was the daughter of Capt. James Higginson. She was married three times and each marriage produced only one child. However, each child established a famous family of Virginia.

Her first husband was Major Lewis Burwell (1621–1653). Their child was Major Lewis Burwell, Jr., (1653–1710), who was the great-grandfather of the Benjamin Harrison (1726–1791) who signed the Declaration of Independence. That Benjamin Harrison was the father of President William Henry Harrison (1773–1841).

The second husband of Lucy Higginson was William Bernard. Their daughter was Elizabeth Bernard who married Thomas Todd. Their daughter was Elizabeth Todd whose granddaughter married the grandson of Col. Robert Carter (1663–1732), who was the richest man in Virginia and who was known as 'King Carter'. He established the Carter family lineage in Virginia. The great-grandson of Elizabeth Todd was General Robert E. Lee (1807-1870). Another great-grandson of Elizabeth Todd married a daughter of Patrick Henry.

The third husband of Lucy Higginson was Philip Ludwell. Their son, Philip Ludwell, Jr., (b. 1672), was the grandfather of Richard Henry Lee (1732–1794), the man who proposed that there should be a declaration of independence. His daughter married Corbin Washington, a nephew of General George Washington.

All of this is new information. It has taken original research by this author, aided by a computer, to discover that one obscure woman, Lucy Higginson, was the matriarch of all of these famous families. One reason for the difficulty in this is that her name is always given differently. Among the various names used for her are Lucy Higginson, Lucy Hickerson, Lucy Burwell, Lucy Bernard, and Lucy Ludwell. It has taken considerable research to prove that all of these women named 'Lucy' are actually one and the same person.

If the sex roles had been reversed, and the name 'Higginson' had been the family name of all of these famous people, it would now be one of the most famous names in American history. Instead, it is a name which we do not even know how to spell or to pronounce correctly. We do not even know when this Lucy Higginson lived. However, from her husbands and from the ages of her grandchildren we can estimate that she must have been born in around 1630.

What we do know is that many of the people who are named in this book are descended from her. For example, Rebecca Burwell, the first great love in the life of Thomas Jefferson, was the great-great- granddaughter of

Lucy Higginson by her first husband, Lewis Burwell. In addition, Elizabeth Moore Walker, the second great love in the life of Thomas Jefferson, whose husband challenged him to a duel over her, was the great-great-granddaughter of Lucy Higginson by her second husband, William Bernard.

Another of the many surprising facts which this database has uncovered is that President William Henry Harrison was a fourth cousin one generation removed from his own vice-president, John Tyler, who later succeeded him as President of the United States. Probably even these two men did not know that. For two blood relatives to run on the same ticket for office would have been politically unacceptable. These relationships are hard to trace because it was the mother's mother's mother of John Tyler who was related to the Harrisons.

Peter Jefferson was born on February 29, 1707. At about that time, the calendar changed. Previously, each year had started in March, not on January 1, as at present. Because of this, the year of the birth of Peter Jefferson is sometimes given as 1708. All dates in January or February going back to this period suffer from this same problem.

The father of Peter Jefferson was named Thomas Jefferson and was born in 1679. His grandfather was also named Thomas Jefferson (1653–1697) and was married to Martha Branch in 1677. The father of Martha Branch was Christopher Branch.

The mother of Peter Jefferson was named Mary Field and was born on February 3, 1680. Her father was named Peter Field, who was born in 1642. He married Judith Soane on October 21, 1678.

Judith Soane, born in 1646, was the daughter of Henry Soane, born in 1618. Judith Soane was married twice. She first married on December 12, 1661 to Henry Randolph (1623–1673), who was the uncle of William Randolph of Turkey Island. That marriage produced two children, Henry Randolph Junior and Judith Randolph. After Henry Randolph Senior died, Judith Soane married Peter Field.

Thus, the ancestors of Peter Jefferson reached America slightly before William Randolph of Turkey Island.

Another family of interest is the Eppes Family. This family has confounded biographers because there were at least six persons named Francis Eppes. One Francis Eppes married into the Randolph family, another married into the Isham family, and yet another married a daughter of John Wayles. The son of this last Francis Eppes married Maria Jefferson. Their son was named, you guessed it, Francis Eppes.

To illustrate the problems in tracing this family, among the six persons named Francis Eppes, there were three who were known as Col. Francis Eppes and two more known as Lt. Col. Francis Eppes. All three persons named Col. Francis Eppes had a son named William. Therefore, there were three different persons named William Eppes, all of whom had a father named Col. Francis Eppes.

The members of the Eppes family spelled their name in various ways, including 'Epps' and 'Epes'. These names were completely interchangeable.

The Isham family were direct descendants of King David I of Scotland, who was an uncle of Robert the Bruce. Mary Isham was the wife of William Randolph of Turkey Island. Therefore, Thomas Jefferson was a direct descendant of the Kings of Scotland.

The Randolph family had the tendency to marry within the family. Indeed, almost all of the leading families of that day engaged in this practice, this custom being derived from the British aristocracy.

This tendency produced complex inter-family relationships which only a computer program can solve. For example, if a man successively married two sisters, this being a common practice in those days, then the father of each child would also be his uncle. In addition, if a man married a woman and then married her niece, he would then be both the uncle and the husband of the second woman.

These multiple marriages occurred not because of divorce or polygamy but because of the death of the spouses. A man would often have four or five wives within his lifetime and many women had three or four husbands. At the same time, divorce was virtually non-existent. A man would marry his fifth wife after the first four had died. For example, Samuel Washington, the full brother of General George Washington, had five wives. All but the last pre-deceased him.

One of the five wives of Samuel Washington was Jane Champe. She had siblings named Mary Champe and John Champe. The aunt of Samuel Washington and his brother, President George Washington, was Mildred Washington, whose father was Lawrence Washington. The father of President George Washington was Augustine Washington who was the son of Lawrence Washington. One of the sons of Mildred Washington, who married twice, was Lewis Willis. The father of Lewis Willis was Henry Willis, who married three times, the last wife being Mildred Washington. The other two wives of Henry Willis each produced a son named 'John Willis.'

An example of the resulting complexity in family relationships can be found in the case of Mildred Willis, the daughter of Lewis Willis, who was the full cousin of President George Washington. The mother of Mildred Willis was Mary Champe. The brother of Mary Champe was John Champe. The wife of John Champe was Ann Carter. The brother of Ann Carter was Langdon Carter. The wife of Langdon Carter was Mildred Willis.

There was nothing remarkable about this circular relationship. However, when Mary Champe and John Champe both died, their surviving spouses, Lewis Willis and Ann Carter, married each other.

From this, a poem on behalf of Mildred Willis was published in the Virginia Gazette for September 23, 1775, which went as follows:

*'My husband's my Uncle. My father's my brother.*
*I also am sister unto my mother.*
*I am sister and aunt to a brother called John.*
. . . .
*This paradox strange as it may be to you.*
*Any day that you please I can prove it to be true.'*

What was meant by this was that the husband of Mildred Willis was also the brother of Ann Carter, who was the step-mother of Mildred Willis. Therefore, 'My husband's my uncle.'

In addition, her father, Lewis Willis, was also the husband of her sister-in-law. Therefore, 'My father's my brother'.

This means also that Ann Carter, her step-mother, was also her sister- in-law. Therefore, 'I also am sister unto my mother.'

Finally, her brother John Willis, was the nephew of Langdon Carter, Mildred's husband.

This case was not especially unusual. One finds similar examples throughout the family relationships during this period. This situation is made more difficult to follow by the tendency of many families to keep using the same names. For example, there were at least three persons named 'Mildred Washington'. This, however, is a minor matter compared with the at least six persons named 'Francis Eppes' and the more than ten named 'Benjamin Harrison.'

It seems that just about the only men of this era who married only one wife and did not die young were Thomas Jefferson and George Washington. Both of them married widows who had produced a child by a previous marriage. Both George Washington and Thomas Jefferson had extensive slave holdings, which perhaps made them more satisfied to have only one wife.

Incidentally, the daughter-in-law of Martha Dandridge, the wife of George Washington, through her first husband, Daniel Park Custis, was Elanor Calvert. Elanor Calvert was the grandmother of the wife of General Robert E. Lee. Elanor Calvert is said to have been the descendant of the illegitimate son of King Charles II (1630–84). King Charles II is considered to have had at least 15 illegitimate children by his five mistresses, some of whom were married to other men. On another branch of the same family tree, Elanor Calvert is said to have been a granddaughter of the illegitimate daughter of either King George I or of King George II.

These bastards in-laws are the closest thing which George Washington ever got to royalty. His direct family line was not especially distinguished.

One result of the tendency towards multiple marriages was that just about every important family in Virginia had some blood tie with just about every other important family. For example, although George Washington and Thomas Jefferson lived in different regions of Virginia and their families had nothing to do with each other, it is possible to find a connection between them. Thomas Jefferson had a sister named Lucy Jefferson. Her husband was Charles Lilburne Lewis. They produced, among other children, Isham Lewis and Lilburne Lewis. Lilburne Lewis married his cousin, Jane Woodson Lewis. Isham and Lilburne Lewis were the nephews who subsequently became notorious for chopping a slave into little pieces as an object lesson to the other slaves. The cousin of Charles Lilburne Lewis was Fielding Lewis. Fielding Lewis married twice. His first wife was Catherine Washington, the cousin of President George Washington. His second wife was Elizabeth Washington, the full sister of President George Washington.

All of the important families of England who came to America arrived first in Virginia. Originally, Virginia was the only British colony. New York, then called 'New Amsterdam', established in 1624, was controlled by the Dutch. New York changed hands several times until England finally got it for good in 1674. The famous colony established at Plymouth Rock, now in Massachusetts, was actually a mistake. The Pilgrims were headed for Virginia but landed at Plymouth Rock in error. They decided to stay, which was a poor decision because more than half of them died during the first winter. However, the colony survived somewhat independently from the British who, for a time, did not know where they were, and became famous for burning witches at the stake.

Besides Randolph, other leading early families in Virginia were the families of Burwell, Carter, Cary, Corbin and Bolling. All of these married into the Randolph family. Some of these names no longer exist or are no longer important, because eventually the family only produced girls and the name died.

Thomas Jefferson considered the Burwell family to be among the leading families of Virginia. He did not give a reason for this, but perhaps the reason was that the Burwell family, more immediately than any other, could trace their ancestry back to the British Royal Family. This may explain the fact that Thomas Jefferson was intent on getting married to Rebecca Burwell at an early age. The often heard statement that Thomas Jefferson was not interested in family heritage is probably not true.

Rebecca Burwell would have made an excellent choice for a wife. Many of her descendants became important people. She was also the first cousin of the Benjamin Harrison who was a signer of the *Declaration of Independence* and the father of William Henry Harrison, the President of the United States. However, Rebecca Burwell became the matriarch over a brood of girls. She had seven daughters, but only one son, and that son produced no children. This is part of the reason that the Burwell family name does not exist any longer.

An earlier example of this is provided by the Poythress family. This was probably the first first family of Virginia. They became established in Virginia shortly after the establishment of the first colony in Jamestown in 1607. However, their problem was too many girls. Peter Poythress, whose father died in 1732, had a total of nine sisters and eight daughters. These seventeen women married into every important family in Virginia. All seventeen of them produced children. For this reason, every important family in Virginia who has been here for any length of time claims descent from someone named 'Miss Poythress'. However, the name 'Poythress' almost died out because Peter Poythress had no brothers. Also, he had only one son, William Poythress, who produced no children. However, a male cousin named Poythress continued that family name in Richmond, Virginia.

These were among the first families of Virginia who survived. Virginia was first settled at Jamestown in 1607, but almost all of the early settlers died within a few months of arrival there. The reasons for this were starvation, disease, attacks by the Indians and the fact that Jamestown itself was located in a malaria infested swamp. Even now, the site of Jamestown is virtually uninhabited.

There is one respect in which Thomas Jefferson was scientifically backward. He, like other members of the Randolph family, simply failed to recognize the inherent evil in incest. For example, William Randolph of Turkey Island had six sons who produced children. This family was inbred to such an extent that later on down the line there was one man who was a direct descendant of five of these sons.

Thomas Jefferson also followed this practice. Both of his daughters married their cousins. His daughter, Maria, married Jack Eppes. Both of them were grandchildren of John Wayles, by different marriages of John Wayles. They were related in other ways as well. His other daughter, Martha, married her third cousin. They were also related to each other in several different ways.

This was done with the approval of Thomas Jefferson. It was the common belief at that time that intermarriage was necessary to strengthen the purity of the blood. We now know, of course, that the opposite is true. In a letter dated April 23, 1807 to Randolph Lewis, Thomas Jefferson stated: 'Nobody feels more strongly than I do the desire to make all practicable sacrifices to keep man & wife together who have imprudently married out of their respective families.'

After Maria Jefferson died, her husband, John Eppes, promptly married another woman. There was nothing scandalous or unusual about this. In preparing the genealogical database which was created for the purposes of this book, this author was astounded to note how many men went through three or four wives, not because of divorce, something which almost never happened in those days, but because the wives died so quickly, often in childbirth. John Wayles and his three wives who died before him were among the innumerable of examples of this. A man would get his next wife almost before the last one was cold in the ground. A man would marry his first wife in March of one year and his second wife in July of the next year, after the first one had died in childbirth. There were some women who went through three or four husbands, but these were less frequent, because women died quicker in those days.

The Randolphs had one regrettable tendency: Incest. The Randolphs almost always married first or second cousins. This was apparently based on their misguided belief in their own genetic superiority and the need to preserve the strength of their blood.

Exceptions to this were Jane Randolph and her father, Isham Randolph, both of whom married outside of their family. However, almost all of the other Randolphs either married cousins or else did not marry at all. For this reason, the Randolphs are no longer a factor. Their power, their influence, and even their memory has almost vanished today.

Thomas Jefferson himself perpetuated this tendency towards incest by allowing his daughter, Martha, to marry her third cousin, Thomas Mann Randolph, Jr. His other daughter, Maria, married her first cousin, John Eppes. Among the twelve full brothers and sisters of Thomas Mann Randolph, Jr. were Judith (b. 1772) and Ann Cary 'Nancy' Randolph (1774–1837). Their father was Thomas Mann Randolph, Senior (1741–93) by his first wife, Ann Cary (1745–89). Shortly before he died, Thomas Mann Randolph, Senior took an 18-year-old second wife, Gabriella Harvie, who produced a son, whom he also named Thomas Mann Randolph, Jr. (1791–1851), adding to the confusion.

The father of Thomas Mann Randolph, Sr., was William Randolph (1713–45) by his wife, Mary Judith Page, whom he married in 1735. William Randolph was the son of Thomas Randolph of Tuckahoe (1683–1730). Thomas Randolph of Tuckahoe was the second son of William Randolph of Turkey Island. Thomas Randolph of Tuckahoe married Judith Fleming in 1712.

Richard Randolph of Bizarre (1770–96), who was arrested and charged with infanticide in 1793, was the son of John Randolph of 'Mattoax' (1739–75), who married Frances Bland in 1769. John Randolph of Mattoax was the son of Richard Randolph of 'Curles' (1686–1748) and of Jane Bolling (1704–66). Jane Bolling was the fourth generation in direct descent of Pocahontas, the famous Indian maiden who saved the life of Captain John Smith. Richard Randolph of Curles was the fourth son of William Randolph of Turkey Island.

Although Thomas Jefferson was not a direct descendant of Pocahontas, he married his daughters to at least one man who was. Thomas Mann Randolph Junior was a direct descendant of Jane Rolfe and of her grandmother, Pocahontas (1585–1617). John Eppes was a direct descendant of Robert Bolling, but by his second wife, Anne Stith, not by his first wife, Jane Rolfe.

The story of Pocahontas has been told many times but, nevertheless, it bears retelling here because, as usual, the well known and often repeated version does not describe what actually happened.

According to Captain John Smith, Pocahontas did in fact save his life by jumping in the way while his head was on the execution block about to be pounded into mush on the orders of her father, Chief Powhatan. Everyone agrees that Chief Powhatan had the right idea, and if Pocahontas had not jumped in the way, the Indians would not have been decimated so quickly later on. Of this, there is no dispute. The question is: What exactly was reward of Pocahontas for this?

The official version is that thereafter she got married to 'Gentleman John Rolfe' and they sailed off to England where she was well received by the British nobility. It is presumed that she had fallen in love with the Englishman and had voluntarily gone off to live with him happily ever after.

However, the original source documents tell us instead, that upon reaching the age of 18, Pocahontas was captured and kidnaped by Captain Sir Samuel Agrall on or about April 13, 1613. The reason given for this was that they suspected that her father, Chief Powhatan, had stolen some arms and ammunition from them. They intended to hold Pocahontas as a hostage for the return of these arms. Presumably, what happened to her next was what might easily have happen to any young woman in her situation. Then, about one week later, her father, Powhatan, approached the colonists, asking them for the return of his daughter. He was told that they had their own plans for her and had no intention of giving her back. Powhatan apparently accepted the *fait accompli* and went back to his Indian village, whereas Pocahontas was taken to Jamestown and was delivered to Governor Gates.

Three months later, Powhatan offered five hundred bushels of corn for the return of his daughter. He never offered to return the arms and ammunition which they believed that he had stolen, however. This offer of corn was refused. Later, Governor Gates returned to England but, before doing so, handed Pocahontas over to his successor, Governor Dale.

John Rolfe (1585–1622) was a man whose wife had accompanied him to America but the wife had died shortly after their arrival in 1610. On the way over, they had been ship wrecked in Bermuda. A daughter had been born there, whom they named Bermuda, but the child had died within a few months. With no living wife, John Rolfe somehow arranged to become the husband of Pocahontas. The marriage took place on or about April 5, 1614, by which time Pocahontas had been held a prisoner for nearly one year. She became pregnant and her baby, Thomas Rolfe, was born in Virginia in 1615. She was converted to Christianity and given the name 'Rebecca'. She and the child were taken to England, where they arrived in 1615. Unfortunately, two years later, she suddenly became ill and died almost immediately of unknown causes in Gravesend, England. John Rolfe after that married yet again and returned to Virginia. He is believed to have been killed in a famous massacre by the Indians which took place on March 22, 1622. That massacre resulted in the death of 350 colonists, that being nearly half of the total white population of Virginia at that time.

It was not at all surprising that Pocahontas died so quickly. Rather, it was surprising that she lived so long. Most of the Indians died of various white man's diseases immediately upon exposure to them. This, however, went both ways, with the white colonists often succumbing to Indian diseases. One of the rewards which the Europeans got as a result of colonizing America was the disease of syphilis which became a great epidemic in Europe shortly after the colonists got it from the Indians for the first time and brought it back to Europe with them.

Pocahontas, of course, would have been better off minding her own business and allowing the head of Captain John Smith to pounded into mush. She would probably have lived to a ripe old age as a happy, although unknown, Indian princess.

Thomas Rolfe, the son of Pocahontas, was raised up by an uncle in England. When he reached maturity, in 1640, completely on his own, he came back to his birthplace of Virginia. He was given land by the Indians, who accepted him as their brother. This made him a wealthy man. He married an English woman, whose actual name is not known, although her name is usually given as Jane Poythress, since the Poythress family is believed to have been in Virginia at that time. They had only one child, Jane Rolfe. Jane Rolfe married Robert Bolling in 1675. She died, apparently in the aftermath of childbirth, in 1676. Her son was Col. John Bolling (1676–1729), who married Mary Kennon. They had one son and five daughters. These six children and their children married into almost all of the prominent families of Virginia, including the Randolphs, making just about every significant family in Virginia a relative of a descendant of Pocahontas.

After the death of Jane Rolfe, Robert Bolling took a second wife named Anne Stith. They are known to have had at least two sons who produced more Bollings. These Stith Bollings, not the Pocahontas Bollings, were the ancestors of John Wayles Eppes. The grandmother of John Wayles Eppes was Martha Bolling. Her father was Robert Bolling. However, this Robert Bolling was the son on Anne Stith.

The best, and perhaps the only, source which deals clearly with this confusing situation is the 1958 book *Colonial Families of the Southern States of America* by Stella Picket Hardy, p. 76.

There have been as many as six persons named Robert Bolling. Unfortunately, except for the above source plus the Bolling family Bible, no genealogical record of the Stith Bollings has been maintained, perhaps out of a desire on the part of everybody named Bolling to claim to be a descendant of Pocahontas.

The Randolphs married the Pocahontas Bollings. One of the daughters of Col. John Bolling and Mary Kennon was Jane Bolling, who married Richard Randolph of Curles and was the great-grandmother of Thomas Mann Randolph Junior.

The entire story above obviously hangs by several slender threads. Nobody can say whether it is completely true or not. It is amusing to learn that the *National Inquirer* style of writing was not invented in this century. More than 150 years ago, the Reverend E. D. Neill, Doctor of Divinity, tried to sell books by impugning the chastity and the virtue of Pocahontas. He described her as a common promiscuous slut and said that both she and John Rolfe were adulterers, having had sex together while being married to others. He further said that Pocahontas had three husbands, the first being an Indian man and the third being an additional husband she took while in England.

However, the documentation supporting his claim turned out to be a listing of her husband in England as being a man sometimes named 'Thomas Wrolfe' and sometimes named 'Thomas Wrothe'. As can plainly be seen, this 'Wrolfe' or 'Wrothe' was obviously the same person as John Rolfe. All this was happening while the plays of Shakespeare were still being written. There was no uniform spelling system at that time. The Randolphs also spelled their names in several different ways at that time, including even 'Randall'.

The decline and fall of the Randolphs can be attributed to a number of factors. Starting in around the year 1800, the Randolphs no longer produced so many children. Many of the members of the Randolph family died without issue. Branches of the family became extinct. Most of the Randolphs today are not descendants of William Randolph of Turkey Island, but rather are descendants of his uncle, Henry Randolph, who had only one son, who in turn also had only one son. The Randolph tendency towards incest was certainly harmful in the long run. The strange behavior and possibly even mental illness of Thomas Mann Randolph, Jr., may have been in part caused by this. No doubt the American tendency toward democracy, where a man received a high government position because of his merit rather than because of who his grandfather was, eroded the influence of the Randolphs.

An eccentric person like Thomas Mann Randolph, Jr., would never have three times been elected Governor of Virginia for one year terms had it not been for his Randolph family name.

One cannot say for certain that incest was the cause of this, but there were a number of Randolphs who were deaf mutes or had other mental deficiencies. Elizabeth Jefferson, one sister of Thomas Jefferson, was mentally retarded. After she died, he kept a clipping entitled *Elegy on the Death of an Idiot Girl*. Another sister, Jane Jefferson, never married and died at the age of 25, although history does not tell us exactly what was wrong with her. Several of the other siblings of Thomas Jefferson also seemed to have something wrong with them. His only brother, Randolph Jefferson, was regarded as a simpleton. In *Jefferson at Monticello*, p. 22, one of the slaves evaluated him as follows:

> *Old Master's brother, Mass Randall, was a mighty simple man: used to come out among the black people, play the fiddle and dance half the night; hadn't much more sense than Isaac.*

In addition, there was a highly publicized incident, largely forgotten today, involving the murder of a newborn child, which certainly did not help the public reputation of the Randolphs. This incident is the origin of the well-known Southern saying, 'There is always that one nigger in the woodpile'. 'In the woodpile' was where the freshly murdered possibly half-black infant Randolph child was placed.

Thomas Mann Randolph Jr. had twelve full brothers and sisters. One sister was Ann Cary 'Nancy' Randolph. She was born on September 16, 1774. On October 1, 1792, when this incident took place, she was just 18 years old and unmarried. Her older sister was named Judith, who was born on November 24, 1772. Judith, in accordance with the Randolph family custom, was married to her first cousin, Richard Randolph of Bizarre, who was born in 1770. Richard and Judith had been married in 1790.

All three had been living in the same house together at Bizarre. 'Bizarre' was the name of the estate of Richard Randolph, located near Farmville. It seems possible that the following strange but well-known incident is how the term 'bizarre' acquired its present meaning in the English language.

According to one version of the story, the first born child of Richard and Judith had died. Thereafter, Judith Randolph became depressed and Richard Randolph took up with Nancy Randolph, who promptly became pregnant.

The second version of the story was that Nancy had been engaged to be married to the chronically sickly Theoderic Bland Randolph, who was born in 1771 and died in February, 1792, just before the marriage ceremony was scheduled to take place. John Randolph of Roanoke later expressed the view that Nancy, prior to the marriage, had already become pregnant with the child of Theoderic, and she did not want the baby after Theoderic Randolph had died.

However, the prevalent view outside of the Randolph family was that Nancy had a black slave lover named Billy Ellis, and that this relationship had caused her to become unmarried and pregnant.

Martha Jefferson Randolph apparently must have known about the unwanted pregnancy, because she sent to the Randolph plantation a concoction sometimes useful for producing abortion. Later on, Richard Randolph, the husband of Judith, who was the sister of Nancy, hired both Patrick Henry and John Marshall, two of the most eminent lawyers in America at the time, for defense against the charges of infanticide. Richard Randolph was suspected of having fathered the murdered child. Richard was acquitted, but died shortly thereafter under mysterious circumstances. His brother believed that he had been poisoned with arsenic by Nancy.

There are a multitude of sources which confirm this basic story. Among these are the notes of one of the attorneys for the defense, John Marshall, who later on became the Chief Justice of the United States Supreme Court.

The details are as follows: The incident involving the birth and immediate murder of the illegitimate child occurred on the night of October 1, 1792, at Glenlyvar, the home of Randolph Harrison and his wife, Mary Randolph, a first cousin of Thomas Jefferson, in Cumberland County, Virginia. Randolph Harrison was a first cousin of future President William Henry Harrison, who, in turn, was the grandfather of President Benjamin Harrison. Five members of the Randolph family, including Richard Randolph, Judith Randolph and Nancy Randolph, had arrived that day as guests. Screams were heard in the middle of the night coming from the room where Nancy was staying. These were heard by Randolph Harrison and his wife, who, shortly thereafter, heard the footsteps of a man walking down the stairs and later on returning. The next morning, they found Nancy and Nancy's bed covered with blood. A trail of blood led from the bedroom to the woodpile behind the house. A Negro slave told them that the unmarried Nancy had suffered a miscarriage. Later, another slave said that a fetus had been deposited on a pile of shingles between two logs on the woodpile.

Richard Randolph was thereafter arrested on a charge of infanticide and held without bail. On April 29, 1793, Richard was formally charged with murder. Three famous attorneys, including John Marshall and Patrick Henry, were retained to defend him. The notes of John Marshall, dated June 28, 1793, state that Nancy was also a defendant to the charge of murder.

At the beginning of the trial, it was not yet proven that a living child had even been born. The other possibility was a miscarriage. The prosecution did eventually establish that Nancy had been manifestly pregnant and had given birth to a living child. However, the Negroes who were the most likely witnesses to the murder and who actually saw the body of the dead child lying in the woodpile were not competent to testify in court. As a result, a jury of 16 magistrates eventually returned a verdict of not guilty.

However, the matter did not end there, because nobody really believed that Richard and Nancy were not guilty. Thomas Jefferson, in a letter to Martha Jefferson Randolph dated April 28, 1793, stated that he had read about this incident in the *Richmond Gazette*. He expressed the view that Richard, and not Nancy, was the guilty party. 'In either case I see guilt but in one person, and not in her', wrote Jefferson.

However, others took an opposing view. John Randolph of Roanoke, one of the famous men in America at that time, was the younger brother of Richard Randolph of Bizarre. He was also the future Chairman of the House Ways and Means Committee, the Ambassador to Russia, a powerful orator and a brilliant United States Senator. He never married and hated women. He viewed the acts of Nancy in dragging his innocent brother into this affair as typical of all women. In a letter dated March 12, 1824, to his niece, he said:

> *I have seen such dreadful consequences ensue from the indulgence of a propensity to satire by women that I never discern the slightest propensity towards it in a female without shuddering. This vice . . . . consigned my most amiable and unfortunate brother to a dungeon, and might have dragged him to a gibbet [hangman's noose], blasted the fair promise of his youth, and rendered an untimely death a welcome and happy release from a blighted reputation.*

In fact, Richard Randolph died in June, 1796 (the exact date of death is unaccountably missing from the Randolph family history) and John Randolph of Roanoke believed that he had been poisoned with arsenic by Nancy.

However, one remarkable thing came out of this. From the writings which he left behind in the short 26 years of his life, it is apparent that Richard Randolph of Bizarre was a brilliant, gifted and progressive thinker who would have become as famous as his younger brother had he lived. Richard Randolph was an even more vehement opponent of slavery than was Thomas Jefferson himself. He was more of a fiery abolitionist than the actual abolitionists who followed him. In his will, Richard Randolph decreed freedom for all of his slaves, numbering in excess of 200. More than that, he ordered four hundred acres of land from his considerable estates to be given to them.

Here are some of the words of the last will and testament of Richard Randolph of Bizarre, as recorded in the Will Book for 1797 in the Clerk's

Office of Prince Edward County, Virginia:

> *To make retribution, as far as I am able, to an unfortunate race of bondsmen, over whom my ancestors have usurped and exercised the most lawless and monstrous tyranny, and in whom my countrymen (by their iniquitous laws, in contradiction of their own declaration of rights, and in violation of every sacred law of nature; of the inherent, inalienable and imprescriptible rights of man, and of every principle of moral and political honesty) have vested me with absolute property; to express my abhorrence of the theory as well as infamous practice of usurping the rights of our fellow creatures, equally entitled with ourselves to the enjoyment of liberty and happiness; to exculpate myself . . . . from the black crime which might otherwise be imputed to me of voluntarily holding the above mentioned miserable beings in the same state of abject slavery in which I found them on receiving my patrimony at lawful age; to impress my children with just horror at a crime so enormous and indelible; . . . . for the aforesaid purposes and, with an indignation, too great for utterance, at the tyrants of the earth, from the throned despot of a whole nation to the most despicable, but not less infamous, petty tormentors of single wretched slaves, whose torture constituted his wealth and enjoyment, I do hereby declare that it is my will and desire, nay my most anxious wish that my Negroes, all of them, be liberated, and I do declare them by this writing free and emancipated to all intents and purposes whatsoever.*

After his untimely death, a free Negro settlement of his former slaves was established on his former land. It was called Israel Hill. However, it failed abysmally, as the former slaves quarreled over the land. This example was used thereafter by pro-slavery extremists as an argument against emancipation. In reality, it was simply an argument against communal living and communism.

The controversy over the entire matter of infanticide continued until the deaths of all of the people involved. According to John Randolph of Roanoke (so-called to distinguish him from all of the other John Randolphs), Nancy Randolph approached many men thereafter, including himself, looking for a man to marry her, but no man would touch her, knowing that she had murdered her own illegitimate child. Finally, another truly great person in American history, Gouverneur Morris (1752–1816) of New York, who devised the present monetary system of 'dollars' and 'cents', who was a Framer and signer of the Constitution of the United States, who had been involved in preparing the final draft of that document, and who personally got the constitutional clause inserted establishing a presidential veto, agreed to take in Nancy as a simple housekeeper, apparently without knowing her history or even who she was. This happened in 1814, while he was the Governor of

New York and already an old man.

One thing led to another, and soon thereafter Gouverneur Morris married her. He was later informed about the incident of murder, but he always expressed complete happiness and satisfaction with having Nancy as his wife, up until the time he of his death two years later. They left one child, Gouverneur Morris Junior, apparently the only child for both of them.

John Randolph of Roanoke, then a member of Congress, wrote Nancy a letter in 1814 in which he stated that he himself had withheld evidence from the court which would have led to her and his brother's conviction and hanging for murder, just to save the Randolph family name. He stated that Nancy herself had strangled the child immediately upon birth and then had handed the dead body to Richard to be taken out to the woodpile. He further stated that three years later Nancy had murdered Richard with arsenic poisoning, because he alone knew her secret. Here are a few words of the sweet letter which John Randolph of Roanoke wrote to Ann Cary 'Nancy' Randolph on October 31, 1814:

> *His hands received the burthen, bloody from the womb, and already lifeless. Who stifled its cries, God only knows and you. To the prudence of Randolph Harrison, who disqualified himself from giving testimony by refraining from a search under the pile of shingles, some of which were marked with blood — to this cautious conduct it is owing that my brother Richard did not perish on the same gibbet by your side, and that the foul stain of incest and murder is not indelibly stamped on his memory and associated with the idea of his offspring.*
>
> *. . . .*
>
> *My brother died suddenly in June, 1796, only three years after his trial. I was from home. Tudor [Randolph], because he believes you capable of anything, imparted to me . . . . his misgivings that you had been the perpetrator of that act, and, when I found your mind running upon poisonings and murders, I too had my former suspicions strengthened. . . . . But your intimacy with one of the slaves, your 'dear Billy Ellis', thus you commenced your epistles to this Othello!, attracted notice. You could no longer stay at Bizarre.*
>
> *. . . .*
>
> *When I first heard of you living with Mr. Morris as a housekeeper, I was glad of it. . . . . The idea of his marrying you never entered my head. Another connection did. My first intimation of the marriage was its announcement in the newspapers. . . . . What do I see? A vampire that, after sucking the best blood of my race, has struck her harpy fangs into an infirm old man. . . . . If he be not both blind and deaf, he must sooner or later unmask you unless he too dies of cramps in his stomach. . . . . Repent before it is too late. May I*

The phrase near the end, 'unless he too dies of cramps in his stomach,' refers to the common symptom of arsenic poisoning. George Wythe, one of the signers of the Declaration of Independence, was murdered in 1806 by arsenic placed in his coffee by a great nephew, George Wythe Sweeney, as was readily proven by cutting open his inflamed stomach and intestines after he died. His 15-year-old putative mulatto son, Michael Brown, had been murdered at the same time in the same way and the crime was proven in the same way. The sole motive for this double murder had been that both Michael Brown and George Wythe Sweeney had been named in the will of George Wythe. George Wythe Sweeney had just gotten out of jail for forging bad checks and wanted money quickly to pay his gambling debts. Richard Randolph of Bizarre was apparently, according to the above quoted letter, also murdered by arsenic poisoning in the same way.

It is noteworthy that, according to the above letter, even after Nancy had murdered the newborn child, and even after she had also murdered John's brother Richard Randolph with arsenic poisoning, she continued to live at Bizarre. It was only when she was caught exchanging letters with her Negro lover, Billy Ellis, that she was kicked out of the house.

The above letter, while addressed to Nancy, was actually delivered to Gouverneur Morris. He kept it for nearly three months and gave it to his wife, Nancy, on January 15, 1815. The next day, she wrote a long reply. Numerous copies were made, apparently by her or at her direction, and these copies have found their way into the archives of various historical societies. However, she never sent the original letter to John Randolph of Roanoke.

There are numerous sources regarding this entire incident, but the best is William Cabell Bruce, *John Randolph of Roanoke 1773– 1833* (New York, 1922), Vol. I, pp. 106-23 and Vol. II, pp. 273-295. A typical two paragraph whitewash can be found in Dumas Malone, *Jefferson and the Ordeal of Liberty*, p. 172. There is also a novel about this incident entitled *The Bizarre Sisters* (New York, 1950) by Jay and Audrey Walz.

There were at least two other murders by members of the Randolph family at about the same time. John Randolph (1743–1803), the son of Henry Randolph IV, was found murdered, having been shot in the head. His son, Richard Bland Randolph, was arrested for the murder. He spent considerable time in jail over this charge. Although he was ultimately acquitted for lack of evidence, it is generally assumed that he was guilty.

One of the most grizzly murders in American history involved two nephews of Thomas Jefferson: Lilburn and Isham Lewis. They were the sons of his sister, Lucy Jefferson (1752–1784), who married Charles Lilburn Lewis. They murdered one of their own slaves in Tennessee, where they were living at the time.

However, it was not the murder of an obscure slave which made this event noteworthy, but the way in which it was done. The slave had apparently been guilty of some minor infraction of house rules or had knocked over something by accident. In order to impress upon the other slaves that this sort of thing ought not to be done, Lilburn and Isham assembled all of the other slaves together, put the guilty slave on the chopping block, and then, with a hatchet, cut off first one hand, then the other hand, then one foot, then the other foot; slowly piece by piece chopping off various body parts until the poor victim was mercifully dead.

What is remarkable about this is that all of the other slaves just stood there and watched, although they could easily have overpowered Lilburn and Isham and rescued their brethren.

This episode was repeatedly invoked by abolitionists as a typical example of the cruelties of slavery. It has been mentioned in many books. There is currently in print a book only about this entitled *Jefferson's Nephews*, available now at a bookstore near you.

# Chapter Seventeen

## The Contribution of "Down From The Mountain"

Judith Price Justus, in her 1991 book, *Down From The Mountain*, has made a number of excellent discoveries and observations which enhance this entire story. These discoveries are so important and come so close to the scheduled publication date of this book, that a special chapter is required devoted only to them.

Judith P. Justus is a white school teacher in Perrysburg, Ohio, who has a wide ranging interest in historical personalities, including, among others, General George Armstrong Custer and Sally Hemings.

Unlike so many other books, her book never bothers to rehash the well known facts of this story. Instead, she strikes out into unknown territory and provides facts, almost all of which are not available from any other source. In particular, in the concluding chapters of *Down From the Mountain*, she makes a strong case tending to show that the original concubine of Thomas Jefferson was actually Mary Hemings, who was born in 1753. Mary, according to Judith P. Justus, was shunted aside when Sally Hemings, twenty years her junior, grew up. Because of this, in 1792, Mary requested that she be sold to Col. Tom Bell.

Mary was the mother of Joe 'Fossett', who was born in 1780, and of Betsy Hemings, who was born in 1783. That would possibly make Thomas Jefferson the father of both of these children.

The most important items of evidence regarding this are as follows:

The family and descendants of Joe Fossett who are alive today all claim that Joe, known in the *Farm Book* only as 'Joe 80', was the son of Thomas Jefferson. See *Thomas Jefferson's Negro Grandchildren, Ebony Magazine*, November, 1954, Vol. 10, No. 1, pp. 78-80.

This claim was rejected by Fawn Brodie and others, who say that Joe was the son of William Fossett, a white carpenter who briefly worked at Monticello. Nevertheless, the descendants of Joe 80 continue to insist that Thomas Jefferson was the father of Joe.

It must be pointed out that this claim is based entirely on the oral tradition of the Fossett family. No scandal was ever published regarding Mary Hemings, the mother of Joe. Sally Hemings was known in the newspapers of that time as the concubine of Thomas Jefferson. The name of Betsy has been mentioned as a possible second concubine. The name of Betty Brown has also been mentioned in this capacity. However, the name of Mary Hemings has never come up. Her name is only found in obscure entries in the *Farm Book*. There was nothing special about her. It is only the family of Joe Fossett which insists that she was the concubine of Thomas Jefferson.

The primary bit of evidence proving that this is true comes in the statement by Isaac Jefferson that Mary was taken by Thomas Jefferson to Williamsburg when he served as the Governor of Virginia from 1779 to 1781. The *Farm Book* says that Joe was born November, 1780. How is it possible that William Fossett, who worked at Monticello, was the father of Joe 80, when Mary, the mother of Joe 80, was in Williamsburg and Richmond with Thomas Jefferson from 1779 until 1781, while he was governor?

The original capital of Virginia was in Williamsburg. The capital was moved to Richmond in the Spring of 1780. The *Memoirs of Isaac Jefferson*, which are to be found in *Jefferson at Monticello*, p. 4, edited by James A. Bear, Jr., describe the carriage that took Thomas Jefferson and his entourage from Monticello to Williamsburg in 1779. Bob Hemings was the driver. James Hemings was the body servant. Martin Hemings was the butler. Mary rode in the wagon. Sally Hemings, still a child six years old, was mighty handsome. Her older half-sister, Betty Brown, was also along on the journey.

Thus, we know that Mary was taken to Williamsburg by Thomas Jefferson in 1779. This was probably in the early part of 1779, because the Governor of Virginia would normally take office early in the year. We also know from the same memoirs of Isaac Jefferson that Mary was still in the capital, in the residence of Thomas Jefferson, when the British under the famous turncoat General Benedict Arnold attacked Richmond on January 5, 1781. 'Isaac was out in the yard. His mother ran out and cotch him up by the hand and carried him into the kitchen hollering. Mary Hemings, she jerked up her daughter the same way.'

Mary and her infant son Joe are listed by Isaac Jefferson as among those who were taken prisoner by the British, and who were personally present as prisoners at the Battle of Yorktown in October, 1781.

Thus, we know that Mary was not in Monticello from 1779 to 1781. Also, Monticello was three days drive by wagon from Richmond. Therefore, William Fossett was probably not the father of Joe 80 and Thomas Jefferson very likely could have been the father.

Judith P. Justus also points out that Joe 80 never used the name 'Joe Fossett' until the will of Thomas Jefferson in 1826 gave him that name.

All this has important implications. It might mean that Thomas Jefferson maintained a concubine, Mary Hemings, even before his wife, Martha Wayles Jefferson, died in 1782.

Another possibly important piece of evidence concerns the fact that the Philadelphia Directory for 1793 gives a listing for a 'Mary Hemmings' on Collowhill Street in Philadelphia. At that time, Philadelphia was the capital of the United States of America. Thomas Jefferson lived in Philadelphia from 1790 to 1793 as the Secretary of State under President George Washington. Although it seems unlikely that Mary Hemings, a slave, would have had her own listing in the *Philadelphia City Directory* (this was not a telephone directory, as the telephone had not been invented yet), it also seems unlikely that there would have been anybody else in America by the name of Mary Hemmings. Hemings is a rare name. It does exist in England, but anybody in America with that name is probably a descendant of Betty Hemings.

James A. Bear says that Mary was sold at her own request to Col. Tom Bell in 1792. This statement is based upon a published letter dated April 12, 1792, from Thomas Jefferson to his overseer, Nicholas Lewis, directing that this sale be made 'according to her desire'. Judith P. Justus suggests that this unusual request was the result of jealousy by Mary at being supplanted by Sally as the number one consort of Thomas Jefferson. However, Judith P. Justus also points out that there is no proof that this sale was ever consummated. Mary may have eventually changed her mind and decided to remain with Thomas Jefferson, even if it meant being the number two or number three concubine. Also, this sale may have been just a ruse for her to gain her freedom, as was often the case. She might have made it to Philadelphia the following year in 1793 as a free woman. Judith P. Justus also believes that Mary returned later to Monticello of her own accord and continued to live there until the death of Thomas Jefferson.

However, on this last point, Judith P. Justus has given an invalid reason for reaching this conclusion. It is true that there are two Marys on all of the lists on the last few pages of the *Farm Book*, ending in 1824. There are Mary Bet's and Mary Moses's. Mary Bet's could plausibly be Mary, the daughter of Betty Hemings, but the *Farm Book* makes it clear that that Mary was actually the Mary who was born in 1801 and was the daughter of Betty Brown. Also, Mary, the daughter of Moses, is clearly a different person and is mentioned on many other pages of the *Farm Book*.

Another factor, not mentioned by Judith P. Justus, is that there is some reason to believe that Edy, the wife of Joe Fossett, may also have been the concubine of Thomas Jefferson. The primary basis for this belief is that it is well established that Edy was in the White House while Thomas Jefferson was President. Joe Fossett was not there. Two of the children of Edy, James (1805) and Maria (1807), were born while Thomas Jefferson was President.

Although James (1805) is reported elsewhere to have died as an infant and Thomas Jefferson is said to have purchased a coffin for the funeral, Judith P. Justus states on page 122 of her book that he died in 1880 in Charlottesville, Virginia and his will was probated in the Albemarle County Circuit Court. However, there were at least five slaves named James at any given time at Monticello.

The main point is that it is possible that Thomas Jefferson was the father of Joe Fossett and it is also possible that Thomas Jefferson was the father of at least some of the children of Edy, who was known as Joe's wife.

The best proof for all of this is that many of the descendants of Joe Fossett became important and distinguished people, one of which was the co-founder of the NAACP. They are less likely to have been descendants of a mere carpenter like William Fossett.

It must also be mentioned that Edy was presumably pure black. Therefore, her children, regardless of who the father may have been, had no chance to pass for white. However, perhaps Edy was not completely black. On page 122 in *Down from the Mountain*, there is a reference to *Early Charlottesville, Recollections of James Alexander 1828–1874*, p. 84, published by The Michie Company in Charlottesville, 1942, which indicates that a daughter of Col. Tom Bell married Jesse Scott, the celebrated fiddler, who may have been a son or a grandson of Joe and Edy. One wants to know: Was this a white daughter or a slave daughter of Col. Tom Bell? Did Mary produce a child for Col. Tom Bell, or was she too old for that? This book refers to Jesse Scott as 'half-Indian', which is a way in Virginia of implying that he was half-black.

An article entitled *Thomas Jefferson's Negro Grandchildren*, in Ebony Magazine in November, 1954, had this to say:

> Perhaps the best known of Negro descendants of Jefferson are the great grand children of one of these slaves, Joseph Fossett, an iron worker who married the ex-president's favorite cook, Edith. He had seven children.
> Ebony, November, 1954, Vol. 10, No. 1, pp. 78–80.

The same *Ebony* article quotes the granddaughter of Anna Elizabeth, also known as 'Betsy', and identified in the article as Jefferson's grand-daughter, as saying, "My grandmother, rocking in her favorite chair, used to tell me about him [Thomas Jefferson] all the time. She called him 'Grand Pa'."

The *Ebony* article was debunked by historian Fawn Brodie, who claimed that this was based upon ignorance and upon a mistaken belief that Thomas Jefferson fathered children by slaves other than Sally. Brodie felt that the authors of this article simply did not know that the father of Joe Fossett was William Fossett. Brodie seemed to feel the strange need to defend the virtue of Thomas Jefferson, implying that he was always a one-woman man.

However, Fawn Brodie apparently did not know what every reader of

*Ebony Magazine* probably did know, which is that a great-grandson of Joe Fossett was William Monroe Trotter who, along with W.E.B. DuBois and H. Claude Hudson, founded the predecessor of the National Association for the Advancement of Colored People (NAACP) in 1905.

The original name of the NAACP was the Niagara Movement. It was changed to the present name in 1910. The NAACP was the leading black political organization in America, which brought about the eventual desegregation of the public schools and other public facilities.

William Monroe Trotter founded the *Boston Guardian*. He personally met twice with President Woodrow Wilson in the White House. He is perhaps best known for an often quoted letter he wrote to President Wilson complaining about racial discrimination in federal employment facilities. That letter is quoted in full in the 1991 book *Chronology of African-American History* by Alton Hornsby, Jr., pp. 455-457. The eloquence and style displayed in that letter shows that no average man could have written it. Yet, there is no hint or clue that the author of the letter was a descendant of Thomas Jefferson.

The mother of William Monroe Trotter was Virginia Isaacs. Virginia Isaacs was the granddaughter of a Jewish merchant named David Isaacs (1760–1835) who had a store on Main Street in Charlottesville. Thomas Jefferson sometimes sent his slaves to buy items from that store. David Isaacs had seven children by a mulatto woman named Nancy West. He acknowledged all of these children in his will. Two of these children married the grandchildren of Betty Hemings. A daughter, Julia, married Eston Hemings Jefferson. A son, Tucker Isaacs (1809–74), married Ann Elizabeth Fossett, the daughter of Joe Fossett.

Sometimes the name Fossett is spelled Fosset or even, in the case of *Ebony Magazine*, as Faucett. However, the spelling 'Fossett' is used throughout here for the sake of uniformity as it is clear that the same person is being discussed. Only one possible person with a name like that had the first name of Joe and a wife named 'Edy'.

Ann Elizabeth Fossett is the same person who is known as Betsy 1813 in the *Farm Book*. 'Betsy' was the nickname for Elizabeth. However, this particular Betsy is not the Betsy who was the possible concubine of Thomas Jefferson, because this Betsy would have been only 13 years old when Thomas Jefferson died in 1826 at the age of 83. The Betsy believed possibly to have been the concubine of Thomas Jefferson was either Betsy, the daughter of Mary, who was born in 1783 or else was Betty Brown, the sister of Mary, who was born in 1759.

Another son of Joe Fossett was Peter Fossett. After Joe Fossett was given his freedom in the will of Thomas Jefferson, he went to Cincinnati. However, some of his children were sold as slaves and left behind. One such child was Peter Fossett. He escaped twice, was sold on the auction block and was about to be sold a second time in Richmond in 1850 when friends got together and raised enough money to buy him and send him to his father in Cincinnati. There, he established a catering business and, almost immediately, became rich and famous. He became The Reverend Peter Farley Fossett and is regarded as the Founding Father of the Negro Ohio Baptists. He also became a 'conductor' on the underground railroad which led runaway slaves out of Virginia and what is now West Virginia across Ohio, sometimes reaching as far as Canada, the only place where they were completely safe. This so-called 'underground railroad' was really a system of safe houses whereby runaway slaves could move from house to house in the night, eventually crossing Ohio. It ran though mainly Chillicothe, Ohio, which is near the West Virginia border, and extended through Cincinnati to the Great Lakes.

Peter Fossett and William Monroe Trotter were the two most famous descendants of Joe Fossett, but several others were important and distinguished persons as well. This again shows that some distinguished person must have been the ancestor of these persons.

It appears that the two leading anti-slavery Negro preachers in Ohio and, indeed, the entire United States of America at the time were Lewis Woodson and Peter Fossett, who undoubtedly must have known each other, even if they did not know that they were distant relatives and actual descendants of Thomas Jefferson. Here is an example of the writing and speaking style of Lewis Woodson, which is found in the *Minutes of the Christian Anti-Slavery Convention* in Pittsburgh, Pennsylvania, April 15, 1850, as quoted in Carter G. Woodson's book, *The Negro and the Mind*, p. 493:

> *A Christianity without humanity, without benevolence, without mercy, without justice, is no Christianity at all. It is a liable upon the character of true Christianity and the example of the teachings of its Divine Author. His life was spent in doing good to the bodies, as well as the souls, of men; in rendering them happy on earth, as well as preparing them for heaven. The Author of Christianity never intended that slavery should become part and parcel of it. The examples which he set, the principles which he uttered, the Great Principles which he laid down, show that this was not his intention. On the contrary, if they were reduced to practice and fully carry out, they would extirpate slavery from the earth.*

Thomas Jefferson himself could have hardly succeeded in writing better than that. Even the writing style is somewhat reminiscent of the *Declaration of Independence*. However, there is one important difference. Lewis Woodson and Peter Fossett were clearly Christian Baptist preachers. Thomas Jefferson claimed that he had a religion but that it was his private business. Many detractors claimed that Thomas Jefferson had no religion at all. Indeed, the well known *Virginia Statute on Religious Freedom* written by Thomas Jefferson was intended to protect persons like Thomas Jefferson himself from persecution by others professing a particular religion.

One question which will be raised is that if Thomas Jefferson really was the father of Joe Fossett, why did he wait until his death to free him, by which time Joe was already 46 years old? Why not unofficially free him at the age of 21 or 22 as in the case of Beverly and Harriet? Also, why were the children of Joe not freed in the will.

The answer might be that, as oral tradition has it among the slaves, Thomas Jefferson made a deal with Sally that if she agreed to return with him from France, her children would be freed upon reaching age 21. He made no such agreement with his other concubines, such as Mary, the mother of Joe. Also, he may have been not completely sure that he was the father of Joe 80 and may have suspected that another man might be the father. Also, his will does seem to contemplate that the children of Joe would all get their freedom somehow, even though this implied term of his will was not carried out.

Judith P. Justus has also located and published a letter written by Thomas Jefferson Randolph in rebuttal of the statement given by Israel Jefferson to the *Pike County Republican*. She regards the publication of this letter as one of the major achievements of her work. This letter was never before published and probably was never mailed to the *Pike County Republican*. However, it tends to confirm and not to refute some of the otherwise shaky sounding statements of Israel Jefferson. In particular, Thomas Jefferson Randolph acknowledges that Israel Jefferson did, in fact, come to Edgehill to visit him in 1866, one year after the Civil War had ended, and found him in a state of financial distress. Israel Jefferson had remarked that all Thomas Jefferson Randolph had left was 'one old blind mule.' Thomas Jefferson Randolph stated that it was even worse than that, as even the rings had been removed from the fingers of all of the females in his family, as a consequence of the Civil War.

Thomas Jefferson Randolph also recounted, quite accurately, his personal legislative record in favor of the abolition of slavery, following in the footsteps of his grandfather. He kept asking why his family is being slandered by the claim that his grandfather produced children from his slaves, after all that he alone among all Virginians had done to try to bring about the abolition of slavery by peaceful means.

Comparing the statement of Israel Jefferson and the reply of Thomas Jefferson Randolph, there is no doubt that the two men knew each other well and were talking about the same things, things which no outsider would probably ever have known. Therefore, the reply of Thomas Jefferson Randolph serves to confirm the statements made by Israel Jefferson.

Another discovery of Judith P. Justus was that the first Negro woman ever to graduate from the exclusive Vassar College at Poughkeepsie, New York was one Anita Hemming. This occurred in 1897 and caused a great scandal at the all-white all-girls college at that time. Anita Hemming had been admitted at Vassar as white, had attended for four years, had completed all her courses and then, just a few days prior to graduation, it was suddenly discovered that she was a 'Negress'. This caused a big problem for the school officials, who did not know what to do about such a situation. Finally, they decided that they had no choice but to give her her diploma and let her graduate, as all of her courses had been completed.

The Boston Newspapers of that time did not mince words over this situation. "NEGRO GIRL AT VASSAR", screamed one headline. "VASSAR'S NEGRESS, MISS HEMMING", said another. The headlines continued: "She Was Graduated this Year After Confessing Her Father's Race — THE HANDSOMEST GIRL THERE — Yale and Harvard Men Among Those Who Sought Favor with the 'Brunette Beauty'."

> POUGHKEEPSIE, N.Y., Aug. 15. Society and educational circles in the city are profoundly shocked by the announcement in a local paper today that one of the graduating class of Vassar College this year was a Negro girl, who, concealing her race, entered the college, took the four years course, and, finally, confessed the truth to a professor a few days before commencement.
> The facts were communicated to the faculty, which body in secret session decided to allow the girl to receive her diploma with the class.
> Vassar is noted for its exclusiveness and every official of the college refuses to say ought regarding the girl graduate. She has been known as one of the most beautiful young women who ever attended the great institution of learning and even now women who received her in their homes as their equal do not deny her beauty. At the reception on Founders Day, Philalethian Day, and the other holidays of the college year none of the fair students was more eagerly sought by the men from Yale, Harvard and the other universities who attended these events.
> Her fellow students called her the 'beautiful brunette'. Her manners were those of a person of gentle birth and her intelligence and ability alike were recognized by her class-mates and professors. . . .

The first article about this scandal appeared in The World newspaper and was entitled "NEGRESS AT VASSAR". It said:

> Vassar College Girls are agitated over the report that one of the students in the senior class of '97 is of Negro parentage.
> She did not disclose the fact until just before graduation, when remarks she

*made to her roommate led to an investigation which brought out the facts.*
*The girl says that when she was young she was clever and bright and a*
*wealthy white woman offered to educate her, seeing in her possibilities of*
*noble womanhood if properly reared.*
*She studied hard, passed the required examination and entered Vassar.*

Subsequent articles explained further that her father was Robert J. Hemming, who had recently come to Boston from the South. Her benefactor had been a wealthy white woman who recognized her beauty and intelligence and had sent her to a private preparatory school. Her roommate at that school had been the future wife of lawyer named Henry Lewis, who had also assisted her.

Later on, she was caught in her deception as a result of constantly bragging that her family were 'Blue Bloods' and often speaking of the splendor of their homes. The term 'blue blood' means that the person is of high or noble birth. Her roommate became suspicious about this and went snooping around her family to find out exactly how blue their blood actually was. She hit upon the truth.

Any student of history should have immediately realized from these newspaper articles that this was not just any ordinary Negro girl but was undoubtedly a descendant of Thomas Jefferson and of the 'decidedly good looking' Dusky Sally, who was known for her beauty at Monticello. However, none of the newspapers of that day ever made this connection or came to the realization of who this mysterious girl really was.

The photographs of her which were published in the newspapers of that time show a strong resemblance to the photographs of Amelia Elizabeth Perry Pride, another possible descendant of Thomas Jefferson, who became the principal of the Negro Public School in Lynchburg, Virginia. Indeed, the resemblance between the two women is so strong that they could almost be the same person, except that Anita Hemming was 14 years younger.

Anita Hemming eventually became Mrs. Andrew Love (1872–1960). Social Security records do not show the death of this person, so perhaps she went to England. It seems possible that she is a relative or ancestor of Edward Graham Jefferson, the retired Chairman of the Board of DuPont Chemical Corporation, whose father was named Edward Hemmings Jefferson. His wife is named Naomi Nale Love, from England.

In any event, there can be little doubt that when a partially black woman with a name such as Anita Hemming, establishes herself as both the most beautiful girl at Vassar College and at the same time one of the top students, then she must have been a recipient of the legendary beauty of Sally Hemings and the high intelligence of Thomas Jefferson.

Another discovery of Judith P. Justus is that a bed which is possibly the bed used by Thomas Jefferson at Monticello still exists in Chillicothe, Ohio, having apparently been brought there by Eston Hemmings and his wife Julia Isaacs. All of the furniture at Monticello was sold shortly after the death of Thomas Jefferson to pay his debts. This bed in Ohio could well have been purchased at the auction by the Jewish merchant, David Isaacs, given to his daughter, Julia, and later taken by her and her husband to Ohio.

In addition, a pair of spectacles, a silver hair buckle and an inkwell belonging to Thomas Jefferson had been given to Sally Hemings and had been inherited by Madison Hemings upon the death of his mother. In 1938, a descendant of Madison Hemings offered these items to Monticello. The official reply dated November 1, 1938, which came back from Monticello, was, 'we really have quite enough of these little mementos so that it would be indifferent whether we bought any more.'

The personal eyeglasses of Thomas Jefferson would be immensely valuable today. They would be put on display at Monticello, which receives thousands of tourist dollars every day. We would then be able to find out how bad his eyesight was. However, their present whereabouts are unknown. No doubt, Monticello refused this offer in part because Sally Hemings was officially considered to be a non-person to them at that time.

Finally, on a personal note, Judith P. Justus mentions a descendant of Thomas Jefferson named Cyrus Creighton Cassel who was born in 1845 and fought in the Civil War. He was the son of T. James Cassel (1814–1876) and the daughter of Frances L. Woodson (1814–1899) who was the daughter of Tom Woodson, who was the son of Thomas Jefferson. It so happens that the maternal grandmother of this author had the family name of 'Cassel' and the brother of this author is named Creighton. Therefore, anybody with the unusual name of Creighton Cassel would seem to be a likely ancestor of this author himself. As the old Southern saying goes, 'There is always one nigger in the woodpile.'

The saying 'there is always one nigger in the woodpile' means that regardless of how lily white one might be, there is always that one small possibility that somewhere back there is black African blood in every family. Of course, under the theory of the superiority of genetic diversity, having a little bit of black ancestry should make one stronger, healthier, more resistant to disease and longer living. However, most whites in the South do not look upon this constantly looming possibility that way.

In reality, it is extremely remote that this author might be a descendant of that Creighton Cassel, the great grandson of Sally Hemings, as the Cassel side of the family tree of this author can be traced back to Scotland, where they were collateral descendants of John Paul Jones. However, one can never be completely sure. As the old saying goes, 'There is always that one nigger in the woodpile.'

# Chapter Eighteen

## Famous Descendants of Thomas Jefferson

There are an exceptional number of famous people in both the white and black communities that are actually closet descendants of Thomas Jefferson. These include the retired Chairman of DuPont Chemical Corp., who was previously the head of Research and Development of that corporation, the co-founder of the NAACP, a recently appointed federal judge, the first black assemblyman in the history of the State of California, a member of the executive committee of the Woman's Christian Temperance Union and the first Negro girl ever surreptitiously to attend Vassar College. All were descendants of Thomas Jefferson, although nobody knew about their ancestry.

Much better and more detailed work on the subject of what ever happened to the descendants of Sally Hemings has been done by a number of women, of whom Minnie Shumate Woodson and Judith P. Justus are the most prominent. Minnie Shumate Woodson and her friends have been working on this since 1979. Judith P. Justus is a relative newcomer, who was given access to the material developed by Minnie Shumate Woodson, and who has developed new material of her own.

One of the most intriguing discoveries is the fact that apparently Beverly Hemings, after having been given his freedom by Thomas Jefferson, went to England, where he turned white. There is now an Englishman who is a naturalized American citizen who was until 1986 the Chairman and Chief Executive Officer of the E. I. duPont Chemical Corporation. He also is or was a member of the board of directors of A T & T Corp., Chemical New York Corp., Chemical Bank and Seagram Corp. His name is Edward Graham Jefferson. He was born in 1921 and has a Ph. D. in Chemistry from King's College, University of London. His father was Edward Hemmings Jefferson and his grandfather was named Beverly Jefferson. He has been listed in *Who's Who in America*. By the way, he says that he doesn't know and, anyway, he could care less about who his ancestors were and is tired of the questions on this subject.

A number of researchers have traced the genealogies of the other children of Sally Hemings and this work is still going on. In general, it seems that many of the descendants of Thomas Jefferson and Sally Hemings have had a solid record of accomplishment. Among them have been a number of prominent writers and businessmen. In fact, it seems that on the average, the children of Sally Hemings and their descendants have done better than the children of Thomas Jefferson through his white daughters, Maria and Martha. Few of the legitimate descendants of Thomas Jefferson have ever accomplished anything which was not attributable to being a descendant of Thomas Jefferson.

Eston Hemings Jefferson, the last born son of Sally Hemings, had a son named John Wayles Jefferson. He joined the Union Army during the Civil War and became prominent as a writer of articles for the newspapers. He is described in his military papers as being red-headed, just as Thomas Jefferson was. He was wounded at Vicksburg, settled in Memphis after the Civil War and founded the Continental Cotton Company there. He never had children, perhaps out of a fear shared by other people in his position that a black baby would appear.

Eston's daughter, Anne, married Albert Pearson. Their son, Walter Beverly Pearson, became President of the Standard Screw Company and at his death left an estate of two million dollars.

Two sons of Madison Hemings fought on the Union side and died in the Civil War. However, one daughter, Ellen Wayles, moved to California. Her son, Frederick Madison Roberts, became the first black man ever to be elected to the State Assembly of California, where he served for twenty years. He became a close friend of Earl Warren and helped found the University of California at Los Angeles. He ran unsuccessfully for Congress in 1938 and was defeated by Helen Gahagan Douglas, who later lost to Richard Nixon. In all his years in California politics, he never revealed that he was a direct descendant of Thomas Jefferson. Had he done so, perhaps Nixon would never have become president.

He did, however, tell his wife about this family secret just before their marriage and said, 'We just don't talk about it.'

Thomas Woodson, the first-born son of Sally Hemings, married a mulatto slave, so their children became black. Tom Woodson became the distributor of an abolitionist newspaper and a leader in the black community. The youngest daughter of Tom Woodson was Sarah Jane Woodson (1825–1907). She graduated from Oberlin College in Ohio in 1856. She became a university professor and was the first Afro-American woman to serve on a college faculty. She was a noted public speaker and the author of books and published essays. In the later years of her life, she became a prominent leader and a member of the executive committee of the famous Woman's Christian Temperance Union ('WCTU'). Under her married name of Sarah Woodson Early, she crossed America giving speeches against the use of alcohol. Her organization, after her death, was credited with bringing about the nationwide Prohibition on the sale of alcohol.

The oldest son of Thomas Corbin Woodson was Lewis Frederick Woodson, who moved to Pittsburgh, where he wrote against slavery under the pseudonym 'Augustine'. He argued that whites and blacks should live in separate communities, which indeed Thomas Jefferson had also argued. He is regarded as one of the founders of black nationalism. See *The Father of Black Nationalism, Another Contender*, Floyd J. Miller, *Civil War History*, Vol. XVII, No. 4, December, 1971.

While this book was being written, the news came out that a new federal judge had been appointed by President George Bush named Timothy K. Lewis, who openly admits to being a descendant of Thomas Jefferson and Sally Hemings thorough Lewis F. Woodson. The name 'Lewis' is, in fact, the family name of some of the descendants of Sally Hemings. Lewis was also the name of a white family closely connected with Thomas Jefferson. Included in that family were Charles Lilburne Lewis, a brother-in-law of Thomas Jefferson, and Meriwether Lewis, the personal secretary in the White House of Thomas Jefferson.

However, the significant fact is not only that Judge Timothy K. Lewis is a descendant of Sally Hemings and Thomas Jefferson, but more importantly the fact that he is prepared openly and publicly to admit to this fact. That is the first time that any prominent person has ever made this admission. This may mean that the taboo which has long surrounded the subject of the slave children of Thomas Jefferson is about to be lifted. On the other hand, it appears that Judge Lewis did not reveal to the press his descent from Sally Hemings until after his Senate confirmation hearings had been completed and after his appointment as a federal judge had been confirmed. Compare the *Pittsburgh Press* for October 4, 1990 with the *Pittsburgh Press* for July 1, 1991. The latter, at page B2, states:

> *Lewis is a descendant of President Thomas Jefferson. This is a fairly well documented part of his family history - but as far as Lewis is concerned, Jefferson is not the family story. Lewis Woodson is.*
>
> *Lewis' great-great-great-grandfather, Lewis Woodson, settled in Pittsburgh in 1831. He was the son of Thomas Woodson, the oldest son of Thomas Jefferson and Sally Hemmings, a slave who was Jefferson's mistress.*
>
> *Lewis Woodson . . . . was an abolitionist and a leader of the Underground Railroad.*

The *Woodson Family Source Book*, edited by Minnie Shumate Woodson of Washington, D.C., provides the genealogy of Timothy K. Lewis, the federal judge recently appointed by George Bush.

The father of Judge Timothy K. Lewis was James K. Lewis, born in 1923.

The mother of James K. Lewis was Lulu Proctor, born in 1894. Her father was Jacob Proctor born in 1868. His mother was Virginia Woodson, born in 1843. All of the above were born in Pennsylvania.

The father of Virginia Woodson was Lewis F. Woodson born in 1806 in what is now West virginia but was then Virginia. The father of Lewis Woodson was Thomas Corbin Woodson who was born in 1790. The parents of Thomas Corbin Woodson were Sally Hemings and Thomas Jefferson.

Thus, Thomas Jefferson was the great-great-great-great-great-grandfather of United States District Judge Timothy K. Lewis.

The above is only a partial list of the accomplishments of the children of Thomas Jefferson by Sally Hemings alone. There are also those believed to have been descendants of other concubines of Thomas Jefferson, such as Mary Hemings. One of these was The Reverend Peter Farley Fossett, a famous evangelist preacher. Another was William Monroe Trotter, a co-founder of the NAACP. William Monroe Trotter earned his M.A. degree from Harvard University in 1896, which was a major accomplishment for a 'colored' man at that time, or even now and even for a white person. Harvard University is regarded as the number one university in America. A master's degree from there is 'bankable.' William Monroe Trotter is most famous today for his 1914 letter to President Woodrow Wilson. Here is the beginning of that letter.

> One year ago, we presented a national petition, signed by Afro-Americans in thirty-eight states, protesting against the segregation of employees of the national government whose ancestry could be traced in whole or in part to Africa, as instituted under your administration in the Treasury and Post Office departments. We appealed to you then to undo this race segregation in accord with your duty as president and with your pre-election pledges. We stated that there could be no freedom, no respect for others, and no equality of citizenship under segregation for races, especially when applied to but one of the many racial elements under government employ. For such placement of employees means a charge by the government of physical indecency or infection, or of being a lower order of beings, or a subjection to the prejudices of other citizens, which constitutes inferiority of status. We protested such segregation as to working positions, eating tables, dressing rooms, rest rooms, lockers and especially public toilets in government buildings. We stated that such segregation was a public humiliation and degradation, entirely unmerited and far-reaching in its injurious effects, a gratuitous blow against ever-loyal citizens and against those many of whom aided and supported your evaluation to the presidency of our common country.

Notice the high writing style of the above quotation. Notice, most importantly, that its style makes it sound like something which Thomas Jefferson himself might have written.

The complete letter can be found in *Chronology of African-American History*, by Alton Hornsby Jr., Detriot, 1991, pp. 455-457.

Meanwhile, the white children of Thomas Jefferson from Martha Wayles have accomplished just about nothing at all, in spite of the tremendous advantages they have had of just being white, plus being known as descendants of Thomas Jefferson.

Minnie Shumate Woodson, who keeps track of the achievements only of the direct descendants of Thomas C. Woodson, has a list of university professors, ministers, teachers, civil engineers, several Lt. Colonels, a Colonel, a Lt. General of the Army who was also a university president, two United States District Court Judges, a Professor of English, and a Senior Vice-President of a Fortune 500 Corporation, all of whom are descendants of Thomas C. Woodson. The Howard D. Woodson High School in Washington, D.C. is named after one of them.

It seems extremely unlikely that all of these prominent people could possibly be the descendants of one obscure slave, unless that one obscure slave happened to be the son of Thomas Jefferson.

One might feel entirely justified in concluding that these people have got us poor white folk surrounded, especially since we don't know who they are.

Studies have shown that there is a high correlation in IQ levels between husbands and wives. Surprisingly, the correlation of IQ's of husbands and their wives is higher than that of parents and their children. Articles have been published about this surprising phenomena in places such as *Science* magazine.

This means that a smart man is likely to marry a smart woman. It explains why, assuming that, for example, Tom Woodson was a smart man, he might have a great-great-great-great-grandson who is a federal judge, even though his genes only form 1/64 th of the genes of that federal judge.

# Chapter Nineteen

## Areas for Further Study

It is hoped that this book will not be the last, but rather will be the first word on this subject.

Growing up as a boy in Lynchburg, Virginia, I remember hearing the story that Thomas Jefferson had fathered children from his black slaves. I believe that I first heard it from my mother, in fact.

This was before any of the current sources I have used were even written, not counting the *Farm Book* by Thomas Jefferson himself. It shows that the story has been around for a long time.

Old people still living in Lynchburg say that they remember hearing this story from their elders. Some of the elders of these elders could easily have been alive when Thomas Jefferson and Sally Hemings were still alive.

Sally Hemings was almost certainly born in Cumberland County, Virginia in a place where a town called 'Guinea Mills' is still a dot on the map. This is about 40 miles east of Lynchburg. We know this because Sally and her mother were at Guinea when Thomas Jefferson inherited them from John Wayles. Sally was then less than one years old. 'Guinea' was the name of one of the farms owned by John Wayles.

John Wayles purchased six tracts of land in Bedford County in 1770 and 1771, shortly before he died in 1773, which were inherited by Thomas Jefferson. Lynchburg has expanded considerably since that time and much of what was formerly Bedford County is now within the limits of City of Lynchburg. The house where this book is being written was built in Bedford County, but the land was annexed and is now part of Lynchburg. One of Jefferson's farms, comprising 2,000 acres, is less than two miles from where this book is being written. That farm, however, was one of those sold shortly after he inherited it from John Wayles. It is now a residential area, covered with houses, and is fully within Lynchburg. Poplar Forest, the second home of Thomas Jefferson and the place where he kept the majority of his slaves, is about seven miles from here. Most or a substantial part of the original 5,000 acre Poplar Forest estate is now within Lynchburg. The original now reconstructed buildings of Poplar Forest are still in Bedford County, just a stone's throw across the city line. All of the original Tomahawk Farm is now within Lynchburg.

When I started thinking about writing on this subject, I was concerned that I might create a scandal. As it turns out, the problem is exactly the opposite. No scandal is possible because the story is known by everyone around here.

Every person I have talked to, even random people on the street, seem to know something about Sally Hemings, John Wayles and the slave children of Thomas Jefferson. Even more interestingly, they cannot remember where they first heard about it. They say that it is part of the oral tradition of Lynchburg. None of them have read the writings of Fawn Brodie, Douglass Adair, Virginius Dabney, Minnie Shumate Woodson, James A. Bear, Jr., or Barbara Chase-Riboud, yet all of them know that Thomas Jefferson fathered children by his slaves.

The idea that plantation owners in general fathered children by their slaves is widely accepted and indeed is written on the faces of so many of the black people around here.

Since it is universally accepted that plantation owners around here engaged in the practice of producing children by their slaves, the only real question is whether everybody did it or just a few exceptional owners did it.

There is an economic theory that the good businesses will drive out the bad. According to this theory, any successful farmer will prosper and eventually take over the land of the unsuccessful farmers.

Slave growing was a good business. Slaves were worth money. A mulatto slave would fetch more on the slave market than a slave who was pure black.

A plantation owner with an eye towards successful business might well conclude that the best way to make money was to impregnate his female slaves himself. Undoubtedly, any slave woman of fertile age was going to produce children, no matter what. Thus, the only question was: Who would the father of those children be? If a random black slave was the father, the child would be worth less on the slave market than if the father was a white man.

Any white plantation owner who had any qualms about this practice could just as well sell his farm and go into another line of work.

According to this line of reasoning, most of the successful plantation owners did this, not just a few.

The first Virginia census which counted black people the same as whites was the census of 1850. Blacks were listed as pure black or as mulatto. A high percentage were listed as mulatto, showing the prevalence of this practice. By the time of the 1860 census, there were 500,000 mulatto slaves in the South plus 350,000 slave owners. Thus, every slave owner had, on average, produced more than one slave child.

Still, we cannot say that the case is proven. More work has to be done.

The problem is not a shortage of research material. Rather, the problem is too much material. Every writer on this subject has made mistakes. No doubt, this book also contains mistakes, but hopefully not so many.

Unfortunately, it is impossible to follow every lead to its conclusion. That would take several lifetimes. Here is one point which has not yet been followed up:

We know the last name of Betty Hemings from the *Farm Book*. Thomas Jefferson always spelled it with one 'm'. However, even back then, others spelled it with 'mm'. On the other hand, the will of John Wayles gives her name as 'Betty Hennings', which is a different name altogether.

This small item could lead us to a major revision of what we now know about this subject. Researchers long ago searched diligently through the records of all slave ships entering the Port of Williamsburg in the period of 1735. No ship has ever been found with a captain by the name of Captain Hemings. In addition, there is no record of any such captain in England. Perhaps they are looking under the wrong name. Perhaps his name was Captain Hennings. Also, Hennings was the name of an important family living in Virginia at that time. Perhaps the name of the captain was something entirely different, and Hennings was the name of the family which first owned Betty. The authoritative work on the law of Virginia of that time, which has been consulted in the course of the research necessary for this book, is entitled *Henings' Statutes of Virginia at Large*. Also, the 1868 letter by Henry Randall gives the name of Sally as 'Henings'.

Pursuing this line of research, some industrious person might come up with a new explanation as to the origin of Betty Hemings.

The starting point for all research into this subject is the *Farm Book* of Thomas Jefferson. It is like the old *Doomsday Book* of historical England. Everything in the *Farm Book* is, by definition, correct. The *Farm Book* is the bible. It cannot be wrong.

The only exception to this rule is when the *Farm Book* itself appears to contain a contradiction. For example, the name Wormley is sometimes spelled Wormly. This causes no problem, because there is obviously only one person by that name.

A bit more checking, however, is required in the case of Nancy, whose name is sometimes spelled Nance. It takes a while, but finally it can be established that this is also one and the same person.

On the other hand, there is the case of Critta and Cretia. Here, we reach a different result. This looks like the same person, but actually these are two different people. Cretia is short for Lucretia and was purchased as a slave in 1805 when Thomas Jefferson was president. Critta was the sister of Sally Hemings.

Finally, we have the case of Jame, Jamy and James. Here, there is really a problem. We cannot be sure which of these are the same people or different. Several important people in the story had the name James, including James Hemings, James Hubbard, another James Hubbard, James the husband of Critta, James Lewis's, James Bedf., and James Ned's.

On this point, I believe that I have found a mistake by James A. Bear, Jr., an exceptionally careful researcher, when he says that James Hubbard was the son of Critta. I feel certain that James Hubbard was not the son of Critta. However, I could be wrong about that. It could easily be that Bear is right and Thomas Jefferson and the *Farm Book* is wrong. However, Thomas Jefferson, by definition, cannot be wrong.

It is not merely dogma which leads us to that conclusion. No entry in the *Farm Book* has ever been found to be wrong.

Anybody who wants to study this subject needs to go out and buy his own copy of the *Farm Book*, which can be had from the University of Virginia Press for thirty dollars. Statements by others about what the *Farm Book* contains are unreliable.

For example, in his article attacking the Sally Hemings story, Virginius Dabney wrote: 'The *Farm Book* tells us that Harriet was born in 1795 and died two years later.' *Virginia Cavalcade*, Autumn 1979, Volume XXIX, Number 2, p. 57.

However, this is not correct. The *Farm Book* only mentions her birth. Squeezed into the very bottom of page 31 of the *Farm Book* is an illegible entry showing that 'H--- Sally's' was born in 1795. We know from subsequent entries that this H--- was Harriet.

There is nothing at all in the *Farm Book* about the death of Harriet. We know about that from only one source, a letter from Martha Jefferson to her father dated January 22, 1798, in which she reported that a few days after his departure from the farm on December 4, 1797, Harriet had died, but Tom and Goliah had recovered. This is how we know that Harriet died in 1797, two years after birth. This is also how we know that there was a child named Tom, presumably Tom Hemings, the first born child of Sally Hemings, who is not mentioned anywhere in the *Farm Book*.

I believe that I have discovered many things which have been overlooked by everybody else. It has been stated that Sally had two children who died: Harriet who was born in 1795 and Edy who was born in 1797, but both died in 1797.

However, one possibility is that Harriet and Edy are different names for the same person. There is no record in the *Farm Book* of a child named Edy being born in 1797. Also, it never happens that the names of Harriet and Edy appear together on the same list. On any list during the relevant period, either the name of Edy is listed below Sally or the name of Harriet is listed below Sally. Never both.

This is how we establish if two people are different or the same. We know that Critta and Cretia are different people because their names constantly appear together on the same lists. We know that Nancy and Nance are the same person because that never happens. Either one or the other name is always there, but never both. We surmise that Jame and James are different people because just once their names appear together on the same list.

By the same reasoning, Betty and Bett are the same person. However, Sally and Sall are different people. Martin who was born in 1755 is the same person as the Martin who was born in 1756. (This discrepancy is the only place among the thousands of entries in the Farm Book where Thomas Jefferson is inconsistent when it comes to dates. However, this case is understandable, since Martin was born 18 years before being inherited from John Wayles by Thomas Jefferson.)

There is one book which I strongly advise anybody interested in this subject not to read. That is *Sally Hemings* by Barbara Chase-Riboud. I realize that it sounds bad to say that any book should not be read. However, once a wrong idea is burned into anybody's brain, it becomes difficult to erase. This book contains many wrong ideas.

For example, on page 337, Barbara Chase-Riboud depicts the slave auction in 1827 when the former servants of Thomas Jefferson were sold. She depicts Critta 'sold at 100 dollars despite her age' and Nance sold for 650 dollars.

In fact, Nance was much older that Critta. Nance was born in 1761, so she would have been 66 at the time. She is listed in the final inventory of Thomas Jefferson's estate as 'an old woman having no value'. Even Sally Hemings herself, aged 54, was given a value of $50. Critta would have been 58. There is no possibility that Nance could have been sold for $650.

Of course, it will be said that *Sally Hemings* by Barbara Chase-Riboud is a novel which is not intended to represent actual fact. The author merely took a bit of license (quite a bit, in fact, for this is just one of a thousand examples). However, these little pieces of the puzzle are important. One needs to know when Nancy was born, when Critta was born and when Sally was born. Undoubtedly, Barbara Chase-Riboud did not bother to check her exact facts. She just threw together a novel over the weekend, put it in the mail to her publisher, and went to work on the next one.

With some reluctance, better example of why the book *Sally Hemings* by Barbara Chase-Riboud is pure trash can be provided. On page 29, she has the mother of Betty Hemings running away six times. This already seems unlikely because she had just gotten off the boat from Africa and presumably could not speak English and did not know the way around. Because of this repeated running away, she is beaten every time and finally John Wayles brands her with a hot brand with the letter 'R', for 'runaway'. He intends to brand her on the cheek, but when the hot brand approaches her skin, his hand slips and the brand lands on her right breast instead. After that, she never tries to run away again.

To call this 'trash' is a considerable understatement. However, a better word to describe this vile falsification does not suggest itself. A little hard core pornography featuring oral sex and multiple orgasms with Sally Hemings in bed with Thomas Jefferson would be expected and not entirely unwelcome in this sort of exploitation book. However, to describe John Wayles, who was in fact an eminent and respected lawyer from England, as a man who would personally engage in such atrocities, is unspeakable. Worse yet, the reader is left with the impression that there might be an element of truth to this story.

Just to set the record straight, the truth is that John Wayles probably never personally owned the mother of Betty Hemings. In fact, nothing at all is known about the mother of Betty Hemings, not even her name. After arriving in America and giving birth to Betty, there is no further record of her. It is entirely likely that she died shortly thereafter, perhaps even in child birth. She appears to have had no other children. There is also no record of John Wayles branding his slaves or engaging in any other such cruel atrocities. Tradition had it among the slaves at Monticello that John Wayles was the father of six of the children of Betty Hemings. Therefore, it is true that he probably did have sex with his female slaves (we cannot even be completely sure of that) but so did just about every other plantation owner during that period. There is nothing to indicate that John Wayles was in any way a cruel or inhuman person. Many of his descendants, including descendants of Sally Hemings, named themselves after him, even after gaining their freedom.

As a further example of the purely revolting trash found in the *Sally Hemings* novel, on page 282, Barbara Chase-Riboud has Dabney Carr Jr. and his brother, Peter Carr, getting into a serious fight in the tunnel under Monticello because both of them want to have sexual intercourse with Critta at the same time. Instead of agreeing to flip a coin and take turns over the poor girl, as two such eminent and distinguished gentlemen might have done in real life, they practically kill each other trying to be the first one. This, of course, is a cheap ploy by Barbara Chase-Riboud to convince the reader that neither one of them ever had sex with Sally Hemings, the sister of Critta.

While writing this book, this author has read *Burr* by Gore Vidal. That is a good example of the proper way to write a historical novel. Gore Vidal takes the known true facts about a person and molds them into an interesting yarn, while never actually deviating far from the truth. In this way, the reader is both entertained and learns a little bit about history. The slight falsifications and exaggerations in this sort of novel are obvious to the reader and nobody objects, especially since it helps to make the story more interesting. Indeed, many of the statements in that book which appear to be wild and unbelievable actually turn out to represent true facts. For example, it is actually true that in 1834, when Aaron Burr was 78 years old, his wife of less than one year filed a suit against him in court in which she alleged that he had conducted an adulterous affair with a 21-year-old girl.

The approach of Barbara Chase-Riboud instead was to get all the known true facts so completely mixed up that there is hardly even one true statement in her entire book, and then to add in a bunch of completely false facts which just sprang from her head. All this, with the result that the reader believes that he has added to his knowledge of history and has gained something from her book, whereas in reality he knows less history than when he started. One can only be thankful that Barbara Chase-Riboud failed in her effort to get her book made into a television mini-series.

At the other extreme, we have *Thomas Jefferson, an Intimate History* by Fawn M. Brodie, a professor of history at UCLA. This is a painstakingly detailed and accurate work. True, it contains some small mistakes and oversights and I like to think that I have improved on it in some ways, but this is definitely required reading for one interested in this subject.

However, Virginius Dabney doesn't think so. He dismisses the entire story as told by Fawn Brodie as 'absurd'. He quotes Dumas Malone in a private letter to him as saying about Brodie's work 'the resulting mishmash of fact and fiction, surmise and conjecture is not history as I understand the term'. These are strong words, when spoken by one professional historian about the work of another.

However, on more careful examination, the actual complaint of Dumas Malone concerns the fact that Fawn Brodie filled her book with a 'mishmash', as he aptly puts it, of pseudo-psycho-sexual Freudian type analysis, which is obviously pure baloney. (There is a better, unpublishable, word to describe many of Brodie's theories). She talks at length about the shape of the plow as compared with the shape of a woman and the deep and profound significance in the complex emotional and so on about the structure of Jefferson's brain, etc. She also inserts a lot of Freudian dogma, without ever mentioning the name of Freud, such as the theory of Freud that every daughter has the subconscious desire to seduce her father. Brodie claims to be able to find such a subconscious desire in the innocent letters which Martha dutifully wrote to her father, in response to his instructions to write him frequently. Truly, Malone is right when he says that this type of nonsense 'is not history as I understand the term'. This style of writing may appeal to a certain class of person who feels that he or she is proving himself or herself to be highly intelligent by being able to read this kind of stuff, but it is useless to any person seeking solid historical facts.

However, the 'mishmash' is only part of Brodie's book. She also has lots of solid, hard facts, with detailed footnotes. Not even one of her significant facts has been shown to be in error.

In addition, it must be pointed out that Dumas Malone is the author of the Pulitzer Prize winning *Jefferson in His Time* and is the official biographer in residence of Thomas Jefferson at the University of Virginia. When somebody comes out with a book implying that Thomas Jefferson may have had sex with his slaves, Dumas Malone had better try to tear that book apart, unless he wants to go out and look for another job.

Incidentally, when the University of Virginia went on a student strike a number of years ago, an unauthorized student newspaper appeared called *The Sally Hemings*.

The main thing which one needs to know is that the 1974 book by Fawn Brodie was written in a style which was in vogue at that particular time. The first book of this variety was the 1968 biography of the life of *Martin Luther* by Erik Erikson. After the publication of this successful book, Erikson wrote biographies of other famous people, including *Gandhi*. Other authors such as Fawn Brodie jumped on the bandwagon with the publication of similar biographies of famous people such as Thomas Jefferson here. These books all followed the same successful formula. Indeed, Brodie mentions her personal friendship with Erik Erikson in the acknowledgments section of her book.

This is the reason that Fawn Brodie's analysis of the *Declaration of Independence* on page 116 of her book so closely resembles Erik Erikson's analysis of the 95 thesis nailed by Martin Luther on the church door. Brodie considers the *Declaration of Independence* to resemble the complaints of a child who feels that he has been unjustly disciplined by his parent. This is exactly the psychological relationship postulated by Erik Erikson between Martin Luther and the Pope.

To further illustrate this point, in her acknowledgments section, Brodie lists five persons who were allowed to read sections of her book prior to publication. All of them were psychoanalysts. It appears that not one actual historian was allowed to review her book prior to publication. She does mention the name of a real historian, Page Smith, but it appears he was not allowed to read her book and that only the five psychoanalysts were allowed an advance look it. The other historians she mentions in her thanks, including Dumas Malone, subsequently repudiated her work.

(Incidentally, nobody at all has read my book prior to publication. In addition, nobody has been asked permission for the use of their name here.)

It is with great relief that we can report that the sort of psycho-sexual biography pioneered by Erik Erikson, of which Fawn Brodie's book is one example, is no longer popular with the reading public. No longer do small minds try to psychoanalyze the greater mind of a person who died nearly two hundred years ago.

Especially objectionable are Fawn Brodie's obscure Freudian theories, expressed on page 294 of her book, hardback edition, and pages 387-388, paperback edition, about how Martha Jefferson Randolph had this deep subconscious desire to seduce her father, during the time period when she was producing twelve children for her husband. These twelve children were born in the period 1791 to 1818.

One of the letters which Fawn Brodie cites as proof that Martha wanted to seduce her own father was dated March 31, 1797. However, this letter says something quite different from what Fawn Brodie implies. Thomas Jefferson wanted the children of Martha brought to Monticello for inoculation against smallpox. This was a highly experimental and dangerous procedure. This was not Jenner's smallpox vaccine, as Jenner did not publish his findings in England until 1798. This inoculation must have been something different. Many people died from such inoculations, including Jonathan Edwards, the famous philosopher and the grandfather of Aaron Burr, who died in this manner in 1758. Martha Jefferson Randolph, in this letter, expressed the fear that her children might die from this dangerous inoculation. For that reason, she was postponing sending them to Monticello. Her expressions of love for her father in that letter were to reassure him in view of the fact that she was not ready to send her children to Monticello for the purpose of these inoculations.

Other letters between father and daughters expressing love for each other were natural to compensate for the fact that they spent years apart and rarely saw each other while Thomas Jefferson was holding political office and his daughters were residing with their husbands.

Fawn Brodie, being a woman herself, should know that a woman like Martha Jefferson Randolph in the process of producing twelve children, does not much feel like seducing anyone, much less her own father. Still, throughout her book, Brodie keeps finding innuendoes which, according to her, show daughters wanting to seduce their fathers and fathers wanting to seduce their daughters. Again, she never mentions that this is all just Freudian dogma, with no proven basis in actual fact.

In one of her rare moments of caution, Fawn Brodie stops just short of implying that Thomas Jefferson had sexual intercourse with his own sister, Jane. On page 76, in her chapter entitled *A Problem with the Forbidden*, Brodie pointedly compares his relationships with Rebecca Burwell, Elizabeth Walker and Maria Cosway to his relationship with Jane Jefferson. She notes that Jane died at age 25 without ever having married. Brodie is not prepared to go so far as to directly suggest incest. She leaves the alert reader with only the vague wisp of a thought that this might have been something other than the normal brotherly-sisterly relationship.

Fawn Brodie manages to find some sort of subconscious sexual innuendo in every little thing which Thomas Jefferson ever did. For this reason, her version of his story can never be accepted as real history, even though there is merit to some of her observations and conclusions.

One surprising conclusion reached by Fawn Brodie is that Thomas Jefferson made a mistake in recording the date of the death of the infant Jack Skelton, who was born in 1768 and was the only surviving son of the first marriage of his wife, Martha Wayles Jefferson. Brodie says that although Thomas Jefferson recorded the date of death as June 10, 1771, Jack Skelton actually died on June 10, 1772.

From this strange assertion, Brodie reaches a number of other surprising conclusions. Thomas Jefferson and Martha Wayles Skelton were married on New Year's Day, January 1, 1772, in Charles City County. They immediately went by horseback to Monticello, passing through a blizzard on the hundred mile journey and finally arriving several days later at what is now known as the 'honeymoon cottage' on the Monticello estate. From this, Brodie concludes that Martha Skelton Jefferson abandoned her son, Jack, and left him on the estate of John Wayles and probably did not even return to attend the funeral of her son six months later.

The sole basis for Brodie's conclusion that Thomas Jefferson wrote down the date wrong is that in his fee book, he records the purchase of an item for Jack on February 26, 1772. From this, Brodie concluded that Jack must still have been alive on that date.

However, there are a number of other possible explanations for this, all of which are far more likely than that Thomas Jefferson wrote down the date wrong and that his wife, Martha, abandoned her infant son. Thomas Jefferson might have been late in paying his bills or the item might have been ordered from England and did not arrive until after the death of the child. In addition, the calendar itself was adjusted at about this time. Previously, the calendar year commenced in March. It is not even clear why Brodie raises this point. She seems to feel that it shows a character flaw in Thomas Jefferson and fits in with her psychological theories about him. In particular, her claim that he married a woman who had a living child is apparently intended to confirm Brodie's peculiar theory that Thomas Jefferson was only attracted to 'forbidden women'. She keeps repeating this theme throughout her book, not only in the chapter entitled: *A Problem with the Forbidden*.

The fact is that Thomas Jefferson never wrote down a date wrong. There are thousands of dates in his *Farm Book* and elsewhere. Not one of them has ever been shown to be wrong. The only possible exception is where he states that Martin Hemings was born in 1755 and, at another place, states that he was born in 1756. However, Martin Hemings was born as a slave of John Wayles and was about 17 years when inherited by Thomas Jefferson, so

Thomas Jefferson would not have known his exact year of birth.

Thus, the only reasonable conclusion is that Jack Skelton died on June 10, 1771, the date given by Thomas Jefferson, and that Martha Wayles Skelton was a widow without living children at the time that Thomas Jefferson married her.

Going further on this, Fawn Brodie theorizes that after Jefferson was apparently rejected by Rebecca Burwell in 1764, for the remainder of his life, he only touched 'forbidden women'. These women were: Elizabeth Walker, Martha Wayles Skelton, Maria Cosway and Sally Hemings.

Elizabeth Walker was clearly 'forbidden' in that she was his best friend's wife. It is true that Maria Cosway was also 'forbidden' in that she was married, but her husband did not seem to mind too much that his wife was openly and notoriously having sex with other men. However, Thomas Jefferson did not know that and indeed did not know much at all about Maria Cosway when he started his affair with her.

The claim that Martha Wayles Skelton was 'forbidden' is based solely on the fact that she was a widow with a child. However, Thomas Jefferson, in other correspondence, suggests a reason for choosing such a woman for a wife. The fact that she already had a child proved that she was not barren and that therefore she was capable of producing children. Thomas Jefferson wanted children.

Much of what we know about the life of Thomas Jefferson comes from Henry Randall, his most important nineteenth century biographer. Randall had the opportunity to interview personally Thomas Jefferson Randolph and others who were alive when Thomas Jefferson was alive. Randall is the only source for much of the information we have about Thomas Jefferson. The problem created by this is that when Randall made a mistake, every subsequent biographer copied him.

It was Randall who first reported the, frankly, preposterous theory that all of the children of Sally Hemings were fathered by Peter Carr. However, Randall cannot be blamed for that, as he clearly got that idea from Thomas Jefferson Randolph.

Here are two other apparent mistakes by Randall:

He says that the first husband of Martha Eppes, who was the wife of John Wayles, was Llewellen Eppes, who died in 1743. However, Llewellen Eppes did not die in 1743. He died in 1759. His father, Col. Littlebury Eppes, died in 1743. This thunderbolt of news comes from *Tyler's Quarterly Magazine*, Vol. 6, p. 266 (1925). Proof can be found in the *Virginia Historical Magazine*, Vol. 22, p. 435 (1914), which shows court records stating that in December, 1743, the will of Littlebury Eppes was presented by Llewellen Eppes, one of the executors.

A greater discovery is that Bathurst Skelton, the first husband of Martha

Wayles, the wife of Thomas Jefferson, did not die in 1768, as reported by Henry Randall and every biographer since. Rather, Bathurst Skelton, who was born in 1744, died in 1771. His will was proved in the Charles City County Court on September 25, 1771. See *Virginia Historical Magazine*, Vol. 10, p. 330 (1903).

It must be recalled that Thomas Jefferson married Martha Wayles on January 1, 1772. This means that the first husband of Martha had just been dead a few months when she married Thomas Jefferson. This is probably the reason that Randall found it more acceptable to say that he had died in 1768.

There was nothing unusual about this quick re-marriage. In those days, as soon as one spouse died, the surviving spouse married almost immediately, within a few months. This is the reason that Col. Samuel Washington, the brother of President George Washington, was able to get married five times in his lifetime, without ever divorcing any of his wives. If Martha Wayles had waited nearly four years before marrying a second time, as Henry Randall states, she would have been just about the only woman of that era who did so.

However, imagine what the late Fawn Brodie would have said if she had known that Thomas Jefferson married Martha Wayles only a few months after Martha had become a widow. Already, Brodie devotes a full chapter to her theory that Thomas Jefferson was only interested in 'forbidden women'. Imagine what she would have made of the fact that Thomas Jefferson got married to a woman whose first husband's body was just barely cold in the ground.

In spite of all of these glaring weaknesses, there is considerable value in Fawn Brodie's book. It is just about the only one volume complete biography of the life of Thomas Jefferson available on the market today. It is filled with facts and footnotes not readily available from other sources. Indeed, the book is to be recommended, provided that one exercises caution and notes the point at which Fawn Brodie leaves the realm of solid facts and launches into her own pet theories.

I would take the criticism of Dumas Malone and others like him much more seriously if they had a specific factual criticism beyond sweeping generalizations. However, the actual criticisms leveled are indeed rather silly. For example, there is the claim by Douglass Adair that the 1873 interview of Madison Hemings was completely fake and must have been composed by a political enemy of Thomas Jefferson who had access to 'any well regulated library'.

In reality, all the political opponents of Jefferson had already been dead for nearly fifty years, and the detailed information provided by Madison Hemings, who lived at Monticello for thirty years, from 1805 to 1835, could not have been found in any library, regardless of how well regulated.

Then, there is the sweeping statement by Virginius Dabney that 'the true story of Peter or Samuel Carr's relationship with Sally Hemings would not have served her purpose'. Note the words 'true story', as though this story has been written in stone.

The names of Peter and Samuel Carr got into this from an interview of Thomas Jefferson Randolph, the grandson of Thomas Jefferson, which was given many years after Thomas Jefferson had died. Thomas Jefferson Randolph was asked to explain the fact that all the children of Sally Hemings looked exactly like Thomas Jefferson. Indeed, Thomas Jefferson Randolph himself provided this information. He provided various anecdotes about how visitors at Monticello had mistaken, in the dusk or from a distance, the servants at Monticello for Thomas Jefferson himself. One of these visitors who had made this mistake was none other than John Quincy Adams, future President of the United States.

In order to explain this strange phenomenon of visitors constantly getting the slave children at Monticello mixed up with Thomas Jefferson, the master of the house, Thomas Jefferson Randolph has said that it must have been Peter or Samuel Carr, his nephews, who were responsible for these pregnancies. It is from this statement that Virginius Dabney gets his 'true fact'.

However, there is no proof that Sally Hemings even knew Peter and Samuel Carr, although there can be no real doubt that she did. At the same time, there are volumes of evidence that Sally Hemings and Thomas Jefferson were living constantly together over a period of 39 years. John Adams, John Quincy Adams and Aaron Burr all mention Sally Hemings as being with Thomas Jefferson on important occasions. The *Lynchburg Virginia Gazette*, which sent a reporter to Charlottesville in 1802 when the story first broke in the newspapers, said that their reporter could find 'nothing but proofs of their authenticity'.

Still, we cannot say that the story has been proven. More work has to be done.

Actually, we have more proof of a connection between Thomas Jefferson and Sally Hemings than we have of most of the great and established events of world history. Most items found in the standard history books can only be proven from one or two original sources. However, because of the sensitive nature of the story between Thomas Jefferson and Sally Hemings, we have to provide two or three times more evidence than one needs to prove any normal historical fact.

Some of the facts fit together so nicely and perfectly that it seems like a dream that it could have really happened like that. For example, here we have in April, 1789, Thomas Jefferson suddenly going out and buying a whole bunch of new dresses and other clothing for Sally Hemings and renting a private apartment for her in the space of just a few weeks. Also, in April, 1789, his daughter, Martha, suddenly declares that she wants to become a nun. Then, in the beginning of 1790, almost exactly nine months later, the baby is born.

Could it really be true that it happened just like that? Surprisingly, everybody, including not only Dumas Malone, but even Fawn Brodie, has overlooked the nine-months connection between the purchase of the dresses and the birth of the baby. Perhaps, they spend too much time reading history books. They forget about how things happen in real life.

Still, we need more proof.

Most researchers of this subject have used as their primary sources the *Farm Book* of Thomas Jefferson, the *Account Book* of Thomas Jefferson, and the 18,000 collected letters of Thomas Jefferson. Census records have also been checked, but there is nothing conclusive there because, prior to 1850, the names of slaves were not included in the census, only the numbers. Slaves were not really people, yet.

One good place not to check is the record of slave sales in New Orleans, where it was reported that a daughter of Thomas Jefferson was sold at public auction for one thousand dollars in 1838. Many people have already been through those slave records trying to prove this and have come up with nothing.

However, somebody over in France with the energy and enthusiasm to do this could actually try to find the house of Madame Dupre, where Thomas Jefferson rented a room for Sally Hemings. This has never been checked. After the passage of two hundred years, it would probably be difficult to locate the house and obtain any documents connected with it, especially with Dupre being such a common name in France, but one cannot say that this is entirely impossible, unless somebody tries. Just a short note from Madame Dupre mentioning that Thomas Jefferson also often spends the night in the same room with Sally Hemings would be useful proof about this. We know that the official residence of Thomas Jefferson in Paris was the Hotel de Langeac, so information or records might be available from there.

An easier source here would be to check the official records of the White House to show who was living there when Thomas Jefferson was president. I have gone out on a limb in this book by stating that when Thomas Jefferson became President, he moved most of his household slaves, including presumably Sally Hemings, to the White House. I have no proof of this, but I am confident that this is what actually happened because it fits in with everything we know about Thomas Jefferson's lifestyle. He had no wife, four of his six legitimate children were dead and the remaining two daughters were married. If he did not bring his slaves with him to the White House, this would mean that he lived there alone, which would have been utterly impossible for Thomas Jefferson to do, as he was always surrounded by his own people.

The only proof we have about this right now is the one incident in July and August, 1806, where Edy, an 18-year-old slave, was living in the White House and Joe Fossett, her husband, ran away from Monticello to go to Washington to be with her. Thomas Jefferson sent the police to look for him and Joe was apprehended in the yard just walking out the door of the White House. He had apparently been living inside the White House for a few days with Edy.

Incidentally, their child, Maria, was born on October 27, 1807, according to page 128 of the *Farm Book*. This means that Joe and Edy got back together again, even after Thomas Jefferson had Joe arrested, assuming that Joe and not Thomas Jefferson was the father of that child.

At this time, the White House had just been built, so it was apparently just a question of knocking on the front door to get in. The elaborate security system which presently exists was obviously not there at that time. The White House indeed was then located out in the middle of an empty field where farming was done.

However, from this small incident, we can reasonably infer that the other household slaves, and not just Edy, were in the White House at this time. Presumably, the White House itself would have records of this. Edmund Bacon, in his memoirs, states that Thomas Jefferson had eleven slaves from Monticello with him in the White House.

This is, of course, important. If it can be established that Sally Hemings was living in the White House during a substantial part of Jefferson's presidency, that would be strong evidence proving that he was the father of the three children born to Sally Hemings while Thomas Jefferson was President. It would also end the contention that Peter or Samuel Carr might have been the father of these three children, as they had their own plantations near Charlottesville.

This, however, would just be evidence, not proof. Somebody else could possibly be the father even if Sally Hemings spent the entire eight years of Jefferson's presidency sleeping in his bed in the White House, and, since Thomas Jefferson occasionally visited Monticello while he was president, he could be the father even in the unlikely event that she never came to Washington at all.

Incidentally, this entire subject has been overlooked by everybody. Even Fawn Brodie assumes that Sally Hemings never left Monticello and that Thomas Jefferson had to come there while he was president to father her children. This is a surprising blind spot, in view of the fact that it is believed that Thomas Jefferson took Sally Hemings with him to Philadelphia for his inauguration as Vice-President.

We know that from the papers of Aaron Burr, who was the vice-president under Thomas Jefferson during his first term of office. While he was still vice-president, Aaron Burr went from being one of the most important and prominent persons in American politics to being one of the most despised and disreputable persons, by his single act of killing Alexander Hamilton at the Weehawken Dueling Ground in New Jersey in 1804.

Both Alexander Hamilton and Aaron Burr were at that point political enemies of Thomas Jefferson. As a result, hardly anybody studies the papers of Aaron Burr any more. Still, there might be more information there about Sally Hemings, if somebody bothers to look.

None of this, however, would really constitute proof. By its very nature, there is never conclusive proof of who went to bed with whom and when. Even evidence that they spent time in the same bedroom together would not provide conclusive proof in this case. Sally Hemings was the chambermaid and the personal attendant of Thomas Jefferson. She cleaned his bedroom. That was supposedly her job. The fact that, according to at least one visitor to Monticello, nobody had the authority to enter the bedroom and private study of Thomas Jefferson and even his daughters could not go there, except for obviously the cleaning ladies, still does not prove this relationship conclusively.

It also must be mentioned that anybody who has ever tried to do some serious writing (such as writing this book for example), knows that it is absolutely essential to seal one's self off, preferably in a private room free from interference from the outside world. Since Jefferson wrote 18,000 letters which survive today, we know that he must have spent most of his waking hours reading and writing every day. Thus, it comes as no great surprise to learn that even his daughters were not allowed to enter his private study, regardless of how loving a father he may or may not have been. Only his chambermaid would have been allowed to go in there.

It also must be mentioned that it is still possible that a bunch of old letters will be uncovered which will shed further light on this subject. Indeed, many of the documents we now have were only fairly recently revealed. Most of the letters regarding Maria Cosway were kept secret by the family until the 1940's. The New York Times on May 18, 1974, published a previously unknown letter by the granddaughter of Thomas Jefferson on the Sally Hemings affair. That letter had been kept secret by the family for all these years. There may still be a box of old letters, such as the volume of letters for the years 1788 and 1789 which went mysteriously missing, which will eventually surface when somebody dies.

There is, however, a way to prove the the relationship between Sally Hemings and Thomas Jefferson, but the proof lies on the cutting edge of modern technology. This is through a study of the DNA of the descendants of Thomas Jefferson.

Every cell of the body of every human being contains DNA, which is a strand billions of molecules long. No two human beings have the same DNA. This is the reason that no two people are the same. We all have different faces and different personalities. This is controlled by the DNA.

Only in the last few years has the technology been developed to cut the strands of DNA into small pieces and compare the ends. By this laborious and difficult process, it is now possible to prove absolutely that one person is the father or mother of another.

Just a few years ago, this was not possible. Even the advanced HLA and RBC tests could only produce a 99% result at best. With DNA testing, proof can come at more than the 99.99999% level.

The problem is that this is still expensive and difficult. It has not yet even been introduced into many paternity cases in court, although it no doubt will be soon.

Once it becomes possible to identify the father of a child to a more than 99.99999% level of confidence, it also becomes possible to identify the brother, the uncle and the cousin three times removed. As the blood relationship becomes more remote, the testing obviously becomes more difficult and expensive, but the point remains that it can be done.

What must be done is that tissue or hair samples of several known blood descendants of Thomas Jefferson have to be taken and the DNA broken down. This would then be compared to the hair samples of the known or believed descendants of Sally Hemings.

It would be important for the tests to be done on several people, not just one person from each group. One reason for this is that nobody really knows who his father was. With so many generations having passed, it is entirely possible that a person who has every reason to believe that he is a descendant of Thomas Jefferson actually is not, perhaps because the person he thinks was his great-grandfather was not really his great-grandfather, for example.

However, if enough different people from enough different branches of the Thomas Jefferson family tree were tested, this problem could be substantially eliminated.

Another problem will be to get the white descendants of Thomas Jefferson to consent to this test. Undoubtedly, every descendant of Thomas Jefferson has heard the story of Sally Hemings, and it is problematic as to whether they would agree to have their hair tested and compared with that of a black person. The answer to this would be to pay them some money to do this. For money, most people will do anything.

The easiest way to explain the difficulties involved is in the following terms: The last child of Thomas Jefferson by his wife was born in 1777, and the last child of Sally Hemings was born in 1808. We will assume that since then, at least six generations have passed. This would mean that the present descendants have 1/64 (one sixty-fourth) the DNA of Thomas Jefferson, or even less, since DNA divides into two strands.

In short, what we are doing is comparing 1/64 of the DNA of one person to 1/64 of the DNA of another, and we have no idea which 1/64 will come up the same. This will obviously involve the testing and comparison of thousands of molecules along the DNA strand to find out if enough of them come up the same.

A more certain or easier result could be obtained by digging up the dead body of Thomas Jefferson himself. However, before everybody gets out his shovel, perhaps the museums should be checked. It only needs one authenticated snippet of the hair of Thomas Jefferson preserved in a museum somewhere to obtain a real strand of Thomas Jefferson's DNA, assuming that a DNA strand can survive nearly two hundred years in storage without breaking down. There is apparently a museum in Boston which has a lock of the hair of Thomas Jefferson plus a lock of the hair of Lucy, a child who died.

In short, the proof is there. It would be expensive and time consuming to obtain this proof, but it could be done.

However, the astute reader will have already noticed one problem with all of this. This goes back to the allegation that the reason that the children of Sally Hemings looked just like Thomas Jefferson was because they had been fathered by Peter Jefferson Carr, his nephew.

In fact, the problem is even bigger than that, because on the other side of the family tree, Sally Hemings is known or believed to be the half-sister of Martha Wayles Jefferson, the wife of Thomas Jefferson.

In other words, here is the problem: Assuming that it is true that, as everybody says, John Wayles was the father of both Martha Wayles Jefferson and of Sally Hemings, then the children of Martha Wayles Jefferson and the children of Sally Hemings would both have the same DNA to the same extent.

By the way, poor John Wayles does not have any descendants prepared to defend him, but the possibility exists that he is just being made the scapegoat for all of this. However, we will assume that John Wayles really was the father of both. In fact, he also left three other daughters by his second wife. One of them became the mother-in-law of Maria Jefferson. That is the 'Aunt Eppes' to whom she referred in her 1786 letter to her father, when she said that she did not want to come to France.

In short, even if a genetic similarity between the children of Sally Hemings and the children of Martha Wayles Jefferson is proven, this could just be the result of them both having the genes of John Wayles.

Worse than that, on the other side of the family tree, we have Peter Jefferson Carr and Samuel Jefferson Carr, who were the sons of the sister of Thomas Jefferson. They would also have similar genes to those of Thomas Jefferson. If one of them made Sally Hemings pregnant, as has been alleged, that could well explain any genetic similarity between the white putative descendants of Thomas Jefferson and the black putative descendants of Thomas Jefferson.

In short, unless the information we now have is completely wrong, there will definitely be a genetic link between the white putative descendants of Thomas Jefferson and the black putative descendants of Thomas Jefferson, irrespective of whether Thomas Jefferson personally impregnated the lady in question.

At the same time, this means that any proven descendant of Sally Hemings can state with confidence, even without the benefit of testing, that he or she is a collateral descendant of Thomas Jefferson. Some of the same genes will be there, irrespective of whether Thomas Jefferson put them there or some relative did the job.

Still, it might be possible to obtain more conclusive proof. The method to be followed would be similar to carbon dating to determine how old something is.

Carbon dating works because certain elements have a half-life. Half of the element disappears or deteriorates over a period of a known number of years. The other half remains just like new.

With this knowledge, by measuring what percentage has broken down and what percentage remains the same, a determination can be made as to precisely how old an object is.

With DNA testing, it should be possible to be much more precise and accurate, because exactly half of the DNA chain is passed from one generation to the next. With carbon dating, only the approximate age of an object can be determined, with a margin of error of a few hundred years. However, with DNA testing, it should be possible to determine exactly how many generations back the two persons are related.

Let us assume that the present generation of believed descendants of Thomas Jefferson are six generations removed from Thomas Jefferson himself. If the genetic similarity comes from John Wayles, that would be seven generations back. If Peter Jefferson Carr contributed genes, that would also show a similarity seven generations back, because the origin of the same genes would be Peter Jefferson, the father of Thomas Jefferson and the grandfather of Peter Jefferson Carr. However, those genes would appear to be twice as strong as the genes of John Wayles, because Thomas Jefferson was the full brother of his sister, whereas Sally Hemings was only the half sister of Martha Wayles Jefferson. In other words, both Peter Jefferson and his wife Jane Randolph should have contributed genes to the present generation whereas, from the other side, John Wayles alone would have contributed genes to both family groups.

In short, by extremely precise and detailed measurement, it should be possible to prove exactly where the genes in the present generation of children came from.

Again, this subject is right on the cutting edge of modern technology. Until now, nothing like this has ever been done. A great amount of scientific work is being conducted in this area right now. It is not clear whether this sort of testing can be successfully concluded right now, or if will take some years more. There have been some optimistic suggestions that the entire DNA strand will be unraveled and understood by the year 2010, but most scientists think it will take longer than that. Fortunately, it is not necessary to solve the entire DNA chain. Only the comparison of the ends of a few tiny snippets are enough to establish a genetic link between two persons.

Again, it is not clear whether it is possible to do this yet, or whether it will take a few more years, but, undoubtedly, it can be done and will be done eventually. Some day we all will know the absolute truth of whether the children of Sally Hemings are descended from Thomas Jefferson. We will also know the answer to other related questions, such as whether Tom Woodson and Madison Hemings, both of whom left a multitude of descendants, were the actual sons of Thomas Jefferson. We might even flush the descendants of Harriet out of hiding. All it takes is some person or group with the energy, the enthusiasm, the time and the money to get to the bottom of this question.

Armed with the information contained in this book, the reader should be able to go through almost every standard biography of Thomas Jefferson available at the bookstores and find blatant errors.

One title available now on the bookstands consists of portraits of every First Lady in the history of America. When it comes to Thomas Jefferson, one finds the famous portrait of Martha Jefferson Randolph who, according to that book, served as the First Lady while Thomas Jefferson was president. It goes further to state that she gave birth to the first baby ever born in the White House in 1806.

Of course, the reason that the authors found it necessary to include the portrait of Martha Jefferson Randolph is that Thomas Jefferson had destroyed every portrait of his wife, Martha Wayles, after she died. He had also destroyed every portrait of his mother, Jane Randolph, after she died. For this reason, we have no idea what those two women looked like. The authors of the above book had to put somebody's picture into this empty space, so they chose Martha Jefferson Randolph's, the only picture they had.

However, we know that at most Martha Jefferson Randolph spent only a few weeks in Washington during the eight years while Jefferson was President. It is true that she did give birth to a child in the White House in 1806. However, she was in Washington, not because she was the President's daughter, but because her husband, Thomas Mann Randolph, Jr., had been elected to the United States Congress. During most of those eight years that Jefferson was president, she was at Edgehill, or at Tufton, a farm owned by Thomas Jefferson.

The other daughter, Maria, resided at estates owned by the Eppes family, including Eppington, which was in Chesterfield County at Bermuda Hundred, which was across the river from Hopewell, just south of Richmond.

Neither Martha nor Maria liked Washington, D.C., which was a new city with primitive facilities just being constructed. They preferred the comforts of their family estates. They often wrote their father asking him to come to visit them, but never volunteered to go to Washington. Except for the period of six weeks in November and December, 1802, in which Martha and Maria stayed in the White House with their father to show solidarity during the height of the Callender and Sally Hemings scandal, they never came to Washington except to accompany their husbands, both of whom had been elected to Congress on the coattails of Thomas Jefferson.

It is true that Martha Jefferson Randolph did give birth to a child in the White House in 1806, this being possibly the first baby born there. However, Martha was in Washington, not because her father was the President, but because her husband was a United States Congressman. After Thomas Jefferson had been elected President, both of his sons-in-law, John Wayles Eppes and Thomas Mann Randolph, Jr., had been elected to Congress. Thomas Jefferson privately opposed the candidacy of Thomas Mann Randolph, Jr., but the voting public did not know that. After being elected, they came to live in Washington. Thomas Jefferson tried to get them to live together with him in the White House, but as usual they could not get along, so Thomas Mann Randolph, Jr. moved out and eventually shared a rented room with another man. It was during the period when Thomas Mann Randolph, Jr., was living in the White House that Martha Jefferson Randolph gave birth to a baby there.

Of course, one does not expect the author of the above book to say that Sally Hemings was the First Lady while Thomas Jefferson was President and that Harriet, Madison or Eston Hemings may have been the first presidential baby born in the White House.

Incidentally, although John Wayles Eppes was first elected to Congress in 1802 on the coattails of Thomas Jefferson, he continued to serve with distinction there even when Thomas Jefferson was no longer president. More than that, he was elected to the Senate in 1816. He resigned due to ill health in 1819 and died in 1823.

Because of errors like those mentioned above, one needs to re-check and double check everything ever said about Thomas Jefferson. There is a tendency after an author has made an error, for subsequent authors to repeat the same error.

For example, every source, including this one, has said that after Thomas Jefferson died, his land and slaves had to be sold at auction to pay his enormous debts. But, is this really true?

Although Thomas Jefferson kept fastidious records of his debts, there is little proof that he ever bothered to pay them. Some of these debts were actually inherited from his mother when she died in 1776. These same debts still remained unpaid fifty years later when Thomas Jefferson himself died in 1826. Perhaps the statement that these debts were ultimately paid off by Thomas Jefferson Randolph is completely false. Who knows, perhaps they were paid in Confederate money.

The story of Thomas Jefferson and his debts has never been fully explained. Here are the rough outlines of what we know about this:

Many of the debts of Thomas Jefferson were apparently connected with the land he owned. Much of this land had come with debts attached. The debts were owed to persons in England who had never been to America. Apparently, the King of England would grant land to his favorites or to corporations formed to develop the newly emerging territories, who would then sell the land to persons such as John Wayles, who speculated in both land and slaves. When John Wayles died, Thomas Jefferson inherited both the land and the debt. The will of John Wayles states: 'I therefore direct that my estate be kept together, and the whole Tobacco made thereon shipped unto the said Farrel and Jones of Bristol, until his debt and interest shall be lawfully and completely paid and satisfied.'

History does not tell us whether Thomas Jefferson actually paid the debts to Farrel and Jones, or whether he merely added them to his long list of creditors.

During the American Revolutionary War, the newly formed American government issued its own money to pay the troops. However, this new money rapidly depreciated and eventually became worthless. Many of the troops never got paid. Alexander Hamilton, much later, was the first person to put the United States on a sound financial basis and to issue dollars which had lasting value. Meanwhile, Thomas Jefferson and others paid their debts in British pounds or in pounds of tobacco.

The virtually worthless money issued by the Continental Congress during the Revolutionary War was used by Thomas Jefferson to pay his land debts to the absentee British. However, he did not pay the money to his creditors directly. Instead, he paid it to the Virginia land office. The British creditors presumably never actually got the money.

After the Revolutionary War was over, Justice Samuel Chase of the United States Supreme Court ruled that these payments to the Virginia land office were legally invalid and that the land owners in America were still legally obliged to pay their debts to the British. This decision was of questionable legal validity. Samuel Chase was reputed to be a Torie sympathizer. England was the enemy. It is a universally recognized principle of international law that there is no obligation to pay debts owed to the enemy. Indeed, the problems created by these absentee landlords in England was one of the reasons for fighting the Revolutionary War.

This is the reason that Fawn Brodie and other authors keep saying that poor Thomas Jefferson was so excessively honest that he wound up having to pay his debts twice. However, the funny money used by Thomas Jefferson to pay these debts the first time had not really satisfied that obligation. In addition, there is no evidence that he paid these debts to the British a second time either. He simply carried the debts on his books, with no intention of ever paying them. Meanwhile, he kept advocating a law that every 19 years all debts be erased.

Fawn Brodie claims that the debts where eventually paid by Thomas Jefferson Randolph. However, it is difficult to believe that this is true. He probably just wrote them off. By that time, some of these debts were nearly one hundred years old.

After the death of Thomas Jefferson in 1826, there were two public auctions at which slaves were sold. The first took place at Monticello on January 15, 1827. The second was apparently at Bedford. It concerned primarily the Bedford slaves and took place on January 1, 1829.

Why these auctions were conducted in the winter is a mystery. Perhaps, they wanted to discourage potential bidders from attending.

On August 7, 1826, prior to either of these auctions, an inventory list of the slaves was prepared, with a valuation assigned to each slave.

The full list, which is illegible anyway, will not be reproduced here, but these are some of the highlights.

'Sally Hemings' (b. 1773) was valued at $50 (fifty dollars). It might be considered pathetic that a person so important to the life of her master was considered to be worth so little after his death. However, it was probably to her advantage to receive such a low valuation as it lessened the likelihood that the creditors of the estate would insist that she be sold to pay the debts of Thomas Jefferson.

Even better off was Betty Brown. About her, it was said 'Negro Woman Betty Brown worth nothing'. She was born in 1759 and therefore was 67 years old.

'Critta' (b. 1769), Sally's older full sister, was worth $50.

Another entry is 'Negro to be free in July next, worth for year $125, full value $400'. This would be Joe Fossett.

Directly below this is 'Edy & her child Daniel' followed by Patsy, Betsy, Peter, Isabella, and William.

The above slaves are Edy, the wife of Joe Fossett, and their six children. This raises an important point. Although Joe Fossett, along with Madison, Eston, Burwell and John Hemings, were all named in the will of Thomas Jefferson as persons to be freed, they were not to get their freedom immediately. It appears that Joe Fossett was due to be freed in July, 1827, one full year after the death of Thomas Jefferson.

At the same time, Joe's wife and children were not scheduled to be freed. In fact, they were sold.

Among the wife and children of Joe Fossett, Edy (b. 1787) and her child Daniel (b. 1825) were worth $200, Patsy (b. 1810) was worth $300, Betsy (b. 1812) was worth $275, Peter (b. 1815) was worth $200, Isabella (b. 1819) was worth $150 and William (b. 1821) was worth $125. Thus, the entire family, not counting Joe Fossett, was worth $1250.

Edy was born on April 10, 1787. This is the reason that her mother, Isabel, was not able to go to France in 1787 and Sally was selected for the journey instead. Joe was born in November, 1780. (See page 24 of the *Farm Book*). This proves that Joe Fossett was conceived in Richmond, not at Monticello, because his mother, Mary, was in Richmond and Williamsburg during the period 1779-1781 when Thomas Jefferson was governor of Virginia. The *Memoirs of Isaac Jefferson*, p. 10, states that Joe Fossett, still a baby, was personally present at the *Battle of Yorktown* in October, 1981, where he and other slaves of Thomas Jefferson were held prisoner by the British, after having been captured in Richmond.

'Negro man Isaac the Carter' was worth $80. This might be Isaac Jefferson (b. 1775), whose memoirs were published in 1847.

'Negro man Israel' was worth $350. This undoubtedly was Israel Jefferson, whose memoirs were published in 1873 in the *Pike County Republican*. He was born in 1800.

'Negro man Davy Senior' (b. 1755) worth nothing. 'Negro man Davy Junior worth $250'. Perhaps this was Davy Bowles. Davy Bowles traveled freely and was given important assignments such as being sent to purchase nails, so he often seemed to be free. There were actually several Davys. This might be the one who was born in 1784.

'Negro man Ned' (b. 1760) worth $50. 'Negro woman Jenny' (b. 1764) worth nothing. These would be the parents of Israel Jefferson. He said that his parents were named Edwin Gillett and Jane. It has been shown that Ned was a nickname for Edwin and Jenny was a nickname for Jane.

'Negro man Barnaby' (b. 1783) worth $400. 'Negro man Gill' (b. 1792) worth $375. These would be the brothers of Israel Jefferson.

'Negro woman Nance' (b. 1761) worth nothing. Negro woman Doll (b. 1757) worth nothing. 'Negro man John a gardener' (possibly b. 1753) worth nothing.

Since Thomas Jefferson died at age 83, most of those old enough to have played an important role in his life were worthless by the time that he died.

'Negro woman Mary Bet's daughter' worth $50. We are anxious to know who this was. Mary, the daughter of Betty Hemings, was born in 1753 and would have been worthless. Besides that, she had been sold in 1792 to Col. Tom Bell and had not been at Monticello since. Mary, the daughter of Betty Brown, was born in 1801 and would have been worth much more than $50, assuming that she was strong and healthy.

There are other lists of the slaves at Lego and Tufton. These were farms near to Monticello. The slaves on these lists were field hands and are not important to this story.

There is a list dated December 5, 1826 of the slaves in Campbell County. Actually, Thomas Jefferson did not have a farm in Campbell County. However, what is now the independent City of Lynchburg (where this book is being written) was, at that time, in Campbell County. Poplar Forest, which was and is in Bedford County, was even then only a few miles from Lynchburg. Poplar Forest was less than two miles from the county line of Campbell County. Bedford City, the county seat of Bedford County, is 30 miles from here. Therefore, this inventory of slaves of Campbell County is actually an inventory of the salves at Poplar Forest, Tomahawk and Judith Creek, which were nearer to Lynchburg than to Bedford City.

A slave named Hannah at Poplar Forest is listed as being worth $300. However, the slave named Hannah (b. 1770) that we know about was old and would have been almost worthless.

There are many other familiar sounding names on these lists. However, these are not the people we have in mind. For example, Burwell the butler, who was born in 1783, was one of those named in the will to be freed. A slave named Burwell at Lego was worth $400. This is not the Burwell we know about, however, but another Burwell who was born in 1809.

Minerva at Tufton, who was born in 1771, was worth nothing, but she still had a lot of life left in her. The 1850 census shows that Minerva was still living at Edgehill with Thomas Jefferson Randolph, 24 years later. Bagwell (b. 1768), the husband of Minerva (b. 1771) and the father of many children, was worth $50.

At the January 15, 1827 sale, it appears that Ursula (b. 1787), a former cook on the White House staff, along with her four youngest children, the oldest being age 7, were sold for $745. Ursula was the wife of Wormley (b. 1781).

Edy, a cook at the White House and the wife of Joe Fossett, was sold with two of her children, Daniel (b. 1825) and William (b. 1821), for $505.

Patsy (b. 1810), the daughter of Joe and Edy, was sold for $395. It is to be recalled that on the inventory list she was valued as being worth $300.

Tom (b. 1813), the son of Wormley and Ursula, was sold for $400. Louisa (b. 1816), the daughter of Wormley and Ursula, was sold for $260. Caroline (b. 1818), the daughter of Wormley and Ursula, was sold for $190.

Someone named Betsy was sold for $450. Who was this person? The name 'Betsy' has often been mentioned as the name of a concubine of Thomas Jefferson. Was this the daughter of Joe and Edy who was born in 1812? Whoever this was, there was something special about her. The amount of $450 was the highest price paid for any woman on the list.

The above four slaves, Louisa, Caroline, Tom and Betsy, were all purchased by a man named John Winn. Whoever he was, he clearly had an interest in young women.

Finally, Thomas Jefferson Randolph bought a total of 16 slaves for a total of $6200. Almost all of these are from the list at Lego. These are the same slaves that he leased from his grandfather, Thomas Jefferson, in 1817. Now, he was purchasing the same slaves. Among the 16, he paid $120 for Minerva and her husband Bagwell together and $470 for Burwell (b. 1809). This explains the fact that we know that the Burwell on the Lego list is not the same as the Burwell who was freed.

The list of 16 slaves purchased by Thomas Jefferson Randolph and their years of birth are as follows: Bagwell (1768), Minerva (1771), Willis (1806), Archy (1808), Jordan (1811), Robert (1811), Washington (1805), Eliza (1805), Moses (1792), Gloster (1807), Phil (1796), Sanco (1797), Nanny (1800), Joshua (1806), Burwell (1809), and Cornelius (1811).

The second auction sale, which took place on January 1, 1829, is less interesting. Thomas Jefferson Randolph brought nine slaves, paying a total of $935. These were James (1772), Rachel (1773), Edmund (1813), Bedford John (1785), Virginia (1793), Ben, Esther, Bagwell, and Jerry (1777). Ben, Esther and Bagwell were children whose birthdates were not recorded because their parents, Bedford John and Virginia, were leased to Thomas Jefferson Randolph at the times of their births.

John M. Perry bought four slaves, including Lania (b. 1805) and child, for which he paid a total of $770 for the four. Were these possibly ancestors of the family of Amelia Elizabeth Perry Pride of Lynchburg, who say that they are descended from a man named John Perry?

Samuel Carr bought Jackson (b. 1818) for $225. Note that he did not buy any of the women available, which shows that he was not much interested in that.

William Garland bought Gill (b. 1792), the brother of Israel Jefferson, and Esther (b. 1795), the wife of Gill, for a total of $590.

Dr. Robley Dunglison bought Waggoner David for $270. This might be

Davy Bowles, who often drove a wagon and was the husband of Fanny (b. 1788).

Unfortunately, that's all there is. There isn't any more. What happened to so many of the people who are important to this story? What happened to Wormley, to Isaac Jefferson, and to Israel Jefferson? In his memoirs, Israel Jefferson tells us that he was sold in 1829. However, the documentation is not available here. There is no bill of sale for him. What happened to Peter (b. 1815), the son of Joe Fossett, who became The Reverend Peter Farley Fossett, the famous evangelist preacher? The answer is: We don't know.

We can only hope that the complete documentation surfaces some day. In the meantime, we will have to be satisfied with what we have.

The census records for 1850 show that Thomas Jefferson Randolph still owned 46 slaves. Unfortunately, their names were not given, only their ages, sex and race, whether black or mulatto.

For example, the first entry after the name Thomas Jefferson Randolph is '79 F B'. This means that he owned a 79 year old female black. Since this was 1850, she would have been born in 1771.

Looking at the *Farm Book*, we find that a woman named Minerva was born in 1771. Her name is last seen on page 160, where she is on the list of Negroes leased to Thomas Randolph. She could be the same person who was at Edgehill with Thomas Jefferson Randolph in 1850. Indeed, it is almost certain that she was exactly that person.

Of the 46 slaves listed on the census of 1850, 27 were 24 or older, which means that they were alive when Thomas Jefferson was alive. It seems unlikely that Thomas Jefferson Randolph would make any new purchases of slaves, in view of the fact that he had little money, so these were probably the same old slaves which Thomas Jefferson had owned, along with their children.

Here are the vital statistics regarding these 46 slaves. Someone with the energy to do so can try to compare these with the lists in the *Farm Book* and determine which ones these might have been:

There were 10 black females. Their ages were 79, 58, 52, 50, 24, 22, 17, 15, 14, and 1. There were 16 black males. Their ages were 75, 63, 58, 53, 50, 45, 45, 43, 42, 41, 41, 30, 25, 23, 19, and 17. There were 5 mulatto females. Their ages were 70, 50, 16, 5, and 3. Finally, there were 15 mulatto males. Their ages were 46, 45, 40, 40, 39, 29, 27, 23, 22, 20, 20, 18, 16, 14 and 9.

It appears that Thomas Jefferson Randolph did not follow his grandfather's habit of keeping large numbers of mulatto females and children close by him.

By the time of the census of 1860, just at the time of the start of the Civil War, there were only 34 slaves left. Included were 17 black females. Their ages were 96, 67, 66, 66, 66, 62, 59, 57, 40, 7, 5, 5, 4, 2, 2, 1, and 9 months. There were 7 black males. Their ages were 53, 52, 38, 6, 4, 1, and 8 months. There were 3 mulatto females. Their ages were 5, 3, and 2. Finally, there were 7 mulatto males. Their ages were 56, 53, 48, 40, 2, 1 and 1.

The above two lists do not reconcile. Few of those on the 1850 list appear to be on the 1860 list. The best that can be said is that probably Thomas Jefferson Randolph freed or sold most of the male blacks, since he needed money and these were the ones who were the most valuable on the slave market. He kept the females, most of whom were old and had little value as slaves. Perhaps, he even took in a few more old female slaves. One cannot explain the fact that 18 of his slaves, more than half, were small children, since all but one of the women he owned were too old to produce children. Perhaps, just before the census, he sold all the young female slaves and kept their children.

The presence of a 96-year-old black female slave looks like an error, although he might have taken in such a slave from somebody else's farm for free.

Thomas Jefferson Randolph was born in 1792, so by the time of the 1860 census he was 68 years old.

In short, the 1860 census appears to be entirely wrong, but it is hard to imagine that a census taker would lie.

Moving to another subject, it is reported on p. 634 of Fawn Brodie's book that when Martha Jefferson Randolph left her husband and went to Boston, her husband's sanity was restored and he got a job mapping the Florida order, but when she returned, he became crazy again. However, it is possible that Fawn Brodie has made another mistake and that the person who got a job mapping the Florida border in 1827 was actually another Thomas Mann Randolph Junior, the son of the second wife of Thomas Mann Randolph Senior (1741–1793). This would be an easy error to make. As usual, Fawn Brodie does not give any footnote which would make it possible to verify her information.

That second marriage of Thomas Mann Randolph Senior, age 49, was to 18-year-old Gabriella Harvie, and took place just three years before he died. It was bitterly opposed by his family, including Martha Jefferson Randolph, who was concerned that because of this second marriage, she and her husband might not get Edgehill, where they were planning to live.

This second marriage produced only one surviving child, but that child was probably the most successful offspring of Thomas Mann Randolph Senior, even though that son inherited nothing and his father died while he was an infant. The second Thomas Mann Randolph, Jr., had a total of fifteen children by his two different wives.

From everything we know about the man, it seems unlikely that Thomas Mann Randolph Junior the First ever went out and actually got a job. It seems rather more likely that Thomas Mann Randolph Junior the Second was the one who committed that foul deed.

The Edgehill estate, which was owned by Thomas Mann Randolph, was four miles away from Monticello. It came as part of a land grant to William Randolph from the king. After William Randolph died in 1745, title passed to his son, Thomas Mann Randolph Senior. Then, in 1793, just before his death, Thomas Mann Randolph Senior deeded the property to his oldest son, Thomas Mann Randolph, Jr. This had to do with the fact that on September 20, 1790, Thomas Mann Randolph Senior had taken an 18-year-old second wife. However, for the next 29 years, Thomas Mann Randolph Junior was not able to get the title to Edgehill recorded in his name in the county clerk's office, due to the lack of the required cooperation by the three witnesses to the deed, one of whom was a relative of Peter Carr. Apparently, the three witnesses realized that once Thomas Mann Randolph Junior got the title recorded in his name, he would immediately sell the estate and squander the money, as he had done with all of the other money which had ever fallen into his hands, leaving his wife and eleven surviving children homeless and destitute.

Thomas Mann Randolph Junior and his wife, Martha Jefferson, had received two estates in dowry in 1790 pursuant to their marriage contract. One was called Varina and was in Henrico County near Richmond. Both were eventually lost to creditors due to the financial irresponsibility of Thomas Mann Randolph Junior. By 1799, they were living at Monticello. Sometimes, they lived at another farm called Tufton. They moved like nomadic gypsies. Nobody today can be sure exactly where they lived. It was at about this time that they first moved to Edgehill. Previously, there had been no house at Edgehill, only the land. At the time that they moved to Edgehill, Thomas Jefferson was serving as vice-president. In 1809, when Jefferson concluded his presidency, they again moved back to Monticello.

In 1822, the three witnesses who, all this time, had been preventing the title to Edgehill from being recorded in the name of Thomas Mann Randolph Junior, agreed to have the title recorded, but only so that the title could be passed immediately to his son, the more financially responsible Thomas Jefferson Randolph.

As a result, Martha Jefferson Randolph and her children had a place to live, even after Monticello itself and all of the furniture was sold for a mere $7,000, following the death of Thomas Jefferson.

The record on this point is confusing. Land records appear to show Varina, the original estate which Thomas Mann Randolph Junior received in dowry, being lost early after the marriage in 1790, but somehow later on Martha Jefferson and her husband were living there again. Perhaps other members of the Randolph family acted to keep Varina in the family name or perhaps the 950 acres which Thomas Mann Randolph Junior received in dower from his father did not constitute the entire Varina estate, just as the part of Poplar Forest which the young couple received from Thomas Jefferson did not constitute all of that. Martha was conveyed 1000 acres of Poplar Forest as part of the marriage deed. The entire Poplar Forest estate amounted to 5,000 acres.

In any event, one point which is completely clear is that the entire Randolph family and everybody associated with them understood that Thomas Mann Randolph Junior, three times Governor of Virginia, was financially irresponsible and no money or anything of financial value should ever be allowed to pass into his hands.

As late as 1875, Thomas Jefferson Randolph was still living at Edgehill. Monticello, of course, had another owner. The Varina estate was long gone and presumably had been subdivided, with many different owners.

When Thomas Jefferson was alive, Henrico County was larger than it is today. Nowadays, Henrico County is completely north and east of Richmond. At that time, it extended all the way south of Richmond as far as Petersburg. It included Bermuda Hundred, which is just across the Appomattox River from what is now Hopewell. Bermuda Hundred is now in Chesterfield County. The Varina estate owned by Thomas Mann Randolph Senior is presumably the same as the estate by that name owned by a member of the family of William Randolph of Turkey Island, the great-grandfather of Thomas Jefferson, one hundred years earlier.

One of the great men in American history was George Wythe (1726–1806). Not only was he the teacher and mentor of Thomas Jefferson, but he also was the teacher of John Marshall, who later became Chief Justice of the United States Supreme Court. George Wythe was a signer of the *Declaration of Independence* and was one of the Framers of the *Constitution of the United States*, although he did not sign that latter document. He was among the many participants in the Constitutional Convention of 1787, who, for various reasons, failed or refused to sign the final document.

Because of these great achievements, it seems almost unbelievable that the end of the life of George Wythe came at age 80 when he was murdered by a grand-nephew who needed money to pay his gambling debts.

George Wythe is said to have fathered a son, Michael Brown, by his slave, Lydia Broadnax. If Thomas Jefferson did not engage in the practice of producing children from his slaves, he was just about the only one. Unfortunately, history tells us that George Wythe, his concubine and their son were poisoned by arsenic in 1806 by a white relative enraged that the concubine and the child had been named in his will. Wythe and the child died. Only the concubine survived. The murderer was acquitted because the only witnesses who could testify against him were black, and their testimony was inadmissible in court. See Julian Boyd, *The Murder of George Wythe*, William and Mary Quarterly, Vol. X11, No. 4, pp. 513-74 (Oct. 1955); *Judicial Cases Concerning Slavery and the Negro*, Helen T. Caterall, Vol.1, pp. 108-09.

George Wythe was a brilliant lawyer. He was married twice, but neither of his wives produced any children. Finally, one of his slaves bore him a son. He loved the child dearly and taught him Latin and Greek. For this unpardonable sin, he was murdered in 1806 at age 80 along with his son by arsenic poisoning by a grand nephew wanting to get his full inheritance. Thomas Jefferson later wrote that no crime of greater iniquity was ever committed within the memory of modern history.

Even today, after the passage of nearly two hundred years, it is difficult to believe that such a murder could have happened. George Wythe was the greatest legal mind in early American history. As a law professor, his students included John Marshall, Thomas Jefferson and Henry Clay. As a jurist, in 1782, he was among the first to enunciate the proposition that the courts had the authority to declare a legislative act to be unconstitutional. His star pupil, John Marshall, made this principle the law of the land in his famous 1803 decision of *Marbury v. Madison*. As a member of the House of Burgesses, George Wythe led the fight for the repeal of the hated Stamp Act.

How is it possible that after such a brilliant and distinguished career, this man was murdered at age 80 by a juvenile delinquent great-nephew who wanted to inherit some money quickly in order to pay his gambling debts?

There is no firm proof that George Wythe was the father of the slave child, Michael Brown, as he never acknowledged his paternity in writing. However, we can safely conclude that he was the father from the following facts: (1) He had given Michael Brown his freedom. This was most commonly done by a slave owner with respect to his children. (2) More importantly, he had named Michael Brown as the equal beneficiary, along with his greatnephew, in his will. The fact that Michael Brown, a 15-year-old mulatto boy, was due to receive half of the entire estate of George Wythe, constitutes virtual proof that he was his son. (3) Perhaps even more importantly, in his will, George Wythe appointed Thomas Jefferson as the legal guardian to raise up Michael Brown. Clearly, he would not have burdened Thomas Jefferson with the duty to care for just any random mulatto child. This means that Thomas Jefferson was aware of the true relationship between George Wythe and Michael Brown.

On the other hand, it is not completely certain that Lydia Broadnax was the mother of Michael Brown. Perhaps some other unknown slave woman was the mother. This hardly matters, however. The important fact is that George Wythe was the father.

As to the motive for the murder, there was no doubt. The will of George Wythe had provided that his estate be divided approximately equally between Michael Brown and George Wythe Sweeney. However, it also provided that if Michael Brown pre-deceased George Wythe, the entire estate would go to George Wythe Sweeney. Therefore, in order to get all of the money, George Wythe Sweeney had to murder simultaneously both George Wythe and Michael Brown.

George Wythe made a cardinal error. He left his will out in the open on the top of a desk in his study. The findings of the police investigation showed that George Wythe Sweeney entered the study, read the will and, just a few minutes later, took a coffee pot over to the fire place, put arsenic in the coffee, and left the house quickly. George Wythe, Michael Brown and Lydia Broadnax thereafter all drank the coffee. Only Lydia Broadnax survived.

Thomas Jefferson was the founder of the University of Virginia, which is in Charlottesville. Charlottesville is a university town. Few of the letters of Thomas Jefferson make any mention of Charlottesville. It must have been a small village at that time, and grew big as the university grew. Many of the personal papers of Thomas Jefferson, coming to some 100 volumes, are being held there, the other two main repositories being the Library of Congress and the Massachusetts Historical Society. Included are his complete records of the purchase and sale and birth and death of his slaves. He left behind a grand total of 18,000 private letters.

The second home of Thomas Jefferson was at Poplar Forest, which is now right on the outskirts of Lynchburg, less than seven miles from where this author is now sitting. Poplar Forest was actually bigger in area than Monticello. It was a vast plantation where his purely black slaves toiled the fields. The partly white mulatto slaves were kept where Jefferson actually lived most of the time, at Monticello. The farm land is poor at Monticello, which is situated on a mountain top. Most of the serious farming took place at Poplar Forest.

Another interesting fact is that the Governor of Virginia is a white skinned mulatto black, just as Sally Hemings must have been. Governor Wilder became a candidate for President of the United States, and his candidacy was taken seriously. At least, he seemed to be better than some of the other candidates the Democrats put up. Unfortunately, he was forced to abandon his quest for the presidency because the American electorate was not prepared to consider a conservative budget-cutting white black man for the highest political office.

Some local wags here in Lynchburg have even raised the question of whether Governor Wilder might possibly be a descendant of Thomas Jefferson.

It is interesting to note that while many blacks carry the name of 'Jefferson', there are hardly any whites by that name. In fact, there is a joke that the last two white persons in America named Washington and Jefferson were the presidents by that name. These names are used nowadays almost exclusively by black people.

Although it is beyond the scope of this book, it must be noted that George Washington is also often thought of as having fathered children by his black slaves. Indeed, this practice may even have led to his death. Every history book says that Washington died from a cold which he contracted while returning from his slave's quarters, which he visited frequently. Washington had no children at all by his white wife, Martha Dandridge, although she had had two children by her previous husband.

In 1619, slavery was introduced in Virginia, for the reason that not many white people were willing to risk their lives by going there. The main peril faced by the slaves was the boat ride over from Africa. The slaves were so badly treated that typically 25% to 50% of them would die and their bodies would be thrown overboard on the nine weeks long voyage. It is difficult to understand why so many slaves died, regardless of how badly they were treated. Perhaps many of them were sick already, which is how they came to be captured and sold as slaves. There is, of course, the well known theory that 'the smart ones got away.' Perhaps it was true that the healthy ones got away.

The slaves who arrived in 1619 were the first permanent black immigrants to reach the Americas. However, they were not the first blacks to reach the Americas. One of the sailors on the initial voyage of discovery by Columbus in 1492 is believed to have been possibly a black seaman. Thirty of the group who accompanied Balboa when he discovered the Pacific Ocean were black. The man who first discovered and explored what became the states of Arizona and New Mexico was black. His name was Estevancio and he was from Morocco. He was originally a slave, but in 1528, he and the rest of his party in the ill-fated Navaraez Expedition was shipwrecked first in Tampa Bay and then on Galveston Island off of the Texas coast. Only four survived. He reached Mexico City in 1536 and was selected to lead a party in search of gold. He was sent ahead alone with Indian guides to explore the Arizona territories, but was killed by the Indians there in 1539. See *Chronology of African-American History*, Alton Hornsby, Detroit, 1991, pp. 1-2.

Dr. Livingstone in Africa reported large scale killings by Africans of each other as the various tribes of Africa tried to capture each other to sell the other into slavery in exchange for merchandise. A common tactic was that an entire village would be set on fire in the night. When the inhabitants tried to flee, they would be captured and sold to the slave traders. It was estimated that ten Africans died for each one successfully boarded onto a ship bound for America. Also, of those successfully boarded, only about half survived for long enough to begin work as field hands in the Americas.

After being captured, the slaves were held in dungeons in forts maintained by the Portuguese, primarily along what was known as the 'Gold Coast' of Africa, which is now in the area of Ghana. This is where the word 'negro' came from. When the Pope drew the famous 'Line of Demarcation', he gave Africa to the Portuguese and all of South America except for Brazil to the Spaniards. This put Portugal into the primary business of selling slaves. 'Negro' is a Portuguese word meaning 'black'.

Slavery was the biggest business in Africa, bigger even than gold, diamonds and ivory, all of which Africa had. This was a triangular business relationship. English trading ships brought goods such as textiles from England to Africa to be bartered for slaves. The slaves were then taken to America and exchanged for commodities such as tobacco which was taken back to England.

Once they reached America, the slaves probably had a better survival rate. They presumably knew better how to forage in the woods and live off the land than the white settlers who were used to living in houses in England. At one point in very early Virginia history, the number of slaves is believed to have exceeded the number of white people. This was not a matter of great significance, however, because, as late at 1622, after a massacre by the Indians, there were less than a thousand white colonists still alive in Virginia.

As soon as Virginia became safe for habitation, white people started coming in much larger numbers and the slaves as a percentage of the population dwindled. By 1648, there were 15,000 colonists in Virginia. It was during this period that the ancestors of Thomas Jefferson arrived. By 1700, the number of slaves was reduced to as little as 14 per cent of the population. The population of Virginia was 70,000, of which 10,000 were slaves.

With the development of cash crops like tobacco and cotton, slavery became a profitable business. At this point in Virginia history, the slave population began to rise again. Slave importation greatly increased during the period 1700–1740. In 1735, the mother of Betty Hemings arrived in America. The 1873 interview of Madison Hemings tells us that John Wayles wanted to keep the newborn infant Betty Hemings because racial mixing was just getting started at that time and the child was a great curiosity. For this reason, he refused to sell the child to her father, Captain Hemings, at any price. By 1756, the population of Virginia was 292,000, of which 120,000 was slaves.

By the time Thomas Jefferson reached maturity, slaves constituted 45% of the entire population. In the states of the Deep South such as South Carolina, slaves constituted the overwhelming majority.

Slavery made it easy for any member of the gentry class to become rich. A man of noble birth such as Peter Jefferson or John Wayles could simply register a land title with the clerk of the court. He could then order an entire consignment of slaves from Africa. When the ship load of slaves arrived, he could simply set them to work clearing the land and establishing a farm. All this, with no money down, as they say. There was nothing left for the slave owner to do but to sit on the veranda and sip mint julep, while all of the actual work was done by the slaves.

This was clearly the procedure followed by John Wayles. He was actively engaged in the business of importing slaves. He would bring entire ship loads of slaves from Africa, advertise them in the newspapers and sell them at auction. This is perhaps the reason that he owned such a large number of slaves at the time that he died.

With this in mind, the original story as told by Madison Hemings has to be rechecked. No doubt, the story is a summary of what happened, not the entire story. It seems unlikely that it could have happened quite the way Madison said. Madison himself seemed to have some doubts about that part of this story. He qualified it by saying, 'Such is the story that comes down to me.'

Madison Hemings states that his mother had become pregnant on the slave ship by the owner of the ship, whose name was Captain Hemings. Then, after the child was born, Captain Hemings realized that the child was his and tried to buy the newborn infant at any price.

However, the voyage from Africa took only about nine weeks. Captain Hemings would have had to wait in the Port of Williamsburg for another seven months to see how the child came out. A seaman like him could not afford to stay on dry land for very long.

However, Madison Hemings did not say that the captain waited. Rather, he said that the captain just happened to be in Williamsburg at the time that the child was born. This is entirely possible. Captain Hemings would have had time to make the circle once or twice more, going from Williamsburg, to England, from there to Africa and from Africa back to Williamsburg again, to see his newly born infant daughter.

If we could find any record of a man by the name of Captain Hemings, that would help, but we can find no such man. The name 'Hemings' does exist in England, but is quite rare.

However, this is not a crucial point. We can say for sure that Betty Hemings was half-white and half-black. Her father was white. Her mother was black. We would like to know the exact name of her father, but this information, while important and useful, is not an essential element to the story of the slave children of Thomas Jefferson.

All of the above facts provide a basis for further research into this subject. It is hoped that somebody will be prepared to solve all of the mysteries which remain, plus those new mysteries which might be created.

# Chapter Twenty

## Conclusion

Every book needs a conclusion. In this case, the conclusion is obvious.

We have to say that the case regarding whether Thomas Jefferson had children by Sally Hemings is practically proven. Of course, everybody understands that, by its nature, this sort of claim can never be absolutely proven. Absent some advanced DNA genetic test, nobody will ever know for sure whether Thomas Jefferson did do it or didn't do it. However, from the facts, from common sense, and from what we know about human nature, we must consider that he did it.

From the very date when Sally Hemings first arrived in France in 1787 until the death of Thomas Jefferson in 1826, there is no record of Thomas Jefferson ever having had so much as a cup of tea with any other woman. At the conclusion of his presidency in 1809, he stated that he had not attended a ball for more than forty years. Before the Sally Hemings scandal hit the newspapers, his political contemporaries believed that Thomas Jefferson was a bloodless man, without passion, who had no sex life at all. His later letters to Maria Cosway were primarily for the purpose of discouraging her from coming to America to join him, as she was always threatening to do. Here was a man who was a notorious woman chaser, who once stood in the hallway in the early morning hours in his shirt waiting to seize a passing woman, who wrote one of the great love letters in the history of the English language but who suddenly appears to have lost all interest in the opposite sex starting in 1787.

At the same time, in the ensuing 39 years, Thomas Jefferson and Sally Hemings were constantly together. They traveled together. Neither was married during this period. Children were born. It was said that Thomas Jefferson was the father of these children. He never denied it. He made sure that these children all got their freedom before he died or, in the case of the minor children, were freed just after his death. Almost all of his other slaves were sold at public auction.

Thomas Jefferson gave Sally a bunch of dresses in April, 1789. Nine months later, a baby was born. Thomas Jefferson went to Monticello on the occasion of the funeral of his daughter, Maria, in April, 1804. Nine months later, another baby was born.

In addition, Sally was known to be the half sister of his deceased beloved wife Martha. They both had the same father: John Wayles. Undoubtedly, they looked alike. For this reason, Thomas Jefferson would have felt a strong physical attraction towards 'Dusky Sally', as they called her.

This is like the pieces of a jig saw puzzle. If even one piece doesn't fit right, the entire puzzle has to be taken apart and started again. In this case, all the pieces fit perfectly. There is no flaw.

Consider if Sally had been a free white woman who spent 39 years with Thomas Jefferson but never married him. She would be considered in a court of law as his common law wife. They lived together openly and notoriously under the same roof for many years, the judge would say.

It is only because Sally Hemings was a partly-black slave that there is any doubt about this subject. However, we have to say that in the light of the totality of all of the evidence, the case is proven as much as any case of this sort can be.

That is still not quite the end of it, however. It so happens that the descendants of John Hemings and of Joe Fossett are also claiming Thomas Jefferson as their ancestor. We should at least examine their claims. In addition, there is an oral tradition which says that Thomas Jefferson had a second concubine named Betsy.

There were at least two Betsys. The oldest one was born in 1783, so she would have reached child bearing age just in time to produce children for Thomas Jefferson in his old age. She was the daughter of Mary, the oldest daughter of Betty Hemings. However, she did not stay long on the farm. She is nowhere listed after 1796.

Therefore, it has generally been assumed that this 'Betsy' was actually Betty Brown, born in 1759, the older sister of Sally.

Here, the case is much weaker. There is no record of either Betty or Betsy ever leaving the farm and traveling anywhere with Thomas Jefferson. Other than being his slaves, their names were not associated with him in any way, except through rumors. Betty Brown was the half sister of Sally, but her father was a black slave, so she would not have had the physical attraction which Sally had as the daughter of John Wayles.

However, there is the one significant fact that although Betty Brown had six children, she never had a husband. All of the other women on the farm, with the single exception of Sally, had husbands listed in the *Farm Book*.

In addition, Betty Brown was listed as a seamstress. Sally was also listed as a seamstress. They were the only two official seamstresses at Monticello.

In general, the rule was that Thomas Jefferson always recorded the name of any child born on the farm in the *Farm Book* together with the name of the father, unless the father was white. Thus, those relatively few cases where children were born with no father listed are all cases of the child having a white father.

According to this, all of the children of Betty Brown had a white father. However, we have no information as to who that father was.

In addition, at the Tomahawk Farm in Bedford County (now in the City of Lynchburg), there was a slave named Hannah. One of her sons, Billy B., born in 1799, had been transferred from Tomahawk to Monticello by the time he was 14 years old. The rule was: All the slaves at Tomahawk were pure black. All the slaves at Monticello were partly white. Hannah was pure black. Therefore, Billy B. must have had a white father. We have no way of knowing who his father might have been, but we know that Hannah had great personal affection for Thomas Jefferson because of the letter she wrote him.

Unfortunately, this transfer was not successful. Billy got in fights, was put in jail and eventually started a revolution of sorts. He was last heard from roaming the countryside with a gang of runaways.

John Hemings and Joe Fossett were two of the five on the list to be freed upon the death of Thomas Jefferson. This creates the presumption that Thomas Jefferson might be their father. However, this seems unlikely. John Hemings is considered to have been the son of John Neilson, a carpenter, designer and architect who worked for Thomas Jefferson for a time. John Neilson designed at least one of the buildings at Poplar Forest and may have done some of the design work on the University of Virginia.

John Neilson did not remain long with Thomas Jefferson, but years later, his son, John Hemings, knowingly or not, continued some of the work his father had started. John Hemings is also believed to have personally built much of the furniture at Monticello, but none of it is known for certain to survive today.

Joe Fossett is believed to have been the son of a white apprentice named William Fossett who worked for a short time at Monticello. The mother of Joe was Mary who was born in 1753 and was the oldest half-sister of Sally. The wife of Joe Fossett was Edy, born in 1787. Joe and Edy had six children together. There is no clear evidence that any of the children of Edy or of Mary were fathered by Thomas Jefferson. Therefore, we conclude that the claim of the descendants of Joe Fossett to be descended from Thomas Jefferson to be unfounded.

As to the fact that Joe Fossett and John Hemings were freed the same time as Madison and Eston Hemings, there is another possible reason for this: John Hemings was 75% white. The father of John Hemings was John Neilson. His grandfather was Captain Hemings. Several other mulattos on the farm were also 75% white, but John Hemings had been especially valuable as a carpenter and as a supervisor of the construction at Poplar Forest.

Joe Fossett was apparently only 62.5% white. His father was William Fossett, his grandfather was apparently a black slave and his great-grandfather was Captain Hemings. This makes it rather unclear as to why he was on the list of the five to be freed. It is reported that Joe Fossett was freed because of the many valuable services performed for Thomas Jefferson over the years.

We are surprised to learn that the Joe Fossett who was freed by the terms of Thomas Jefferson's will is the same person as the Joe who was ordered arrested at the White House by the police in 1806.

As to Burwell, a son of Betty Brown, who later became known, according to James A. Bear, as Burwell Colburn, there is no hint or clue as to why he was on the list of five to freed, except that he was a personal servant to Thomas Jefferson in the last years before he died. The only other observation we can make is that all five on the list to be freed had white fathers.

It is a curious fact that Burwell had been given the same name as Rebecca Burwell, the first great love in the life of Jefferson to whom he had perhaps proposed marriage in 1764. The significance of this is difficult to imagine.

Incidentally, although the name Burwell Colburn has been used on pages 23 and 129 of this book, the only source for the name 'Colburn' is an article by James A. Bear in the Autumn, 1979 issue of *Virginia Cavalcade*. This information has to be checked. Among other things, it seems possible that the correct name was 'Corbin', instead of 'Colburn'. Corbin was the name of a prominent family in that area of Virginia.

It is not clear what happened to the families of the five to be freed. The one most directly affected by this was Joe, who had a wife, Edy, and six children. They were apparently on the list to be sold. However, Joe presumably had the opportunity to buy them back once he got his freedom. A freed black man was in an enviable position to the extent that he could select whichever woman he wanted for a wife and buy her on the slave market. A freed black woman could also buy a husband in the same manner.

There is one additional significant bit of evidence. This comes in the form of anecdotes told by or about people who visited Monticello and noticed that a large number of mulatto children there looked exactly like Thomas Jefferson.

Unfortunately, we cannot be certain from these anecdotes of when these visitors went to Monticello. If they visited before Thomas Jefferson became president in 1801, that would be strong evidence that Thomas Jefferson did father children by another woman such as Betty Brown because, with the exception of Tom who was born in 1790 and was sent away in 1802 or 1803, the other children of Sally Hemings were just babies or were not born yet. However, in the somewhat more likely event that the visitors came later, such as around 1820, there would have been four approximately teen-age children around at that time who were the children of Sally Hemings. One of those visitors was John Quincy Adams, who was elected President in 1824. It could easily be that he visited Monticello in 1820 or thereabouts since Thomas Jefferson was still a leader of his political party. Therefore, we cannot come to any conclusion about this.

However, there are several reasons for the conclusion that Thomas Jefferson was not the father of the children of Betty or Betsy. First, Madison Hemings stated in 1873 that only the children of Sally had been fathered by Thomas Jefferson. Second, it appears that no special treatment was given to Betty or her children. Burwell, one son of Betty Brown, was freed, but the others were not freed. They may have been sold as slaves after the death of Thomas Jefferson. This may have included Wormley, another son of Betty Brown, who dug the grave of Thomas Jefferson. Wormley and all of his children were apparently sold. Even Betty Brown herself, who was still alive at age 68 at the time of the auction, was apparently sold. It appears that all but one of the children of Betty Brown were sold at this auction. Therefore, it seems unlikely that these were the children of Thomas Jefferson.

As for Betsy, she disappeared from the list of slaves in the *Farm Book* long before. She became the property of John Wayles Eppes, the son-in-law of Thomas Jefferson, who took a second wife after his first wife, Maria Jefferson, had died. The gravestone of Betsy has been found in Buckingham County showing that she died in 1857.

There is an additional reason for believing that Jefferson was the father of Madison and Eston, but not the father of the other three on the list of five. The will of Thomas Jefferson decreed that Madison and Eston would be freed upon reaching maturity, but until that time both would be in the custody of John Hemings. Madison was not much affected by this because he was just then reaching maturity anyway. However, it appears to have been the pattern that the children of Jefferson were all freed upon reaching maturity. Both Beverly and Harriet were allowed to go north at about age 22. Apparently, Madison and Eston were to be treated in the same way.

However, Burwell, Joe, and John Hemings were all mature. John was born in 1775, Joe in 1780. Burwell was born on December 24, 1783. Thus, Burwell, the youngest, was nearly 43 years old when Thomas Jefferson died. It is therefore unlikely that these three were his sons.

Thus, the conclusion is as follows: Thomas Jefferson was almost certainly the father of all the surviving children of Sally Hemings. This includes Beverly, Harriet, Madison, Eston and presumably Tom, assuming he was born and survived.

Jefferson might have been the father of the children born to Betty Brown, of one of the children born to Hannah and of various other children around the house, including the children of Edy, but there is no strong evidence for any of this. We must consider these claims to be unproven.

# Epilogue

When I first started writing this book, I feared that it might cause a big scandal in the area of Virginia from which I come. Now, I have exactly the opposite fear, which is that it will be greeted with a big yawn.

The story that Thomas Jefferson fathered children by his black slaves is well known around here. It is said that they even teach it in the public schools.

In fact, there are many cases somewhat analogous to it in American history. The best known example of this concerned Grover Cleveland. During the 1884 presidential campaign, he was accused by his opponents of having fathered an illegitimate child. Instead of denying it, as was expected, he acknowledged the child, sent the mother some money, and was elected president in a great upset victory.

A much lesser known but more similar case concerns Richard M. Johnson, the Vice-President of the United States under Martin Van Buren from 1837 to 1841. He was accused of fathering two children by a black woman. He accepted the accusation and won the election. It has been reported that he even went through a marriage ceremony with the woman at some point, but this is not certain.

There was an incident while Richard M. Johnson was Vice-President. He tried to put his two mulatto daughters on the same platform with him, but was prevented from doing so.

An almost completely forgotten episode concerns George McGovern, who was the presidential candidate against Nixon in 1972. When he first won the nomination, he appeared to have a good chance. However, early on, his candidacy was rocked by a variety of problems. One concerned the claim that he had fathered an illegitimate child, which he denied.

A newspaper reporter said that he had personally seen the birth certificate of the child in the Indiana county clerk's office, with McGovern's name on it. The next morning, after this story had appeared in all the newspapers in the nation, a swarm of reporters descended on that county clerk's office. However, the birth certificate had been removed overnight. They could tell by a break in the numbers that one birth certificate was missing, but nobody was ever able to locate it.

This was not the only problem McGovern had. He eventually went down to ignominious defeat, in spite of the Watergate scandal, which was to force his opponent, Richard M. Nixon, to resign two years later.

A different sort of case concerns Abraham Lincoln. Scholars who have studied his case say that his father probably was not Thomas Lincoln, the husband of his mother, Nancy Hanks. It is said that Nancy Hanks got married when she was already pregnant by another man. A photograph of that man is available, and it is said that Abraham Lincoln looked exactly like that other man.

Benjamin Franklin is a notorious case. It is said that he had fathered possibly as many as 18 illegitimate children. He firmly believed that this was a good idea and made no effort to hide it. Of course, he never ran for election, being too old when America finally got its independence.

Everybody will raise their hand and mention the persistent problems involving the Kennedys. This case is so well known that it is hardly worthy of mention. However, there is still a lesson to be learned from this.

Ted Kennedy would probably have been elected president in 1968, except that he chose not to run, preferring to wait a little longer. However, that turned out to be his last good chance because, in 1969, a girl was found dead in the water.

The incident itself about the girl being dead was not what hurt Kennedy. Accidents do happen. What hurt him is that he lied about it and, to this very day, has never told the truth.

Anybody who has ever studied that case in detail has quickly realized that the story told by Ted Kennedy about how it happened was truly ridiculous. Since then, he has shut up and refused to say even one word more about the subject. Every time he tries to run for President, this issue comes up again.

Even now, if Kennedy told the truth, he could possibly get some political redemption, assuming that the truth is not that he personally strangled the girl himself. However, Kennedy refuses to talk, and will probably carry the truth to his grave.

We have to say that the girl did not die in vain. Kennedy probably would have been elected president eventually had this not happened, and he probably would have been one of the worst presidents America ever had.

An even more recent example involving presidential politics concerns Gary Hart. Early in the 1988 campaign for the presidential nomination, Hart had double the popularity on the opinion polls of any other candidate and was considered a 'shoo-in'.

Unfortunately, somebody discovered a photograph of him sitting with a beautiful girl in his lap. Moreover, it was established that Hart had gone on a long ocean cruise on a private yacht with the woman in question, Hart being a married man. Beyond this, nothing was ever proven. Still, for this reason and for no other, his popularity immediately started dropping and he had to withdraw from the race.

Therefore, from these few examples, we have a trend. If a man actually fathers a child and admits it, in the long run this will help him. At least, the women will vote for him.

On the other hand, if a man dallies with a woman other than his wife and allows her to sit on his lap for example, but does not actually produce any children, he can be politically ruined.

Thomas Jefferson probably did the right thing. Because of the racial sensitivity of the issue, he could not admit that he had fathered children by Sally Hemings. To do so would have been to admit that he had committed a crime, because miscegenation was against the laws of Virginia at the time. However, he remained silent, which was the proper thing to do because the children were almost undoubtedly his. He was rewarded by winning a resounding victory for re-election. He won the 1804 presidential election by 162 electoral votes to 14, one of the most lopsided results in American history.

There is also a much longer list of white–black people who can be determined to be majority white by pure observation but who either don't know or aren't willing to reveal from where they got their white blood.

Most readers will be surprised to learn that the famous black militant separatist, Malcolm X, was clearly more white than black. This author knows about this from personal knowledge, because he saw Malcolm X at close range at a distance of not more than three feet just after he had given a speech on the steps of Sproul Hall at the University of California at Berkeley in 1965, just a few months before he was assassinated in New York's Harlem. Malcolm X was a heavily freckled but mostly white man, who was clearly only a little bit black. He was sensitive about this subject. In his autobiography and other writings, he said that he cursed the blood of the white man which flowed in his veins, the man who had 'raped' his grandmother.

However, anybody who saw Malcolm X up close would have to agree that the blood of more than just one white man flowed in his veins, because he was clearly majority white. Indeed, his biographies state that prior to his birth it was intended to name him after his grandfather, Earl Little, but when it was seen at birth that he was almost completely white, his parents refused to give him that name and called him Malcolm Little instead. Little wonder that he later decided to call himself Malcolm X.

Television documentaries of Malcolm X always cast a deeply dark black actor in his role, to hide the true color of the man.

The late Alex Hailey of *Roots* fame, who in fact was also the ghost writer of the *Autobiography of Malcolm X*, is another famous person who can be seen to be partly white even though no doubt most of his roots really do come from Africa.

Another black man who was really mostly white was Justice Thurgood Marshall of the United States Supreme Court. This author also got a close look at him, because this author argued a case orally before the full panel of the United States Supreme Court. The name of that case was *S.E.C. v. Samuel H. Sloan*, 436 U.S. 103 (1978).

Before becoming a Supreme Court justice, Thurgood Marshall was one of the most successful lawyers in Supreme Court history. Representing the NAACP, he argued and won 36 Supreme Court cases in a row. No other lawyer in history has ever won 36 cases in a row in the United States Supreme Court.

Of course, Marshall had an advantage. He was on the right side of the law. These were all racial desegregation cases.

However, the case of Governor L. Douglas Wilder of Virginia urgently demands attention, because he actually ran for President of the United States and had a real chance to gain the Democratic nomination, especially since nobody good wanted to run against George Bush.

Wilder has been on national and even international television quite a lot. Anybody who has seen him on television will immediately realize that this is actually a white man who is only a little bit black.

Wilder has a remarkable history. He served in the United States Army during the Korean War and fought among the vastly outnumbered American troops in the famous *Battle of Pork Chop Hill*, which was the last battle of that war. Anybody who has ever seen the movie by that name will understand what the odds against him surviving that battle actually were.

Wilder was awarded the Bronze Star and is officially credited, along with two other soldiers, with capturing 19 Chinese prisoners in the *Battle of Pork Chop Hill*. However, he takes no credit for that, saying that the soldier who actually did this job was killed in the battle.

Wilder acquired his financial expertise by working as an elevator operator in Richmond's financial district. He listened to and learned from the words of the financial wizards as they rode up and down his elevator.

Wilder won his election for Governor of Virginia as a financial conservative. That is the key to his success. He gets the conservative white vote because he is a cost-cutting tight-fisted conservative and he gets the black vote because he is partly black. Most Virginians are fed up with the big spending ways of his white predecessors.

This unusual combination is what made Wilder the first black governor of any state in the history of the United States, since Reconstruction. (There are many old jokes dating back to the Reconstruction era, which came after the conclusion of the Civil War, regarding black men in states like North Carolina who worked as a gardener for the governor's mansion after completing their own term of office as Governor of North Carolina. Most white southerners were not allowed to hold public office in those days.)

The combination of being regarded as black plus being a fiscal conservative was what made Wilder the first truly serious black candidate for President of the United States. Actually, he was a much better candidate than most people realized. There was a tendency to group him together with Jessie Jackson, although those two are extreme opposites. Jessie Jackson is a rabid leftist-liberal who has never been elected to public office in his life. Wilder is an arch-conservative career politician who has never lost an election in the last 22 years. If Wilder were not black, if he were the same man, but only white, he would probably have been the leading candidate for the Democratic Presidential Nomination. He was certainly a better public speaker than any other democratic candidate. However, being part black made those who had not seen him not take him seriously.

However, the question here is: How exactly did Wilder get to be part white and part black? Also, is it even barely possible that he too is one of those unknown descendants of Thomas Jefferson who have got us surrounded?

So far, Wilder has never publicly answered that question. All he will say is this:

His father's parents were slaves. His mother's mother was a freed Negro. He doesn't know or has not yet told who his mother's father was.

From taking a good look at Governor Wilder and from this sketchy history, it can be considered virtually certain that his mother's father was a white man and that Governor Wilder either does not know or does not want to reveal who he was.

Still, there is more to it than that, because Wilder is clearly more than 50% white.

What he does tell us is that his paternal grandfather was James W. Wilder who was born a slave on November 18, 1838 in Goochland County, West of Richmond. His paternal grandmother was Agnes W. Johnson who was born on December 8, 1839 in Richmond.

They were married in a slave marriage on April 25, 1856, at Braggs farm in Henrico County, north of Richmond. They had thirteen children. The first, Emma and Sally, were born as slaves. Then James and Agnes Wilder were sold separately. Fortunately for them, the Civil War came shortly thereafter and they got their freedom. After the war, they got back together again and produced most of the rest of their children. Wilder's father was the youngest. His name was Robert Judson Wilder and he was born in Richmond on July 10, 1886.

Much less is known about the maternal grandparents of Governor Wilder. The only thing which is known is that his mother was named Beulah Olive Richards and she was born in the village of Ruthville, Charles City

County, near Williamsburg, on April 26, 1892. Her mother, Mary Richards, was, according to Wilder, a free Negro woman. We know from this book that free Negro men and women often got to be that way by being freed by their master-fathers. Thomas Jefferson was just one example of many masters who freed their children from slavery.

Mary Richards brought Beulah, the mother of Governor Wilder, to Richmond when she was a baby. They lived briefly with Mary's mother, who was known only as Pinky. Later, Mary took Beulah took Newark, New Jersey, where Mary worked as a domestic for a white family and married the family's chauffeur. When Mary died in about 1906, Beulah returned alone to Richmond, where she lived on Church Hill with her grandmother Pinky and her Aunt Kate, who also worked as a domestic for a white family. She met Robert Wilder there and married him on July 13, 1913. The future Governor Wilder was born on January 17, 1931.

From this we can infer that his mother's father was probably white and that his mother's mother's father, who produced a child from Pinky, was also probably white. There still must be more white in him than that, however. Probably, his father's parents were also part white.

There is nothing in any of this which links him in any way to Thomas Jefferson except for the remote coincidences that his mother was born in Charles City County, where the estate of John Wayles was located, and his father's parents lived in Henrico County, where Bermuda Hundred and Eppington, the Eppes family estates, were located. None of this, of course, proves anything.

Nevertheless, if he again becomes a presidential candidate, Governor Wilder may be inclined or even compelled to tell us more about his family history. One should be checking any new names which may come out of this.

One of these days, perhaps not very long from now, somebody is actually going to start digging up the graves of the children of Sally Hemings and others and testing the DNA to see if they really were descendants of Thomas Jefferson. The grave sites of Madison Hemings, Eston Hemings Jefferson and Thomas Woodson are well known. A lock of the hair of Thomas Jefferson is available in a museum.

One is reminded of the efforts of a small but persistent group of Americans who keep trying to dig up the grave of William Shakespeare in England. This movement was started by a school teacher in New England more than one hundred years ago who learned that William Shakespeare in his life never attended school. Being a school teacher herself, she believed that is was impossible for a man without formal schooling to have written the greatest works in the history of the English Language.

After further investigation, she concluded that in fact there never was any such person by the name of William Shakespeare. From this sprang a variety of theories, such as one which is well known which says that all of Shakespeare was written by Sir Walter Raleigh while he was a prisoner for 13 years in the Tower of London prior to being executed by King James in 1618.

Indeed, the plays of Shakespeare often attacked the British Royal Family. Whoever wrote those plays had good reason for wanting to use a pseudonym.

Having fully convinced herself that there was no such person as Shakespeare, the school teacher then financed her own trip to England and went to the grave of Shakespeare at Stratford-on-Avon in the night with shovel in hand prepared to dig him up.

In fact, the tombstone of Shakespeare states: 'Cursed be he who moves these bones.'

This unusual admonition against digging up this particular grave convinced this school teacher even more that no bones at all would be found in the grave. She believed that the only thing which would be found in the coffin of William Shakespeare would be a bag of rocks.

Sad to relate, the authorities stopped her from digging up the grave of Shakespeare. The British have no inclination whatever to dig up the grave of their national idol. It is only the Americans who keep trying to do that.

Eventually, the school teacher in question went back to America without ever having achieved her goal.

However, Americans clearly do not have any qualms about digging up the graves of their past presidents. Probably, that is how this controversy regarding Sally Hemings and Thomas Jefferson will eventually be resolved.

# Acknowledgments

First, I want to apologize to the reader for not providing more extensive citations and footnotes than I have. My original intention was to try to make this book easy reading, and not a mass of trivia. I can assure the reader that I have a source for everything I have said. In the vast majority of cases, the original source for anything I have said is *Thomas Jefferson's Farm Book*. The source or sources will become obvious to anybody who chooses to research the subject more deeply.

I, personally, am not impressed by footnotes. I see a book on the life of Thomas Jefferson, or on almost any other subject for that matter, with copious footnotes. I then go to the library, check out the books cited, and look at the original sources for those footnotes. As often as not, I find that the original source says nothing of the kind. Other researchers have reported the same results. I am prepared to guarantee that in my book, when I give a page and line number for any citation, the reader can look up that exact page in the library and find that what I have said is right there on that page.

The reader will have noticed that many of the books I have cited were published in 1991. This shows that there has been a resurgence of interest in this area. This caused a great problem for me. Every time I went to the local library, there was a new, just arrived book, waiting to be cataloged, which sent me back to the word processor to revise everything I had. The uneven style of my book is one result of these repeated revisions.

The reader may have noticed that my book is lumpy, to put it mildly. In case the reader has noticed a fluctuation in the writing style of this book, there is a simple explanation for this. In the beginning, this book was supposed to contain short sentences and small words for easy light reading. The idea was to write a book which the reader could get through in three hours, and still learn most of everything one might want to know about the slave children of Thomas Jefferson.

The problem with this is that as this author read more and more of the letters of Thomas Jefferson, his writing style began to change and his sentences and ideas became more complex and convoluted. A typical example of the writing style of Jefferson can be seen in the last paragraph of the *Declaration of Independence*, which is actually only one sentence long. That is the paragraph which states: 'We .... solemnly .... declare .... that these colonies are and of right ought to be free and independent states . . . . ,' etc., etc.

In short, if the reader has any problem getting through this book, he can blame it all on the bad influence of Thomas Jefferson.

Probably the best and certainly the most accurate work on this subject was done by James A. Bear, Jr. He is the source for much information which cannot be found anywhere else. For example, the fact that James Hemings committed suicide in Philadelphia in 1801 and that Robert Hemings married a woman named Dolly and thereafter lived on the corner of 7th and Grace Streets in Richmond, Virginia, and died there in 1819, cannot be found anywhere else.

Bear also quietly corrects the misstatements made by other writers, without making an issue over it. For example, he apparently agrees with my conclusion that there was no separate child named Edy who was a daughter of Sally Hemings.

Unfortunately, Mr. Bear has only written one article on this particular subject that I am able to locate. That article is entitled, *The Hemings Family of Monticello*. It appeared in *Virginia Cavalcade*, Volume XXIX, Autumn 1979, Number 2, page 78, published by the Virginia State Library in Richmond, Virginia 23219.

Even in this one short article, Mr. Bear displays his vastly superior knowledge of this subject matter. It is unfortunate that he has not published more about this. Most of his other publications are essentially collections of letters of Thomas Jefferson. Incidentally, it should come as no great surprise that Mr. Bear knows more about this subject than anybody else, because he was the resident director of Monticello.

Another source which I have used liberally is *The Family Letters of Thomas Jefferson*, also published by the University Press of Virginia in Charlottesville, and edited by Mr. Bear and by Edwin Morris Betts. This book is the source for my quotations of a number of important letters between Thomas Jefferson and his daughters, including the 1798 letter in which Martha informed her father that Harriet, the daughter of Sally Hemings, had died. Mr. Bear is also the co-author of the *Monticello Guide Book*.

Perhaps an even more important contribution has been made by Minnie Shumate Woodson of Washington, D.C., who was kind enough to write me several personal letters expressing her views. If what she says is correct, she has solved the long standing mystery of what happened to Tom, the first born son of Sally Hemings. Her views have been explained in the chapter I have devoted to the subject.

The existence of Tom is vital to this story. If we can prove that Tom existed, we have virtually proven that Sally Hemings was the concubine of Thomas Jefferson. Thus, the research done by Minnie Shumate Woodson is of utmost importance. Her book is entitled *The Sable Curtain*.

There is not the slightest doubt that there once was a man named Tom Woodson. In the 1970's, an interview was taken of an elderly gentleman in Ohio who had known Tom Woodson personally while a small child. The first question he asked the interviewer was: 'Was Tom Woodson a white man or a black man?' From this interview, we know that Tom Woodson was light skinned, but that he lived in the black community. Therefore, the only question which remains is: Was this Tom Woodson the same man as 'Yellow Tom', the son of Thomas Jefferson, who was made famous in the writings of James Thompson Callender?

The third major source is *Thomas Jefferson: an Intimate History* by the late Fawn Brodie. The criticism by Dumas Malone is correct, in that all of her sources were previously known. That, indeed, is why I have listed her as third, not first. However, it took Fawn Brodie to assemble all the material and present it in the right way. Dumas Malone never did that, at least not with regard to the Sally Hemings story.

It must be mentioned that the story of Sally Hemings is only a small part of *Thomas Jefferson: An Intimate History*. That book deals with his romances or affairs with Elizabeth Walker and Maria Cosway as well with as his innocent love for Rebecca Burwell. However, all of this is necessary for an understanding of what kind of man Thomas Jefferson was.

There were also two articles by Fawn Brodie in *American Heritage Magazine*. These articles are better than her book, because they are shorter and more to the point. The first is in the June 1972 issue of American Heritage. It is entitled *The Great Jefferson Taboo*. This article was a summary of her then not yet published book, *Thomas Jefferson: an Intimate History*. It is only about 15 pages long, and yet contains every significant fact about Sally Hemings which can be found in the 812 page subsequently completed soft cover edition of book. Being shorter but saying the same things, it is preferable to reading the book itself.

The second article by Brodie was in the October, 1976 issue of American Heritage and is entitled: *Thomas Jefferson's Unknown Grand-Children*. This article arose because, after the publication of her book, Brodie was contacted by many people who had been harboring the family secret that they were descended from Thomas Jefferson. As a result of these contacts, she was able to learn what had happened to the children of Madison, Eston, Beverly and Tom. Only the fate of Harriet has eluded researchers until this day.

Importantly, this article contains photographs of seven of the possible unauthorized descendants of Thomas Jefferson, plus a family tree.

As noted previously, this research work has since been carried on by Minnie Shumate Woodson among others, so that by now the entire family tree of these descendants has just about been solved.

One book I did not appreciate at all was *Sally Hemings, a Novel*, by Barbara Chase-Riboud. I consider her book to be a step backwards. Apparently, all that she must have done is take the part of *Thomas Jefferson: an Intimate History* which deals with the Sally Hemings story, invent a bunch of additional facts of her own, and flesh it out into a novel. Not only did she fail to contribute any new information, but she leads the reader down the trail of false facts. Incidentally, her piece of worthless drivel was a *Literary Guild* selection.

A useful little book which I found helpful when I first started researching this subject was *The Secret Loves of the Founding Fathers*, by Charles Callan Tansill, Devin–Adair Company, New York 1964. This contains short sketches about George Washington, Thomas Jefferson and Benjamin Franklin, among others. All of the information contained therein is available elsewhere, but not in such handy form.

I must give full credit to Virginius Dabney for being the one who convinced me that Sally Hemings really was the concubine of Thomas Jefferson. He wrote an article intending to prove that she was not the concubine. However, the arguments and points he presented were so weak that he convinced me of exactly the opposite of his thesis. The article by Dabney appeared on page 53 in the same issue of *Virginia Cavalcade* as the article by James A. Bear mentioned above.

The same issue of *Virginia Cavalcade* contains a third article, this one about the life of *James Thompson Callender* by Charles A. Jellison. All three articles are 'must' reading.

After I had substantially completed the first draft of my book, a book appeared by Dabney entitled *The Jefferson Scandals*, published by Madison Books in Lanham, Maryland, 1991. Naturally, I was terrified at this, because I feared that Dabney might have discovered something new which would send my proposed book to the chopper. Fortunately, I was gratified to discover that this book was actually written in 1981 and was just an expansion of his earlier *Virginia Cavalcade* article, and that all of his sources were the same sources that I have used, except that I have more recent sources, which he did not have.

It short, it appears that he does not know anything more about this subject than I do. The only difference between us is that, starting from the same original sources, we reach exactly the opposite conclusion. Probably the reason for our opposing views is that Virginius Dabney was born in Lynchburg, but spent his life in Richmond, whereas I was born in Richmond, but grew up in Lynchburg.

The only thing he really adds to his original *Virginia Cavalcade* article is a detailed criticism of the books by Barbara Chase-Riboud and Fawn Brodie. Regarding the book by Chase-Riboud, he obviously agrees fully with my conclusion that this is a terrible book and a disservice to the reading public.

Regarding his criticism of Fawn Brodie's book, he attacks her attempts at a 'psychosexual analysis' of the inner workings of Jefferson's mind. In fact, Fawn Brodie does keep trying to read hidden sexual meanings into almost everything written by Jefferson. Obviously some, if not all, of her attempt at psychoanalysis is utterly without merit. I agree with Dabney to the extent that I also do not see any value in Brodie's 'psycho-historical' analysis of everything Thomas Jefferson did.

Dabney also devotes many pages of his book to debunking the thoroughly discredited story that a daughter of Thomas Jefferson was once sold at a slave auction in New Orleans for one thousand dollars. I agree with his conclusions there, also.

However, the problem with Dabney's approach is that he never directly addresses the hard solid factual evidence which tends to prove the relationship between Sally Hemings and Thomas Jefferson. In other words, he seems to feel that by successfully attacking the apparent inadequacies and outright errors in the writings of Barbara Chase-Riboud, Fawn Brodie, James T. Callender and others, he has thereby proven that Thomas Jefferson never went to bed with Sally Hemings. Obviously, he hasn't done that.

Other sources for my book include *Thomas Jefferson, A Reference Biography*, Merrill D. Peterson, Editor, Charles Scribner & Sons., 1986, p. 429. From this, I have taken the quote about the *Congo Harem* maintained by Jefferson. I have also quoted *Fame and the Founding Fathers*, (New York 1974) by Douglass Adair, published posthumously, in which he claims to have 'proven' that the Sally Hemings story was untrue. Again, the weakness of his arguments led me to the opposite conclusion.

Here locally in Lynchburg, a number of publications have been helpful. An edition of *Lynch's Ferry*, Vol. 4, Summer 1991, which is a semi- annual magazine published by Warwick House Publishing, 720 Court Street, Lynchburg, Virginia 24504, contains several articles on the restoration of Poplar Forest, regarded as the Summer Home of Thomas Jefferson. These articles were especially useful because this is the area where Thomas Jefferson maintained his second home.

There is one source above all which everybody uses. That is the famous *Thomas Jefferson's Farm Book*. I have picked it up an average of once every three minutes while writing this book. It is Edited by Edwin Morris Betts and is published by the University Press of Virginia, in Charlottesville. However, anybody buying their own copy of the *Farm Book* had better also buy a magnifying glass. Many entries are tiny and illegible, which may account for some of the bitter disagreements about what the *Farm Book* contains.

The reason that I have not included in this book footnotes in the normal style and manner, a decision which which nobody agrees, is that I felt that the reader needs to know right away the source for anything written and especially the date on which it was written. There is a big difference between what Thomas Jefferson wrote in 1787 and what he wrote in 1821, and the reader needs to know about this right away, without attempting to thumb through the back of the book. Most of the direct quotes in this book are from letters. In that case, I have included the date of the letter and to whom it was written. This is the information which the reader needs to know immediately. I have not told where the letter can be found. The reason for this is that most of these letters can be found in several different places. Any letter dated through 1792 can be found in the 24 volumes now published of *The Papers of Thomas Jefferson* by Princeton University Press. Most of the other letters can be found in such places as *The Family Letters of Thomas Jefferson*, *The Domestic Life of Thomas Jefferson* and *Thomas Jefferson's Farm Book*. There are also books devoted entirely to his correspondence with Maria Cosway and with John Adams.

There are also quotes of things said, as opposed to things written, by Thomas Jefferson. However, since I know that Thomas Jefferson was not much of a talker, I tend to be suspicious of these quotes. This probably sounds contradictory, but if I am not confident of the source, I just leave out the potential citation.

An example of this is the book by Winthrop Jordan, *White over Black*. This book is quoted extensively in Fawn Brodie's book and indeed appears to have been one of the primary inspirations for her book. I, however, have used it hardly at all. This book would be quite useful to me because it essentially supports my thesis, but I have shied away from it because it is filled with outrageous statements which cannot readily be confirmed from other sources. Similarly, there is the highly regarded 1961 book *The Negro in the American Revolution*, by Benjamin Quarles. There were many useful things in this book, but I decided not to use them.

To give one example of this, Quarles mentions the fact that during the American Revolution, the British offered freedom to any slave who ran away to them. Of this fact, there is no doubt. This is the reason that the *Farm Book* shows that more than 30 slaves of Thomas Jefferson ran away, although, according to Isaac Jefferson, they were actually taken prisoner.

Quarles states that a total of 30,000 slaves ran away during that war. Of these, 27,000 died of smallpox and other diseases. (This tendency is also confirmed by the *Farm Book*.) Of the 3,000 who survived, most were sold back into slavery in the islands of the West Indies such as the Bahamas. Of the few who remained, most were sent to Nova Scotia. These were the only ones who has their promise of freedom fulfilled. They were eventually shipped to Freetown, which is now the capital of Sierra Leone in West Africa.

The above facts are certainly interesting and important and I fully believe them to be true. However, they are so outrageous that I felt uneasy including it in the main text of the book. Therefore, I have included it here.

A book published in October, 1991 is *The Buffalo Ridge Cherokee: The Colors and Culture of a Virginian Indian Community*, by Horace R. Rice, Madison Heights, Virginia, 1991. This book recounts the efforts by the Cherokee Indians in Amherst County, which boarders Lynchburg, to avoid deportation to Oklahoma by mixing with the blacks. It also has photographs to prove that there still are pure or almost pure red Indians living in the mountains north and west of Lynchburg, although their numbers have been reduced to a mere handful.

Again it must be said that the one book which is just plain bad is *Sally Hemings* by Barbara Chase-Riboud. Naturally, I had to read it, as it is my obligation to read everything ever written on this subject. However, I had to force myself to read this book. It was truly a painful experience. It is clear that Barbara Chase-Riboud had only read one book on the life of Thomas Jefferson, and that was Fawn Brodie's book. The mistakes made by Barbara Chase-Riboud could not have been made if she had read anything more than that one book. To cite just another one of innumerable examples, she repeatedly calls the Virginia House of Delegates the *House of Burgesses*. That was the name of the body which existed under the authority of King George III prior to the Revolutionary War. The House of Delegates was created after the United States got its independence. In her book, Barbara Chase-Riboud has Thomas Mann Randolph Junior serving in the *House of Burgesses*, a body which actually ceased to exist while he was an infant.

In order to cover up her total lack of knowledge of the subject matter about which she was writing, Barbara Chase-Riboud states in her acknowledgments section: 'A bibliography would be long and out of place here.' In reality, it would not be long at all, as clearly she only read parts of one book plus a few magazine articles. She artificially increased the length of her short bibliography by listing as separate sources all of the various documents included in the appendices to *Thomas Jefferson, An Intimate History*. The result of this trick was that one reviewer mistakenly stated that her book had an 'impressive bibliography'. It is not clear where Barbara Chase-Riboud even learned the term 'House of Burgesses', as Fawn Brodie never mentions that body in her book. Probably, she got it from the article in the *William and Mary Quarterly* about the *Murder of George Wythe*, which is the one article that she says that she read. George Wythe was old enough to have served in the House of Burgesses.

I must add that one reason why I am so angry about the book by Barbara Chase-Riboud is that I, myself, was initially misled by it.

I have often been critical herein of Fawn Brodie's book *Thomas Jefferson, an Intimate History*. The reason is that her book does contain many errors, false footnotes and invalid assumptions. However, perhaps I have gone too far. There is also considerable merit to her book, in spite of the errors.

First, it must be pointed out that, contrary to popular belief, her book is not the story of Sally Hemings. Rather, it is a complete biography of the life of Thomas Jefferson. Only one chapter is devoted entirely to Sally Hemings, but the name of Sally Hemings does come up in other chapters.

I am happy about the fact that Fawn Brodie's book is now somewhat difficult to obtain and therefore I did not read it in full until I had almost completed my own book. The reason I say this is that because I was already fully familiar with the subject matter, I was able to spot the errors in Fawn Brodie's book immediately and therefore was not misled. At the same time, her book is filled with facts and contains a lot of information which was new to me, especially about other aspects of the life of Thomas Jefferson which had nothing to do with the story of the slave children of Thomas Jefferson. If Fawn Brodie had stuck to the facts and not attempted to psychoanalyze Thomas Jefferson, she would have sold less copies but her work would have been recognized by historians. Which is more important: To sell a lot of copies of your book, or to have your work recognized by the great scholars in the field? It is, of course, far more important to have your work recognized than to try to make some money off of a book.

I do not claim to be an expert on every aspect of the life and times of Thomas Jefferson. It is true that my book does mention in passing at some point or another almost every significant event in the life of Thomas Jefferson, with the exception of the XYZ Affair. (You say that you want to hear about the XYZ Affair? I will save it for another book, if ever there be one). However, the exact area of my expertise is confined to the slaves and the slave children of Thomas Jefferson. When I want to write about some other aspect of the life of Thomas Jefferson, I just look it up in the *Encyclopedia Britannica* or even in the *World Almanac and Book of Facts* (which is more at least than some authors seem to have done). A simple source like the *Encyclopedia Britannica* is where I learned that all authors are wrong in saying that Sally was inoculated with Edward Jenner's smallpox vaccine in 1787. That vaccine was not first tested until 1796. However, it must be noted here that Jenner's smallpox vaccine did become available to Thomas Jefferson in 1801 and he used it along with other vaccines after that date.

Incidentally, I am not the only one who uses the *Encyclopedia Britannica*. The words of Fawn Brodie about the life of Jonathan Edwards, the famous philosopher-grandfather of Aaron Burr, appear possibly to have been copied word for word from the *Encyclopedia Britannica*. However, this is perfectly legal. It is assumed under copyright law that books about the same historical figures will say the same things.

If one asked me to recommend a single book to read about the life of Thomas Jefferson, I might easily recommend Fawn Brodie's book, in spite of the errors which I know that it contains. I rather prefer it to the standard milk-toast variety of biography which talks a lot about what a great and good man Thomas Jefferson was, and actually says nothing.

The reader must be warned that the writing style of Fawn Brodie is difficult. Although I read every word of her book, I had to force myself to do so. I suspect that I am one of the few people who have actually read her best selling book. I cannot believe that more that five percent of the people who bought her book managed to get through it.

Finally, I have devoted an entire chapter to the contribution of *Down from the Mountain* by Judith P. Justus of Perrysburg, Ohio. Not only did I gain much factual information from her book, but she provided further additional information in private correspondence with me. In fact, some of her most interesting points came in her private letters which contained information she had been afraid to publish in her book. In those cases, I have not given her credit for being the source, as she does not want that information revealed. I recommend her book highly for any person interested in more details about the lives of the descendants of Thomas Jefferson.

Our books do not compete with each other because hers in reality concerns a different subject matter, namely, what happened to the children. The same thing can be said, and for the same reason, about *The Sable Curtain* by Minnie Shumate Woodson.

Both Judith P. Justus and Minnie Shumate Woodson have gleaned much of their information about the slave children of Thomas Jefferson from yet other genealogists who have been working on this subject for much longer than either of them but who have not yet published their findings. I am informed, for example, that there is a woman somewhere in Ohio who has been working on this for more than 20 years. However, I do not know her name. Anyway, whoever that is, I want to thank her too because undoubtedly there are some things in this book which were originally her findings.

Since I have mentioned that I have been given information which other authors have been afraid to publish, I must add that I am not afraid of this at all. I can assure the reader that in no case whatever have I asked any person for permission to publish anything which appears in this book. I am just chomping at the bit for somebody such as the Chairman of DuPont to sue me for slandering his good name by accusing him of being a descendant of Thomas Jefferson.

In the course of writing this book, I visited the Family History Library maintained by the Mormon Church in Salt Lake City, Utah. The purpose of this library is to enable church members to get their ancestors into heaven by finding out who they were, in accordance with the Mormon Religion. As a result, the Mormon Church has by far the world's largest genealogical database. Unfortunately, however, it turns out that they have little information on the relatives of a presumed atheist like Thomas Jefferson, because his family members have not entered data into their database. I have to some extent attempted to correct this problem by sending the Mormon Church a floppy disk with 1200 names on it.

Starting with a computer program I purchased from the Mormon Church called 'Personal Ancestral File' or 'PAF', I created my own database of more than 3,000 persons who were near or distant relatives of Thomas Jefferson and/or Sally Hemings. This was a difficult job, probably never done before on a computer, and because of it I can state with authority that, for example, Rebecca Burwell was a second cousin one generation removed from President William Henry Harrison, a fact not previously known. In addition to that, she was also his third cousin, his fourth cousin and his fifth cousin, all at the same time, but all on different branches of the family tree. This is a result of the practice at that time of marrying cousins. It would be virtually impossible to calculate these complex relationships without the aid of the trusty computer program from the Mormon Church.

This database of the relatives and in-laws of Thomas Jefferson extends to almost every famous person in Virginia at that time. For example, Presidents George Washington, William Henry Harrison, John Tyler, Zachary Taylor, Benjamin Harrison and James Madison are all linked together in my database. The reason for this is that, like the royal families of Europe, the leading families of Virginia tended to marry each other. Thus, all of these people are related, if not by blood, then by in-laws.

This is the reason that one sees in my book the statement that President John Tyler was exactly the fourth cousin of William Armistead Burwell, the personal secretary to Thomas Jefferson while he was president. This and similar statements were all calculated on my computer.

Unfortunately, I must add that a bug in the computer program developed by the Mormon Church caused my data to self-destruct after I had entered 3000 names. This turns out to be a problem which everyone making extensive use of the Personal Ancestral File program has faced. A ran up a big long- distance telephone bill to Salt Lake City trying to get to the bottom of this problem. The Church claims that they have got this problem corrected in their latest version of PAF and that it should be possible to reconstruct my data, which I will get around to trying to do some day.

Of course, I had to have the data to enter into my database. This came from many sources, including dozens of private family histories I consulted. Among these were the various family histories of the Randolph family, including the voluminous histories by Wessel Randolph. However, by far the best one-volume source of genealogy proved to be *Colonial Families of the Southern States of America*, 1958, by Stella Picket Hardy. Strangely, this book omits the Randolph and Eppes families, but does deal with almost every other family of importance during that era of Virginia history.

The other major source in this area was *Genealogies of Virginia Families*, Genealogical Publishing Co., Baltimore, 1981, in 14 volumes. This consists of reprints of articles from other publications such as the *William and Mary Quarterly* and *Tyler's Historical Magazine*. Some of those articles were originally published more than one hundred years ago, when many of the people mentioned in this book were still alive.

There are numerous additional sources besides these just mentioned, but most of them have already been cited in the text itself, so they will not be repeated here.

Lastly, I must give the greatest thanks of all to the *Jones Memorial Library* in Lynchburg, Virginia, which is an excellent library devoted exclusively to genealogy and history, especially Virginia history. That library has abstracts of original court order books, church parish records and other documentary items for most counties of Virginia dating back to the seventeenth century. Most of these were published in book form, but in limited editions, in the nineteenth century. The *Jones Memorial Library* staff provided me with excellent sources which I might well otherwise have overlooked. Almost all of my sources originally came from them. It is no exaggeration to state that without their help, the writing of this book would have been impossible.

It is especially necessary for me to thank individually Philip Wayne Rhodes, Lewis Averett and Rebecca Glasser of the staff of the *Jones Memorial Library*. They kept me supplied with piles of books on the life of Thomas Jefferson plus made over one thousand photocopies of source documents. They had obviously been through this material themselves. They always seemed to know exactly what I needed. Some of the books they showed me were nearly two hundred years old and apparently are not available in many other libraries, or at least they seem not to have been cited by any other source. Without their assistance, I would never have undertaken this project.

Incidentally, the Jones Family, which provided the grant which established the *Jones Memorial Library*, is also a branch of the Randolph family, which is the family of Thomas Jefferson.

I must also thank other patrons of the same library and even random people walking around of the streets of Lynchburg, Virginia. All of them seemed to have heard the story that Thomas Jefferson produced children from his slaves, not from any book, but as part of the oral tradition of the Lynchburg area. Sally Hemings was born in Cumberland County, which is near Lynchburg. I did not even catch the names of most of the people I talked to about this subject, but many of them gave me ideas which I found useful for this book. I would say that it would have been virtually impossible for me to write this book with such completeness in any place other than in Lynchburg, Virginia or in nearby Charlottesville.

# Appendix

It was originally intended that the full text of all documents and letters of major significance would be included in this appendix. However, in view of the length plus the fact that most of these documents are already quoted extensively and are readily available in other books, it was decided to scrap that idea.

Therefore, this appendix only includes those documents which the reader would not easily be able to obtain elsewhere. For example, there is a letter by Adrien Petit which is translated for the first time into English. There is also the will of John Wayles, which is of great importance to this story and which has never previously been published in any book. It and the subesquent will was obtained from a 1925 issue of *Tyler's Quarterly Historical Magazine*, Vol. 6, pp. 268-270.

The following letter has apparently never been published before in the English language. It can be found in the original French in volume 24, page 262 of *The Papers of Thomas Jefferson* which was just published in 1991. It is a letter from Petit, the French man-servant of Thomas Jefferson. This same Petit had been sent by Thomas Jefferson from Paris to England to collect Maria and Sally Hemings upon their arrival by boat in 1787. Later, after serving Thomas Jefferson faithfully in France, Petit had been brought to America in 1792.

The importance of this letter comes from the last line, where it says, 'say hello to Jimmy and Sally'. James Hemings is known to have been in Philadelphia at this time, serving Thomas Jefferson as a chef. Therefore, Sally must have been in Philadelphia as well.

The following translation was provided by Mr. and Mrs. Gilbert Guedj of Madison Heights, Virginia, whe were referred to the author by Joan Dorr, also of Madison Heights. They remark that the author of this letter must have been poorly educated.

### Letter of Adrien Petit

*July 28, 1792*
*Sir: I am sorry to bother you. I have to do so after being insulted by Francios's wife, telling me that I am a Sodom, that I like men, and that's among other*

*expressions that only a cheap woman can say. You can believe me sir that after insults it is impossible to live close to such a woman who pretends to be a pawn. She has to be fed in this house, and does what ever pleases her. You can ask Jimmy all about it, sir. What really made them mad is that I locked the passage's door with a padlock for security reasons. I prefer to open the door myself, to know how many people were going through the garden to their house. I also removed the apartment's keys. To be in good terms with them, I need to let them have every-thing there is in the house and let them do everything willingly. I asked Robert and Joseph to clean Mr. Eppes' room. It was 12 days after his departure. The room was dirty. Of course, Franciose blamed me for it. He was Mr. George Meite's coach. Well, sir, I am sorry to leave you. I am keeping my book close to me so that we can keep up with our account. I am getting ready to go to France. I have to leave you because of this cheap woman. I would not stay in this house for all the gold in the world. I wish to see you soon so that we can take care of our business, the sooner the better. I hope, sir, that you will write me a few lines for my own satisfaction. It is a shame to come from such a far away country for such a short time. There is nothing that will keep me from leaving. I regret not seeing Mrs. Randolph and her husband. Even though I haven't met them, I'll ask you to present them my most humble respects.*

*I am your most humble and obedient servant.*

*Adrien Petit*

*P.S. Say hello to Jimmy and Sally.*

## THE WILL OF JOHN WAYLES

It is important to read this will carefully and note the dates. The original will is dated April 15, 1760, which was 13 years before John Wayles died. At that time, Elizabeth Lomax was his wife, but she died one year later, in 1761. In 1772, his daughter, Martha Wayles, married Thomas Jefferson. As a result, there is a codicil to the will dated March 5, 1772 which appoints Thomas Jefferson as his executor. Finally, there is a second codicil dated February 12, 1773. There, John Wayles mentions his granddaughter, Martha Jefferson, who was just born in 1772, and his grandson, John Wayles Eppes, who was a babe in arms, having been born in 1773. Finally, he appoints his remaining children, Elizabeth, Tabitha and Anne, executors after they reach maturity. Since his daughter Martha (1748–1782) was already 25, this means that her three half-sisters, Elizabeth, Taitha and Anne, were much younger than her.

One wonders whether Elizabeth Lomax was the mother of Elizabeth, Tabitha and Anne Wayles. The mother of those three daughters is unknown. Their mother definitely was not Tabitha Cocke, a name given by some sour-ces. However, the Lomax family history says that Elizabeth Lomax never had children and that she died less than one year after being married to John Wayles.

Note that 'Betty Hennings' is the only slave whose full name is given in the will of John Wayles, showing that already by 1760 she had acquired special status in his home. One wonders what his wife, Elizabeth Lomax, thought about that.

*In the name of God, Amen. I, John Wayles of Charles City County, make this my last Will and Testament.*

*Imprimis, I give unto my dear wife Elizabeth all and singular the slaves with their offspring that were devised unto her by the last will and testament of Reuben Skelton, deceased, to her and her heirs forever she paying all my just debts out of the same.*

*Item, I give unto my said wife the Land and Plantation whereon I now dwell and twenty slaves also the Stocks of Horses, Hogs &c the Eqipage, and Household Furniture to her, during her natural life in lieu of her dower and after her decease to my children as underneath directed.*

*Whereas my daughter is amply provided for by a settlement made by myself and her mother, and the Slaves contained in the settlement have been devised to me by her mother, now I hereby give and confirm unto my said daughter Martha all and singular the slaves mentioned in the said settlement to her and her heirs forever, except Betty Hennings and Jenny the cook, which I desire may be part of twenty-five slaves divided as above to my Dear Wife, to continue with her during her natural life, and after her death to my said daughter Martha.*

*Item, I give and bequeath unto my three Daughters Elizabeth, Tabitha and Anne all & singular my lands tenements & Hereditaments, and also all my slaves and all other my estate both real and personal unto them and their heirs forever, to be equally divided among them.*

*Item. It is my desire that, if my Daughter Martha thinks her portion not equal to her Sisters, that her portion may be thrown into Hotchpotch with her three sisters above and equally divided among them. And lastly I do hereby appoint and request it as a favor that Francis Eppes and my children as they respectively attain to lawful age would be executors to this my last will wholly written with my own hand this 15th day of April, 1760.*

*J. Wayles. (Seal)*

*Published and Executors altered this 5th March, 1772. I appoint Thomas Jefferson, my son-in-law, likewise to be a joint Executor hereof.*

*Feb. 12, 1773*

*Whereas I, John Wayles of the County of Charles City and Parish of Westover, have before made my will, which by this codicil I would confirm and enlarge until I have more leisure and better health adjust so important a piece of business; Messieurs Farrell and Jones have on every occasion acted in a most generous manner to me I shall therefore make them every grateful return in my power. I therefore direct that my estate be kept together, and the whole Tobacco made thereon shipped unto the said Farrell and Jones, of Bristol, until his debt and interest shall be lawfully and completely paid and satisfied, unless my children should find it to their interest to pay and satisfy the same in a manner that may be agreeable to the said Farrell and Jones. I would have new quarters settled at Saml James's and in Bedford to increase the crops. I give to Robert Skipwith, Esqr., two hundred and fifty pounds, to be paid as soon as the same can be conveniently collected. I desire that my executors may purchase for my three grandchildren, viz: Richard Eppes, John Wayles Eppes and Patty Jefferson, each, a female slave between twelve & fifteen and they are to be adjudged in a court as their property, the same to be purchased any time within five years after my death. And I now, as I have done heretofore, appoint my children my Executors as they respectively come of age.*

*J. Wayles. (Seal)*

*This codicil was published and declared in our presence.*
   *Anderson Bryan*
   *Henry Skipwith*


## THE WILL OF BATHURST SKELTON

Bathurst Skelton was the first husband of Martha Wayles. After his death, Martha Wayles married Thomas Jefferson. Bathurst Skelton was also the brother of Reuben Skelton, who had been the first husband of Elizabeth Lomax.

*In the name of God, Amen. I, Bathurst Skelton, make this my last will and testament. Imprimis, whereas my wife Martha will be entitled to sundry slaves at the death of her father, by virtue of a marriage settlement made betwixt him and her mother, all which slaves I give to her and hers forever in case my son dies under age, or unmarried, but if he attains to lawful age or marriage, then the said slaves to be equally divided betwixt them, my wife and my son. I devise the guardianship of my son John to John Wayles and my wife, and make them executors to this my last will. In witness whereof, I put my hand and seal this 30th day of September, 1768.*

*Bathurst Skelton. (Seal)*

*Published and declared to be his last will and testament in the presents of us.*

*Jos. Harris     N.B., and at his request his name was signed by Jos. Harris and further that he give to his wife his Faton and horses.*
*Chris: Mantove*

*Francis Eppes*
*Proved in Court, September 10, 1771, by the oath of Joseph Harris, who declared that he wrote the said will and of Francis Eppes.*

The above will requires careful reading. John Skelton, the son of Bathurst Skelton and Martha Wayles, died on June 10, 1771 at age four. The will indicates that he might have been in bad health already in 1768.

Fawn Brodie in her book, *Thomas Jefferson: An Intimate History*, page 88, makes a rather silly mistake. She gives September 30, 1768 as the date of the death of Bathurst Skelton. Actually, that was the date of his will. He died in 1771. Fawn Brodie may have copied this error from biographer Henry Randall.

## LETTER FROM THOMAS JEFFERSON TO JOHN ADAMS

The following letter constitutes the 'smoking gun'. It proves that Jefferson thought it a good idea for the best man on the farm to impregnate all of the females. The best man was, of course, Thomas Jefferson himself.

John Adams, no doubt interested in learning the truth about the Sally Hemings scandal, had lured him into this discussion with free references to sex in his letters to Jefferson.

However, the following letter is of great importance for many other reasons as well. It sets forth Jefferson's philosophy of 'one man, one vote', which today is known as a 'Jeffersonian Democracy'. It also expresses ideas which are so commonplace today that the letter almost seems rather boring. For example, Jefferson's ideas for a free school to teach reading, writing and arithmetic to the children and the establishment of a public university for the brightest and the best are all common ideas now, but they were not in Jefferson's time. Similarly, his ideas of local governments, frequent elections and public meetings to give the common people the opportunity to express their ideas to the politicians were not yet accepted. These were all radical ideas in the time of Thomas Jefferson, ideas which John Adams, among many others, opposed.

Notice that Jefferson also seems to advocate world revolution, which is one reason Karl Marx liked him so much.

It is remarkable that this letter has been generally overlooked. Almost the only place where it can be found is in *The Adams–Jefferson Letters*, Edited by Lester J. Cappon, University of North Carolina Press, Vol. II, pp. 387-392.

Thomas Jefferson could read and write Greek and apparently Adams could as well, this being a required accomplishment for every educated man in those days. Part of the following letter was written in original Greek. Apparently, Jefferson was better at Greek than Adams, because Jefferson then translated the Greek parts into English. Those translations into English are in the version of the letter presented here, with the Greek omitted entirely. Enthusiastic readers who want to see the full text in original Greek can consult *The Adams–Jefferson Letters*.

*Monticello Oct. 28, 1813*

*Dear Sir*

*According to the reservation between us, of taking up one of the subjects of our correspondence at a time, I turn to your letters of Aug. 16 and Sep. 2.*

*The passage you quote from Theognis, I think has an ethical, rather than a political object. The whole piece is a moral exhortation, and this passage particularly seems to be a reproof to man, who, while with his domestic animals he is curious to improve the race by employing always the finest male, pays no attention to the improvement of his own race, but marries with the vicious, the ugly, or the old, for considerations of wealth or ambition. It is in conformity with the principle adopted afterwards by the Pythagoreans, and expressed by Ocellus in another form. Which, literally as intelligibility will admit, may be thus translated. 'Concerning the interprocreation of men, how, and of whom it shall be, in a perfect manner, and according to the laws of modesty and sanctity, conjointly, this is what I think right. First to lay it down that we do not commix for the sake of pleasure, but for the procreation of children. For the powers, the organs and desires of coition have not been given by God to man for the sake of pleasure, but for the procreation of the race. For as it were incongruous for a mortal being to partake of divine life, the immortality of the race being taken away, God fulfilled the purpose by making the generations uninterrupted and continuous. This therefore we especially lay down as a principle, that coition is not for the sake of pleasure.' But Nature, not trusting to this moral and abstract motive, seems to have provided more securely for the perpetuation of the species by making it the effect of the oestrum implanted in the constitution of both sexes. And not only has the commerce of love been indulged on this unhallowed impulse, but made subservient also to wealth and ambition by marriages without regard to the beauty, the healthiness, the understanding, or virtue of the subject from which we are to breed. The selecting of the best male from a harem of well chosen females also, which Theognis seems to recommend from the example of our sheep and asses, would doubtless improve the human, as it does the brute animal, and produce a race of veritable aristocrats. For experience proves that the moral and physical qualities of man, whether good or evil, are transmissible in a certain degree from father to son. But I suspect that the equal rights of men will rise up against this privileged Solomon, and oblige us to continue acquiescence under 'the degeneration of the* race of men' which Theognis complains of, and to content ourselves with the accidental aristoi produced by the fortuitous concourse of breeders. For I agree with you that there is a natural aristocracy of among men. The grounds of this are virtue and talents. Formerly bodily powers gave place among the aristoi. But since the invention of gunpowder has armed the weak as well as the strong with missile death, bodily strength, like beauty, good humor, politeness and other accomplishments, has become but an auxiliary ground of distinction. There is also an artificial aristocracy founded on wealth and birth, without either virtue or talents; for with these it would belong to the first class. The natural aristocracy I consider as the most precious gift of nature for the instruction, the trusts, and government of society. And indeed it would have been inconsistent in creation to have formed man for the social state, and not to have provided virtue and wisdom enough to manage the concerns of the society. May we not even say that that form of government is the best which provides the most effectually for a pure selection of these natural aristoi into the offices of government? The artificial aristocracy is a mischievous ingredient in government, and provision should be made to prevent its ascendancy. On this question, What is the best provision, you and I differ; but we differ as rational friends, using the free exercise of our own reason, and mutually indulging its own errors. You think it best to put the Pseudo-aristoi into a separate chamber of legislation where they may be hindered from doing mischief by their coordinate branches, and where they may also be a protection to wealth against the Agrarian and plundering enterprises of the Majority of the people. I think that to give them power in order to prevent them from doing mischief, is arming them for it, and increasing instead of remedying the evil. For if the coordinate ranches can arrest their action, so may they that of the coordinates. Mischief may be done negatively as well as positively. Of this a cabal in the Senate of the U.S. has furnished many proofs. Nor do I believe them necessary to protect the wealthy; because enough of these will find their way into every branch of the legislation to protect themselves. From 15 to 20 legislatures of our own, in action for 30 years past, have proved that no equalization of property are to be apprehended from them.

I think the best remedy is exactly that provided by all our constitutions, to leave to the citizens the free election and separation of the aristoi from the pseudo-aristoi, of the wheat from the chaff. In general they will elect the real good and wise. In some instances, wealth may corrupt, and birth blind them; but not in sufficient degree to endanger the society.

It is probable that our difference of opinion may in some measure be produced by a difference of character in those among whom we live. From what I have seen of Massachusetts and Connecticut myself, and still more from what I have heard, and the character given of the former by yourself, who should know them so much better, there seems to be in those two states a traditionary reverence for certain families, which has rendered the offices of the government nearly hereditary in *those families. I presume that from an early period of your history, members of these families happened to posses virtue and talents, have honestly exercised them for the good of the people, and by their services have endeared their names to them.*

*In coupling Connecticut with you, I mean it politically only, not morally. For having made the Bible the common law of their land they seem to have modeled their morality on the story of Jacob and Laban. But although this hereditary succession to office with you may in some degree be founded on real family merit, yet in a much higher degree it has proceeded from your strict alliance of church and state. These families are canonized in the eyes of the people, on the common principle 'you tickle me, and I will tickle you'. In Virginia we have nothing of this. Our clergy, before the revolution, having been secured against rivalship by fixed salaries, did not give themselves the trouble of acquiring influence over the people. Of wealth, there were great accumulations in particular families, handed down from generation to generation under the English law of entails. But the only object of ambition for the wealthy was a seat in the king's council. All their court was then paid to the crown and it's creatures; and they Philipised in all collisions between the king and the people. Hence, they were unpopular; and that unpopularity continues attached to their names. A Randolph, a Carter, or a Burwell must have a great personal superiority over a common competitor to be elected by the people, even at this day.*

*At the first session of our legislature after the Declaration of Independence, we passed a law abolishing entails. And this was followed by one abolishing the privilege of Primogeniture, and dividing the lands of intestates equally among all their children, or their representatives. These laws, drawn by myself, laid the axe to the root of Pseudo-aristocracy. And had another which I prepared been adopted by the legislature, our work would have been complete. It was a Bill for the general diffusion of learning. This proposed to divide every county into wards of 5 or 6 miles square, like your townships; to establish in each ward a free school for reading, writing and common arithmetic; to provide for the annual selection of the best subjects from these schools who might receive at the public expense a higher degree of education at a district school; and from these district schools to select a certain number of the most promising subjects to be completed at an university, where all the useful sciences should be taught. Worth and genius would thus have been sought out from every condition of life, and completely prepared by education for defeating the competition of wealth and birth for public trusts.*

*My proposition had for a further object to impart to these wards those portions of self-government for which they are best qualified, by confiding to them the care of their poor, their roads, police, elections, the nomination of jurors, administration of government in small cases, elementary exercises of the militia, in short, to have made them little republics, with a Warden at the head of each, for all those con-*

cerns which, being under their eye, they would better manage than the larger republics of the county or state. A general call of ward-meetings by their Wardens on the same day through the state would at any time produce the genuine sense of the people on any required point, and would enable the state to act in mass, as your people have so often done, and with so much effect, with their town meetings. The law for religious freedom, which made a part of this system, having put down the aristocracy of the clergy, and restored to the citizen the freedom of the mind, and those of entails and descents nurturing an equality of condition among them, this on Education would have raised the mass of the people to the high ground of moral respectability necessary to their own safety, and to orderly government, to the exclusion of the Pseudalists; and the same Theognis who has furnished the epigraphs of your two letters assures us that 'Curnis, good men have never harmed any city'. Although this law has not yet been acted on but in a small and inefficient degree, it is still considered as before the legislature, with other bills of the revised code, not yet taken up, and I have great hope that some patriotic spirit will, at a favorable moment, call it up, and make it the key-stone of the arch of government.

With respect to aristocracy, we should further consider that, before the establishment of the American states, nothing was known to history but the man of the old world, crowded within limits either small or over-charged, and steeped in the vices which that situation generates. A government adapted to such men would be one thing; but a very different one that for the Man of these states. Here every one may have land to labor for himself if he chooses; or, preferring the exercise of any other industry, may exact for it such compensation as not only to afford a comfortable subsistence, but wherewith to provide for a cessation from labor in old age. Every one, by his property, or by his satisfactory situation, is interested in the support of law and order. And such men may safely and advantageously reserve to themselves a wholesome control over their public affairs, and a degree of freedom, which is in the hands of the Canaille of the cities of Europe, would be instantly perverted to the demolition and destruction of every thing public and private. The history of the last 25 years of France, and of the last 40 years of America, nay of its last 200 years, proves the truth of both parts of this observation.

But even in Europe a change has sensibly taken place in the mind of Man. Science has liberated the ideas of those who read and reflect, and the American example had kindled feelings of right in the people. An insurrection has consequently begun, of science talents and courage against rank and birth, which have fallen into contempt. It has failed in its first effort, because the mobs of the cities, the instrument used for its accomplishment, debased by ignorance, poverty and vice, could not be restrained to rational action. But the world will recover from the panic of this first catastrophe. Science is progressive, and talents and enterprise on the alert. Resort may be had to the people of the country, a more governable power *from their principles and subordination; and rank, and birth, and tinsel- aristocracy will finally shrink into insignificance, even there. This however we have no right to meddle with. It suffices for us, if the moral and physical condition of our own citizens qualifies them to select the able and good for the direction of their government, with a recurrence of elections at such short periods as will enable them to displace an unfaithful servant before the mischief he mediates may be irremediable.*

*I have thus stated my opinion on a point on which we differ, not with a view to controversy, for we are both too old to change opinions which are the result of a long life of inquiry and reflection; but on the suggestion of a former letter of yours, that we ought not to die before we have explained ourselves to each other. We acted in perfect harmony through a long and perilous contest for our liberty and independence. A constitution has been acquired which, tho neither of us think it perfect, yet both consider as competent to render our fellow-citizens the happiest and the securest on whom the sun has ever shown. If we do not think exactly alike as to its imperfections, it matters little to our country which, after devoting to it long lives of disinterested labor, we have delivered over to our successors in life, who will be able to take care of it, and of themselves.*

*Of the pamphlet on aristocracy which has been sent to you, or who may be its author, I have heard nothing but through your letter. If the person you suspect it may be known from the quaint, mystical and hyperbolical ideas, involved in affected, new-fangled and pedantic terms, which stamp his writings. Whatever it be, I hope your quiet is not affected at this day by the rudeness of intemperance of scribblers; but that you may continue in tranquillity to live and to rejoice in the prosperity of our country until it shall be your own wish to take your seat among the Aristoi who have gone before you. Ever and affectionately yours.*

    *Th: Jefferson*

*P.S. Can you assist my memory on the inquiries of my letter of Aug. 22?*


## LETTER FROM THOMAS JEFFERSON TO EDWARD COLES

The following letter provides perhaps the most authoritative view of Thomas Jefferson regarding slavery. It is a letter to Edward Coles, a neighbor of Thomas Jefferson, who inherited a large number of slaves, took them to Illinois, bought land for them, gave them their freedom and, in recognition for these good deeds, was elected Governor of Illinois in 1822.

This letter is cited by everybody to prove whatever point he or she is trying to make regarding slavery. Fawn Brodie says that this letter proves that Jefferson had sex with his slaves. Virginius Dabney says that this letter proves that Jefferson never had sex with his slaves. In fact, this letter has nothing whatever to do with sex with slaves.

What this letter does show is that while Jefferson was opposed to slavery, in the end, he was prepared to maintain the status quo, while pressing for a gradual change.

This letter starts slowly, but gets better in the middle, especially where Jefferson virtually predicts the forthcoming American Civil War.

Modern spelling and punctuation are used for the ease of the reader.

*Monticello August 25, 1814*

*Your favor of July 31 was duly received, and read with peculiar pleasure. The sentiments reached through the whole do honor to both the head and the heart of the writer. Mine on the subject of the slaves of Negroes have long since been in the possession of the public, and time has only served to give them stronger root. The love of justice and the love of the country plead equally to the cause of the people, and it is a mortal reproach to us that they should have pleaded it so long in vain, and should have produced not a single effort, nay I fear not much serious willingness to relieve them and ourselves from our present condition of moral and political reprobation. From those of the former generation who were in the fullness of age when I came into public life, which was while our controversy with England was on paper only, I soon saw that nothing was to be hoped. Nursed and educated in the daily habit of seeing the degraded condition, both bodily and mental, of those whose unfortunate beings, not reflecting that that degradation was very much the work of themselves and their fathers, few minds had yet doubted but that they were legitimate subjects of property as their horses or cattle. The quiet and monotonous course of colonial life had been disturbed by no alarm and little reflection on the value of liberty. And when alarm was taken at an enterprise on their own, it was not easy to carry them the whole length of the principles which they invoked for themselves. In the first or second session of the legislature after I became a member, I drew to this subject the attention of Col. Bland, one of the oldest, ablest and most respected members, and he undertook to move for certain moderate extensions of the protection of the laws to these people. I seconded his motion, and, as a young member, was more spared in the debate: but he was denounced as an enemy to his country, and was treated with the greatest indecorum. From an early stage of our revolution other and more distant duties were assigned to me, so that from that time till my return from Europe in 1789, and I may say until I returned to reside home in 1809, I had little opportunity of knowing the progress of public sentiment here on this subject. I had always hoped that the younger generation, receiving their early impressions after the flame of liberty had been kindled in every breast, and had become as it were the vital spirit of every American, that the generous temperament of youth, analogous to the motion of their blood, and above the suggestions of avarice, would have sympathized with oppression wherever found, and proved their love of liberty beyond their own share of it. But intercourse with them, since my return, has not been sufficient to ascertain that they had made towards this point the progress I had hoped. Your solitary but welcome voice is the first which has brought this sound to my ear, and I have considered the general silence which prevails on this subject as indicating an apathy unfavorable to every hope. Yet the hour of emancipation is advancing in the march of time. It will come; and whether brought on by the generous energy of our minds, or by the bloody process of St. Domingo, excited and conducted by the power of our present enemy, if one stationed permanently within our country, and offering asylum and arms to the oppressed, is a leaf of our history not yet turned over.*

*As to the method by which this difficult work is to be effected, if permitted to be done by ourselves, I have seen no proposition so expedient on the whole, as that of emancipation of those born after a given day, and of their education and expatriation at a proper age. This would give time for a gradual extinction of that species of labor and substitution of another, and lessen the severity of the shock which an operation so fundamental cannot fail to produce. The idea of emancipating the whole at once, the old as well as the young, and retaining them here, is of those who have not the guide of either knowledge or experience of the subject, for, man, probably of any color, but of this color we know, brought up from their infancy without the necessity of thought or forecast, are by their habits rendered incapable as children of taking care of themselves and are extinguished promptly wherever industry is necessary for raising the young. In the meantime, they are pests in society by their idleness, and the depredations to which this leads them. Their amalgamation with the other color produces a degeneration to which no lover of his country, no lover of excellence in the human character can innocently consent.*

*I am sensible of the partialities with which you have looked towards me as the person who should undertake this salutary but arduous work, but this, my dear Sir, is like bidding old Priam to buckle the armor of Hector 'trementibus aevo humeris et inutile ferrumcengi.' No, I have overlived the generation with which mutual labors and perils begat mutual confidence and influence. This enterprise is for the young; for those who can follow it up, and bear it through to its consummation. It shall have all my prayers, and these are the only weapons of an old man, but in the meantime are you right in abandoning this property, and your country with it? I Think not. My opinion has ever been that, until more can be done for them, we should endeavor, with those whom fortune has thrown on our hands, to feed and cloth them well, protect them from ill usage, require such reasonable labor only as performed voluntarily by freemen, and be led by no repugnancies to abdicate them, and our duties to them. The laws do not permit us to turn them loose, if that were for their good; and to commute them for other property is to commit them to those whose usage of them we cannot control. I hope then, my dear Sir, you will reconcile yourself to your country and its unfortunate condition; that you will not lessen its stock of sound disposition by withdrawing your portion from the mass. That, on the contrary you will come forward in the public councils, become the missionary of this doctrine truly Christian, insinuate and inculcate it softly and steadily through the medium of writing and conversation, associate others in our labors, and when the phalanx is formed, bring on and press the proposition perseveringly until its accomplishment. It is an encouraging observation that no good measure was ever proposed which, if duly pursued, failed to prevail in the end. We have proof of this in the history of the endeavors in the British parliament to suppress that very trade which brought this evil on us, and you will be supported by the religious precept 'be not wearied in well doing.' That your success may be as speedy and complete, as it will be of honorable and immortal consolation to yourself I shall fervently and sincerely pray as I assure you of my great friendship and respect.*

*Th: Jefferson*

## THE WILL OF THOMAS JEFFERSON

At first glance, the last will and testament of Thomas Jefferson does not seem to say much. However, upon each rereading, more secrets about the life of Thomas Jefferson are revealed.

For example, he refers to Burwell, John Hemings and Joe Fosset as his 'servants', but he calls Madison and Eston Hemings the 'apprentices of John Hemings'. Is this because Madison and Eston were his sons and the other three were not? Or is this because the other three were simply much older?

We learn, for example, that Burwell has a profession. He was a painter. We already knew that the other two had professions. Joe was an iron worker, tool maker and blacksmith. John Hemings was a carpenter.

We learn that Anne Scott Jefferson, the only surviving sister of Thomas Jefferson and the widow of Hastings Marks, was still alive and living at Monticello. We need to know this because *The Family Letters of Thomas Jefferson* by Bear and Betts, on page 15, states that she died in 1805. In fact, she died in 1828 at age 73.

The James Madison of Montpellier mentioned in the will is, of course, the former President of the United States.

Mainly, we learn the lengths which Thomas Jefferson had to go to keep his only surviving daughter, Martha, out of poverty and destitution brought on by the financial irresponsibility of her husband, Thomas Mann Randolph, Jr., who, during his life, immediately squandered any funds which happened to fall into his hands. No doubt, their relatives breathed a sigh of relief when this unfortunate man died in 1828.

Many of the place names given in the initial part of this will are within walking distance of where this book has been written, such as Waterlick Road, for example.

This will does not contain the signatures of the normal two witnesses. This may indicate that Thomas Jefferson wanted the provisions kept secret until after his death.

*I Thomas Jefferson of Monticello, in Albemarle, being of sound mind and in my ordinary state of health, make my last will and testament, in manner and form as follows.*

*I give to my grandson Francis Eppes, son of my dear daughter Mary Eppes, in fee simple, all that part of my lands at Poplar Forest lying west of the following lands, to wit, Beginning at Radford's upper corner near the double branches of Bear Creek and the public road, & running thence in a straight line to the fork of my private road, near the barn, thence along the private road (as it was changed in 1817), to it's crossing of the main branch of North Tomahawk Creek, and from that crossing, in a direct line over the main ridge which divides the North and South Tomahawk, at the confluence of the two branches where the old road to Waterlick crossed it, and up from that confluence up the Northernmost branch (which separate McDaniel's and Perry's fields) to its source, & thence by the shortest line to my western boundary. And having, in a former correspondence with my deceased son in law John W. Eppes contemplated laying off for him with remainder to my grandson Francis, a certain portion in the Southern part of my lands in Bedford and Campbell, which I afterwards found to be generally more indifferent than I had supposed, & therefore determined to change its location for the better; now to remove all doubt, if any could arise on a purpose merely voluntary & unexecuted, I hereby declare that what I have herein given to my said grandson Francis is instead of, and not additional to what I had formerly contemplated.*

*I subject all my other property to the payment of my debts in the first place.*

*Considering the insolvent state of the affairs of my friend & son in law Thomas Mann Randolph, and that what will remain of my property will be the only resource against the want in which his family would otherwise be left, it must be his wish, as it is my duty, to guard that resource against all liability for his debts, engagements or purposes whatever, and to preclude the rights, powers and authorities over it which might result to him by operation of law, and which might, independently of his will, bring it within the power of his creditors, I do hereby devise and bequeath all the residue of my property real and personal, in possession or in action, whether held in my own right, or in that of my dear deceased wife, according to the powers vested in me by deed of settlement for that purpose, to my grandson Thomas J. Randolph, & my friends Nicholas P. Trist and Alexander Garret & their heirs during the life of my said son in law Thomas M. Randolph, to be held and administered by them, in trust, for the sole and separate use and behoof of my daughter Martha Randolph and her heirs. And, aware of the* nice and difficult distinctions of the law in these cases, I will further explain by saying, that I understand and intend the effect of these limitations to be, that the legal estate and actual occupation shall be vested in my said trustees, and held by them in base fee, determinable on the death of my said son in law, and the remainder during that same time be vested in my said daughter and her heirs, and of course disposable by her last will, and that at the death of my said son in law, the particular estate of the said trustees shall be determined, and the remainder, in legal estate, possession and use become vested in my said daughter and her heirs, in absolute property forever.

In consequence of the variety and indescribableness of the articles of property within the house at Monticello, and the difficulty of inventorying and appraising them separately and specifically, and its inutility, I dispense with having them inventoried and appraised; and it is my will that my executors be not held to give any security for the administration of my estate. I appoint my grandson Thomas Jefferson Randolph my sole executor during his life, and after his death, I constitute executors my friends Nicholas P. Trist and Alexander Garret joining to them my daughter Martha Randolph after the death of my said son in law Thomas M. Randolph.

Lastly, I revoke all former wills by me heretofore made; and in witness that this is my last will, I have written the whole with my hand on two pages and have subscribed my name to each of them this 16th day of March one thousand eight hundred and twenty six.

TH. Jefferson

I Thomas Jefferson of Monticello in Albemarle make and add the following Codicil to my will, controlling the same so far as its provisions go.

I recommend to my daughter, Martha Randolph, the maintenance and care of my well beloved sister Anne Scott Marks, and trust confidently that from affection to her, as well as for my sake, she will never let her want a comfort.

I have made no specific provision for the comfortable maintenance of my son in law Thomas M. Randolph, because of the difficulty and uncertainty of devising terms which shall vest any beneficial interest in him which the law will not transfer to the benefit of his creditors, to the destitution of my daughter and her family and disablement of her to supply him: whereas property placed under the exclusive control of my daughter and her independent will, as if she were a femme sole, considering the relation in which she stands to both him and his children, will be a certain resource against want for all.

I give to my friend James Madison of Montpellier my gold- mounted walking staff of animal horn, as a token of the cordial and affectionate relationship which for nearly now a half century, has united us in the same principles and pursuits of what we have deemed for the greatest good of our country.

I give to the University of Virginia my library, except such particular books only, and of the same edition, as it may already possess, when this legacy shall take *effect. The rest of my said library remaining after those given to the university shall have been taken out, I give to my two grandsons in law Nicholas P. Trist and Joseph Coolidge.*

*To my grandson Thomas Jefferson Randolph I give my silver watch in preference to the golden one, because of its superior excellence. My papers of business going of course to him, as my executor, all others of a literary or other character I give to him as of his own property.*

*I give a gold watch to each of my grandchildren, who shall not have already received one from me, to be purchased and delivered to my executor, to my grandsons at age 21, and granddaughters at that of sixteen.*

*I give to my good, affectionate, and faithful servant Burwell his freedom, and the sum of three hundred Dollars to buy necessities to commence his trade of painter and glazier, or to use otherwise as he pleases. I give also to my good servants John Hemings and Joe Fosset, their freedom at the end of one year after my death: and to each of them respectively all the tools of their respective shops or callings: and it is my will that a comfortable log-house be built for each of the three servants so emancipated on some part of my lands convenient to them with respect to their wives, and to Charlottesville and the University, where they will be mostly employed, and reasonably convenient also to the interests of the proprietor of the lands; of which houses I give the use of one, with a curtilage of an acre to each, during his life or reasonable occupation thereof.*

*I give also to John Hemings the service of his two apprentices, Madison and Eston Hemings, until their respective ages of twenty one years, at which period respectively, I give them their freedom. And I humbly and earnestly request of the legislature of Virginia a confirmation of the bequest of freedom to these servants, with permission to remain in this state where their families and connections are, as an additional instance of the favor, of which I have received so many other manifestations, in the course of my life, and for which I now give them my last, solemn, and dutiful thanks.*

*In testimony that this is a Codicil to my will of yesterday's date, and that it is to modify so far the provisions of that will, I have written it all with my own hand, in two pages, to each of which I subscribe my name this 17th day of March one thousand eight hundred and twenty six.*

Th. Jefferson

# Bibliography

Adair, Douglass, *Fame and the Founding Fathers*, New York 1974

Adams, John, *Diary and Autobiography of John Adams*

Alberts, Robert C., *The Notorious Affair of Mrs. Reynolds*, American Heritage Magazine, February, 1973, p. 8

Alderman Library, University of Virginia at Charlottesville, archives of

Alexander, James, *Early Charlottesville, Recollections of James Alexander*, The Michie Company, Charlottesville, 1942

Ambler, Polly, letter of, *Atlantic Monthly*, Vol. 84, p. 538, 1899

Bear Jr., James A., *The Hemings Family of Monticello*, Virginia Cavalcade, Vol. XXIX, Autumn, 1979, Number 2, p. 78

Bear Jr., James A. and Edwin Morris Betts, *The Family Letters of Thomas Jefferson*, University Press of Virginia

Bear Jr., James A. and Edwin Morris Betts, *Thomas Jefferson's Farm Book*, University Press of Virginia, 1987

Bear Jr., James A., *Jefferson at Monticello*, University Press of Virginia

*Bolling Family Bible*

Boyd, Julian P., *The Murder of George Wythe*, William and Mary Quarterly, Vol. XII, No. 4., pp. 513-74 (Oct. 1955)

Brodie, Fawn, *The Great Jefferson Taboo*, American Heritage Magazine, June, 1972

Brodie, Fawn, *Thomas Jefferson, An Intimate History*, New York, 1974

Brodie, Fawn, *Thomas Jefferson's Unknown Grandchildren*, American Heritage Magazine

Brown, William Wells, *Clotel, or the President's Daughter, A Narrative of Slave Life in the United States*, London, 1853

Brown, William Wells, *Clotelle, A Tale of the Southern States*, 1864

Bruce, William Cabell, *John Randolph of Roanoke 1773-1833*, New York 1922

Bruckburger, Father R. L., *Image of America*

Burr, Aaron, *Diary of Aaron Burr*

Callender, James Thompson, *History of the United States for the Year 1796*

Campbell, Charles, *Memoirs of Isaac Jefferson*

Cappon, Lester J., *The Adams–Jefferson Letters*, University of North Carolina Press

Caterall, Helen T., *Judicial Cases Concerning Slavery*, Vol. 1, p. 108-9

Catanzariti, John, *The Papers of Thomas Jefferson*, Princeton University Press

Chase-Riboud, Barbara, *Sally Hemings, a Novel*

Chestnut, Mary Boykin, *Mary Chestnut's Civil War*

Chestnut, Mary Boykin, *A Diary from Dixie*

*The Civil War*, television documentary

Dabney, Virginius, *The Jefferson Scandals, a Rebuttal*, Lanham, Maryland, 1991

Dabney, Virginius, *History of the University of Virginia*

Dabney, Virginius, *Virginia Cavalcade*, Volume XXIX, Autumn, 1979

Deeds Book, City of Lynchburg

Dennie, Joseph, *Philadelphia Port Folio*, 1802

Diamond, Dr. Bernard, Paper presented at the 1968 convention of the American Ortho-Psychiatric Convention in Chicago, Ill.

*Domestic Life of Thomas Jefferson*
duPont Chemical Corporation, E. I., *Annual Report to Stockholders*
Ebony Magazine, *Thomas Jefferson's Negro Grandchildren*, November, 1954, Vol. 10, No. 1, pp. 79-80
Edwards, Jonathan, *Original Sin*, 1758
*Encyclopedia Britannica*
*Encyclopedia of Virginia Biography*
Erikson, Erik, *Martin Luther*
Family History Library, archives of, Salt Lake City, Utah
Fisher, George D., *Descendants of Jacquelin Ambler*, Richmond, Virginia, 1890
*Genealogy of Virginia Families*, Genealogical Publishing Company, Baltimore, 1981
Graham, Pearl N., *Thomas Jefferson and Sally Hemings*, Journal of Negro History, XLIV, P. 89-103
Hamilton, Madison and Jay, *The Federalist Papers*
Hardy, Stella Picket, *Colonial Families of the Southern States of America*, 1958
*Henings' Statutes of Virginia at Large*
Hornsby, Alton Jr., *Chronology of Early African—American History*, Detroit, 1991
Jellison, Charles A., *James Thompson Callender*, Virginia Cavalcade, Autumn, 1979
Jefferson, Thomas, *Notes on the State of Virginia*
Jefferson, Thomas, *A Summary View of the Rights of British America*
Jefferson, Thomas, *Map of Virginia of Peter Jefferson*
*Jefferson's Nephews*
Jones Memorial Library in Lynchburg, Virginia, Archives of
Jordan, Winthrop, *White over Black*
Justus, Judith Price, *Down From the Mountain*, Perrysburg, Ohio, 1991
Langhorne, Elizabeth, *Monticello, A Family Story*
Lee, General Light—Horse Henry, *Memoirs of the War*, 1812
*Liberator, The*, Boston, 1838
Lynchburg Virginian of Sept. 25, 1837, obituary of Mrs. Francis T. Perry
Lynch's Ferry (magazine), *The Restoration of Poplar Forest*, Vol. 4, Summer, 1991, Lynchburg, Virginia
Malone, Dumas, *Jefferson and the Ordeal of Liberty*
Malone, Dumas, *Jefferson in his Time*
Massachusetts Historical Society, Archives of
Mc Laughlin, Jack, *Jefferson and Monticello, The Biography of a Builder*, New York, 1988
Meade, The Right Reverend William, *Old Churches, Ministers, Families of Virginia*, Philadelphia, 1857
Miller, Floyd J., *The Father of Black Nationalism, Another Contender*, Civil War History, Vol. XVII, No. 4, December, 1971
Miller, Lucy, *Behind the Old Brick Wall, A Cemetery Story*, Lynchburg, 1968
Moir, Anne, *Brain Sex: The Real Difference Between Men and Women*
*My Head and My Heart*, Letter of Oct. 12, 1786 from Thomas Jefferson to Maria Cosway
*New York Times, The*, May 18, 1974, Letter dated October 24, 1858 from Ellen Randolph Coolidge to her husband
Nichols, Frederick D. and Bear Jr., James A., *Monticello, A Guide Book*
Personal Ancestral File, The Mormon Church, Salt Lake City, Utah
Peterson, Merrill D., *Thomas Jefferson, A Reference Biography*, Charles Scribner & Sons, 1986
Pierson, Reverend Hamilton Wilcox, *Memoirs of Edmund Bacon*, published in Jefferson at Monticello by Bear and Betts
*Pike County Republican*, Waverly, Ohio, 1873, interviews of Madison Hemings and Israel Jefferson
*Pittsburgh Press, The*, (newspaper) October 4, 1990 and July 1, 1991
Quarles, Benjamin, *The Negro in the American Revolution*
Randall, Henry Stephens, *Life of Jefferson*
Randolph, Wessel, *The Family of Henry Randolph I*

Rice, Horace R., *The Buffalo Ridge Cherokee, The Colors and Culture of a Virginian Indian Community*, Madison Heights, Virginia, 1991

Robertson, Wyndham, *Pocahontas and Her Descendants*, Richmond, 1899

*The Sally Hemings*, University of Virginia unofficial student newspaper

Tinsell, Charles Callan, *The Secret Loves of the Founding Fathers*, Devin-Adair Company, New York 1964

Tyler's Quarterly Historical and Genealogical Magazine, Richmond, Virginia, Vol. 6, P. 266, 1925

United States Census, 1850 and 1860

Van Pelt, Charles B., *Thomas Jefferson and Maria Cosway*, American Heritage Magazine, August, 1971

Vidal, Gore, *Burr*

Virginia Gazette, Lynchburg, Virginia, March, 1771

Virginia Historical Magazine, Vol. 6, p. 228 (1899)

Virginia Historical Magazine, Vol. 10, p. 330-1 (1903)

Walz, Jay and Audrey, *The Bizarre Sisters*, New York, 1950

*Who's Who in America, 1986-7*

Will of Thomas Jefferson

Will of Richard Randolph of Bizarre

Woodson, Carter G., *The Negro and the Mind*

Woodson, Lewis, *Minutes of the Christian Anti-Slavery Convention, Pittsburgh, 1850*

Woodson, Minnie Shumate, *The Sable Curtain*, Washington, D.C., 1990

Woodson, Minnie Shumate, *Woodson Family Source Book*

World, The (newspaper), *NEGRESS AT VASSAR*, Boston, 1897

*World Almanac and Book of Facts*

Wright Jr., Richard B., *Centennial Encyclopedia of the African Methodist Episcopal Church*, Philadelphia, 1916, p. 255-6

# Index

# Years

1619: 105, 253
1715: 8, 87
1743: 87, 184
1746: 63
1751: 10, 163
1760: 88
1761: 17
1762: 17
1763: 34
1764: 33, 135
1768: 135, 230
1770: 221
1771: 221, 230
1772: 230
1773: 8, 90, 221
1774: 14, 15, 61, 135, 148, 149
1775: 149
1776: 9, 242
1777: 168, 237
1779: 35, 207
1780: 207
1781: 10, 14, 140, 141, 165, 166, 207
1782: 3, 8, 9
1783: 134, 149, 168
1784: 9, 65, 170
1785: 60, 143, 145
1786: 8, 9, 35, 73, 75, 142, 171, 238
1787: 9, 10, 69, 73, 74, 170
1788: 67
1789: 11, 67, 68, 76, 77, 128, 170, 171, 178, 233-4, 256
1790: 4, 11, 74, 75, 77, 140, 167, 172, 234, 249, 259
1791: 171
1792: 67, 80, 91, 130, 200, 245
1793: 167, 195, 200
1794: 135
1795: 4, 53, 135
1796: 10, 21, 37, 65, 164, 201

1797: 4, 42, 43, 82, 134, 159
1798: 4, 36
1800: 6, 28, 32, 145, 149, 155, 159
1801: 11, 18, 32, 36, 40, 41, 53, 138, 140, 145, 159, 165, 172, 269
1802: 4, 5, 38, 41, 46, 47, 153, 233, 241
1803: 41, 150
1804: 44, 91, 150, 153, 163, 256, 263
1805: 13, 24, 28, 36, 81, 84, 91, 223
1806: 45, 82, 143, 235, 240, 241, 250
1808: 36, 133, 149, 238
1809: 34, 35, 78, 181
1810: 136
1814: 202
1815: 22
1816: 241
1817: 246
1819: 144, 241, 269
1820: 13, 94, 101
1821: 70
1823: 241
1824: 15, 22, 73, 180
1825: 70, 94
1826: 8, 15, 22, 94, 112, 127, 133, 243, 245
1827: 51, 64, 135, 243, 245
1828: 64, 174
1829: 172, 247
1834: 226
1835: 38, 134
1838: 38, 48, 98, 234
1850: 2, 211
1853: 38
1857: 156
1861: 158
1862: 55, 143, 145
1863: 101, 157
1873: 82